Music Is My Life

JAZZ PERSPECTIVES

Lewis Porter, Series General Editor

OTHER BOOKS OF INTEREST

Music Is My Life

Louis Armstrong, Autobiography, and American Jazz

Daniel Stein

The University of Michigan Press
Ann Arbor

Published in the United States of America by
The University of Michigan Press
Manufactured in the United States of America
⊚ Printed on acid-free paper

2015   2014   2013   2012   4   3   2   1

A CIP catalog record for this book is available from the British Library.

Library of Congress Cataloging-in-Publication Data

Stein, Daniel, 1975–
     Music is my life : Louis Armstrong, autobiography, and American jazz /
     Daniel Stein.
          p.   m. — (Jazz perspectives)
     Includes bibliographical references and index.
     ISBN 978-0-472-07180-7 (cloth : alk. paper) — ISBN 978-0-472-05180-9 (pbk. :
     alk. paper) — ISBN 978-0-472-02850-4 (e-book)
          1. Armstrong, Louis, 1901-1971.   2. Jazz musicians—United States—Biography.
     3. Jazz—History and criticism.   4. Autobiography.   I. Title.
     ML419.A75S75   2012
     781.65092—dc23
     [B]   2012011073

Acknowledgments

This book began as a master's thesis on Charles Mingus's and Louis Armstrong's autobiographical writings and grew into a doctoral dissertation on Armstrong's autobiographics. I am deeply indebted to Winfried Herget at the University of Mainz for supervising the master's thesis and the dissertation in its early stages and for being part of my doctoral committee, as well as to Frank Kelleter at the University of Göttingen for being my dissertation supervisor. I have benefited from their critical suggestions and wish to thank both of them for their intellectual investment in the project, for their professional and personal advice, and for their crucial sponsorship of my academic activities. I also want to thank Alfred Hornung at the University of Mainz, whose expertise has greatly advanced my understanding of American autobiography and whose professional support I appreciate very much.

At the English Department at the University of Michigan in Ann Arbor, where, thanks to Winfried Herget and Martha Vicinus, I was able to work as a lecturer from 2001 to 2003, I met a host of wonderful and supportive people who shaped not only my outlook on the subjects discussed in this book but also my views on American culture at large. My office mate, Charles Taylor, was a continuing source of knowledge about jazz, while brief talks with Richard Crawford and Travis Jackson reinforced my belief that I was working on a promising project. I had the chance to sit in as a guest in Paul Anderson's magnificent class "Ralph Ellison and the Blues Aesthetic," which turned out to be a formative experience I still treasure. Working for Eric Rabkin, I got a sense of what rigorous critical thought can accomplish. Moreover, my two years at the University of Michigan were very much defined by John Rubadeau and Pat Rubadeau, whom I wish to thank for their endless hospitality and their great sense of humor, as well as by Bonnie Campbell and Terry Jansen, whose open-heartedness always made me feel welcome.

At the University of Göttingen, where I have been a member of the American Studies division since 2003, I have found a highly productive and personally rewarding academic environment. My biggest thanks go to Frank Kelleter, who was, and continues to be, a constant source of advice, inspiration, and intellectual challenge. His astute comments and thoughtful suggestions proved absolutely invaluable throughout the many years in which I grappled with Louis Armstrong's music and writings and struggled with the latest literary and cultural theories. I further want to express gratitude to my fellow colleagues and friends in Göttingen: Heinrich Detering for being part of my doctoral committee; Barbara Buchenau (now at the University of Bern) for our many brainstorming sessions; Harald Kittel for putting everything into perspective; John Coates for musical inspiration and coteaching courses on jazz; Gabriele Rippl (now at the University of Bern) for sharing her vast knowledge of intermedia theory; Philipp Schweighauser (now at the University of Basel) for briefing me on the forms and functions of book proposals; Klaus Herrgen for being the perfect librarian; and Christy Hosefelder for her continual help and assistance. I have also benefited greatly from my fellow doctoral candidates in the American Studies program: Bernadette Kalkert, Kathleen Loock, Eva Morawietz, Birte Otten, Diana Rosenhagen, Stefanie Schulz, Stephanie Sommerfeld, and Alexander Starre.

Beyond this immediate academic environment, I have had the pleasure of bouncing ideas back and forth and discussing the ins and outs of the academic profession with Nassim Balestrini (University of Regensburg), Micha Edlich (University of Mainz), Alexander Fischer (University of Erlangen-Nürnberg), and Christina Meyer (University of Hannover). Reinhold Wagnleitner (University of Salzburg) deserves additional gratitude for his interest in my work on Armstrong, as does Charles Hiroshi Garrett, who allowed me to preview his chapter "Louis Armstrong and the Great Migration" before it was published as part of *Struggling to Define a Nation: American Music and the Twentieth Century* (Berkeley: University of California Press, 2008).

In the fall of 2009, I spent several days at the Louis Armstrong Archives at Queens College, New York, and I wish to thank Michael Cogswell for granting me access to Armstrong's original manuscripts and for his willingness to share his insights on particular texts and individual passages. I also want to thank Lesley Zlabinger, my contact person at the archives, who helped me set up my research visit and answered all my questions about print permissions and copyrights, as well as Ricky Riccardi, whose blog "The Wonderful World of Louis Armstrong" offers superb analyses of Armstrong's life and music and whose monograph *What a Wonderful World: The Magic of Louis Armstrong's Later Years* (New York: Pantheon, 2011) was published just a little bit too late to play more than a cursory role in the following pages. I did not get a chance to visit the Hogan Jazz Archive at Tulane University, but I communicated in writing with Bruce Boyd Raeburn and Lynn Abbott, whose readiness to help me with my requests and provide me with the materials I coveted was exemplary. I also communicated with Elizabeth Esherwood at the Louisiana State Museum Jazz Collection and wish to thank her for granting me permission to reproduce Edmond "Doc" Souchon's photograph of Louis Armstrong as King of the Zulus in chapter 5. Additional requests were handled efficiently and competently at Oxford University Press (Ben Alexander), Magnum Germany (Norbert Neckritz), and LIFE/Time Inc. (Amy Wong). Finally, I wish to thank Oscar Cohen and Phoebe Jacobs of the Louis Armstrong Educational Foundation, Inc., for granting me permission to cite from Armstrong's writings and reproduce facsimiles of previously unpublished material. I am also thankful for Lisa Cohen's many efforts to process my requests and for her kind responses to my questions.

While none of the chapters of this book was previously published, I have occasionally drawn on essays that have appeared in the following publications and under the following titles: "The Performance of Jazz Autobiography," in *Blue Notes: Toward a New Jazz Discourse*, ed. Mark Osteen, special issue of *Genre: Forms of Discourse and Culture* 37.2 (2004): 173–99; "Hearing, Seeing, and Writing Thelonious Monk: Toward a Theory of Changing Iconotexts," *Amerikastudien/American Studies* 50.4 (2005): 603–27; "Jazz-Autobiographie und kulturelle Intermedialität: Theoretische und praktische Überlegungen zur Beziehung von autobiographischem Text und improvisierter Jazz-Musik," in *Literatur und Musik in der klassischen Moderne: Mediale Konzeptionen und intermediale Poetologien*, ed. Joachim Grage (Würzburg: Ergon, 2006), 327–46; "The Things That Jes' Grew? The Blues 'I' and African American Autobiographies," in *Blues and Jazz*, ed. Lisa Graley, special issue of *Interdisciplinary Humanities* 23.2 (2006): 43–54; "From Text-Centered Intermediality to Cultural Intermediality; or, How to Make Intermedia Studies More Cultural," in *American*

Studies as Media Studies, ed. Frank Kelleter and Daniel Stein (Heidelberg: Winter, 2008), 181–90; "Louis Armstrong as a Model for Intermedia Theory," *Annual Review 2009/10*, Heidelberg Center for American Studies (2010): 164–73. I want to thank the editors of these publications as well as those who organized the conference panels and colloquia at which I presented papers on topics related to this book for their support.

At the University of Michigan Press, editor-at-large Chris Hebert and his assistants Scott Griffith and Susan Cronin were tremendously knowledgeable and immensely supportive. Chris's belief that I could squeeze a worthwhile book from my initial proposal helped me through the rougher moments of the revision process. I have always admired John Szwed's work on American music and culture, and I am humbled by the fact that he accepted this book for publication in the Jazz Perspectives series. I have benefited greatly from his suggestions and from the detailed remarks by the anonymous university press reviewers, and I want to thank all of them for their efforts and insights. I also appreciate the help and advice I received from project manager Marcia LaBrenz and administrative assistant Debra Shafer, as well as the copyeditor's careful corrections and suggestions.

Two generous dissertation awards allowed me to cover the print permission and copyright fees for this book (apart from the cultural capital they also award). My thanks go to the Heidelberg Center for American Studies, where I was privileged to receive the Rolf Kentner Dissertation Prize in October 2010, and to the Graduate School of Humanities Göttingen (GSGG), which awarded me the Christian-Gottlob-Heyne-Preis in November 2010.

Above all, I want to thank my family: my parents, Thomas Michael Stein and Johanna Stein; my brother, Simon Stein, and his wife, Verena Barthel-Stein; my in-laws, Kresimir Petricevic and Beate Petricevic-Rompf; and my wife, Cornelia, who has accompanied this book from the very first day and has provided crucial feedback and smart suggestions countless times.

Contents

"Music is my life, and I live to play"

Louis Armstrong's Jazz Autobiographics

To study jazz, we are often told, means to study something uniquely and centrally American. In his opening remarks to the seminal anthology *The Jazz Cadence of American Culture* (1998), Robert O'Meally calls jazz "a massive, irresistibly influential, politically charged part of our culture" and "the master trope of this American century: the definitive sound of America in our time." Reaching for Du Boisian heights, O'Meally argues that "[t]he sound of the American twentieth century is the jazz line."[1] If jazz is elevated to the status of America's master trope and definitive sound, and if it sonically encapsulates the problem of race that W. E. B. Du Bois diagnosed as the defining issue of the twentieth century, then Louis Armstrong is much more than a musician and entertainer loved by audiences in the United States and across the world.[2] Indeed, his life was so closely interwoven with many of the most central developments in twentieth-century American history that he emerges as a crucial figure far beyond his musical innovations and popular appeal.

As a trumpeter, Armstrong was the major innovator of the 1920s and early 1930s. He was the driving force in the development from traditional New Orleans ensemble playing to the prominent role of the jazz soloist, often stylized as a quintessentially modern artist, a "Master of Modernism," as promotional pamphlets and placards informed audiences in 1927.[3] His studio work with King Oliver's Creole Jazz Band in 1923 resulted in some of the earliest jazz recordings by African American musicians, and while prominent bebop trumpeters such as Dizzy Gillespie and Miles Davis initially attacked Armstrong during the postwar years for what they interpreted as racially self-deprecating and submissive performance antics, they ultimately acknowledged their debt to his musical and personal achievements: "If it weren't for him, there wouldn't be any of us," Gillespie exclaimed during the birthday concert organized by jazz impresario George Wein in 1970. "You can't play nothing on trumpet that doesn't come from him, not even modern shit," Davis would eventually concede.[4] And indeed, players as diverse as Lester Bowie and Wynton Marsalis have paid tribute to Armstrong's style and technique, as well as to his role in American music. Marsalis's commentary in documentaries such as Gary Giddins and Kendrick Simmons's *Satchmo* (1989) and Ken Burns's *Jazz* (2001) leaves little doubt about his devotion to Armstrong, and his solos in Lincoln Center Jazz Orchestra performances of "Portrait of Louis Armstrong" (originally composed for Duke Ellington's *New Orleans Suite* of 1970, featuring Cootie Williams on trumpet) evoke Armstrong's brilliant tone, rhythmic feel, and melodic ingenuity.[5] Bowie, known for his innovative work with the Art Ensemble of Chicago, recorded "Hello Dolly," Armstrong's biggest pop hit, as a duet with pianist John Hicks for his solo album *Fast Last!* (included on the double CD *American Gumbo*; 32 Jazz, 1974). This recording not only recalls Armstrong's acclaimed version of "Dear Old Southland" with Buck Washington on piano (Apr. 5, 1930) and thus illustrates Bowie's interest in connecting his avant-garde trumpeting with Armstrong's lyrical tone. It also adds a sonic dimension to Bowie's understanding of Armstrong as a "true revolutionary" in American music and culture.[6]

As a singer, Armstrong shocked audiences with inventive scat improvisations, and he pioneered vocal techniques that made a lasting impact on singers such as Billie Holiday, Ella Fitzgerald, Nat King Cole, Bing Crosby, Frank Sinatra, Elvis Presley, Tony Bennett, and many more.[7] In her autobiography, *Lady Sings the Blues* (1956), Holiday recalls being transfixed by the suggestive powers of Armstrong's melodic scatting on "West End Blues" (June 28, 1928), and her vocal rendition of "The Blues Are Brewin'" with Armstrong and his orchestra in the movie *New Orleans* (dir. Arthur Lubin, 1947) forcefully illustrates how strongly she was affected by his singing.[8] Ella Fitzgerald's indebtedness to Armstrong's vocal mannerisms and scat techniques is amply documented on the albums *Ella and Louis* (1956) and *Ella and Louis Again* (1957). Bing Crosby's duets with Armstrong in films such as *High Society* (dir. Charles Walters, 1956), on the many radio broadcasts they did together between 1949 and 1951, on the *Bing & Satchmo* album (1960), and on television programs such as the *Edsel Show* (CBS, Oct. 13, 1957), where Armstrong performs "Now You Has Jazz" with Crosby and "Birth of the Blues" with Frank Sinatra, add weight to Crosby's public nod to Armstrong's influence on American music: "I'm proud to acknowledge my debt to the Reverend Satchelmouth. He is the beginning and the end of music in America."[9]

Armstrong's career as a recording artist spans almost fifty years and includes classic tunes such as "Heebie Jeebies" (Feb. 26, 1926), "West End Blues," and "Ain't Misbehavin'" (July 19, 1929), as well as hit singles such as "Blueberry Hill" (Sept. 6, 1949), "Hello Dolly" (Dec. 3, 1963), "What a Wonderful World" (Aug. 16, 1967), and the James Bond song "We Have All the Time in the World" (from *On Her Majesty's Secret Service*, dir. Peter Hunt; Oct. 28, 1969). Beyond the recording studio, Armstrong contributed substantially to the popularization of black jazz on American radio, broadcasting live music from the Savoy Ballroom in Chicago with the Carroll Dickerson band in the late 1920s, speaking over the Southern airwaves as one of the first African Americans in 1931, and being the first black musician to host a major radio program in 1937 (substituting for Rudy Vallée at the *Fleischmann's Yeast Show*).

Apart from his presence on sound recordings and the radio, Armstrong also appeared in more than twenty Hollywood films and published two autobiographies, *Swing That Music* (1936) and *Satchmo: My Life in New Orleans* (1954).[10] His relocation from New Orleans to Chicago (1922) and then to New York (1924–25, 1929) was accompanied by the rise of modern mass media as well as by the monumental demographic shift from country to city and South to North known as the Great Migration. The black musician left his Southern hometown and arrived, via Chicago, in New York at the height of the Harlem Renaissance, where his career coincided with the flowering of sound recording, radio, and film. Initially hailed as a black cultural hero and master musician, Armstrong would become a controversial figure at the commercial high point of his career in the 1950s and 1960s. As a smiling black entertainer, he came to be loved by predominantly white audiences but was scorned by many African Americans as an Uncle Tom. Yet in his role as Ambassador Satch, he was also lauded as an icon of the Cold War and occasionally performed the role of political spokesman for the cause of racial integration.

Armstrong was aware of his complicated place in twentieth-century American culture: "I was a Southern Doodle dandy, born on the Fourth of July, 1900," he once boasted.[11] While it is very likely that he never knew the correct date—he was actually born on August 4, 1901, to a teenage mother and a father who soon abandoned the family—he certainly used the

Fourth of July to present his life story in quintessentially American terms.[12] These terms easily appealed to his mainstream audience and allowed him to claim a status of cultural prominence. Ultimately, however, the birth date is intriguing because it resonates with Du Bois's prediction that race would be the defining issue in the coming century and that African American musicians would weave themselves "with the very warp and woof of this nation."[13] As Ralph Ellison's narrator-protagonist in *Invisible Man* (1952) acknowledges, the rhythmic propulsion of recordings such as "(What Did I Do to Be So) Black and Blue?" (July 22, 1929) suggests "a slightly different sense of time," one that is "never quite on the beat" and, through the pulsating momentum of swing, infuses American culture with an African American sensibility.[14]

The story of Armstrong's life, then, is deeply invested in larger historical narratives: the African American struggle for racial equality, as well as American claims to cultural excellence and exceptionalism, both of which offer convenient conceptual frameworks for what many have interpreted as Armstrong's triumphs over racial discrimination. Take Ken Burns's *Jazz* documentary, which excessively celebrates the lives and music of African American jazz composers and players as examples of what Albert Murray has described as a blues sensibility toward "affirming life in the face of adversity."[15] Burns and scriptwriter Geoffrey Ward focus on the life stories of musicians such as Armstrong, Duke Ellington, Charlie Parker, Dizzy Gillespie, and many others, effectively turning them into larger-than-life figures who overcome the nation's racial burdens by integrating them, through their courageous lives and musical heroism, into an embodied narrative of jazz as America's gift to humanity. It is, however, a very particular version of Armstrong's life story that Burns, Ward, and talking heads like Marsalis and Stanley Crouch fashion, a version that follows jazz critic and Armstrong biographer Gary Giddins's reorientation of the musician's popular image from a grinning entertainer and "modern-day Sambo" toward a vision of his role in American culture as a "black genius."[16] Yet celebrating Armstrong's music as the great art of an unlikely genius whose brilliance, according to Burns, was a "gift from God" diminishes the significance of the musician's struggle for social agency and creative self-determination.[17] It identifies an otherworldly source for Armstrong's inspiration and thereby shortchanges the musician's lifelong effort to promote the very specific origins of his musical prowess: the circumstances of his youth and his participation in the black vernacular culture of New Orleans in the first two decades of the twentieth century. What Burns, Ward, and many other critics also tend to marginalize are the personal ambivalences and ambiguities that shaped Armstrong's professional patriotism. These ambivalences and ambiguities made themselves heard in the "mother lode of autobiographical material" he produced throughout his lifetime, and they require a kind of historically sensitive literary and cultural analysis that is largely missing in the growing body of criticism devoted to this central American figure.[18] Such analysis must by definition shift from a biographical focus and purpose to a more distanced and perhaps also more nuanced critical perspective from which previous biographical interpretations of Armstrong's life and music can be investigated as active participants in the construction and reception of Armstrong's public image and his overall role in twentieth-century American history and culture.

The mother lode of autobiographical material Armstrong produced during his lifetime reveals a very unusual and idiosyncratic, but also a very prolific, writer and storyteller. His two autobiographical books, *Swing That Music* and *Satchmo: My Life in New Orleans*, have been, and continue to be, widely read and discussed by jazz fans, music critics, musicologists, literary scholars, and cultural historians. These narratives, however, grant only partial insight into the musician's life story as they represent only a fraction of a much larger corpus that includes letters, short essays, and longer narratives.

The earliest example of Armstrong's writing is a short letter he sent from Chicago, where he had moved only a few weeks prior to join the King Oliver Band at the Lincoln Gardens on second cornet, to fellow New Orleans musician Isidore Barbarin on September 1, 1922. Armstrong mentions previous letters to Barbarin and another New Orleanian by the name of "Nenest," indicating that he had been writing before that date.[19] The September letter already features many characteristics of the trumpeter's later writings. Armstrong talks about musical institutions and practices typical of the New Orleans of his youth, such as brass bands and funeral parades; he makes reference to the specific context in which he is writing the letter (he is sitting in his room with Joe Oliver) and invests the writing with an oral sensibility by recording laughter as "Ha . . . Ha . . ." while addressing Barbarin in slang terms as "Pops." Even though letter writing was obviously the most common and practical way of keeping in touch over long distances, the fact that Armstrong's preoccupation with writing manifested itself so early and so extensively—he wrote to his wives, friends, colleagues, business partners, fans, and critics almost constantly—is surprising, espe-

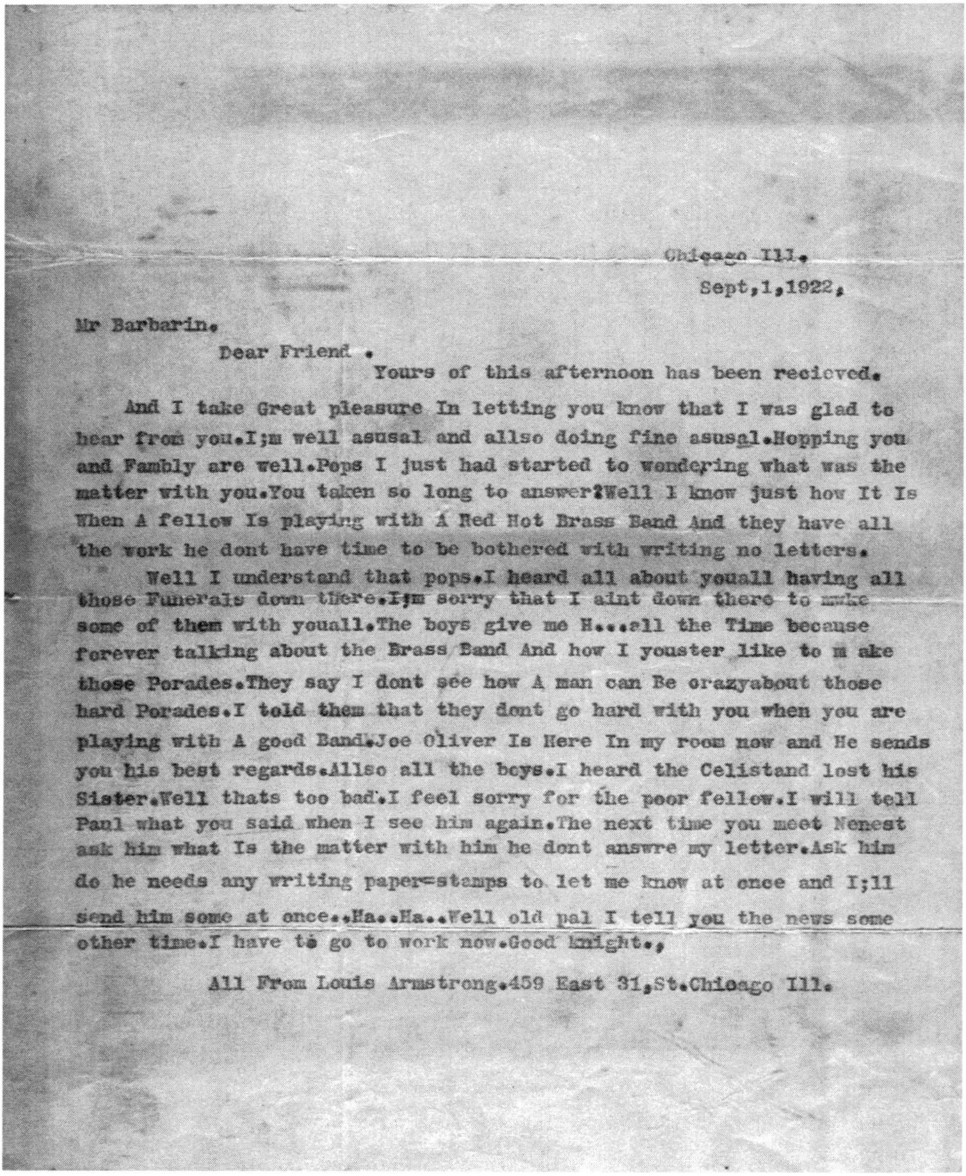

Chicago Ill.

Sept,1,1922,

Mr Barbarin.

Dear Friend .

Yours of this afternoon has been recieved.

And I take Great pleasure In letting you know that I was glad to hear from you.I;m well asusal and allso doing fine asusal.Hopping you and Fambly are well.Pops I just had started to wondering what was the matter with you.You taken so long to answer?Well I know just how It Is When A fellow Is playing with A Red Hot Brass Band And they have all the work he dont have time to be bothered with writing no letters.

Well I understand that pops.I heard all about youall having all those Funerals down there.I;m sorry that I aint down there to make some of them with youall.The boys give me H...ell the Time because forever talking about the Brass Band And how I youster like to m ake those Porades.They say I dont see how A man can Be crazyabout those hard Porades.I told them that they dont go hard with you when you are playing with A good Band.Joe Oliver Is Here In my room now and He sends you his best regards.Allso all the boys.I heard the Celistand lost his Sister.Well thats too bad.I feel sorry for the poor fellow.I will tell Paul what you said when I see him again.The next time you meet Nenest ask him what Is the matter with him he dont answre my letter.Ask him do he needs any writing paper=stamps to let me know at once and I;ll send him some at once..Ha..Ha..Well old pal I tell you the news some other time.I have to go to work now.Good knight.,

All From Louis Armstrong.459 East 31,St.Chicago Ill.

Fig. 1. Louis Armstrong, letter to Isidore Barbarin, September 1, 1922. Courtesy of the Hogan Jazz Archive, Tulane University.

cially since his parents were barely literate and he himself had enjoyed only very little formal schooling.

Letter writing was one of Armstrong's most productive endeavors. Michael Cogswell, director of the Louis Armstrong House Museum and Archives, estimates that the musician wrote more than ten thousand letters.[20] Many of these letters were written on a portable typewriter he carried around with him on his tours. As Kaiser Marshall, the drummer of the Fletcher Henderson Orchestra, recalls, Armstrong "used to write his wife every day" by 1924; "all day in the bus . . . he'd be typing, typing, typing," pianist Teddy Wilson noted about the early 1930s.[21] Lil Hardin, whom Armstrong married after he had left his first wife, the New Orleans prostitute Daisy Parker, stayed in Chicago when her husband moved to New York to play with the Henderson band, and she was the recipient of what must have been dozens, if not hundreds, of samples of Armstrong's early writing. Whenever Armstrong did not have access to his typewriter, as was the case in 1955, when he penned a lengthy missive to his manager Joe Glaser, and in 1969, when he began one of his most impressive essays during an extended hospital stay, he put down his thoughts in longhand.[22]

While many of Armstrong's letters were confined to private circulation, a substantial number of them were sent to jazz critics and music magazines and were subsequently published. The roster of prominent jazz writers who received letters from Armstrong includes the French Hugues Panassié, the Belgian Robert Goffin, and the British Leonard Feather. One of Armstrong's first pieces of published writing was sent to, and printed by, the British music magazine *Melody Maker* in 1933. Penned in his characteristic orally inflected style, it describes the musician's return from his first concert tour through England and informs his English followers about his well-being: "I am now at home, in Chicago, and enjoying myself to the highest. The first thing I had for supper [. . .] was a big pot of good red beans and rice, ha, ha, ha . . ."[23] Armstrong not only saw to it that letters such as this one were published; he frequently used letter writing as a vehicle for communicating his life story to his audiences. A typical letter, sent to the entertainer and television host Ken Murray on May 24, 1950, begins with a conversational paragraph ("'Just a little 'Scribblings") and turns into an autobiographical statement in the second paragraph: "Honest 'Stuff [i.e., Ken Murray]—you remind me of a very popular guy down in New Orleans in our neighborhood called 'Slippers. [. . .] He was the kind of a fellow who could mingle with everybody,—musicians—church folks, he could dance, swim, had all the gals, and was crazy about us kids."[24]

Besides producing a vast collection of letters, Armstrong wrote articles and columns for newspapers, jazz magazines, and the mainstream press. Among them are two installments of a "Special Jive" column for the *Harlem Tattler* (1940); short pieces for American and international music magazines such as *Jazz Hot, Down Beat, The Record Changer, Melody Maker, The Jazz Review,* and *Music Journal* (from the late 1930s to the early 1960s); a book review of Alan Lomax and Jelly Roll Morton's autobiographical *Mister Jelly Roll* in the *New York Times* (1950); and essays on topics as diverse as jazz in New Orleans (*True*, 1947) and Chicago (*Esquire's 1947 Jazz Book*), European tours (*Holiday*, 1950), early recordings (*Esquire*, 1951), his preference for dark-skinned women (*Ebony*, 1954), and his receding health toward the end of his life (*Esquire*, 1969). In addition to these articles, Armstrong voiced his thoughts on an array of issues, musical and otherwise, in many interviews, the most substantial of which appeared in *Life* magazine on April 15, 1966, and was reissued in an updated form in Richard Meryman's *Louis Armstrong—A Self-Portrait* (1971).[25]

Armstrong's "stream of correspondence" and his many magazine articles are part of a larger written output that can be described as the result of a "ceaseless literary activity."[26] A passionate letter writer and essayist, Armstrong was also jazz's most productive autobiographer. While many of the twentieth century's most influential jazz figures published memoirs, none of them has written as extensively about his or her life and music. What is more, only a few of these jazz autobiographers, among them Charles Mingus and Artie Shaw, actually wrote down their experiences themselves. Most musicians enlisted amanuenses to whom they either dictated their stories or delegated the power to rework sketches into full-blown narratives, as did New Orleanian players like Sidney Bechet, George "Pops" Foster, and Jelly Roll Morton or band leaders like Count Basie and (to a much lesser degree) Duke Ellington.[27] Armstrong's engagement with life writing, however, was more substantial. He was not only a dedicated chronicler of his experiences who sought to document, preserve, and explain his life, his cultural background, and his music in different genres of writing over the course of many decades. He also gained much pleasure from the very acts of writing and typing: "Of course I am not so bad myself at 'Swimming.—In fact it's one of my' famous 'Hobbies, outside of "Typing."—I loves that also," Armstrong wrote in the mid-1940s, and in the

"Forward" to a collection of jokes and puns, he noted: "This typewriter and 'swimming and 'baseball—are my soul 'Hobbies. . . .' "[28]

Following the letter to the *Melody Maker* (1933) and a letter titled "A Word from Louis Armstrong" (1934), Armstrong's desire to write his life story found its earliest, if flawed, realization in 1936, when his first longer autobiographical narrative, *Swing That Music*, was published.[29] This text has been called "an unreliable early star biography," a "heavily journalized book," a narrative "bleached by a zealous ghostwriter," "a whitewash," and a "historical curiosity."[30] A contemporary reviewer of *Swing That Music* already complained about the obvious editorial interventions: "It seems to me that old 'Satchmo' might have swung away from his ghost-writing collaborator of his autobiography and given us some of the real low-down on his experiences, swing-banding up and down the Mississippi from New Orleans to Portland and also tell us something about his struttin' stuff over the entire continent of Europe," W. H. Barefield Gordon noted in the *Chicago Defender*.[31] As Gordon's review illustrates, dismissing *Swing That Music* from the analysis of Armstrong's life writings would be a mistake, if only for the fact that discarding the work as ghostwritten and thus somehow not comfortably authentic does not address the most pressing questions it raises: questions of access to the means of public self-presentation (Gordon realizes that the text is ghostwritten, even though no ghostwriter or amanuensis is mentioned); questions of narrative control that foreground a struggle over public representation (Gordon assumes correctly that Armstrong has not been able or willing to speak openly about his experiences); and questions concerning the discursive construction of musical and cultural meanings associated with jazz in 1930s America (Gordon uses racially suggestive expressions such as "real low-down," "swing-banding," and "struttin' stuff").

Dismissing *Swing That Music* would, furthermore, marginalize the book's lasting impact on jazz criticism. After all, several early histories of black music, and of jazz in particular, include references to *Swing That Music*, among them Alain Locke's *The Negro and His Music* (1936), Winthrop Sargeant's *Jazz: Hot and Hybrid* (1938), Robert Goffin's *Jazz: From the Congo to the Metropolitan* (1944), and Marshall Stearns's *The Story of Jazz* (1956). The autobiography also left an imprint on J. S. Slotkin's early academic article "Jazz and Its Forerunners as an Example of Acculturation" (1943), as well as on more recent works, such as Eric Porter's important study of African American musicians as artists, critics, and activists and

Jorge Daniel Veneciano's essay on the swing aesthetics of Armstrong's photo-collages.[32] It further provided the basic narrative trajectory for later filmic attempts to present the story of jazz to a mainstream audience. The recording Professor Hobart Frisbee (Danny Kaye) makes for his "History of Music" project in *A Song Is Born* (dir. Howard Hawks, 1948), for instance, follows the evolutionary narrative provided in the music section of *Swing That Music*. So rather than ignore this first autobiographical narrative or try to determine which parts of *Swing That Music* are authentically Armstrong and which are not—a fruitless endeavor since no manuscript exists—it makes more sense to acknowledge that it has performed substantial cultural work in terms of its impact on American jazz criticism and on popular depictions of jazz history. But above all, it was a first major indication of Armstrong's continuous devotion to life writing, which may explain why he never explicitly dismissed *Swing That Music*. On the contrary, he celebrated its publication as an important step in his writing career in a radio interview in 1940 ("it might not have been a literary masterpiece, but every word in it was my own, so I can read it and understand it"); used it to maximize his popularity by showcasing a copy of the book in the movie *New Orleans*; and made sure to rewrite, recontextualize, and reevaluate it in the many narratives he would produce throughout his life.[33]

Armstrong's second extended published autobiographical narrative, *Satchmo: My Life in New Orleans*, presents a more self-determined autobiographical voice, as comparative readings of the incomplete manuscript (posthumously published as "The Armstrong Story") and the published version demonstrate.[34] While Dan Morgenstern, director of the Institute of Jazz Studies at Rutgers University, has argued that the heavy ghostwriting of *Swing That Music* was reduced in *Satchmo* to a more-or-less intrusive editing by Armstrong's publisher, Prentice Hall, but that "[t]he words are essentially Armstrong's own," others maintain that editorial interventions frequently "changed the entertainer's meaning, as well as his style."[35] Thus, questions about the extent to which Armstrong's autobiographical voice is actually an amalgamation of voices of people with different interests and varying degrees of editorial power are crucial, as Whitney Balliett's review of *Satchmo* in the *Saturday Review* makes clear: "Perhaps if the publisher had let the manuscript alone—Louis has a written style, typographically and otherwise, that makes E. E. Cummings's seem like ladyfingers on a spree—[. . .] his] personality might have come closer to the surface."[36] Armstrong's peculiar writing style certainly matters for our understanding of his written life stories, and it is intriguing that Balliett's assessment—one of the first critical acknowledgments of Armstrong as a writer of literary merit—reveals a familiarity with the musician's writing techniques that must have been based on an intimate knowledge of Armstrong's letters or even the manuscript for *Satchmo*.[37] Here, then, we have an example of contested authorial and editorial voices that cannot be resolved simply by reading and interpreting Armstrong's two officially published autobiographies but also necessitates a close study of unpublished manuscripts and shorter autobiographical narratives such as essays and interviews.

These observations illustrate that questions of ghosting and editing must be addressed head on rather than sidestepped. They point to a rich field of analysis that remains somewhat marginalized in jazz historiography: the politics of autobiographical composition, which determine and delimit the boundaries within which popular minority writers—Armstrong is a minority writer in the double sense of being African American and a nonprofessional author—are compelled to present their lives and careers to the reading public. This is no abstract matter. Charles Mingus's *Beneath the Underdog*, for instance, was whittled down from an 875-page manuscript to a much slimmer and streamlined narrative by Knopf editor Nel King, and Billie Holiday's *Lady Sings the Blues* was largely culled together from interviews and newspaper articles by the white journalist William Dufty.[38] In Armstrong's case, the sequel to *Satchmo*, part of which survived as a manuscript, was allegedly suppressed by his manager Joe Glaser, most likely because of its lengthy celebrations of pot smoking. One passage reads: "This whole second book might be about nothing but gage [marijuana] . . . Of course there'll be a lot of sore heads who'll probably resent this."[39] Knowledge of this and similar instances of editorial pressure, combined with an awareness of Armstrong's tendency to edit himself whenever he wrote for the general public, explains the many divergences between published and unpublished writings and warrants a closer look at the processes of self-representation that shaped the musician's writing practices.

On this view, the wealth of autobiographical narratives available beyond *Swing That Music* and *Satchmo* necessitates a careful mapping out and thorough analysis of Armstrong's writings as a whole. One of the most substantial and significant of these writings is a series of "notebooks" that Armstrong composed in the mid-1940s and sent to the Belgian lawyer and jazz writer Robert Goffin, who turned them into a primitivist biography titled *Horn of Plenty: The Story of Louis Armstrong* (1947). These writings further include the surviving portions of the manuscripts for *Satchmo* ("The Armstrong Story") and the suppressed sequel ("The Satchmo Story 2nd Edition"), Richard Meryman's extensive interview with Armstrong for *Life* (and the extended book version, *Louis Armstrong—A Self Portrait*), a fifteen-page reminiscence published in Max Jones and John Chilton's biography *Louis: The Louis Armstrong Story 1900–1971* ("Satchmo Says," ca. 1970), as well as an unusually frank narrative Armstrong started while he was recovering from an illness in a New York hospital in 1969 ("Louis Armstrong + the Jewish Family").[40] The sheer number and diversity of these texts suggest an understanding of autobiography as a writing *practice*, as a mode of self-representation, instead of a polished and carefully composed *product*. This writing practice complicates common conceptions of autobiography. As we shall see, it escapes the generic limits of written autobiography by spilling over into spontaneously penned letters and essays and into other media of performance, such as music, stage acting, film, and photography.[41]

The implications of Armstrong's presentations of autobiographical narratives across the boundaries of genre and medium are immense, as a brief excursus into Sidonie Smith and Julia Watson's theory of autobiographical performativity may illustrate. Smith and Watson argue that autobiography and other forms of life writing emerge from "processes of communicative exchange and understanding" between a performer and his or her audiences.[42] They result from a series of decisions made in the process of performance, a process that unfolds not only within the discursive space a writer inhabits but also vis-à-vis particular "criteria of intelligibility" held by an imagined or real audience at a specific cultural moment. As a black musician who possessed little formal schooling and even less cultural capital as an author, Armstrong faced audiences who came to his writings with specific expectations. And as a public figure whose daily fare it was to meet the expectations of his fans and critics, he must have been intimately aware of what these expectations entailed. Crucially, as Sidonie Smith reminds us, the audiences of autobiography are never homogeneous, which is why autobiographers like Armstrong find themselves performing "on multiple stages simultaneously," where they are "called to heterogeneous recitations of identity."[43] Anyone who wants to draw an adequately complex portrait of Armstrong should therefore examine the criteria of intelligibility and the expectations of the heterogeneous audiences he faced as an autobiographical performer, as well as the shifting mise en scènes of autobiographical performativity—the places, historical moments, and sociopolitical contexts from which he addressed these audiences.[44]

If Armstrong's repeated autobiographical narratives are viewed as performances for heterogeneous audiences that reveal the self as a communicative subject always in flux, then the result of these performances can be described as an overarching referential space, rather than a fixed textual artifact. Autobiography scholar Leigh Gilmore calls this referential space *autobiographics* in her study of autobiographical writings by women. Gilmore suggests that established conceptions of autobiography, such as religious confession, political memoir, or the literary self-portrait, are inadequate models for assessing the life narratives of marginalized writers. She therefore advocates a conceptual shift toward "discursive contradictions in the representation of identity (rather than unity), the name as a potential site of experimentation rather than contractual sign of identity, and the effects of the gendered connection of word and body." According to this shift, "an exploration of a text's autobiographics allows us to recognize that the *I* is multiply coded in a range of discourses; it is the site of multiple solicitations, multiple markings of 'identity,' multiple figurations of agency."[45] If one pushes the logic of autobiographics beyond the generic boundaries of textuality, where, especially in Armstrong's case, it already transcends more conventional notions of autobiography as a narrowly defined literary genre, and if one thinks of *graphics* as a media-flexible mode of self-inscription, then Armstrong's life story begins to emerge in media other than writing. In fact, this life story is not merely communicated through multiple media, but it attains particular significance through its dispersal across a wide spectrum of interdependent autobiographical performances, including musical recordings and live appearances.

This modified conception of autobiographics allows us to consider works such as the four-LP collection *Satchmo: A Musical Autobiography* (Decca, 1957) as part of Armstrong's construction of a multimedia persona and life story. This album differs substantially from more literary projects such as *A Modern Jazz Symposium of Music and Poetry with Charles Mingus* (1957) or Langston Hughes's recitation of poems set to music by Mingus and Leonard Feather (*Weary Blues*, 1958). It was inspired by the format and success of *Bing Crosby: A Musical Autobiography* (1954), and it presents an interesting mixture of autobiographical narration and musical recordings that uses stories and anecdotes from Armstrong's life as interludes between classic songs re-recorded with the All Stars. The narrative walks the listener through the well-publicized stations of Armstrong's career.[46] Most biographers identify producers Leonard Feather and Milt Gabler as authors of the spoken segments on *A Musical Autobiography;* Gabler seems to have compiled a series of notes based on Armstrong's recollections, which Feather then turned into the final narrative.[47] It remains unclear exactly how much of this narrative retains Armstrong's original recollections and how much was added by Feather, but it is important to realize that Armstrong's life story had been in the public domain for a considerable time when the preparations for this album were made. It had been reported by the musician himself in his two published autobiographies, but also by William Russell in Frederic Ramsey Jr. and Charles Edward Smith's *Jazzmen* (1939), by Robert Goffin in *Horn of Plenty*, and by the many journalists and jazz writers who had covered Armstrong's illustrious career.[48] In one way or another, Gabler and Feather must have drawn on these earlier autobiographical narratives or on some of the many letters Feather had received from Armstrong since the 1940s. Furthermore, the title of the album—*Satchmo: A Musical Autobiography*—echoes the title of Armstrong's second autobiography, *Satchmo: My Life in New Orleans*, published just three years earlier, and thus signals a close link between oral narrative and written autobiography. It also connects autobiographical narrative and music. The songs on the recording are offered as the soundtrack to, and sonic manifestation of, Armstrong's life and thus anticipate a statement he would make to David Dachs a few years later: "Music is my life, and I live to play."[49]

While conceived in the same spirit as Crosby's *Musical Autobiography*—as a means of capitalizing on the musician's star status and making the most of the public interest in his biography—Armstrong's *Musical Autobiography* is also different because it stands alongside the trumpeter's many autobiographical writings. As such, it offers an intertext that aligns writing with spoken narrative and musical performance. When Armstrong says at the end of the recording that "it sure has been a thrill living my life over again" and that he is "Red Beans and Ricely Yours," he not only delivers a perfect example of what Paul John Eakin has recently theorized as a form of "living autobiographically"; he also establishes a connection between musical recording and letter writing.[50] He had been using the beans-and-rice phrase as a sign-off in his letters for many years, and the ending on the recording illustrates that he favored certain expressions independent of the particular medium of communication. At least the more knowledgeable members of his audience would have been aware of this connection between musical autobiography and letter writing since Armstrong had been sending out letters to fans and music magazines for quite some time and since several of these letters had been reprinted in the jazz press.[51] Those who might not have recognized the red-beans-and-rice reference as a typical ingredient of Armstrong's letters might at least have encountered one of the musician's many references to this and other Southern foods on recordings such as "When It's Sleepy Time Down South" (Apr. 20, 1931), "All That Meat and No Potatoes" (his romping duet with Velma Middleton from the *Satch Plays Fats* album, recorded on Apr. 27, 1955), and "New Orleans Stomp" from the *Satchmo Plays King Oliver* album (Sept. 30–Oct. 1–2, 1959). The point here is that these references do not merely pop up in oral narrative, letters, and spoken patter on musical performances. Within the referential space of Armstrong's autobiographics, they constitute an interface that indelibly connects music and autobiography in ways that have not yet been fully explored.[52] They also illustrate how closely Armstrong's personal life, including his allegiance to the New Orleans food of his youth, was connected with its mediations: performing the songs for *A Musical Autobiography* and walking the listeners through the major stages of his career indeed means living his life all over again, as he states at the end of the recording.

Even beyond *A Musical Autobiography*, autobiographical references work the interface between Armstrong's life and his music. These references contribute to the construction of a web of autobiographical significances (to appropriate a phrase from Clifford Geertz) that, in its extent and complexity, is unique in the history of American jazz.[53] In light of the widespread practice of naming jazz tunes after band leaders and soloists, the fact that several song titles from Armstrong's oeuvre feature either his name, the monikers Satchelmouth and Satchmo, or other popular nicknames ("Dipper Mouth Blues," Apr. 6, 1923; "Laughin' Louie," Apr. 24, 1933; "Satchel Mouth Swing," Jan. 12, 1938; "Jack-Armstrong Blues," May 17, 1947), is not necessarily all that remarkable in itself. Think, for instance, of Lester Young's signature tune, "Lester Leaps In," of Jelly Roll Morton's "Jelly Roll Blues," or of Thelonious Monk's "Monk's Mood." Even the fact that many album titles, especially from the 1950s, carry references to Armstrong's name—*Louis Armstrong Plays W. C. Handy* (1954), *Satch Plays Fats* (1955), *Ambassador Satch* (1956), *Satchmo the Great* (1957), *Louis and the Good Book* (1958), *Satchmo Plays King Oliver* (1959)—does not per se account for the special status that autobiographical references attain in Armstrong's oeuvre. Album titles such as *Mingus Ah Um* (1959), *Charles Mingus Presents Charles Mingus* (1960), *Mingus Mingus Mingus Mingus Mingus* (1963), *Miles Ahead* (1957), *Miles Smiles* (1966), *Monk's Music* (1957), *Monk's Dream* (1963), or *Soultrane* (1958) similarly reference the names of their respective band leaders (Charles Mingus, Miles Davis, Thelonious Monk, John Coltrane). In Armstrong's case, however, the Satchmo references in song and album titles establish a more extensive web of autobiographical significances. In the mid-1950s, this web would extend from the album *Satchmo the Great*, which provided the soundtrack for a television documentary by Edward R. Murrow, to the autobiography *Satchmo: My Life in New Orleans* and to the music-cum-narrative offerings of *Satchmo: A Musical Autobiography*.

If album titles establish a web of autobiographical significances on a macrolevel, song titles and spoken comments on individual performances add a series of microlevel references. This is significant because it remains unclear how much input Armstrong had on the selection of album titles in the 1950s. As early as 1930, he referred to himself as "Satchelmouth" on his recordings. This constituted a more clearly self-controlled practice of connecting his name with his musical voice. It opened up a connection between musical performance and autobiographical narration by establishing an implicit pact between the musician and his listeners in the very same way in which autobiographer and reader implicitly agree on a generic pact that guides the reader's expectations of the text's referential nature. According to this pact, the author's name as it is displayed on the book cover signifies an identity of living person, narrative voice, and the character designated by the personal pronoun "I."[54] The same pact can be identified in Armstrong's musical recordings, where the object of narration (the lyric I) and the performing subject (the singer enunciating the lyrics) are cross-referenced by the performer's name, face, and voice. Therefore, the name and face on the covers of his musical recordings and the name on the covers of his two autobiographies visually connect the musical and textual contents presented in each of these media.

Moreover, most magazine articles and interviews place photographs of the musician prominently alongside the text. These photographs are visual reminders of the autobiographical pact, connecting the autobiographical speaker and his music with images of this speaker and thus referencing the person who produces, or at least informs the production of, text, music, and image. But they do so according to the notion of autobiographics outlined above. They open up a space for visual modes of self-performance rather than being tied to a narrowly defined contractual sign of identity, and rather than simply "document autobiography, [they] may also confound verbal narrative" just as much as "autobiography may mediate on, stimulate, or even take the form of photography." Thus, the referential space of Armstrong's autobiographics connects music with text and image but does so by foregrounding "autobiography's and photography's vexed history of referentiality," according to which "text and image complement, rather than supplement each other."[55]

Whenever Armstrong performed his life story, he entered into an autobiographical pact with his audiences, but since he extended this life story across media, he also produced an overarching autobiographics. While performative experimentation is possible and necessary for a performer who is trying to appeal to diverse audiences and is therefore subject to various institutional and discursive pressures, these experimentations are always (re)integrated through the pact that assumes the identity of performer and the object of performance. The frontispiece of *Swing That Music* is a good example in this regard. It reprints the photograph by Anton Bruehl that had accompanied an article on Armstrong in *Vanity Fair* about a year before the publication of the autobiography.[56] While the photograph represents an instance of mediation that was not fully controlled by Armstrong (he probably had no say in which photograph from the session would make it on to the magazine cover), it allowed him to showcase his elegant dress and satisfied smile. Highlighting the image-text interface, the narrator refers directly to this photograph toward the end of *Swing That Music* when he speaks about the Selmer trumpet Armstrong used as his major instrument: "This is the trumpet you see in the picture at the front of this book."[57] Additional references underscore the cross-pollination of autobiographical narrative and music: the autobiography is titled after "Swing That Music" (May 18, 1936), an up-tempo number that Armstrong and his ghostwriter Horace Gerlach composed especially for the book and that showcases the trumpeter's high-note playing.[58] The musical score for the song as well as its lyrics were added at the end of the autobiography, and a recording of the tune was released to coincide with its publication. Finally, the text proper places itself explicitly in the context of Armstrong's music. Writing about the Luis Russell band, which featured him as its star soloist, the narrator notes: "This is the band you hear over the radio when I play."[59] The present tense of the statement implies that the reader may actually turn on the radio and listen to the music described in the text. No sound recordings exist of Armstrong's radio appearances in 1936, but there is recorded evidence of his performances at the *Fleischmann's Yeast Show* (from April to May 1937), which took place only months after the publication of *Swing That Music*. While he did not perform "Swing That Music," the recordings nonetheless give us a good idea of what radio listeners at the time would have heard when they tuned in to an Armstrong broadcast: high-energy performances of a broad spectrum of material ranging from nineteenth-century abolitionist songs like "Darling Nellie Gray," vaudeville numbers like "Chinatown, My Chinatown," and early jazz classics like "Tiger Rag," to pop tunes like "Memories of You" and movie hits like "Pennies from Heaven."[60] The reader of *Swing That Music* would thus have encountered a series of connected references to the different modes and media through which Armstrong presented himself to his audiences: to an autobiographics that hinges on the interfacing of the Barthesian triad of image, music, and text.[61]

Feeding the musical portion of this triad, many songs in Armstrong's repertoire suggest autobiographical contexts through geographical and historical references. "Mahogany Hall Stomp" (Mar. 5, 1929; Lulu White's infamous Storyville brothel), "Basin Street Blues" (Dec. 4, 1928), and "Canal Street Blues" (Apr. 5, 1923; both streets in New Orleans), as well as "New Orleans Function" (Apr. 26–27, 1950), recall well-publicized scenes and locations from Armstrong's life that soon came to be received—and indeed heard—as an integral element of New Orleans jazz. While these songs were frequently written and performed by other musicians, they attained an autobiographical dimension in the moment of performance when Armstrong announced the tunes by stating that "we're now gonna take you all the way down to New Orleans, this time, my good old hometown" ("High Society," Jan. 26, 1933). The many autobiographical narratives he authorized throughout his life heighten this effect since nearly all of them emphasize his personal investment with the New Orleans places and events named in the songs. For instance, Armstrong's composition "Coal Cart Blues" is supplemented by an autobiographical story in *Satchmo*, where the musician describes his job hauling coal in the Andrews Coal Yard: "That was when I wrote *Coal Cart Blues*, which I recorded years later."[62] There is hardly a biographer who has not pointed out this connection, and it serves as a reminder that, whatever the actual connection between song and story, may be autobiographical narratives contribute to musical sense making and vice versa.

An even more striking example is "New Orleans Function," which was recorded in 1950 and is included on *A Musical Autobiography*. Armstrong introduces the number by saying: "Next, we're going to bring back another New Orleans memory: the days when I was second lining behind the brass bands. This is something I'll never forget: the music they played at the funerals." In the middle of the performance, the music turns into popular theater, the musicians mimicking the crying mourners and Armstrong providing voice-over. While bound by the autobiographical pact to Armstrong's life story and thus to a specific historical moment, this recording is also a site of experimentation in the sense that it enables Armstrong and his colleagues to signal a self-reflexive understanding of their role as popular entertainers who provide their audiences with a sonic illustration of one of the most famous New Orleans socio-musical practices. They do so by overly dramatizing the performance, thereby foregrounding the temporal, spatial, and social distance between the New Orleans folk ritual of the early twentieth century and their current status as highly paid professional musicians who revive this ritual for an audience personally unfamiliar with the culture in which it originated. The sonic narrative constructed on this recording thus adds to, but also complicates, Armstrong's numerous written depictions of New Orleans jazz funerals by simultaneously reciting and multiply marking heterogeneous identities: folk musician versus professional musician versus popular entertainer.

Apart from writing and music, film was another powerful medium into which Armstrong extended his autobiographics. Significantly, in most of the twenty-plus movies in which he starred, he played himself, not a fictional character. Even when he did play a role other than that of "Louis Armstrong" or "Satchmo," and even when a role did not necessarily call for it, he was always depicted playing the trumpet, for example in *Going Places* (dir. Ray Enright, 1938), where he is cast as "Gabriel," a stable hand whose music soothes the racehorse Jeepers Creepers. In *Glory Alley* (dir. Raoul Walsh, 1952), he is "Shadow," a boxing coach for Socks Barbarrosa (Ralph Meeker) and a guide for a blind character called the Judge (Kurt Kasznar), and in *Cabin in the Sky* (dir. Vincente Minnelli, 1943), he appears in a short comedy scene as the trumpeter to the devil.[63] Moreover, the advertising for *New Orleans*, a movie that very loosely covers scenes from Armstrong's life in New Orleans, made extensive use of his popularity. He played a concert after the premiere to promote his role in the film, recorded the soundtrack with Billie Holiday, posed with her on publicity shots, and was featured prominently on movie posters. More revealing in terms of Armstrong's autobiographics, however, is the fact that the film appeared in lieu of a multiepisode biopic that Orson Welles had planned to produce with Armstrong playing the central role. Welles had begun to work on the project in 1941. Several screenplays were written, the most substantial of which was Elliot Paul's "It's All True," based on a six-page autobiographical letter Armstrong had sent Welles on October 22, 1945.[64] Armstrong refers to the film in several letters, two of them to Leonard Feather (in one of them, from Sept. 18, 1941, he calls it "my picture") and a third one to his biographer Robert Goffin (where he calls it "the story of my life").[65] The project was, however, never completed, and the chance to cast Armstrong as the protagonist in his own biopic was missed.[66]

Besides written autobiographical narratives (letters, essays, books); oral statements in interviews, on stage, and in the recording studio; and visual material (films, portraits, photos), Armstrong presented his life story in two additional media, albeit not so much to the public, but mostly to himself, friends, and future generations. One is the medium of the photo-collage, with which he became involved in the 1950s and that he kept up as a hobby for the rest of his life. He made reference to this hobby in a 1953 letter to Marili Mardon. Enclosed in a previous letter he had sent a photo of his collages, and now he wrote to explain: "I guess you've wondered why all the regalia (the photo) that I sent to you . . . huh? Well, you know my hobbie (one of them anyway) is using a lot of scotch tape. . . . My hobbie is to pick out the different things during what I read and piece them together and making a little story of my own."[67] These photo-collages consist of scraps from newspapers and magazines, as well as photographs Armstrong had taken or had been given by fans or friends. He creatively reassembled and pasted them into his many scrapbooks, onto the covers of his reel-to-reel tape-box collection, and onto the walls and even the ceiling of his den at his home in Corona, New York.[68] Included were newspaper articles about his concerts; telegrams and postcards sent to him by musicians, actors, and politicians; photographs of himself backstage with fans and fellow players; magazine pictures of Duke Ellington and Billie Holiday; photo stills and promotional material from films such as *Pennies from Heaven* (dir. Norman Z. McLeod, 1936), *Artists & Models* (dir. Raoul Walsh, 1937),

Fig. 2. Louis Armstrong, working on his photo-collages in his home in Corona, New York. Photograph by Dennis Stock, 1958. Courtesy of Agentur Focus/Magnum Photos.

Glory Alley, High Society, The Five Pennies (dir. Melville Shavelson, 1959), and *Hello Dolly* (dir. Gene Kelly, 1969); a newspaper cartoon of himself and manager Glaser; and many photographs of himself and his fourth wife, Lucille. It is not too farfetched to find structural similarities among Armstrong's anecdotal approach to written and oral autobiography (e.g., reminiscences about film shootings, fellow musicians, manager Glaser, his wife Lucille), his habit of quoting material from different sources in his solos and vocals, and the bricolage aesthetic of the photo-collages. These photo-collages, as Jorge Daniel Veneciano notes, "offer iconic (photographic) representations and personally symbolic interpolations of a life and its celebrity world" and thus "constitute autobiography by other means."[69]

Finally, there are more than one thousand hours of recordings that Armstrong made on his Ampex and Tandberg tape players. Besides taping his favorite records (including his own) and his live performances, he taped hundreds of hours of private conversations at his home in Corona, backstage, and in hotel rooms (he took his recording equipment on tour). While not all of these recordings can be conceived as autobiographical in a conventional sense, they nonetheless illustrate a drive to conserve his life story in yet another medium. And since he also dictated some of his letters into the tape recorder and sought to preserve segments of his life story by speaking them into the recording machine, we can certainly think of these recordings as "audio autobiography" and as a "soundtrack of his private and public lives."[70] In one of these recordings, which was recently made available as part of the *Fleischmann's Yeast Show & Louis' Home-Recorded Tapes* CD, Armstrong proofreads a letter to his British biographer Max Jones and explains his motive for this curious practice: "I'm putting it on tape, you know, for my posterity." He told the same thing to Lucille when she stated that she "wouldn't give a shit about your thousands of tapes."[71] Armstrong, we can gather from these remarks, was deeply involved with the mediation and conservation not just of his music but also of virtually everything he experienced and produced throughout his life.

The immensity and diversity of Armstrong's autobiographical output raise a central question: how can we read, hear, and perceive these wide-ranging activities without either strictly segregating them into autobiographical writings and nonwritten communication or merely speculating that writing and expressions in other media are somehow connected? Obviously, we confront a series of performances that urge us to conceive of Armstrong's autobiographics as a mode of communication that is not confined to a single text, published as an authoritative account of a life between the covers of one book, or even to a fixed textual corpus in the sense that *Swing That Music* and *Satchmo* combined would constitute one authoritative story.[72] Rather, we encounter an expressive practice that shapes Armstrong's communication in more than one genre of writing—letters, essays, extended narratives—*and* transcends the limits of textual signification. This practice structures Armstrong's music (singing and trumpet playing), his spoken narratives (interviews, tape recordings, vocal insertions and jive patter on recordings), and his visual performances (on stage, in films, on photographs, and in his photo-collages).

These complex autobiographical phenomena—an endless string of narratives instead of a fixed body of texts, autobiographical performances across media instead of autobiography as a literary genre—are best approached through an intermedial model of music-image-text interfaces.[73] Applied to Armstrong's autobiographical practices, this model produces two central assumptions. The first assumption is that Armstrong follows a *transmedial* impulse in the sense that he is communicating similar ideas and sentiments in and through different media. He performs his life story in every medium at his disposal, and while the shape, form, and details of this story will vary depending on the context of performance and on the medium through which each particular presentation emerges, it is nevertheless the same basic story conveyed over and over again and orchestrated as part his autobiographics.[74] Since the material conditions of each medium influence the content of communication, the question is which specific shapes and forms these autobiographical expressions take on in different media and in what ways each medial variation and each new enunciation of the story references and revises existing versions of a continually growing body of accumulated narratives.[75] The second assumption is that this transmedial impulse, once it is expressed in different media, results in a media mix that can only be described as *intermedial* since it casts Satchmo as a physical, musical, visual, textual, and discursive figure in the field of popular culture. This book accounts for these two related phenomena: it comes to terms with Armstrong as a *transmedial* artist, and it maps the *intermedial* effects of Armstrong's autobiographical performances.

As a transmedial and intermedial study of these performances, this book differs from the biographical, historical, and musicological focus of previous scholarship. It pursues four aims. Recognizing Armstrong's potential as a figurehead for jazz historiography, critics, biographers, and scholars have often raided the musician's written and spoken statements in order to tell their specific versions of jazz history. Yet acknowledging and accounting for the historically and culturally specific moments in which Armstrong wrote and spoke about his life and music is especially significant in a field of cultural production in which musicians have rarely had full and open access to the means of self-representation. In his analysis of jazz musicians as artists, critics, and activists, Eric Porter maintains that "there is still a need for sustained, historical discussions of what African American musicians have said publicly about their music, their positions as artists, the 'jazz tradition' in general, and the broader social and cultural implications of this music." This turn to the jazz musicians' public speech, to their written and spoken statements as a series of "interventions in the jazz discourse" (as Porter puts it in his chapter on Charles Mingus), presents an important moment in the historiography of jazz.[76] Reading Armstrong's autobiographical narratives and epistolary commentary, which span the course of five decades (1922–70), as a series of interventions in shifting jazz discourses means realizing that musicians like Armstrong were actively involved in providing the fodder for modern conceptions of race, culture, and nation. Jazz musicians, as John Gennari rightly notes, are "savvy co-conspirators in the crafting of their public images."[77] Determining the nature and the extent of Armstrong's involvement in the musical, visual, textual, and discursive construction of his public persona is the book's first aim and distinguishes its approach from the largely biographical focus of publications such as Gary Giddins's *Satchmo: The Genius of Louis Armstrong*, Laurence Bergreen's *Louis Armstrong: An Extravagant Life*, Scott Allen Nollen's *Louis Armstrong: The Life, Music and Screen Career*, Terry Teachout's *Pops: A Life of Louis Armstrong*, and Ricky Riccardi's *What a Wonderful World: The Magic of Louis Armstrong's Later Years*.

The second aim is to dig into a textual corpus that Gary Giddins identified as an autobiographical subgenre of jazz literature in 1979 and that William Kenney labeled "jazz autobiography" in a bibliographical essay in 1987.[78] In spite of the handful of scholarly articles that have suggested different theoretical frameworks for the more than one hundred autobiographies by American jazz musicians that have appeared since 1926, when Paul Whiteman published an account of his life, and apart from a few more analyses devoted to single autobiographies, there remains a substantial lack of critical inquiry into this textual corpus.[79] If John F. Szwed is correct to claim that "the black jazz musician [. . .] was perhaps the first truly nonmechanical metaphor for the twentieth century" and that the life of the usually male jazz instrumentalist was shaped by "the double alienation of artist and color," then it makes sense to investigate the ways in which a musician like Armstrong tapped into the metaphorical power of his life and music and to examine the ways in which he narrated and performed his life as a lived process.[80] By doing so, this book sheds light on a segment of American autobiography that has essentially remained a "fugitive literature" not only in the field of jazz studies, where the interest in jazz autobiographies has been scattered, and in the field of literary studies, where critics have overwhelmingly turned to poetic, fictional, and (to a lesser degree) dramatic representations of jazz, but even more so in the field of autobiography studies, where it is almost nonexistent.[81]

Recent criticism has opened the field of jazz studies to analyses of the music's relationship with other media and art forms. Robert O'Meally, Brent Hayes Edwards, and Farah Jasmine Griffin, for instance, emphasize the need to account for "cross-fertilizations and links between jazz and creative expression in other media: the visual arts, literature, electronica." They argue that inquiries into music-text relations should not "echo old assumptions about the ways that a novelist emulates or evokes a saxophonist," as more traditional studies of jazz poetry and narrative fiction have frequently advocated, but that such inquiries should "suggest that certain aesthetic issues, certain modes and structural paradigms, show up in a number of media—or, more precisely, operate at the edges of media, at what one might term the interface of sound and script and pigment."[82] This paradigm shift from an *intra*disciplinary perspective on jazz literature toward an *inter*disciplinary and *intermedial* analysis of jazz and other media has two central implications. On the one hand, it encourages readings of musicotextual relations between jazz and autobiography that are sensitive to the communicative exchange that takes place between expressions in these media while, at the same time, dismantling the overly narrow formalist and structuralist requirement that autobiographical discourse must mimic jazz music in order to qualify as a form of intermedial literature. On the other hand, this shift makes clear that one would be ill-advised to marginalize, or even ignore, the manifold expressive forms chosen by musicians and focus solely on their music, thereby underestimating the significance of their appearances in film, on television, and in photographs. Indeed, the cross-fertilizations that result from the interdependencies among these media code jazz as an intrinsically intermedial phenomenon. Theorizing, mapping, and analyzing this phenomenon—especially its role in the construction of Armstrong's autobiographics, but also in response to those studies of music-text relations that downplay the performative and intermedial implications that arise from the jazz musician's role as both producer and subject of music and autobiography—is a third aim this book pursues. Armstrong utilized the autobiographical mode as his most powerful and central form of expression in all media of communication. In that regard, autobiography is neither an addendum to his music nor simply a collection of jazz anecdotes. Instead, it provides the structure through which all of his communication emerges, and it largely determines the popular and critical reception of his Satchmo persona. While it makes sense, from a literary standpoint, to think of Armstrong's autobiographies as a corpus of related writings, it makes even more sense, from an intermedial perspective, to emphasize the cross-references among expressions in various media and the cultural work they perform within the referential frame that is constituted by the musician's autobiographics.

This intermedial space is structured to a substantial degree by historically contingent representations and discourses of musical "blackness." When Armstrong entered the mass-mediated entertainment culture of the urban North in the 1920s, he encountered deeply held racial stereotypes and widely embraced cultural narratives that had evolved from the minstrel shows in the nineteenth century and were now entering the era of modern mass mediatization. The arrival of jazz and its growing popularity presented black musicians with a basic conundrum. In order to gain an audience eager to attend their shows and buy their records, they offered themselves and their music to listeners who had routinely used black music as a canvas for cross-racial projections and interracial fantasies. New media such as sound recording and radio, as well as the rapidly changing social makeup of cities like Chicago and New York, did not abolish minstrel constructions of "black" sounds and sights. In this period of heightened cultural flux, new projections were added to more established racial fantasies. While "blackness" on stage had long operated as a signifier of comic exuberance and intellectual inferiority, it frequently came to be embraced in primitivist terms as a means of sexual stimulation and as an escape from the constraints of modern life. These new projections limited the creative possibilities of the musicians but simultaneously provided them with new cultural capital, which players like Armstrong used strategically in their struggle for social agency, commercial success, and creative freedom. Armstrong, in this sense, is an autobiographer who also functions as "a mediator in intercultural, interethnic, and interracial affairs."[83] Therefore, the book's fourth aim is to make sense of a historical development from the construction of "blackness" on the minstrel stage to performances of "blackness" during the Jazz Age and into the era of the civil rights movement. The idea is to examine the ways in which changing stage representations and racial discourses structured Armstrong's autobiographics, its reception, and its cultural repercussions and to do so by tracing an evolving intermedial cultural poetics of blackface minstrelsy that is not beholden to the popular entertainer versus master musician dichotomy or to the narrative of Armstrong's jazz as great American art by an unlikely black genius.[84]

In order to attain these aims, this book is divided into six chapters. Based on the assumption that the aesthetics of jazz and autobiography require a specific understanding of intermedia relations, it makes a distinction between music-text interfaces that result from shared aesthetic, narrative, and performative principles and can be allocated on the level of autobiographical text and musical form (chapters 1, 2, and 3) and a larger frame of reference that ultimately transcends the bounds of individual texts and musical pieces and includes a more expansive kind of cultural intermediality (chapters 4, 5, and 6). The first three chapters thus focus on central performative impulses that shape Armstrong's communication across media: a musicking impulse according to which music is a socially grounded cultural practice that structures both the content and the telling of Armstrong's life story (chapter 1); a versioning impulse that accounts for the performative drive behind Armstrong's music and writing and champions the provisional qualities of improvisation over static models of self-presentation (chapter 2); and a scat/swing impulse that shapes the musician's unedited writings in ways that suggest the excessive signification of scat singing (chapter 3).

Chapters 4, 5, and 6 identify instances of cultural intermediality in terms of a discourse of modern blackface minstrelsy within which Armstrong was frequently positioned and that he himself evoked. Chapter 4 launches an inquiry into the ways in which the minstrel shows of the nineteenth century extended their intermedial influence even after they had largely disappeared from American life. It develops a conceptual frame through which to perceive Armstrong's complicated involvement with the productive ambiguities that the minstrel legacy bestowed upon black jazz musicians in the twentieth century (and not only black jazz musicians, but other artists, entertainers, and public figures, as well). Chapter 5 views Armstrong as a performer whose intermedial interventions in the jazz discourse amplified the double resonances of the postcolonial laughter with which he confronted his audiences and readers. Specifically, it discusses the influence of Bill "Bojangles" Robinson and Bert Williams on the musician's "Reverend Satchelmouth" routines and his depictions of African American religious practices. It further assesses the intriguing confluences between the minstrel gaze and the patterns of the African American migration narrative in Armstrong's writings and music and reconstructs the discourses and debates that surrounded his highly controversial blackface performance as King of the Zulus in 1949.

Chapter 6 examines Armstrong's cultural politics, the unconventional sense of political engagement that earned him political prominence as Ambassador Satch but also caused him to fall out of favor with many African American listeners, who denigrated him as an Uncle Tom and accused him of playing the clown for white audiences by the 1960s. Listening closely to Armstrong's nuanced commentary about his tours to Africa and paying close attention to his written, spoken, musical, and visual reflections on his role as a black entertainer during the civil rights movement, this chapter argues that the musician's complicated, and sometimes contradictory, engagement with the political changes that shaped his life is best understood in terms of a deeply rooted habitus that was determined by the vernacular culture of New Orleans, as well as by the legacy of blackface minstrelsy. The final chapter offers a short coda on Armstrong's intermedial autobiographics by way of a close reading of his baffling "Laughin' Louie" recordings from 1933.

A Note on Citations

Louis Armstrong's handwritten and typed manuscripts are filled with orthographic and typographic idiosyncrasies (apostrophes, dashes, ellipses, underscores, unorthodox capitalization, unusual spelling, and so forth). These idiosyncrasies are represented without editorial interventions because they convey meaning and determine the visual appearance of the texts. The frequent ellipses that shape Armstrong's writings are reproduced without brackets; whenever I cite only parts of a sentence or passage, I use ellipses in brackets to indicate the omission. Many of Armstrong's manuscripts and letters have been published in recent years; in order to increase readability and accessibility, I cite from the published versions whenever possible.

A Note on Recordings

All of Armstrong's recording dates, personnel, and the exact spellings of song titles are taken from Jos Willems, *All of Me: The Complete Discography of Louis Armstrong* (Lanham: Scarecrow, 2006).

"I have always been a great observer"

New Orleans Musicking

Reviewing Louis Armstrong's second autobiography, *Satchmo: My Life in New Orleans*, the music historian Henry Kmen wrote in 1955: "Unfortunately, the earliest jazz musicians were not given to keeping written records, and their music was not, nor could it be, formally composed on paper." For Kmen, *Satchmo* disappoints those interested in the "obscure period" of prerecorded jazz because "Louis has written little that is not already known about the origins of the music" and because "there is little [. . .] here that is concerned with jazz itself." Armstrong's depiction of the musical culture of his youth, Kmen concludes, is merely a "group of vignettes" and a "kind of montage of the life surrounding a poor Negro family in New Orleans during the first two decades of the twentieth century."[1]

In fact, Armstrong's autobiographical narratives accomplish much more than Kmen realized. They document the personal and cultural significance of New Orleans music making, question the very notion of "jazz itself," and intervene repeatedly in the discursive construction of the "jazz tradition."[2] This is why these narratives should not be reduced to mere historical source texts about the past, but can be more fruitfully read as performative engagements that continue to participate actively in shaping our efforts to understand the musical and cultural history of New Orleans jazz. And indeed, Armstrong was very much aware of the discursive power wielded by music journalists and historians and sought to accommodate their interests in addition to furthering his own. As early as 1941, he wrote to Leonard Feather, "I 'Dug'd that write up in the *Down Beat* about the Trumpet players and thought it was pretty nice," and on one of his late tape recordings, he reads from a letter to his biographer Max Jones, stating that he "shall try to answer all of your questions."[3] Taking a more disgruntled stance, Armstrong once told Richard Meryman that jazz historiography basically amounted to the production of popular myths. Here, he sought to reestablish his authority as a jazz autobiographer in the 1960s: "What they say about the old days is corny. They form their own opinions, they got so many words for things and make everything soooo big—and it turns out a—what you call it—a fictitious story."[4] Such disavowal of jazz criticism is a dominant topos among jazz musicians. George "Pops" Foster, for instance, announces that his autobiography "is gonna straighten a lot of things out," while Sidney Bechet asserts: "You know there's people, they got the wrong idea of Jazz. [. . .] And the real story I've got to tell, it's right there." Danny Barker is even more confrontational: "Many books came on the scene together with many falsehoods, lies and cooked-up stories. I read much of this crap and then I was told that I should write some truth, and explanations of many jazz subjects that were not clearly explained."[5] These statements suggest an understanding of jazz autobiography "as a *reaction against* previous writing on jazz," as a chance to offer alternate takes on the musicians' personal histories and the history of their music.[6] While "[j]azz critics may think of what they are doing as an exercise in formal analysis," as John Gennari observes, "musicians read jazz criticism as a first draft of *their* history," seeking to revise, correct, or build on previous representations of their lives and music.[7]

Armstrong's memories of New Orleans music are therefore triply coded: they aim to set the record straight by relating his version of past events, they afford him prominence as a cultural icon whose life story resonates with American myths of race and black music, and they deliver the raw material for others to present his life story to the public. If jazz autobiographers intervene in the shifting discourses of jazz, offer alternate takes on jazz history, and revise drafts written by others, the question is how they realize these objectives. As participant observers whose understanding of the past is necessarily shaped by the pitfalls of memory as well as by complex personal significances and strategic concerns, they nevertheless speak with special authority as cultural insiders and musical creators. This authority rests on specific linguistic and narratological means, which is why this chapter sets out to conduct a series of literary close readings of Armstrong's autobiographical recollections. The goal is to reconstruct the historical contexts in which Armstrong produced his depictions of early New Orleans jazz and to investigate the ways in which his language and narrative perspective determined his versions of the story. The usefulness of such a literary approach lies in its ability to contextualize, amend, and sometimes question the conclusions musicologists and jazz historians like Kmen have drawn about Armstrong's role in the development of jazz.

A good case in point is Armstrong's "Jazz on a High Note," the essay he wrote for *Esquire* in 1951 to celebrate his classic Hot Five and Hot Seven recordings from the 1920s. Armstrong recalls about the origins of "Struttin' with Some Barbecue" (Dec. 9, 1927):

> This tune was derived and thought of during the days when [drummer] Zutty Singleton and I were playing at the Savoy Ballroom on the South Side of Chicago . . . And, after the dance was over every night, Zutty and I would drive out to 48th and State Street . . . There was an old man there who made some of the most delicious barbecue that anyone would love to smack their chops on (their lips) [. . .] . One night, while Zutty and I were manipulating those "Chime Bones" (barbecue), a thought came into my head . . . I said to Zutty—"Say, Zoot, as I sit here eating these fine-tasting ribs, it dawned on me that I should write a tune and call it 'Struttin' with Some Barbecue'" . . . Zutty said, "Dush, that's a real good idea" . . . So then and there, "Struttin' with Some Barbecue" was born. . . .[8]

For musicologists and jazz historians, Armstrong's claim to having composed the piece with drummer Zutty Singleton rings false. As Joshua Berrett argues, certain harmonic properties of the song (especially the major seventh chord that underlies the opening melody) are atypical of Armstrong's musical vocabulary but very common in the classical compositions studied by his wife and comusician, Lil Hardin. This makes plausible Hardin's claim to being the actual composer of the tune: "the individual musical details of this piece tell another, more complex story" than Armstrong's anecdote implies, Berrett concludes.[9]

While certainly convincing in musicological terms, this conclusion illuminates only parts of this other, more complex story. Read as an autobiographical statement made for a specific purpose and directed at a specific readership, Armstrong's words attain a historical significance of which purely musicological perspectives may remain unaware. In the early 1950s, jazz was becoming recognized as an art form and as a musical genre whose history was worth preserving, and Armstrong was setting out to become an all-American jazz icon. In 1951, he had already started working on his second autobiography, to be published three years later as *Satchmo: My Life in New Orleans*. His obvious wish to put a personal stamp on "Struttin' with

Some Barbecue" and his apparent desire to retroactively supply the song with an autobiographical context—his friendship with Zutty, his love of Southern food, the dominance of male jazz musicians over women like Lil Hardin, and jazz's indebtedness to moments of spontaneity and social interaction—may be taken as indications of a drive toward memorializing past achievements and redrafting the popular narrative of New Orleans jazz into a personalized historiography of the music. The passive voice at the beginning of this statement ("was derived and thought of") alerts the careful reader to the complex history of the piece. Hardin may have been the actual composer, but perhaps Armstrong thought that he had made it his own by adding his personal style to it. It is very possible that Hardin composed the chord progressions and melody of the tune but that the band collaborated on the actual arrangement of the piece. The phrase "Chime Bones," for instance, evokes Armstrong's first solo captured on sound recording on "Chimes Blues" with King Oliver's Creole Jazz Band (Apr. 5, 1923), and so he may also have thought that he owned certain songs once he had recorded a trumpet solo for them. All in all, the anecdote says much about Armstrong's creative process (connecting musical innovation with personal recollection and vice versa) and about the power of autobiographical interventions in the historiography of jazz. The story of two Southern émigrés enjoying down-home food up North and twisting the English language to express their sentiments resonates deeply with stories of the Great Migration and occupies a central position in Armstrong's autobiographics.

Musical recordings and personal testimony, as this example attests, must be read *in conjunction with* and not *against* each other, if we are to get a sense of the historical complexities and personal significances of jazz.[10] The best way to accomplish this is to analyze Armstrong's depictions of his life by making the narratological distinction between *story* and *narrative discourse* in addition to tracing the evolution of his autobiographical and musical consciousness to the formative influences of his childhood in New Orleans. In narratological terms, Armstrong's depictions capture music making and its social integration on the level of content (story), as well as on the level of narrative transmission (discourse): vernacular music is reflected by a vernacular approach to autobiographical telling, and instead of formal musical analysis, the reader encounters portraits of particularly memorable players, performances, and practices.[11]

Again and again, Armstrong's autobiographical narratives return to the musical culture of New Orleans and to the people among whom he grew up. They also cover events from his career after his departure from New Orleans in 1922, but the musician's vigorous insistence on the personal relevance of his New Orleans youth and the moral as well as musical lessons he had internalized there suggest that we may read these narratives as crucial enunciations of a life invested in, and shaped by, the musical culture of the city: "I only live in Chicago. My Home's New Orleans," he told the *New Orleans Item-Tribune* in the 1920s.[12] Thus, rather than being sensational narratives of success, Armstrong's recollections of prerecorded New Orleans jazz are best understood as representations of what Christopher Small has labeled "musicking": music as "an activity, something that people do."[13] According to this understanding, music emerges from an encounter between human beings who communicate through the "medium of sounds organized in specific ways"; it is a social activity embedded in a specific time and place.[14] "To music is to take part, in any capacity, in a musical performance," Small maintains, "whether by performing, by listening, by rehearsing or practicing, by providing material for performance (what is called composing), or by dancing."[15] And indeed, Armstrong regularly describes music as a cultural practice through which New Orleanians communicate and through which they organize their lives in particular sociocultural settings. The self presented in Armstrong's life narratives comes into existence through musicking's powerful impact on the autobiographical subject, and the autobiographer makes sense of his self through his social role as a musician. Musical performances allow early black jazz musicians to "extend [. . .] the self into the made world" and feel a "sense of agency"; they constitute "not just [. . .] a collection of sounds, but [. . .] a way of living in the world."[16] In that sense, musical achievements birth an "I" from which musical style and creativity flow, as Armstrong acknowledged many times: "Music has been in my blood from the day I was born"; "My life has always been music"; "My whole life, my whole soul, my whole spirit, is to b-l-o-w this h-o-r-n."[17]

Armstrong once referred to his life as "an open book." Coupled with his belief that "your environment makes you," this provides the rationale for his recollections of New Orleans musicking.[18] But what kind of musical culture and life do the autobiographies describe? What kind of "I" is birthed in and through these recollections? And what are the narrative techniques through which these recollections are voiced? These questions are best split into a series of questions that address the different components of musicking, the historical moments Armstrong describes (story), the autobiographical vantage point from which he describes them, and the language he employs to formulate his recollections (narrative discourse): who plays music, what songs are played, and how are they played? What is the cultural position of the black musician in New Orleans in the 1900s and 1910s? What are the musical materials on which musicians draw and out of which they create new styles? And what, according to those who heard it, did the music sound like? In terms of setting, what are the places of musical performance, and how do these places influence the performance? What are the institutions and rituals through which musical performances are regulated? What effects does the music have on its audiences? What are the personal and cultural meanings for the music's practitioners? In terms of narrative transmission, when does Armstrong tell which specific stories? To whom does he address them? How does he verbalize his recollections of past events? And what kind of narrative voice and autobiographical speaker are constructed?

In order to answer these questions, it makes sense to start with *Swing That Music*, Armstrong's first autobiography, because its narrative construction of events is most obviously shaped by the ghostwriter's hand, which controls the narrative discourse and is responsible for a notion of New Orleans music very much opposed to the musicking Armstrong remembered in later accounts. *Swing That Music* takes an analytical approach to its subject. As the narrator claims, "this book isn't supposed to be so much about me as about swing; where it came from, how it grew and what it is." This narrator simultaneously glorifies and marginalizes Armstrong's role in the development of the music: "It is just an accident that swing and I were born and brought up side by side in New Orleans, travelled up the Mississippi together, and, in 1922 [. . .] were there in Chicago getting acquainted with the North—and the North getting acquainted with us."[19] Here, meaningful human communication is reduced from a causal connection between music and the moment of its creation to a myth of coincidental origins. The account insinuates a sense of passivity that is striking. Swing was born by accident, not created by ambitious musicians, and Armstrong and the music simply "were there" in Chicago in 1922, which implies that the music had an identity apart from the musicians who played it and had somehow arrived in Chicago of its own volition.

Swing That Music places New Orleans musicians at the beginning of jazz while erasing the specific cultural value of their musical innovations. The musicians of Armstrong's youth, the narrator holds forth, didn't know Bach from Beethoven, or Mozart from Mendelssohn, and maybe hadn't even heard of them, and, strange as it may sound, I think that is exactly why they became great musicians. Not knowing much classical music, and not many of them having proper education in reading music of any kind, they just went ahead and made up their own music. Before long, and without really knowing it themselves, they had created a brand new music, they created swing. They made a music for themselves which truly expressed what they felt.[20]

This passage is rich in implications, and several observations about its endorsement of early jazz, anachronistically called "swing," can be made. It is certainly true that many working-class African American musicians of Armstrong's generation began their careers as so-called ear musicians who lacked knowledge of European music theory. What this passage neglects, however, are two important facts. First, many musicians branched out as soon as they could and gathered as much musical knowledge as possible. Armstrong, for instance, accepted employment on the Streckfus entertainment ships (1918–21), vessels that traveled up and down the Mississippi to supply entertainment and dance music for racially segregated and mostly white guests. He did so in order to gain new insights into music, plus money and notoriety. This is how he justified accepting Fate Marable's offer to play on the Streckfus steamers: "When he asked me to join his orchestra I jumped at the opportunity. It meant a great advancement in my musical career because his musicians had to read music perfectly. [. . .] I wanted to do more than fake the music all the time because there is more to music than just playing one style."[21]

Second, the narrator of *Swing That Music* contrasts a Eurocentric notion of musical training with an African American absence of musical knowledge, an absence that allegedly enabled the creation of jazz.[22] This view rests on a primitivist premise. Music unhampered by the straitjacket of rules and conventions is reified as being more spontaneous, more emotional, and more authentic than allegedly civilized music. However, as Armstrong's later autobiographical depictions reiterate and as his recordings from the early 1920s with King Oliver's Creole Jazz Band illustrate (the first of which was made in early Apr. 1923 for Gennett), the vernacular culture of New Orleans possessed a rich array of musical institutions and rituals through which Armstrong and fellow players gained musical expertise in the blues and other styles of music and that they used as a basis for developing new sonic expressions. In light of Armstrong's later accounts, it is safe to say that the musicians did not "just [. . .] ma[k]e up their own music" and that they did not simply "express [. . .] what they felt," as *Swing That Music* claims. Neither did they simply follow "musical instinct." They were not "natural swing players" but had learned to play their instruments and repertoire from older and more experienced musicians, who had acquired their musical knowledge from the preceding generation.[23] All of Armstrong's later narratives resist the teleology endorsed in *Swing That Music*; they substitute the notion of jazz's unselfconscious and untutored origins with detailed descriptions of African American working-class culture and its vernacular traditions.

The stark discrepancy between *Swing That Music*'s view of jazz as a music that came naturally to black New Orleanians and Armstrong's revision of this view makes one wonder whether this first narrative of Armstrong's life should even be considered as part of his autobiographics. It should be, and for good reasons. Only if we recognize *Swing That Music* as the template for Armstrong's later narratives can we read these narratives as evidence of Armstrong's active and conscious engagement with previous representations of his life story. What is more, the topos of jazz as natural music never fully disappeared from his autobiographics. It continued to shape the popular understanding of jazz long after *Swing That Music* had faded from public consciousness, as a 1955 interview with *U.S. News & World Report* indicates. The interview contains a section titled "Natural Music" in which Armstrong superficially affirms this topos but complicates it at the same time. When asked whether jazz originated in New Orleans, he answers: "All up and down the Mississippi—and old blues, and things like that. But it was the sound at all times. Natural music, shore [*sic*]. It's the same thing. You can't write it—you just feel it. Now with 'The Saints'— 'Saints Go Marchin' In'—it's a hymn, and it comes from the brass bands playin'."[24] Armstrong certainly picks up on the idea of natural music here, and so do the editors of the magazine, who probably prompted him to discuss it (which would explain the affirmative "shore"). But the musician's account is actually very specific about the fact that the music is not instinctive at all. Armstrong mentions the region in which it could be heard ("All up and down the Mississippi"), names the various styles and songs (old blues, a hymn like "The Saints Go Marchin' In") a musician had to master as part of distinct musical organizations (brass bands), and notes that it is a "sound at all times" that a musician could not learn to create by studying musical scores ("You can't write it") but had to learn how to "feel" by being involved in particular cultural practices. That Armstrong affirms the narrative of natural music in his *Jazz Casual* interview with Ralph Gleason in 1963 signals that the piece in *U.S. News & World Report* was no isolated incidence and that the discourse was not confined to the print medium.

The ideological underpinnings of *Swing That Music* thus provide the historical and discursive contexts for later interviews. In 1936, they forced the narrator to perform a number of rhetorical somersaults. The discrepancy between the self-consciously authoritative and knowledgeable voice—allegedly Armstrong's—and his fellow untutored New Orleans musicians is the result of a convoluted logic that seeks to celebrate the musical sophistication of swing music and its popular appeal to white listeners in the 1930s with Armstrong as a black poster child. In order to make this argument plausible, the narrator first presents the autobiography as a tribute to the Original Dixieland Jazz Band and then finds supposedly less sophisticated origins for this music that nonetheless already contain the seeds of the "genius" of swing.[25] *Swing That Music* is dedicated to the Original Dixieland Jazz Band (ODJB), a group of white New Orleanians of Italian and Anglo descent who recorded what is commonly understood as the first jazz recording in 1917 ("Livery Stable Blues" / "Dixieland Jass Band One Step"). The ODJB's members were billed as the "creators of jazz," and members like Nick LaRocca often claimed that jazz had no African American sources and that they alone had invented the music. Owing to the band's prominent status among early jazz historians, *Swing That Music* contains lengthy passages that celebrate the ODJB as jazz pioneers. These passages take away from Armstrong's role in the creation of jazz and reveal the degree to which the prerecorded history of jazz could be reshaped to legitimize a later style of music, in this case, American swing.

As part of this legitimization process, *Swing That Music* insists on early jazz's "crude and not 'finished'" state as opposed to swing's refinement and subtlety. It constructs an evolutionary narrative that is labeled as such by Horace Gerlach's opening statement in the music section: "Louis Armstrong's story of the evolution of modern American music has traced its growth from the barbaric phase through to today's refined and developed forms."[26] The narrator acknowledges that jazz "had come up slowly out of the old negro folk songs and the spirituals" and that "the regular beat of the jazz syncopation probably came out of the strumming of the banjoes which the slaves had learned to play before the Civil War," but he marginalizes these musical sources when he alleges that the influence of European musical styles delivered the musical refinement that led to swing. Refinement and sophistication seem to follow from a muting of the African American—allegedly crude and barbaric—strains of the music and from the infusion of "elements of the polka and the schottische, the grace of the waltz and the delicacy of the minuet."[27] Racial and musical preconceptions are so deeply intertwined here that it becomes difficult to distinguish between the narrator's interest in reconstructing the historical development from proto-jazz to swing and his tendency to promote a racialized narrative that essentially reifies established distinctions between "low" black folk culture and "high" white cultural sophistication.

Swing That Music valorizes a specific understanding of "free improvisation, or 'swinging'": playing according to one's feelings and improvising instead of following written musical scores. In order to substantiate this narrative, a series of binaries is devised: trained/untrained, classical music/swing, following the written score/improvising. The latter part of each binary is idealized. "If those early swing musicians had gone to music schools and been taught to know and worship the great masters of classical music and been told it was sacrilegious to change a single note of what was put before them to play, swing music would never have been born at all," the narrator explains. Without traditional musical training, the jazz musician "is just plain ignorant [. . .] but has a great deal of feeling he's got to express in some way, and has to find that way out for himself."[28] Armstrong's later accounts do not postulate a state of musical ignorance as the source of early jazz. Instead, they celebrate the communal atmosphere and excitement of New Orleans and offer extensive commentary about the alternative musical education that existed beyond the hallowed halls of white conservatories and music schools. "My first Sincere Applause came from the people whom I was working for," Armstrong writes in his tribute to the Jewish Karnofsky family, who employed him to help their son Morris deliver coal to the Storyville district. "I used to sing for my Boss, Some of those good *Ol* good songs. And he would enjoy them so well—he would applaud for me, so *earnestly* until I would feel just like I had just finished a cornet solo in the *French* Opera House—a place where Negroes were not allowed."[29]

Juxtaposing the ghostwriter's perspective in *Swing That Music* with Armstrong's more self-determined writings illustrates the necessity of accounting for the full space of Armstrong's autobiographics and investigating more elaborately his depictions of the social environment he credited with shaping both his sense of self and his musical consciousness. The complex racial and sociocultural stratification of the New Orleans population and the significance of racial segregation in the development of jazz are noted in "Jewish Family," where Armstrong claims that "I did not get to know any of the White Musicians personally, because New Orleans was so Disgustingly Segregated and Prejudiced at the time."[30] Coining the term "Soulville" for the black district in contradistinction to the white-controlled Storyville, Armstrong points to the influence of racially circumscribed geographical boundaries as the seedbed for the new music.[31] Musical employment meant being allowed to cross racial boundaries temporarily, but it also meant adhering to the racial codes of the time, which prevented any mingling on social terms and limited interracial contact to the service economy:

> The Negroes were only allowed to work in the Red Light District [i.e., Storyville]. As far as to *buy* a little *Trim* [sex]—that was absolutely out of the Question. Most of the help was Negroes. They were paid good Salaries and had a long time Job. The pay was swell, no matter what your vocation was. Musicians—Singers and all kinds of Entertainers were always *welcomed* and *enjoyed*. Just *stay* in your *place* where you belonged. No *Mixing* at the *Guest Tables* at *no time*. Everybody understood Everything and there weren't ever any mix ups, *etc.*[32]

This passage indicates vividly how the racial boundaries between Soulville and Storyville were demarcated by skin color and how blacks were not allowed to meet whites on equal social terms. While work in the entertainment industry brought "good Salaries" and the security of a "long time Job," blacks were forced to appear as servants ("help") or were "*welcomed* and *enjoyed*" only as "Entertainers" who "understood" that to "*stay* in your *place*" was not a matter of politeness, but of survival.

Yet the racial makeup of the New Orleans population was more complicated than the black/white dichotomy implies. As Thomas Brothers notes, "Armstrong thought of New Orleans as made up of three main social groups—whites, Creoles, and Negroes."[33] The geographical separation of African Americans, who lived uptown, and the Creoles of Color, who lived downtown, had social and musical implications. While the Creole musician Isidore Barbarin "didn't know I was colored until [. . .] later years," Armstrong learned as a young boy what his dark skin meant in terms of personal restrictions.[34] Late in his life, he recalled: "Most of the musicians were Creoles. Most of them could pass for white easily—They mostly lived in the Down Town part of New Orleans, called the Creole Section. Most of them were also good Sight Readers. They had Small Bands. [. . .] They went [to] a lot of places with ease, because of their light skin. Places we Dark Skinned *Cats* wouldn't Dare to peep in."[35] By contrast, the Creole attitude toward African Americans is nicely encapsulated in Isidore Barbarin's comment about the black cornetist Buddy Bolden: "He was famous with the ratty people," to which Danny Barker adds: "I soon learned what ratty people, ratty joints and dives meant: it meant good-time people, earthy people [. . .] . So ratty music is bluesy, folksy music that moves you and exhilarates you, makes you dance."[36]

What emerges from these comments is an image of two very different musical traditions. Creoles tended to be thoroughly trained and educated in European classical music, whereas New Orleans blacks derived much of their musical knowledge from the idioms of the blues and plantation music. The Creoles favored skills such as precise intonation and the ability to read and notate music. In addition, "lessons in solfège were designed to [. . .] *train* [. . .] the ear to follow a rigid system of Eurocentric musical syntax." The musical training of African American musicians in the blues, in turn, prepared them for "expressive depth through subtle shading and dramatic bending of pitch, while solfège is designed with just the opposite goal in mind—to internalize the distance between pitches with such precision that there is absolutely no deviation from the measured scale." Following the same rationale, "[t]he Creoles were not interested in adding to a given musical text," but rather wished "to perform that text as precisely as a bricklayer follows the dimensions of a house."[37] The Creole, and in many ways European, view of music is exemplified by clarinetist Lorenzo Tio's struggle to teach his students perfect pitch: "No, no, no, we don't bark like a dog," he reportedly scolded his young Creole music student, clarinetist Sidney Bechet, when he deviated from this pitch. By the time Bechet was himself teaching music lessons, he had thoroughly imbibed the African American approach to tone: "See how many ways you can play that note—growl it, smear it, flat it, sharp it, do anything you want to it," he told one of his students.[38] It is exactly this practice of personalizing modes of communication and creating inflected and swinging variants of conventional forms of expression that would structure Armstrong's approach to autobiographical narration from the 1920s onward.

Armstrong's initial musical training took place in the streets and alleys of the black section in New Orleans, where he did not receive conventional music lessons but became acquainted with vernacular black music through his social surroundings and the people of his neighborhood. In *Satchmo*, the reader meets Lorenzo (spelled "Larenzo" in the manuscript), the junk man who traverses the poor black section of the city tooting a tune on "an old tin horn which he used to blow without the mouthpiece." Armstrong, who must have been around the age of ten, is employed by Larenzo and often listens to him "play a tune on it, and with feeling too"; "[t]he things he said about music held me spellbound, and he blew that old, beat-up tin horn with such warmth that I felt as though I was sitting with a good cornet player." There is also a "pie man named Santiago [blowing] a bugle to attract customers." Santiago "could swing it too, and so could the waffle man who drove around town in a big wagon fitted out with a kitchen." Elsewhere, Armstrong "remember[ed] all the crazy sounds that always seemed to be exploding around you and inside you. *Everything* made music back then: banana men, rag-pickers, them pretty painted streetwalkers all singing out their wares."[39] Apart from conveying information on the story level, where the reader learns about the people who provided Armstrong's vernacular musical education, the specific wording of these passages also communicates an important message on the level of narrative discourse. The double conflation of musical instruments as an active medium ("*Everything* made music") with those who played them ("banana men, rag-pickers, [. . .] streetwalkers") and of music as an outside source of inspiration that has immediate effects as a personal sound heard from within the self ("sounds [. . .] exploding around you and inside you") points to Armstrong's holistic understanding of musical subject (the jazz musician), musical medium (instrument), and musical message (the sounds produced by musicians through their instruments).

Aside from amateur musicians like Larenzo and Santiago, Armstrong heard many professional players on the streets of his hometown. He grew up in and around Jane Alley, which was located in the center of the black red-light district and was surrounded by honky-tonks and cabarets. In his interview with Richard Meryman, he elaborates on this social and musical environment in a passage about Funky Butt Hall (also known as Kinney's Hall) that is worth quoting at length because of the dance hall's mythical status as "the birthplace of jazz."[40] The interactive immediacy and sense of place Armstrong re-creates sixty years after the event invest the passage with a performative dimension that combines the story-level depiction of social ritual with a discursive awareness of its status as vernacular expression. "I have always been a great observer,"[41] Armstrong boasted frequently, and this is how he observed the doings at Funky Butt Hall:

> When I was about four or five, still wearing dresses, I lived with my mother in a place called Brick Row—a lot of cement, rented rooms sort of like a motel. And right in the middle of that on Perdido Street was the Funky Butt hall—old, beat up, big cracks in the wall. On Saturday nights, Mama couldn't find us 'cause we wanted to hear that music. Before the dance the band would play out front about a half hour. And us little kids would all do little dances.
>
> Then we'd go look through the big cracks in the wall of the Funky Butt. It wasn't no classyfied place, just a big old room with a bandstand. And to a tune like *The Bucket's Got a Hole in It*, some of them chicks would get way down, shake everything, slapping themselves on the cheek of their behind. Yeah! At the end of the night, they'd do the quadrille, beautiful to see where everybody lined up, crossed over—if no fights hadn't started before that. Cats'd have to take their razors in with them, because they might have to scratch somebody before they left there. If any of them cats want to show respect for their chick—which they seldom did—they'd crook their left elbow out when they danced and lay their hat on it—a John B. Stetson they'd probably saved for six months to buy. When the dance was over, fellow would walk up and say, "Did you touch my hat, partner?" and if the cat say "yes"—Wop!—he hit him right in the chops.[42]

This passage displays Armstrong's extensive abilities as a narrator. The setting, mood, and word choice perfectly illustrate his command of oral storytelling, and they re-create a vivid image of the activities at the Funky Butt. Oral devices include the tight structure and pacing of the anecdote (consider the literal *punch* line), the use of black dialect (double negatives as in "wasn't no" and "if no fights hadn't started"), slang ("chicks," "cats," "get way down," "chops"), exclamations ("Yeah!" and "Wop!"), and direct speech ("Did you touch my hat, partner?"). The peeping of the children and the illicit sexuality of the dancing add to the overall erotic appeal of the tale, as does the sexual innuendo, which unfolds through a series of intricate puns. Note how the "big *cracks* in the wall" and the "Hole" in the bucket resonate with the "cheek" of the women's "behind[s]" as well as the

title phrase "funky butt"—the slang expression "scratch" for cutting somebody with a razor belonging to the same word field (as in "scratching one's
butt").

Moreover, rather than analyzing the music that provides the sonic
background for this anecdote, Armstrong describes the physical and social
setting, as well as the human interactions taking place during the musical
performance. The music animates the dancers and enables nonverbal interaction between the sexes. Thomas Brothers speaks of "the firm association of musical gesture with moving bodies" and opens up an interesting
perspective on the female dancers' slapping themselves on their behinds:
"What is not said may be taken for granted: the slap was rhythmically syn-
chronized with the music. The conflation of musical and bodily gestures
was part of the African cultural legacy that Armstrong was internalizing."[43]
Buddy Bolden's announcement of the tune "Don't Go 'Way Nobody" further captures the interdependence of music and sexuality: "'Way down,
'way down low / So I can hear those whores / Drag their feet across the
floor / Oh you bitches, shake your asses."[44] That Armstrong recalls fragments of this announcement ("'way down"; "shake") and describes a similar scene illustrates a complex integration of musical performance and
autobiographical recollection.

According to Armstrong's Funky Butt account, jazz is a music of the
lower classes ("wasn't no classyfied place"; "a John B. Stetson they'd probably saved for six months to buy"), as well as a music ingrained in the communal structures of black New Orleans both geographically—Brick Row is
right next to Funky Butt Hall—and socially—kids and grown-ups go out to
dance to it on Saturday nights. Furthermore, it is played in an environment
of unabashed sexuality ("chicks would get way down, shake everything,
slapping themselves on the cheek of their behind") and male violence
("take their razors in with them"; "hit him right in the chops"). This environment may be the point of origin of Armstrong's fascination with sexual
intercourse, which expressed itself in his lifelong infidelity to his wives, in
his love of pornographic writings (he typed short narratives with titles such
as "Doctor Ulrich," "Tortures of Love," and "Exercises in Love"), in risqué
photo-collages (one of his tape covers pits a trumpet-blowing Louis against
a bent-over and scantily clad black dancer), and in his boisterous live duets
with Velma Middleton on "Baby, It's Cold Outside" (in Vancouver on Jan
26, 1951) and "That's My Desire" (on *The Great Chicago Concert*, June 1,
1956).[45] Finally, jazz is not only a music of sexual stimulation but also a mu-

sico-cultural hybrid. The quadrille that ends the dancing for the night had been imported to New Orleans by French settlers and was danced at the fashionable Creole balls around the city, but it is played in the ragged African American style at Funky Butt Hall and is accompanied by a dance Armstrong calls "funkybuttin'."[46]

The depiction of the Funky Butt events illustrates Armstrong's performative engagement with his past: the presentation of vernacular practices on the story level and the use of a vernacular mode of storytelling on the level of narrative discourse. The documentary impulse that drives such vernacular recollections of the music's social functions and cultural contexts is consistent in his work. In order to illuminate these functions and contexts, Armstrong often mentioned the social clubs and organizations that were hugely influential in the lives of black New Orleanians.[47] They constituted social networks and created business connections, but they were most renowned for the parades they sponsored. Clubs like the Broadway Swells, the Bulls, and the Turtles would put on a parade every year, and as was typical of a musically inclined black New Orleanian, Armstrong became a member of one of these organizations, the Tammany Social Club.[48] Another function of these clubs was to arrange for a funeral procession whenever one of their members died. These processions were a source of relief and tied the community together, but they also offered work for brass bands and gave aspiring youngsters a chance to learn from musical elders. The parades were public displays of pride and creativity, as Armstrong recalls: "Everybody with silk shirts, white hats, black pants, streamers across their chests with the club's name, everybody shined up, the Grand Marshal always sharp and strutting, and some guys on horses."[49]

In the culture of New Orleans, strutting and parading frequently offered an unprecedented amount of expressive freedom and social agency. African Americans of Armstrong's generation, the musician wrote late in his life, were often faced with "Old *Fat Belly Stinking* very *Smelly Dirty* White Folks" and "poor white Trash" who would "get so *Damn* Drunk until they'd go out of their minds—then it's Nigger Hunting time. *Any* Nigger. They wouldn't give up until they would find one. From then on, Lord have mercy on the poor *Darkie*. Then they would Torture the poor Darkie, as innocent as he may be. They would get their usual Ignorant *Chess Cat* laughs before they would shoot him down—like a Dog."[50] As a respected musician, however, Armstrong "could go into any part of New Orleans without being bothered. Everybody loved me and just wanted to hear me blow." This, then, contextualizes his glowing remarks about being accepted as a member of the Tuxedo Brass Band in 1921 and his strong sense of personal achievement: "I felt just as proud as though I had been hired by John Philip Sousa or Arthur Pryor."[51]

According to Thomas Brothers, the parades performed a double function. First, they constituted a symbolic victory over racial segregation by allowing black musicians unrestricted motion through areas of the city otherwise off-limits. Second, they "move[d] through the actual battlegrounds of class conflict," thus "asserting cultural autonomy" and "literally broadcast[ing] vernacular culture over the entire city."[52] The parades therefore serve a variety of functions on the story level, yet they also structure Armstrong's autobiographical discourse, with the musician "parading" his life story in front of his reading audience. They assert cultural autonomy by celebrating black music, but they also inscribe African American modes of storytelling into the historiography of jazz. They broadcast black culture throughout New Orleans, but they also disseminate stories about this culture throughout American popular culture. In that sense, these stories create important historical contexts for Armstrong's television and live appearances of the 1950s and 1960s, where he frequently paraded around the stage and thus invited his audience to witness a prominent, and certainly commercialized, New Orleans musicking practice. The *Edsel* television show in 1957, for instance, ends with Armstrong leading Bing Crosby, Frank Sinatra, and Rosemary Clooney across the stage in paradelike formation to the music of "On the Sunny Side of the Street"; the black Armstrong becomes a kind of pied piper, or grand marshal, who determines the course his white followers will take. Moreover, when the All Stars played "When the Saints Go Marchin' In" at an Australian concert in 1964, they recalled the New Orleans parades by strutting across the stage.[53]

Additional functions of the parades emerge from Armstrong's depictions of second lining, as part of which bystanders and community members join the music by clapping, singing, and dancing. Second lining draws the community together, constitutes a ritual of self-affirmation, and offers a training ground for young musicians. Armstrong recalls: "When I was [. . .] 'second lining'—that is, following the brass bands in parades—I started to listen carefully to the different instruments, noticing the things they played and how they played them. That is how I learned to distinguish the differences between Buddy Bolden, King Oliver and Bunk Johnson."[54] Thus, these parades and processions were a source of his musical education, and the realization that every player sounded different—had a personal style—must have been an important lesson for an aspiring musician whose crowning achievement in New Orleans was being selected as a replacement for Joe Oliver (who went to Chicago in 1918, after the closing of Storyville in 1917) as the first cornetist in the Tuxedo Brass Band, the leading orchestra in the city. Armstrong makes an interesting remark about this band: "That Tuxedo Brass Band was really something, both to see and to hear, and it is too bad that in those days we did not have tape recorders and movie cameras to record those boys in action." As this remark indicates, the parades were musical and visual spectacles in addition to being social and spiritual rituals.[55] They laid the groundwork for Armstrong's performances as intermedial spectacles that orchestrate visual, verbal, and sonic expressions in order to create maximum effects, and they also fueled his drive to perform and preserve his life story in multiple media, such as phonograph records, tape recordings, photo-collages, and various genres of life writing.

The absence of tape recorders and movie cameras is compensated, if imperfectly, through Armstrong's narratives about the parades and their spiritual and social functions. The jazz funerals are a good example. A boyhood friend's death is described as "a terrible shock. We all felt so bad that even the boys cried." Communal mourning expresses itself through music: "It was a real sad moment when the Onward Brass Band struck up the funeral march as Arthur Brown's body was being brought from the church to the graveyard. Everybody cried, including me." Once the body had been lowered into the ground and the reverend had spoken, "the band would strike up one of those good old tunes like *Didn't He Ramble*, and all the people would leave their worries behind."[56] Since verbal narrative can only evoke the sounds and sights of the funerals and since the jazz funerals had become a central part of the jazz mythology, Armstrong and the All Stars recorded "New Orleans Function: Flee as a Bird / Oh, Didn't He Ramble" in 1950. But instead of playing into the hands of jazz revivalists, who searched for authentic expressions of prerecorded New Orleans jazz, the musicians create an audio spectacle, melodramatic mourning and mock somber blessings included, that marks the recording as a self-reflexive, even comic, performance based on a well-known social ritual.[57]

Specific cultural practices were not only simulated in the recording studio; they had actually motivated the technical innovations that had led to the new music in the first place. Furthermore, they illuminate the appeal of jazz autobiography as a way of claiming narrative authority over jazz history and promoting a personal perspective on the music. An integral element of the sociocultural practices Armstrong identified as the driving force behind the development of jazz were the "bucking" or "cutting contests" staged by competing jazz bands that advertised their music and other events by playing against rival bands from the backs of utility wagons: "They'd stop at a corner and the band would play. People would come from all the neighborhood and be around the wagon." The bucking contests started when two advertising wagons met: "here come another wagon and pull up too and that's where that bucking contest used to come—each band playing different tunes trying to outplay each other. King Oliver and Kid Ory used to cut them all."[58] In *Satchmo*, Armstrong continues the story: "Kid Ory and Joe Oliver [. . .] often played in a tail gate wagon to advertise a ball or other entertainments. When they found themselves on a street corner next to another band in another wagon, Joe and Kid Ory would shoot the works. They would give with all that good mad music they had under their belts and the crowd would go wild."[59]

Armstrong's depiction of these bucking and cutting contests constitutes a narrative framework for early jazz because it delineates creative competition as a performative ethos that urges the musicians to push beyond established musical conventions and, by doing so, impress their listeners with daring feats of musical innovation. As Thomas Brothers explains, the term "bucking" refers to the practice of tying together two horse-drawn advertising wagons and to the ensuing musical battle over which band could outplay the other. And although "cutting" commonly denotes knife fighting, it makes more sense to place it in the context of slave dancing: "Master and mistress would be there, one of whom would award the prize for the best 'cuttin'' of figgers."[60] The participatory dynamics of bucking and cutting not only shaped new musical techniques like fast fingering and playing in the upper register, which were essential ingredients of Armstrong's trumpet style; they also made a memorable appearance in an All Stars performance in Belgium in 1959, where Armstrong and trombonist Trummy Young strut around the stage, battle each other in a high-energy rendition of "Tiger Rag," and do so in front of a paying audience.[61] They further come up in films such as *A Song Is Born*, where Armstrong is trading fours with Lionel Hampton during a nightclub gig, and *Paris Blues* (dir. Martin Ritt, 1961), where Armstrong as Wild Man Moore battles the expatriate musicians Ram Bowen (Paul Newman) and Eddie Cook (Sidney Poitier).

Beyond these musical and filmic contexts, bucking and cutting contests made an impact on the genre of jazz autobiography, as Kathy Ogren notes when she writes that in these texts, "the participatory performance dynamics of jazz music [are] translated into the musicians' persona." In writing about these participatory dynamics and by placing themselves within these historical moments of musical performance, jazz autobiographers like Armstrong both historicize and reproduce (instead of merely describe) performative practices: "These autobiographical accounts can be seen as literary 'cutting contests,' in which the musician/narrators display their storytelling skills."[62]

A particularly powerful arena for musical participation was the black church. Compared to the competitive performances on streets, in cemeteries, and in honky-tonks, the Sanctified Church presented a more egalitarian environment for musical education. Armstrong writes of his preteen years: "In church and Sunday school I did a whole lot of singing. That, I guess, is how I acquired my singing tactics." He told Jones and Chilton: "Yes, I learned that good music right there in the church. All that music that's got a beat, it comes from the same place, from the old sanctified churches."[63] Elsewhere, he elaborates:

> It 'all came from the Old 'Sanctified 'Churches. [. . .] I was a little Boy around 'ten years old. My mother used to take me to 'Church with her, and the Reverend ('Preacher that is') used to '*lead* off one' of those 'good *ol* good '*Hymns*. And before you realized it—the 'whole 'Congregation would be "*Wailing*—'Singing like 'mad and 'sound *so* 'beautiful. 'I 'being a little boy that would "Dig" 'Everything and 'everybody, I'd have myself a 'Ball in 'Church, *especially* when those 'Sisters 'would get 'So 'Carried away while "Rev" (the preacher) would be 'right in the 'Middle of his 'Sermon.[64]

Armstrong was baptized Catholic, his paternal great-grandmother Catherine Walker's denomination, but his mother was Baptist and joined the Sanctified Church when he was still a toddler. Even though he does not specify what kind of singing tactics he had learned in church, he does indicate that he became acquainted with the harmonic structure of hymns and came to recognize the call-and-response dynamics of the African American sermonic tradition. More important in terms of a performative reading, however, is the connection he establishes between the spirituality of the church and his understanding of jazz. In the wake of the LP *Louis and the*

Good Book (1958), which contains renditions of spirituals and neospirituals, he told Studs Terkel: "That's where you get your feelings of songs, in church. Let's say you sing a spiritual. It still has that feeling of reverence, even though it has a different jazz feeling. [. . .] A lot of people wondered how I could jump from jazz to spirituals. You take an album like *Louis and the Good Book*, and you sing all the spirituals. I'd say, 'Whatever song I'm singing, I'm in a spiritual feeling in the song,' because in church we did the same thing."[65] Armstrong's insistence on his music as an expression of spirit (the term "spiritual" appears four times in this passage, both as noun and adjective) and feeling (this term also appears four times, both in the singular and the plural) is important because it connects the sounds of jazz to a specific sensibility that is culturally concrete (the African American Sanctified Church of Armstrong's neighborhood) and historically significant (it influences the development of jazz).[66]

In extension of this performative reading, additional meanings can be deduced from the phrase "singing tactics" once the autobiographical perspective from which Armstrong presents his recollections is taken into consideration. Armstrong may, in fact, indicate that he was inspired by the way in which Elder Cozy conducted his sermons, thereby alleging that his own later performances were indebted to the ways in which black preachers of the Sanctified Church interacted with their congregations. A 1955 interview substantiates this assumption:

[*Armstrong:*] [T]onight I was expectin' to play "Royal Garden Blues," and out come "The Saints." [. . .]
[*Interviewer:*] You just led it off?
[*Armstrong:*] Yeah. Well, the band gonna fall in. Just like a church—if the preacher's caught on, well, the congregation's sure gonna join right in there.

Here, Armstrong associates his band with the church congregation falling in with the groove initiated by the band leader, who is not merely setting the tempo but has himself "caught on" to the quasi-religious spirituality of the performance and inspires his colleagues to musical excellence.[67]

Armstrong frequently insisted that jazz had emerged from the black working poor. He may have acquired his singing tactics in the Sanctified Church, but he also "play[ed] the blues for the whores" with his trio, which featured a pianist named Boogus and a drummer named Garbee.[68] His stories about the blues culture of his youth are significant interventions in the jazz discourse because they place the blues in a historical context that differs substantially from the sanitized narratives presented in popular songs such as "Birth of the Blues," which Armstrong performed on television at least three times between 1954 and 1957 and which, in a similar manner as *Swing That Music*, racializes the origins of the music while simultaneously erasing any specific reference to black musicians (who are referred to as "some people"). The narrative situation of "Birth of the Blues" is twice removed from Armstrong's autobiographical perspective. Instead of a first-person account, the listener encounters a more distanced authorial narrator who casts his narrative as a matter of myth ("Oh, they say"), implies that the music was innate to one segment of the population ("As only they can"), alleges that the musicians did not consciously create a new kind of music ("didn't know just what to use"), and romanticizes the socio-geographical territory of the blues as a minstrel space of racial harmony ("the Southland"). Armstrong undermined the ideology of B. G. DeSylva and Lew Brown's lyrics in a moment of musical signifying by playing the trumpet chorus from W. C. Handy's "St. Louis Blues" in the All Stars version of the song at NBC's *Colgate Comedy Hour* in February of 1955. This musical gesture points to a blues culture that is more fully fleshed out in *Satchmo: My Life in New Orleans* and is explicitly linked to "Birth of the Blues" in Armstrong's announcement of the tune as part of his conversation with host Eddie Fischer during his concert at the Hollywood Bowl for the *Colgate Comedy Hour* in 1954: "Man, that takes me back to my good old hometown, there, man. Yes, sir, that's where that stuff started. Well, you take cats like Buddy Bolden, Joe Oliver, Bunk Johnson, Freddie Keppard, Manuel Perez, you know [. . .] . And they used to swing around that funky . . . boy, ha, and man, you talkin' bout riffs." Here, Armstrong annotates the lyrics by naming several original jazz creators, by recasting the minstrel Southland as black New Orleans, and by doing all of this in the vernacular jargon of jazz musicians ("cats," "swing," "funky," "riffs").[69]

Armstrong started playing with blues combos in his early teens. The harmonic simplicity of the blues and the fact that no music-reading skills were necessary allowed him to practice melodic improvisation without extensive knowledge of music theory. Yet his commentary about these blues engagements serves a double purpose: it indicates how a particular musical style (a vernacular music based in part on African musical retentions and the musical practices of the slaves) and a particular audience (the black working class) shaped musical developments and determined his musical understanding, but it also conjures up images of raw sexuality in a socio-economic environment peopled by gamblers, prostitutes, and their pimps: "Around four or five in the morning, that's when all them whores would come in to the tonk—big stockings full of dollars—and give us a tip to play the blues."[70] These hustling women and their pimps "were my people my crowd and everything, and still are," Armstrong writes in "The Satchmo Story": "Real people who never did tell me anything that wasn't right."[71] Here, then, the connection between the story and discourse levels becomes explicit. Black New Orleans prostitutes and pimps were an integral part of Armstrong's life world in the past, but he keeps them alive in his memory, perhaps as a simple reminiscence, but certainly also as source material for the creation of continuing life stories.

While the blues trio provided a format that differed from the brass bands and dance orchestras Armstrong heard on the streets and would join in later years, it also represented a vernacular musical style that distinctly marked performer and audience as black and working-class and thus as different from many of those who followed Armstrong's career in the 1950s, when he often talked and wrote about the blues culture of his youth. Several musicians recall the name "dirt music" for the blues, a name that describes the blues as an earthy type of music, as well as a cultural disposition that included performance places like Funky Butt Hall; musical ingredients like pitch inflection, bent notes, vocal shadings, and a stomping rhythm; and an audience that took part in nonmusical practices such as ham kicking, sexually suggestive dancing, violence, and profanity. That one of the performance places for this music carried the name Funky Butt Hall is no coincidence, considering that the term "funky" may derive from the Ki-Kongo word *lu-fuki*, which can mean body odor but also expresses admiration for a particularly grooving performance.[72]

These funky blues roots are extended further when Armstrong traces his success as a popular entertainer to his experiences as a member of a vocal quartet with which he performed on the streets of New Orleans, frequently for white customers in the Storyville district. Describing the quartet, Armstrong situates humor and comedy, central and controversial elements of his famous performance practices, within a public sphere in which entertainers vied for attention and presented their wares for a financial reward. He mentions the quartet's lead singer, Little Mack, and the bass singer, Big Nose Sidney, and then identifies himself, in terms that evoke the topos of natural music, as the tenor who "used to put my hand behind my ear, and move my mouth from side to side, and some beautiful tones would appear." He calls baritone singer Redhead Happy Bolton "the greatest showman of them all" and writes further: "First I must explain how our quartet used to do its hustling so as to attract an audience. We began by walking down Rampart Street [. . .] . The lead singer and the tenor walked together in front followed by the baritone and the bass. Singing at random we wandered through the streets until someone called us to sing a few songs. Afterwards we would pass our hats and at the end of the night we would divvy up. [. . .] Then I would [. . .] dump my share into mama's lap."[73]

Such passages are intriguing because they tell us something about Armstrong's first vocal performances and about the places in which he and his friends displayed their skills. They also place early jazz in an economic sphere that, while removed in time and social context, resembles Armstrong's live shows at the time he was writing this account in that the youngsters peddle their music to predominantly white audiences. The money made, however, is not used to accumulate wealth but is immediately reinvested to provide the bare means of survival; Armstrong's mother receives her son's share in order to feed and clothe the family. This economic dimension rejects the romantic perception of early jazz as a happy music played by ever-frolicking blacks, and it also casts Armstrong's later dealings with the rules of show business and his career in popular music as hustles: as performances determined by his need to make money and sell his wares to audiences eager to pay for them, coupled with a willingness to give away significant portions of his earnings to family and friends. It is, therefore, no coincidence that Richard Meryman quotes the following statement by Armstrong in his 1971 book version of the 1966 *Life* interview: "I come from the old hustling territory."[74]

The accounts of Armstrong's youthful hustling contextualize a comedy skit he and trombonist Trummy Young performed before launching into "My Bucket's Got a Hole in It" at a Stockholm concert on May 25, 1962. Armstrong announces the number by saying that "we're gonna take a little trip to my hometown, New Orleans, Louisiana. And while we're over there, we're gonna take a little trip to the red light dis—" He is interrupted by Young's exasperated high-pitched scream, which is followed by a tongue-in-cheek clarification that pretends to hide the sexual economy of the famous New Orleans red-light district from the cultured audience:

"No, you mean Storyville, man." The skit enacts a double hustle, again on the levels of story and narrative discourse: in early twentieth-century New Orleans, black musicians were part of a service economy in which prostitutes offered their bodies to their tricks and black musicians hustled their music to white paying customers (Armstrong uses the same word, "hustle," for both trades). In the early 1960s, when the skit was performed, Armstrong and Young are still hustling their music to paying and predominantly white audiences. The timeline becomes explicit when Armstrong responds to Young's interruption: "Well, they called it something else in 1917 when I left there."[75]

Armstrong generally depicts his youth in New Orleans as a time of musical advancement, professional opportunities, and careful dealings with appreciative white audiences. These depictions suggest an autobiographer who is interested in creating narrative continuity between past and present and in making sure—for himself and for his readers—that he has not severed his cultural roots despite his success as a musician, actor, and entertainer. Important facets of his efforts are the episodes that cover his time in the Colored Waif's Home for Boys, where he lived from 1913 to 1914, and the time, several years later (1918–21), when he played with a black orchestra led by Fate Marable on the S.S. *Sydney* and other Mississippi entertainment ships owned by the Streckfus brothers. In his early teens, Armstrong was sent to the Waif's Home after having been caught shooting a revolver on New Year's Eve of 1912. In the home, he received his first formal musical training and began to play the cornet. He extended his musical knowledge, began his education in European harmony and musical notation, and learned the rudiments of cornet playing.

The trumpeter's recollections of his time in the Waif's Home depict a young boy on his path to becoming a successful musician: "His approval was all important for any boy who wanted a musical career," Armstrong writes about his teacher, Mr. Davis. He also remembers "being the most popular boy in the Home" and describes the day when he paraded through the black section of New Orleans with the home's orchestra: "All the whores, pimps, gamblers, thieves and beggars were waiting for the band because they knew that Dipper, Mayann's son, would be in [the parade]. But they had never dreamed that I would be playing the cornet, blowing it as good as I did."[76] Armstrong identifies the Waif's Home as the institution that channeled his desire to pursue a musical career: while "[m]usic ha[d] been in my blood from the day I was born," and while he "had an awful urge to learn the cornet," it was Mr. Davis and Mr. Jones who gave him the "chance to sing" and to actually study cornet playing, instilling in him the ambition to become a respected musician.[77] In "Jewish Family," Armstrong speaks of being "a young man trying to accomplish something in life" and of "reach[ing] the *Top* in music[;] I was considered one of the popular cornet players of that area [New Orleans]. And I was making *nice money*."[78] These passages attest to the autobiographer's wish to document the racial roots of jazz ("in my blood"), but they also express a desire to celebrate his musical skills ("reach[ing] the *Top* in music"), his public reception ("one of the popular cornet players"), and his economic success ("was making *nice money*").

The seeds of his musical career, Armstrong wants his readers to know, were sown at the Waif's Home, but the branching out began with his employment on the Streckfus entertainment ships. Playing on these ships constituted a step out of the musical culture of New Orleans and introduced him to new audiences and musical formats. It led him out of the South into Midwestern cities such as St. Louis, where audiences became acquainted with this new kind of music and where he had a chance to jam with local musicians, including the white cornetist Bix Beiderbecke, whom he claims to have met in Davenport, Iowa, on one of these trips.[79] The engagement with the Streckfus company is mostly remembered as a chance to acquire new musical knowledge, particularly reading skills, and to expand his musical repertoire. Armstrong studied music with mellophone player David Jones: "he'd teach me about reading music—how to divide, like two four time, six eight time, had me count different exercises," and "I was very happy in his [Fate Marable's] wonderful orchestra, playing the kind of music I had never played before in my life and piling up all the experiences I had dreamed of as an ambitious kid."[80]

The Streckfus engagement also familiarized Armstrong with the power of white bosses in the entertainment industry. When he revisits this crucial moment in the 1920s from the vantage points of the 1950s and 1960s, he does so to inform readers about his musical education but uses the opportunity to allude to his difficult position as a black entertainer whose manager, Joe Glaser, was Jewish and whose audiences were increasingly made up of white fans at the time of the early civil rights movement. While he speaks repeatedly of his white bosses in New Orleans—honky-tonk and cabaret owners, factory and business owners—it is Captain Joe, the most musical of the Streckfus brothers, who is not only a fan of the orchestra's dance music, and of Armstrong's playing in particular, but also a strict master in control of the band's repertoire.[81] The captain enforces a policy of racial segregation on board, where the musicians are not allowed to interact with the white patrons. Whenever he enters the ship, the band plays especially well: "We almost overdid it, trying to please him," Armstrong recalls, indicating an awareness of the minstrel-inflected role-playing expected of him and fellow musicians.[82] Captain Joe and his brothers are portrayed in positive terms as "some real fine white people'" and as "*real Groove* people," perhaps because Joe is the first of several white patrons who urged Armstrong to perform his music according to the expectations of white audiences and thereby laid the foundation for his career as a star singer, master musician, and popular entertainer.[83] From 1935 onward, Armstrong's manager Joe Glaser would monopolize this role, telling his protégé to "[p]lay and sing pretty. Give the people a show," but in his 1966 interview with Richard Meryman, Armstrong sanctions a double reading of this crowd-pleasing ethos when he attributes the admonition to a New Orleans black elder, who offered an important piece of advice as Armstrong was leaving for Chicago in 1922: "As the oldtimer told me when I left New Orleans, he say, 'Stay before them people'"; "please the people.'"[84] This background narrative complicates the apparent message of racial accommodation for which Armstrong came to be criticized in the 1950s and 1960s because it claims that the wish to please audiences was part of a larger set of performative practices from his New Orleans past that was so integral to his musical understanding that it remained indispensable throughout his life. What is more, it reclaims the very narrative authority that Glaser's remarks had called into question.

It seems that Armstrong never mentioned the dances the Marable orchestra played for black audiences on the Streckfus ships on Monday nights. Drummer Warren "Baby" Dodds, however, who played with Armstrong in this orchestra as well as on many later occasions, recalls that performing for a black crowd "gave us an altogether different sensation because we were free to talk to people and people could talk to us, and that's a great deal in playing music. We were less tense because it was our own people." Bassist George "Pops" Foster further told interviewers that they could play "how we wanted" on Monday nights.[85] By noting that the musicians felt and thus played differently because they performed for a black audience, Dodds and Foster distinguish between playing music as a business for white audiences willing to pay for the service but unwilling to treat the musicians as equals and playing music as an interactive process that combines professional duties with communal performer-audience relations. In doing so, they characterize early jazz as a socially embedded performance, as well as a creative expression that is intimately tied to the contexts of its delivery. Why Armstrong did not cover these Monday-night dances remains a matter of speculation. He might have simply forgotten about them, or he might have decided that playing for, and interacting freely with, appreciative black audiences was becoming increasingly less likely for him as his career went on. It is, of course, also possible that he did talk about them in letters or manuscripts that have not yet been available to researchers.

Thus far, this chapter has focused on how Armstrong's autobiographical narratives have impacted the popular understanding of jazz, its history, and the cultural contexts in which it was played. What has not been discussed in detail is the question of what exactly jazz performers heard in the music and what language they used to characterize it. This is important because much of what we know about early New Orleans jazz is based on autobiographies, oral histories, and interviews. Many bands and musicians went unrecorded, and even those who had the chance to record their music did so only in the 1920s, after they had left the city. (Kid Ory was the first African American to take his band into the studio; in 1922, they recorded "Ory's Creole Trombone" and "Society Blues" in Los Angeles under the name Spike's Seven Pods of Pepper Orchestra.) The sonic absence of early New Orleans jazz therefore presents a central problem. The medium of sound recording was limited historically, because it did not capture New Orleans jazz until several years after its inception, as well as materially, because it was able neither to present the visual elements of the music and the social significances of the performances nor to faithfully reproduce its sonic qualities (drums, for example, could not be recorded for several years). Especially when the jazz historians of the 1930s and later decades (Frederic Ramsey, Charles Edward Smith, William Russell, Rudi Blesh, and others) searched for the "authentic" sounds of early jazz and turned their gaze to the cultural moment that had preceded commercial recordings, the genres of oral history and autobiography provided narrative authority and social agency for Armstrong and the many other musicians who had been closely involved with the development of early jazz. What they remembered about these years possessed authority because they could speak legitimately about prerecorded music from the perspective of the participating musician and because they detailed a culture to which jazz critics and historians had no immediate access.[86]

Like many fellow musicians of his generation, Armstrong disdained an overly technical musical vocabulary when he talked about the music of his youth, and he retained a critical attitude toward the category "jazz." He once stated: "I don't think you should analyze music. Like the oldtimer told me, he say, 'Don't worry about that black cow giving white milk. Just drink the milk.'"[87] With statements such as this, he responded to the attempts of jazz critics and journalists to interpret and theorize his music by distinguishing between the music itself, over which he claimed authority, and the critical discourse this music initiated, about which he remained skeptical. When asked in 1955 what jazz is, he replied: "I wouldn't say I know what jazz is, because I don't look at it from that angle. I look at it from music—we never did worry about what it was in New Orleans, we just always tried to play good. And the public named it. It was ragtime, Dixieland, gut-bucket, jazz, swing—and it ain't nothin' but the same music."[88] Musical categories like jazz or swing, in that sense, are applied to the music by outsiders, and while they may be useful for promoting the music, they do not necessarily capture the personal and cultural significances of those who play it.

Armstrong once noted in a blindfold test in *Metronome*, "Music doesn't mean a thing unless it *sounds* good," a statement that follows an earlier remark about George Lewis's clarinet playing on Bunk Johnson's "Franklin Street Blues" (1942): "You can hear from the first note that this has *soul*. [. . .] That clarinet is trying to tell a story—you can *follow* him."[89] In *Satchmo*, he writes that the New Orleans "brass bands could play a funeral march so sweet and with so much soul you could actually feel it inside," and he told Dan Morgenstern that "soul musicians" like King Oliver and Freddie Keppard "*moved* me."[90] Good music, therefore, has to have "soul"; it only sounds good if it moves listeners by expressing and evoking honest emotions. Furthermore, Armstrong uses the familiar trope of musical improvisation as "saying something" or "telling a story."[91] The storytelling effect results from a moment of successful—"conscientious" and "heartfelt"—communication between musician and audience.[92] Thus, a good musician like Creole clarinetist George Baquet of the Excelsior and Onward Brass Bands would "actually bring tears to your eyes" when he played a tune.[93] The wording of Armstrong's response to George Lewis's playing—"That clarinet is trying to tell a story—you can *follow* him"—further explains why and how good musicians evoke powerful emotions. It might be the clarinet that is telling the story since it is the material medium through which Lewis is communicating, but the listeners will follow *him*, the person behind the story, and will hear the story as a personal account: "What you hear coming from a man's horn—that's what he is!"[94]

In order to make his readers understand the stories told by and through the music, Armstrong portrays the musical storytellers whose lives and playing have influenced him. One of his musical mentors, cornetist Joe Oliver, looms large in the "breadth of archival traces" that Ben Alexander finds in Armstrong cultural productions.[95] Armstrong displays his love for Oliver in every medium at his disposal: in the tribute album *Satchmo Plays King Oliver*, on *Satchmo: A Musical Autobiography*, in his photo-collages, in television interviews, on his tape recordings, and in his writings. "Every other page in my story is Joe Oliver," he recalled in one of his taped reminiscences; he wrote to the *Melody Maker* in 1946 that "[m]y life my soul in music and life is inspired by that wonderful man" and that he had learned "from the master—King Oliver School."[96] Armstrong's various portraits of his idol combine discussions of his music and its effects with statements about his personal treatment of the youngster: "Everything I did, I tried to do it like Oliver"; "Joe Oliver has always been my inspiration and my idol"; "he would come to my rescue, every time I actually needed someone to come into me and sort of show me the way about life and its little intricate things"; "He was a Creator, with unlimited Ideas, and had a heart as big as a whale when it came to helping the underdog in music, such as me"; "He taught me the modern way of phrasing on the cornet and trumpet."[97]

Overall, Joe Oliver is portrayed as a role model whose influence on Armstrong went far beyond musical inspiration: "I was just a little punk kid when I first saw him, but his first words to me were nicer than everything that I've heard from any of the bigwigs of music."[98] Armstrong often recounted how he received Oliver's old cornet as his first professional instrument and how the older man frequently helped him out when money was tight.[99] He began running errands for Oliver and his wife Stella as a teenager, and it was Oliver who sent for the young upstart to join him in Chicago: "Couldn't nobody get me out of New Orleans but him," Armstrong told Ralph Gleason on the *Jazz Casual* television program.[100] When Armstrong finally left the relative security of his hometown for Chicago, where New Orleans jazz musicians had carved out their own small community, he solicited Oliver's help and mentoring: "Sometimes I'd persuade

Papa Joe (I calls *him*) to make the Rounds with me [. . .] . It was real *"Kicks—* listening to music, *Diggin'* his thoughts—comments' *etc.* His Conception of *things*—life—Music, people in general, were really wonderful."[101] Again, there is a double dimension to be considered. For one, there is Armstrong's indebtedness to Oliver in musical and personal terms, which implies that music and its makers are inseparable. Second, these remarks are autobiographically significant. They reveal Armstrong's repeated move to document the influence of his substitute father "Papa Joe" as a way of coping with his uprootedness as a transplanted Southerner in the North and as a means of linking himself to the first generation of jazz musicians.

In musical terms, Armstrong notes Oliver's "fire and [. . .] endurance," his "range," the "wonderful creations in his soul," as well as his "tone" and "famous phrases." In "Joe Oliver Is Still King," he writes: "No trumpet player ever had the fire that Oliver had. Man, he really could *punch* a number. Some might have had a better tone, but I've never seen *nothing* have the fire, and no one created as much as Joe."[102] That Armstrong's language transports culturally and historically specific meanings and offers surplus information about early New Orleans jazz beyond the events it depicts becomes obvious when we compare Armstrong's wording with Gunther Schuller's assessment of Armstrong's own "West End Blues" in *Early Jazz* (1968): "The beauties of this music were those of any great, compelling musical experience: expressive fervor, intense artistic commitment, and an intuitive sense for structural logic, combined with superior instrumental skill."[103] In *The Swing Era* (1989), Schuller hears a "combination of technical agility, note perfection, endurance, power, elegance of style and grace."[104] Personal traits are notably absent from these lists of musical qualities. Though not necessarily expressing a view altogether different from Armstrong's "fire" and "punch," Schuller's universalized vocabulary does not adequately consider the suggestive language Armstrong uses to describe his favorite music. It purges jazz of its vernacular grounding, including its reliance on musical storytelling. While Schuller conceives of early New Orleans jazz as "a relatively unsophisticated quasi folk music— more sociological manifestation than music" and implies that the music eventually had to overcome its limitations by shedding some of its racial traits in order to achieve a status of universal artistry, Armstrong suggests the opposite: music is only meaningful if the musician remains conscious of its original environment and his or her ancestors.[105]

When Armstrong finally joined King Oliver's Creole Jazz Band at the

Lincoln Gardens in Chicago only days after receiving the telegrammed invitation from his idol (Aug. 8, 1922), he and Oliver dazzled audiences with their double cornet breaks, with Armstrong perfectly harmonizing Oliver's improvised lead. "I was so wrapped up in him and lived his music that I could take second to his lead in a split second," Armstrong writes. "That was just how much I lived his music." This passage is less important for its ability to explain the musicians' technical achievements—Armstrong gave many and ultimately conflicting accounts of the duet breaks—than for the fact that it connects musical and personal interaction as expressions of New Orleans musicking. As an improvising musician, Armstrong relies on his intimate knowledge of Oliver's personality and style. He is so wrapped up in Oliver's life that he can anticipate the musician's cornet improvisations and can instantly add the appropriate parts on the second cornet. This is possible because he *lives* Oliver's music.[106]

The relocation from New Orleans to the North, first to Chicago and then to New York, entailed fundamental changes in performance contexts, performer-audience relations, and musical material. With King Oliver's Creole Jazz Band, Armstrong joined an outfit composed mainly of New Orleans musicians (the exception being his future wife, pianist Lil Hardin, born and raised in Memphis, Tennessee) who played in a modernized New Orleans style and whose social networks tended to reproduce down-home life in the Northern city.[107] But in terms of performance venues, stage presentation, and recording opportunities, the changes were massive, and they brought about different forms of musicking. Armstrong arrived in the North when new mass media such as sound recording and radio were rapidly gaining popular appeal and when new venues such as urban dance halls and cabarets affected the dynamics of live performance.[108] These media and venues also influenced his music, his social position, and apparently his sense of self. He began to pepper his musical performances with comedic dancing, soon featured his vocals as a prominent element of his show act, and took his stage antics into the recording studio. While he had performed as a singer in New Orleans and had displayed a talent for comedy during his stay in the Waif's Home, his performances were now received in different, more complexly mediated contexts: on sound recording, the radio, and the movie screen, but also in music magazines and the daily press. "I wasn't in '*Tate's* Orchestra 2 weeks before I was making 'Records with them for the Vocalion Recording Company.—I became quite a 'Figure at the 'Vendome' [theater]," Armstrong notes about his appearances with the Chicago-based Erskine Tate Orchestra, which came to feature him as its star soloist.[109]

Armstrong's remarks about his classic Hot Five recordings express a retrospective awareness of these new contexts and communicate a desire to underpin the new forms of musical performance with a personal narrative. That is to say, musical innovations are personalized in an effort to translate interpretive authority from the New Orleans era, of which Armstrong was one of the eyewitnesses on whom critics were forced to rely in their historical inquiries, to an era in which his musicking practices were much more closely monitored by the public and in which his own views about jazz had to compete against the budding jazz criticism and newspaper coverage of his career. Most prominently ranks an anecdote about the 1926 recording of "Heebie Jeebies," a tune that was written by Boyd Atkins but underwent such massive transformation in Armstrong's version that the Jewish clarinetist and jazz autobiographer Mezz Mezzrow contrasted the original lyrics with a transcription of Armstrong's scat in *Really the Blues* (1946) and described how he heard Armstrong "tear [the] lyric limb from limb, maul it, mangle it, and then make mince-meat out of it."[110] Mezzrow paraphrases Armstrong's anecdote, which means that it was already known, at least among musicians, in the mid-1940s. Armstrong never tired of reiterating it himself, and the version he offers in his *Esquire* essay would quickly reach an even broader audience when Bing Crosby prompted him to retell it on the November 28, 1951, radio broadcast of the *Bing Crosby Show*. In *Esquire*, Armstrong wrote:

> When everybody heard about [how] this record was made they all got a big laugh out of it . . . They also said that this particular recording was the beginning of Scat Singing . . . Because the day we recorded "Heebie Jeebies," I dropped the paper with the lyrics—right in the middle of the tune . . . And I did not want to stop and spoil the record which was moving along so wonderfully . . . So when I dropped the paper, I immediately turned back into the horn and started to Scatting . . . Just as nothing had happened . . . When I finished the record I just knew the recording people would throw it out . . . And to my surprise they all came running out of the controlling booth and said—"Leave That In" . . .[111]

This anecdote is an especially compelling example of musicking, both as content (depicting music making in the studio) and as an autobiographical intervention in the discursive construction of modern black performance. For one, it casts the moment of musical innovation as the result of an accident that sparks off Armstrong's immediate and specifically black creative response. More than a decade before he presented the story in *Esquire*, he had already marked scat as an African American form of vocal improvisation when he told jazz researcher William Russell, "We used to do that in the quartet going down the streets [. . .] . Scat-do-beep-dah ba. Some of those old comedians used to do that."[112] That those who possessed the power to accept or reject the recording—"the recording people" who financed the session—immediately recognized its commercial potential indicates the market value of novel jazz expressions and the demand for black styles of singing. Second, the anecdote implies that Armstrong invented scat singing, even though he is careful to attribute this claim to others ("*They* [. . .] said this [. . .] was the beginning of scat"). Armstrong certainly was not the first musician, and not even the first jazz musician, to scat on sound recording. Don Redman, for instance, scats on Fletcher Henderson's "My Papa Doesn't Two-Time No Time" (Apr. 16, 1924), recorded a few months before Armstrong joined the Henderson band. But both discursive interventions in the historiography of jazz—the claim to having brought scat into the recording studio and the assertion that he had already scatted as a youngster in New Orleans—make for a good story, and they help Armstrong cement his popular appeal as *the* central figure in the transition from New Orleans ensemble playing to jazz as a modern popular music. They also allow him to position himself as a precursor to the beboppers, whose scatting, he suggests in the same essay, derived from his pioneer work.[113] Third, Armstrong wants his readers to believe that one of the major principles of jazz, spontaneity, is not lost through the mechanical recording and subsequent technical reproduction of sound that Walter Benjamin would discuss about a decade after the recording of "Heebie Jeebies."

In "The Work of Art in the Age of Mechanical Reproduction," Benjamin argued that "[e]ven the most perfect reproduction of a work of art is lacking in one element: its presence in time and space, its unique existence at the place where it happens to be." The phonograph record, he maintained, "enables the original to meet the beholder halfway, [. . .] and in permitting the reproduction to meet the beholder or listener in his own particular situation, it reactivates the object reproduced." But the price of "substitut[ing] a plurality of copies for a unique existence" is that "the technique of reproduction detaches the reproduced object from the domain of tradition."[114] As a performance based on a kind of spur-of-the-moment interaction and improvisation that is difficult if not impossible to notate, however, "Heebie Jeebies" complicates Benjamin's conception of the original artwork in the sense that it finds its very material manifestation through the act of technological production. Without this recording, the original performance would have been over—immaterial—within a few minutes. Theodor W. Adorno foregrounds this view when he observes that sound recordings create a kind of herbarium by transferring the living sounds of music to a deadened static sonic text but thereby also preserve an otherwise ephemeral and essentially elusive music that could not otherwise survive.[115] Recording "Heebie Jeebies" certainly entailed fixing an elusive performance based on various New Orleans traditions and musical practices into a static sonic "text" that was removed from its unique place and moment of existence as soon as it was transferred onto a mass-produced artifact. In Armstrong's anecdotal reminiscence, however, a sense of spontaneity—and thus of the aura of an original creation grounded in tradition—is reactivated through the recurring ellipses, which make the writing seem spontaneous and hurried, and by the repeated use of the temporal conjunction "when," which contrasts the singular moment of scat invention with the procession of real-time recording. The fluid semantics of the anecdote—"right in the middle," "moving along," "immediately," "just"—reconnect the music with a narrative as well as visual discourse of physical movement and spontaneous creativity that enlivens the otherwise static musical text.[116]

As the "Heebie Jeebies" recording and Armstrong's depiction of its origins illustrate, the distinction between the story-level appearance of historical events and the narrative discourse through which these events are presented matters because it alerts the more sensitive reader to nuances in Armstrong autobiographics that would otherwise be lost. Consider the fact that "Heebie Jeebies" marked the end of an era in sound recording. The song was recorded in one of the final acoustic sessions in Armstrong's career; less than a year later, he and his musicians would record their music electronically and would sound "closer, clearer, and louder than ever" to those who would play their records.[117] On the level of story, Armstrong does not anticipate the looming transition to this new recording technique, which would reproduce irretrievably gone performances with much greater fidelity and would reactivate the musicians' presence in audiences' living rooms even more convincingly than the older acoustic recordings.

On the level of discourse, however, the anecdote is highly informative, telling us something about Armstrong's efforts in 1951 to present himself as the central figure in the history of jazz singing (he scatted in New Orleans as a kid, popularized it through sound recording, and influenced the style of bebop vocalists) *and* something about a watershed moment in American recording history, when a specific vocal technique gained national attention only moments before a new technology would usher early jazz recording into a new era of commercial success and popularity. This new era and later changes in the field of American jazz would leave their mark on the structure and nature of Armstrong's successive life narratives, and the next chapter charts the trajectory of these narratives from the 1930s until the end of the musician's life.

CHAPTER 2

"I done forgot the words"

Versioning Autobiography

For Louis Armstrong, discussing his Hot Five and Hot Seven recordings for *Esquire* was nothing out of the ordinary. Writing and typing were part of a daily encounter with the past. Two letters from his vast epistolary output elucidate the nature of this encounter. In 1952, he wrote to Betty Jane Holder about his work on *Satchmo:*

> I have to write between shows . . . And you can imagine, trying to write, and shaking hands with your fans at the same time. . . . But I managed to get in there, just the same. . . . So, you can tell everybody, that Ol' Satchmo, has 'Octopus hands . . . I have my tape recorder right here by my right side, which I have, pretty near all of my recordings, on reels . . . So, when I listen to my records, I can get food for thoughts, since I'm writing my life's story. . . .[1]

Armstrong conveyed a similar scene to Marili Mardon a year later: "Why—in my dressing rooms—I just about do a dozen things at once, unconsciously—f'rinstance, giving an interview, to some wiseguy who barged in just at the time I'm typing some of my life's story, and right into a real deep chapter, that I didn't want to lose, and probably wouldn't ever get a hold of that particular phrase again. Ya dig?" A few years earlier, he had already informed Leonard Feather: "My dressing room was so crowded at all times, until every time I made an attempt to write a paragraph they'd look at me so wistfull until I'd stop writing automatically."[2]

At least four photographs document Armstrong's disposition toward daily writing. They provide a visual frame for his life narratives as self-referential performances that invite the reader to witness the very moment of textual production. The best-known of the photographs was taken by Popsie Randolph in the dressing room of New York's Basin Street Club in 1955. It shows Armstrong at the typewriter as he is reading a letter or maybe even proofreading one of his own letters. He is facing a mirror, and the connection with autobiography as a genre of self-reflection is readily apparent. Also visible is his trumpet in its case, as well as a scrapbook he used for his photo-collages. An earlier snapshot was taken by an unknown photographer in the early 1940s, and like Randolph's photograph, it recalls the famous title formula of many slave narratives, "written by himself," which is announced in texts such as *Narrative of the Life of Frederick Douglass, an American Slave, Written by Himself* (1845). Here, we see Armstrong typing in the kitchen of the Band Box, a Chicago nightclub, his trumpet resting behind him on a shelf.[3] The third and fourth photographs, which were taken by Dennis Stock in 1958, depict Armstrong at the typewriter in his den at home in Corona, a place he frequently describes in his writings. Again there is a mirror, this time behind him, as well as photo-collages that include publicity shots from the 1930s and a photograph of Joe Glaser (who, in a sense, is watching over his shoulder). A musical dimension is also visible; the desk lamp to Armstrong's left is shaped like a trumpet. Providing a verbal interface for these images, Armstrong wrote in a letter in 1967, "Daddy—here I am 'sitting at my 'Desk ("5. A M) in my den—at home in Corona," and in the "Forward" to his *Joke Book*, a collection of jokes, sayings, and toasts he circulated among his friends, he noted: "Well folks . . . here I sit at this little Ol Typewriter of mine getting ready to write you the Forward of my book. [. . .] It's actually real early in the morning . . . I've just gotten in off the road playing those hard ass *one nighters.*"[4]

The excerpt from Armstrong's letter to Betty Jane Holder attests to the mnemonic power he ascribes to his own recordings. As the sonic traces of musicking—people and places cast in sound—they jumpstart his memory. The music, it seems, already contains episodes and experiences from his life, and by listening to his recordings, he relives these moments and translates a sonically encoded self (*autos*) and its life (*bios*) to writing (*graphe*): from recording to page via the medium of the typewriter. For readers of his correspondence, musical resonances often become specific. In a letter to Max Jones, Armstrong explains that he is listening to the All Stars concert at Boston's Symphony Hall, and he continues by writing down some of his memories of band members Sid Catlett, Arvell Shaw, Barney Bigard, Earl Hines, Jack Teagarden, and Velma Middleton. Armstrong's writing activities, emblematized by his Octopus hands handling the typewriter and shak-

Fig. 3. Louis Armstrong, typing in his den. Photograph by Dennis Stock, 1958. Courtesy of Agentur Focus/Magnum Photos.

Fig. 4. Louis Armstrong, typing in his den. Photograph by Dennis Stock, 1958. Courtesy of Agentur Focus/Magnum Photos.

ing hands with friends and fans, are motivated by a communicative impulse so urgent that typing, hand shaking, and interviews must be handled at the same time.[5]

In all of these examples, readers are not presented with images of musicking but are rather invited to witness the moment of autobiographical creation: Armstrong's repeated production of stories about his life and music. The purpose of this chapter is to make sense of the performative nature of Armstrong's writing practices and to document the changing historical moments in which he performed this life story for different audiences: typing backstage in 1952 and 1953 or in his den in 1958, for instance. The following sets of questions are of particular interest: first, what kind of a writer is Armstrong? Which criteria of intelligibility can be identified in his narratives in terms of literary influences and autobiographical patterns? And how do strategic concerns with heterogeneous audience expectations and editorial constraints shape these narratives? What are we to make, for example, of the many Mark Twain references in *Swing That Music,* of the parallels to the Franklinian myth of the self-made man or to the rags-to-riches trajectory of the Horatio Alger stories, and of a seeming familiarity with Booker T. Washington's program of racial uplift in *Satchmo* and other narratives? To what extent did ghostwriters and editors shape Armstrong's narratives, and in what ways did their editorial interventions change the language and meaning of these narratives? Second, how exactly do the different autobiographical narratives Armstrong produced over the course of his career reflect and address changing historical contexts and discourses? What can we learn by tracing Armstrong's evolution as an autobiographer from the largely ghostwritten *Swing That Music* to more self-determined later narratives such as *Satchmo: My Life in New Orleans* and the 1966 interview with Richard Meryman for *Life*? And in what ways do these later narratives revise Robert Goffin's primitivist biography, *Horn of Plenty,* which contains egregious distortions and misreadings of the manuscript Armstrong had sent to the Belgian jazz enthusiast? Third, can we think of autobiographical narrative and musical performance as forms of expression that are inextricably linked and mutually influential as part of Armstrong's overarching intermedial autobiographics?

Armstrong received only very little formal schooling, and his knowledge of literature, autobiographical and otherwise, must have been limited.[6] The only literary writer discussed in his writings is Mark Twain, whose Tom Sawyer stories are mentioned in *Swing That Music*—the Mississippi excursion boat passes Jackson Island, for instance; the captain refers to the region as "Mark Twain country."[7] The presence of Mark Twain manifests itself both explicitly and implicitly. Implicitly, it can be located in a phrase such as "My river life on that boat," which echoes the title of Twain's *Life on the Mississippi* (1883), and the narrator's reference to this excursion as "my first big adventure," which evokes the titles of *The Adventures of Tom Sawyer* (1876) and *Adventures of Huckleberry Finn* (1884). Explicitly, the narrator recalls reading *Tom Sawyer* in the Waif's Home "and always want[ing] to meet a boy like 'Tom.'" When Armstrong asks the captain of the *Dixie Belle* about Twain's years as a river pilot, the captain recalls how he "used to sit on [Twain's] knee and hear him tell stories about the river and piloting." As the ship reaches Jackson Island, the captain places one "big strong hand" on the steering wheel and the "other hand on my [i.e., Armstrong's] shoulder. It felt heavy and kind." Upon passing the island, the narrator notes:

> I knew the time had come when I should feel something he wanted me to feel. I remembered from the book about how Tom Sawyer and Huckleberry Finn and their little friend Joe Harper had gone to that island to be "pirates," and had cooked their food over a wood fire and had had a good time, but that seemed a long way back to me, and the island, as far as I could see it in the dark, looked just the same as a hundred other islands we had passed in the river in the long time we had been going since we left New Orleans.[8]

This passage exudes a feeling of paternalism that readers would have known from nineteenth-century representations of the South and that still exerted a formidable influence on American literature in the 1930s, if Margaret Mitchell's bestselling novel *Gone with the Wind*, published, like *Swing That Music*, in 1936, is any indication. But the narrator, most likely the ghostwriter, is not satisfied with merely placing Armstrong within such literary contexts; he ends this story by noting how the scenes from Twain's novel "seemed a long way back to me." This remark may be read as a rejection of the paternalism expressed by the captain's hand on Armstrong's shoulder, but it can be interpreted more convincingly as the narrator's recognition of leaving childhood and becoming a professional musician. As such, it is characteristic of the complex inscription of Armstrong's life story as a series of narratives that jibe with popular images of Southern race relations and simultaneously express an individual autobiographical consciousness.

Beyond the Twain references in *Swing That Music*, Armstrong documented his knowledge of very few books, most of them jazz-related: Ramsey and Smith's *Jazzmen*, which includes a chapter on Armstrong by William Russell; Alan Lomax and Jelly Roll Morton's *Mister Jelly Roll: The Fortunes of Jelly Roll Morton, New Orleans Creole and "Inventor of Jazz"*; the autobiography of Jewish clarinetist Mezz Mezzrow, *Really the Blues*; and a book of Creole sayings and remedies titled *Gumbo Ya-Ya*.[9] The Louis Armstrong House Museum also holds a letter from Armstrong to his friend Jack Bradley in which he wrote down his views about Martin Williams's *The Jazz Tradition* (1970). Moreover, the library at his home in Corona included a fairly substantial number of books, the most significant of which might have been autobiographies by W. C. Handy and Pearl Bailey; a biography of Paul Robeson; presentation copies of Langston Hughes's *Famous American Negroes* (1954); and the two-volume *World's Great Men of Color 3000 B.C. to 1940 A.D.* (1947) by J. A. Rogers, in which he had checked off the entries on African American composer Samuel Taylor Coleridge, Haitian political leader Toussaint L'Ouverture, and the slave autobiographer and public orator Frederick Douglass.[10] Howard Taubman saw "crowded bookshelves that contain a well-rounded collection of fiction and non-fiction, including [. . .] quite a few volumes on jazz," when he visited Armstrong as part of his research for a portrait of the musician in the *New York Times Magazine* in 1950, and Michael Cogswell mentions two copies of Hughes's poetry collection *Ask Your Mama: 12 Moods for Jazz* (1961) but adds that Armstrong was most likely given many of the books by fans and publishers and had probably read only few of them.[11]

The sketchiness of these references and the difficulty of determining the exact extent of Armstrong's reading activities indicate that we are dealing with a writer who was largely unaware of the history and conventions of autobiography and other literary genres. Literary forms and patterns do appear in Armstrong's writings, but more often than not, they were added or attributed to the texts by those who edited and marketed them. Take the ending of *Satchmo*, which smacks of the easy plot resolutions readers would have known from Horatio Alger's rags-to-riches stories such as *Ragged Dick; or, Street Life in New York with the Boot-Blacks* (1867): "I had hit the big time. I was up North with the greats. I was playing with my idol, the King, Joe Oliver. My boyhood dream had come true at last."[12] The surviving manuscript, however, runs much longer and covers life in urban Chicago, which takes away much of the climactic vigor of the final statement in *Satchmo*. In addition, the sentence that served as the basis for *Satchmo*'s conclusion—"To play with such great men was the fulfillment of any child's dream, and I had reached that point in Music"—neither presents the dream's fulfillment as the pinnacle of Armstrong's career nor casts his youth as a teleological movement toward greatness and success.[13] What is more, Armstrong rarely celebrated financial wealth, and his insistence on a working-class lifestyle contradicts the triumphant Horatio Alger–like reading suggested, for instance, by the back-cover blurb of the autobiography's first paperback edition: "FROM SLUM BOY TO JAZZ KING!" As *Ebony* writer Charles L. Sanders announced in a 1964 article, Armstrong was a "Reluctant Millionaire" who presented himself as "just a plain old Louisiana boy" and followed the motto "Eat Good, Stay Healthy and Don't Worry About Being Rich."[14]

More can be said about the complicated relationship between Armstrong's autobiographical narratives and the rags-to-riches formula. It is true that the plot pattern is affirmed by the basic facts of his life. He was born poor and out of wedlock to a teenage mother (the father soon abandoned the family; the mother left him in his grandmother's care) and became a relatively wealthy man in the course of his life. He grew up in a segregated section of New Orleans and moved north to become an internationally acclaimed musician and entertainer, meeting royalty, presidents, and popes.[15] *Swing That Music* taps into this narrative formula from the outset. Recalling Armstrong's arrest as a youngster for shooting a gun on New Year's Eve, the narrator explains: "that shot, I do believe, started my career. It changed my life and brought me my big chance. In the twenty and more years that have passed since, I guess I have played almost all over the world. [. . .] But whenever I have had a few minutes to myself out of all of this running around, [. . .] I [. . .] ask[ed] myself, 'Louis, how come this to happen to you?'"[16] This opening is very much in the vein of traditional autobiography, especially the memoir, in which a famous individual gives an account of his (less often her) origins and details how he (or she) achieved his (or her) present status. This present status is usually the teleological end result of a life retrofitted to present a more or less seamless continuum of experiences. But Armstrong's later autobiographical narratives express a strong yearning for his hometown and the people of his neighborhood, and they publicly reject outward manifestations of wealth and social status—think only of his insistence on detailing his bathroom habits and advertising his favorite laxative, Swiss Kriss, or his love of red beans and rice. This contradicts the narrative trajectory and ideological underpinning of the rags-to-riches story, as well as the promise, made in *Swing That Music*, to depict a personal journey to fame and fortune.

Armstrong's writings have also been associated with "the didactic prescriptions of Benjamin Franklin's autobiography" and a Franklinian gospel of "hard-headed realism, tactical planning, and optimistic activity." While Martin Williams discovers an Emersonian "self-discipline" in Armstrong's life, most critics tend to take this life "as an example of the American myth of the self-made man" who starts out at the bottom and reaches fame by being "open to people and ideas" and by "reach[ing] out and absorb[ing] all that was around him."[17] Yet Franklin's public promotion of self-making and Armstrong's open admission of his relentless indulging in physical pleasures, especially eating and sex, suggest vastly different historical contexts and authorial motivations.[18] Compare Franklin's call for frugality, expressed in the dictum "Eat not to Dulness / Drink not to Elevation," with Armstrong's statement that "I'll probably never be rich, but I will be a fat man."[19] On chastity, compare Franklin's advice to "Rarely use Venery but for Health or Offspring; Never to Dulness, Weakness, or the Injury of your own or another's Peace or Reputation" with Black Benny Williams's advice for Armstrong: "'Always remember, no matter how many times you get Married.—Always have another woman for a Sweetheart on the outside.'"[20] Armstrong also transformed Franklin's famous "Early to bed, and early to rise, makes a Man healthy, wealthy and wise" into a short toast about the laxative "Pluto Water": "Make your life longer, / and worries short, / Take Pluto Water, / But please don't Fart // Early to bed, / Early to rise, / 'Pluto will make you / (Shit)-Healthy—and 'Wise."[21] There is no indication, however, that he consciously revised Franklin's aphorisms or that he had read Franklin's autobiography. It is much more plausible to assume that these aphorisms were so widely dispersed throughout American culture that Armstrong had read about them somewhere or that he had picked them up in his daily conversations with friends, fellow musicians, or even his elders (it is also possible that he encountered them in school). These elders would have been vernacular speakers, or hustlers, prone to punning and revising "white" notions of respectability: "I'd trot down to Liberty and Perdido, where all them old-time hustlers hang around the corner at lunchtime, get their poor-boy sandwich, a can of beer, wear that sack apron around them and all sit around and chat and joke. And I was thrilled to sit among those cats," he told *New York Times* writer Gilbert Millstein.[22]

In the history of American autobiography, the Franklinian narrative of the self-made man delivered the teleological pattern for the myth of racial uplift, epitomized by Booker T. Washington's *Up from Slavery* (1901). Yet in the same way in which Franklin's aphorisms probably did not impact Armstrong's writings directly, Washington's autobiography does not seem to have exerted a specific literary influence. A sentence like "I think that I have always done *great* things about *uplifting* my *race*" can be traced to the rhetoric of the New Negro movement and later the civil rights movement, rather than directly to Washington's philosophy.[23] Moreover, Armstrong was part of a Southern black culture that had imbibed central elements of Washington's philosophy and program without necessarily being aware of his writings and speeches.[24] Thus, while echoes of Washington are scattered throughout Armstrong's writings—from a reference to teeth brushing in *Satchmo* to an insistence on getting an education and learning a trade; from commentary about young musicians who pulled Joe Oliver "down like a barrel of crabs" to his relatives' revisionist attitude toward slavery—the narratives depart substantially from Washington's values whenever they revel in black working-class culture and express delight in stories about eating (and overeating), digestion (including laxatives), and sexual intercourse (including extramarital sex and prostitution).[25]

Rather than writing in the literary tradition of black autobiographers such as Frederick Douglass and Booker T. Washington, Armstrong was a vernacular speaker steeped in the oral traditions of his hometown. For the general reading public, however, vernacular narratives were polished and streamlined by editors and, in the case of *Swing That Music*, handled by a ghostwriter. And indeed, depending on the purpose for which he assembled a particular narrative, Armstrong himself already presented edited versions of his life story. Epistolary exchanges with fans and friends allowed him to stay in touch with the people he liked and update them on his past and present experiences; material he composed for professional writers such as Robert Goffin and Leonard Feather was intended as fodder for the jazz press (as Feather recalls, Armstrong "sent a batch of news to me in New York with a request that I transmit it to the *Melody Maker*" in the early 1940s); and then there was Armstrong's "great urge, especially during his last years, to set the historical record straight."[26]

These different purposes of autobiographical performance called for a flexible approach to self-representation, and self-editing was one way in which Armstrong related his life story to heterogeneous and shifting audiences. Such flexibility is particularly visible in the gap between material intended for publication and more private notes, letters, and conversations taped for posterity. In *Satchmo*, for example, Armstrong mentions his fascination with black New Orleans prostitutes but presents this fascination rather humorously, stating that they "continued to chase me. Of course I must admit I just couldn't resist letting some of the finer ones catch up with me once in a while."[27] In the essay about his four black wives for *Ebony*, he talks about "a whole lot of loving and close contact" with his fourth wife, Lucille. In his letters, however, he substitutes such coy language with explicit machismo when he tells of his sexual prowess and his marital infidelities. Talking about his mistress Sweets, he states: "When two people are in a room by themselves, Kissing will lead to fucking every time [. . .] . Every night' we *Whaled.* I mean, I really *Grined* in that Cunt"; in a later letter to Glaser he writes that Grace Kelly was "as hot as a whores pussy with the pox."[28] Another example is Black Benny's advice about women, which Armstrong relates to Glaser and which appears in less explicit form in *Satchmo*. The language changes from "Bitches' [. . .] showing they '*Asses*'" in the letter to the more benign "I have always been wrapped up in my music and no women in the world can change that" in *Satchmo*.[29] Here, readers encounter differently worded versions of one and the same sentiment. As an autobiographical performer, Armstrong considered his respective audience and used language appropriate for each performative context.

Like many African American authors of the time, Armstrong submitted his writings to white editors and publishers, who tended to enforce particular versions of autobiographical representation. The ghostwriter's role in *Swing That Music*, the influence of editors in *Satchmo*, and the suppression of "The Satchmo Story" by manager Glaser are three prominent examples of restrictive editorial politics and its consequences. Armstrong puts it frankly in his interview with Larry King when he notes that people like Glaser and traveling manager Ira Mangel "don't like for me to talk about the olden days. All the prosty-*toots* and the fine gage and the badass racketeers. But hell, Man, I got to tell it like it was!"[30] However, lest one idealize Armstrong's wish to tell his story free of editorial constraint, and lest one accept Armstrong's skilled construction of a freewheeling public persona at face value, there is a statement he made to his biographer Goffin, whom he paid to transform a series of autobiographical reminiscences (Armstrong calls them "books of stories") into a proper (auto)biography: "There may be several spots that you might want to straighten out—or change around . . . What ever you do about it is alright with me . . . I am only doing as you told me . . . To make it real—and write it just as it happened."[31]

Armstrong's correspondence with Goffin and his relationship with ghostwriters and editors exemplify editorial processes that Sidonie Smith and Julia Watson call autobiographical coaxing and coercing.[32] In the history of African American autobiography, these processes shaped Frederick Douglass's *Narrative of the Life of Frederick Douglass, an American Slave, Written by Himself* as a consequence of William Lloyd Garrison's sponsorship and Booker T. Washington's *Up from Slavery* as a result of directives by editor and publisher Lyman Abbott (only in that sense do Armstrong's writings reside within the same autobiographical tradition). Armstrong's willingness to satisfy the demands of coaxers and coercers may be interpreted as a subservient attitude toward the mediation of his life story by journalists and editors, but a more compelling way to read the letter to Goffin cited above can be gleaned from Hugues Panassié's class-conscious remarks about *Swing That Music.* "Louis enjoyed writing his book, and then probably said to himself that corrections made by people more educated than he improved the draft."[33] Moreover, keeping in mind the distinction between autobiographical performance (the act of telling the story in writing) and autobiographical product (the published text), we can assume that Armstrong favored the moment of storytelling and worried less about how the finished product was polished, marketed, and sold, perhaps because he often had little control over these matters.[34] He did, after all, express a very similar understanding about the business side of music: "And all those headaches of keeping a band, keeping musicians, paying them, watching the box office, commissions, paying taxes, picking songs to record—I don't bother with it. He [manager Joe Glaser] just gives me so much money every month, takes care of everything else. I just want to do the things I know how to do."[35]

The discrepancy between Armstrong's unedited texts and the ways in which editors and publishers controlled his early writing is illustrated by *Swing That Music.* The structure of the autobiography follows the example of the eclectic slave narrative. According to Robert Stepto, the eclectic narrative is determined by the authenticating documents that surround the text. The publisher explains that he has done some basic editing but has preserved the original meaning and style. He offers praise for the writer and his or her story, verifies the authenticity of the account, and guarantees the truthfulness of the narrative.[36] The complex fragmentation of the narrative voice in *Swing That Music* indicates how coaxing and coaching influenced the eclecticism of the autobiographical text. A total of four, perhaps five, different voices can be identified.[37] The first is popular crooner Rudy Vallée, whose introduction lauds Armstrong's musical achievements: "He is truly an artist, in every sense of the word." Vallée speaks with the authority of an autobiographer whose own life story had been published as *My Time Is Your Time* in 1930.[38] Moreover, he had scored a hit with the Walter Donaldson composition "You're Driving Me Crazy" (1930), a song Armstrong also recorded on December 23, 1930. The difference between Vallée's subdued crooning and Armstrong's rendition of the tune is striking because it foregrounds the racially coded position from which the white crooner from New England presents the life story of the black jazz musician from New Orleans in the introduction to *Swing That Music*. Armstrong's swinging version includes a short comedy introduction that casts the performance as a self-conscious offering to a commercial audience ("we just muggin' lightly," drummer Lionel Hampton stutters), black vernacular patter that departs from the scripted lyrics ("mama," "oh, you dogs"), and quite a bit of scatting that radically transforms the lyrics from a sappy love lament into a proud display of musico-linguistic agility. In contrast, Vallée's unswung version sticks to the written lyrics, does not include any comedic hokum, and generally stays within the conventions of respectable "white" crooning.

Vallée obviously appreciated Armstrong's music. Only months after the publication of *Swing That Music*, he invited the trumpeter to substitute for him as host of the *Fleischmann's Yeast Show* (Apr.–May 1937) and thus made him the first black musician to host a major American radio show. His introduction to *Swing That Music* expresses his admiration for the black musician in no uncertain terms, but it also displays an awareness of the expectations of the implied reader, for whom Armstrong's unorthodox singing and trumpet style had to be explained. After all, one critic from *Variety* magazine heard the music the Armstrong orchestra played during the *Fleischmann's Yeast* program as noise that "sounded like a boiler factory in swingtime."[39] Being more sensitive and sympathetic toward Armstrong's music, Vallée combines a largely romantic vocabulary about his trumpet playing ("genius," "evolution," "mastery of the trumpet," "purity of his notes," "artist") with the discourse within which Armstrong's singing had been popularly conceived: "Most of you have heard his records, if you have not heard him [in person], and are familiar with that utterly mad, hoarse, inchoate mumble-jumble that is Louis' 'singing.'" After having leveled with the readers, Vallée continues: "And yet when you study it, you will come to see that it is beautifully timed and executed, and to perceive that a subtle musical understanding and keen mind are being manifest through this seemingly incoherent expression." About "Armstrong's vocalizations," Vallée remarks: "They often seem to be the result of a chaotic, disorganized mind struggling to express itself, but those who know anything about modern music recognize his perfect command of time spacing, of rhythm, harmony, and pitch and his flawless understanding of the effects he is striving to achieve." Combined here are the two discourses that had marked Armstrong's critical and popular reception: a discourse of minstrel primitivism ("utterly mad, hoarse, inchoate mumble-jumble") and a discourse of modern artistic genius and musical mastership ("beautifully timed and executed"; "subtle musical understanding and keen mind"; "perfect command"; "flawless understanding").[40]

The second voice in *Swing That Music* appears in the form of Armstrong's vernacular and anecdotal accounts of his youth in New Orleans and his musical career in Chicago and New York. These anecdotes frequently seem edited, resulting in erased or muted references to racism, drug use, and sexual activities. Armstrong's cultural background is included for local color and as evidence of his development from an uneducated and unrefined black youngster to a sophisticated swing musician. The third narrative voice is hidden throughout the text proper. It intermingles with Armstrong's anecdotes and explains swing music to the lay reader. The voice most likely belongs to Horace Gerlach, the cowriter of the autobiography's title song, "Swing That Music," who takes over once the autobiographical narrative ends and thereby adds a fourth voice to the text. In the music section of the book, he familiarizes the reader with what are presented as the best (and mostly white) swing players and supplies musical notations of their playing. The fifth voice, one could argue, is provided by Armstrong's singing and trumpet playing on the recording of "Swing That Music," which coincided with the publication of the autobiography.

Unlike *Swing That Music*, Armstrong's second autobiography, *Satchmo: My Life in New Orleans*, contains the single voice of the author, albeit in edited form. Comparing *Satchmo* with the surviving parts of the manuscript, "The Armstrong Story," several instances can be identified in which

Armstrong's words were changed in order to tone down his attitude toward matters of race. In the original manuscript, Armstrong had written that his mother "came from a little town in Louisiana called Butte Louisiana, when they were all but slaves. . . . And her parents, were all Slaves."[41] In *Satchmo*, the phrase "when they were all but slaves" is excised, which leaves the historical reference to slavery but drops Armstrong's comment about his mother's youth in the post-Reconstruction South of the 1880s and 1890s, when she was still treated like a slave. In another passage, Armstrong recalls King Jones, a prominent figure of Chicago's nightlife. The text of the published autobiography intimates that Armstrong accused Jones of trying to pass for white: "He acted as though he was not a colored fellow, but his real bad English gave him away."[42] The manuscript, however, reveals Armstrong's assumption that Jones was from the West Indies and could speak neither the black vernacular of jazz musicians nor Standard English (and was thus not "colored" according to Armstrong's nomenclature). Armstrong had written: "I don't think Jones was a colored fellow. I think he was from some Island. He tried to be everything but colored but that real bad English gave him away."[43] The edited version suggests that Black English is inferior to Standard English, and it reinforces stereotypes of linguistic deficiency because it omits the geographical reference to "some Island" and thus casts Jones as an African American unable to speak Standard English instead of a West Indian versed in the patois of his home country.

Despite these editorial intrusions, Armstrong seems to be responsible for confrontational statements such as "no matter how tough an ofay may seem, there is always some 'black son of a bitch' he is wild about and loves to death just like one of his own relatives."[44] But even here, criticism is expressed in code, through a more or less subtle form of sarcasm that voices Armstrong's thoughts on the ideology of paternalism ("just like one of his own relatives") that was peculiar to the plantation South and was still powerful in the 1930s. Calling the white Southerner "ofay," he signals his disapproval of racial segregation. By referring to the black person the Southerner proclaims to love as a "'black son of a bitch'" and by indicating that he is quoting an actual speaker (the phrase appears in quotation marks), he points to the racist attitude lurking behind the benign face of paternalism. The Southerner thinks of the black man not as a son, but as a *son of a bitch*. Even the discrepancy between the South's professed love of its black population and the realities of lynching—a discrepancy famously dramatized in Billie Holiday's recordings and performances of Abel Meeropol's lynch-

ing poem "Strange Fruit"—emerges in Armstrong's account: the Southerner loves the black son of a bitch *to death*.[45]

In general, Armstrong's written voice can be identified through stylistic
peculiarities (dashes, apostrophes, explanations in parentheses, italics, insertions, ellipses, and so forth), by word choice, and by comparing it with
statements made in other versions of his life story. In the passage cited
above, the usage of "ofay" is typical of his private and some of his public
writings, and the observation that blacks need white protectors can be located in several verbal and written statements. In another instance, Armstrong's voice remains somewhat subdued, but his point about his time
aboard the Streckfus entertainment ships comes across nonetheless:

> We were colored, and we knew what that meant. We were not allowed to
> mingle with the white guests under any circumstances. We were there to
> play good music for them, and that was all. However, everybody loved us
> and our music and treated us royally. I and some of the other musicians in
> the band were from the South and we understood, so we never had any
> hard feelings. I have always loved my white folks, and they have always
> proved that they loved me and my music.[46]

This statement attests to shifting attitudes toward color barriers and racial
segregation, as well as to Armstrong's growing control over his narrative
voice. In *Swing That Music*, he had only alluded to the practice of keeping
separate quarters on the ship: "we boys in the orchestra [. . .] slept in the
same part of the boat and had our meals at the same table and in fact we
were together most all of the time."[47] In *Satchmo*, he states his position
more decidedly, recalling "some ugly experiences" and "nasty remarks" but
conceding that "most of us were from the South anyway. We were used to
that kind of jive, and we would just keep on swinging as though nothing
had happened. Before the evening was over they *loved* us."[48] This passage
is an example both of what William Kenney calls "situational ethnicity,"
which Armstrong employed in order to appeal to different audiences, and
of ambiguity as a major element in the musician's writings.[49] Situational
ethnicity creeps into the passage when Armstrong confines his criticism to
the South of his youth and makes no connection to 1950s America and
when he softens this criticism by preserving a stoic attitude, ending the
passage with a remark about audience appreciation. Ambiguity comes into
play through the specific language he uses to compose this passage—the

whites are "ofays" and their behavior is called "jive"—and in the surviving bit of original textual index, the italicized *"loved,"* which may signify irony and signal Armstrong's awareness of the social role he was forced to play. Like Armstrong's recollections of musicking, this account can thus be read on two levels: on a level of story, where the autobiographical protagonist acts stoically in the face of racial discrimination, and on a level of narrative discourse, where the autobiographical narrator presents past events with an ironic undertone.

The doubly coded nature of Armstrong's narratives makes them especially effective as performative engagements with specific audiences. These engagements produce multiple versions of the musician's life story in order to satisfy heterogeneous audiences and occasionally ward off editorial interventions. While one finds no self-conscious use of autobiographical conventions, then, one does find a clear understanding of, and often a catering to, the changing expectations of mediators such as Horace Gerlach and audiences like the readers of *Swing That Music* and *Satchmo*. What remains to be seen beyond questions of editorial control is how the different autobiographical narratives Armstrong produced over the course of his career reflect and address the changing historical contexts of, and debates about, American jazz. As discursive interventions in contemporary debates and in the historiography of jazz, these narratives are fascinating documents of a musician's attempts to claim narrative authority over the interpretation of his life and music without sanctioning a single authoritative version. They warrant close attention as integral parts of Armstrong's evolving autobiographics and as evidence of an unusual writing career by a very unlikely author.

This writing career began with *Swing That Music*, which was published shortly after Armstrong had signed on with manager Joe Glaser upon his return from a lengthy hiatus in Europe. The autobiography is filtered through the lens of the British Horace Gerlach, but it performed its cultural work in the context of the American swing era.[50] In terms of the publication date, it is worth noting that the beginning of the swing era is conventionally dated by Benny Goodman's appearance at the Palomar Ballroom in Los Angeles in the summer of 1935, which preceded the autobiography by about a year and probably motivated its publication. *Swing That Music* acknowledges Goodman's fame and taps into the clarinetist's popularity: it names Goodman's band as an exceptional swing orchestra, includes Goodman's photograph, and features his scored improvisation over "Swing That Music" (May 18, 1936) in the music section (Goodman does not play on the actual recording). The autobiography introduces Armstrong's life story to a predominantly white swing audience, celebrates the musician as a star of the new music, and casts him as a "featured soloist in an arrangement written and edited by others."[51] These objectives are emphasized by a photographic movement from the "blackness" of early jazz (Armstrong's photograph as frontispiece) to the racial integration of swing, symbolized by the photographs of Armstrong and the Benny Goodman band in the music section, which includes white players like Goodman and Tommy Dorsey, as well as the black pianist Claude Hopkins.[52] What we find here is a narrative trajectory that prefigures many of Armstrong's film roles, for instance in *A Song Is Born*, where his New Orleans jazz ultimately leads to the kind of swing played by white stars like Benny Goodman and Charlie Barnet. What we also find is a gesture of black authentication of white cultural production that traces back to the minstrel shows of the nineteenth century. In these shows, black culture (or what was taken to be black culture) served as a supposedly authentic creative source for white minstrels, who blackened their faces with burned cork and performed allegedly black folk dances, music, and comedy sketches. A related trajectory from black folk source to white cultural production appears in films such as *The Glenn Miller Story* (dir. Anthony Mann, 1954), *High Society*, and *The Five Pennies*, in which Armstrong adds color and comedic hotness but also a sense of musical brilliance and cultural authority to the white and essentially cool Glenn Miller (Jimmy Stewart), Dexter (Bing Crosby), and Red Nichols (Danny Kaye).

It is safe to say that the ghostwriter and editors of *Swing That Music* sought to make Armstrong palatable for the mostly white swing audience through various references to popular discourses and images of the American South (including the Mark Twain references discussed above). These references include episodes about Armstrong's life on a Streckfus entertainment ship (here called the *Dixie Belle*; in later accounts the *Sydney*), which is described as one of ease and relaxation. Whenever Armstrong does not play music, he "laze[s] around."[53] This recalls Hoagy Carmichael and Johnny Mercer's composition "Lazybones" (1933), which portrays a (probably) Southern black man dozing away in the sun and loafing around all day, as well as Paul Robeson's character Joe, who pays tribute to the Mississippi as the "Ol' Man River" in the movie version of *Show Boat* (dir. James Whale, 1936) and is called "the laziest man that ever lived on this river" by his wife.[54] Published a few months after this movie version, *Swing That Music* directly refers to Jerome Kern and Oscar Hammerstein's 1927 stage adaptation of Edna Ferber's novel *Show Boat* (1926) and repeats the claim to racial authenticity popularized by early minstrel performers such as Thomas D. Rice and Daniel Emmett: "Mr. Jerome Kern sure knew what he was doing when he wrote *Ol' Man River*, for Miss Ferber's 'Show Boat.' He must have been down there."[55]

Furthermore, the opening pages of *Swing That Music* evoke images of the pastoral South when the narrator writes, "That smell of magnolias is my earliest memory of home." The connection between the South as a signifier of a blissful space, implied by the reference to the magnolia myth, and Armstrong's popular music is made explicit in an interesting turn of phrase: "Those big, white flowers do swing their scent."[56] The repeated use of the jazz term "swing" could be interpreted as a subtle indication of Armstrong's critical distance from the discourse reproduced in *Swing That Music*. The magnolia myth is acknowledged, and its power is used to establish Armstrong's benevolent image for a white readership—note the redundant but suggestive reference to magnolias as *"white* flowers"—but the remnant of jazz jargon also manifests a black vernacular perspective.

Nonetheless, in the matter of a few pages, all the stereotypes of popular culture's South are present: Armstrong recalls his great-grandparents' life in slavery; mentions his mother's job as "a house servant in a fine old white family" who "helped bring up all of their children"; notes that "[s]he certainly was one grand cook and could swing the biscuits"; and then turns to images of black youngsters "shootin' dice and fighting," as well as black kids "go[ing] down to the Mississippi and sit[ting] on the docks and sing[ing] together."[57] This type of minstrel pastoralism is contextualized by Armstrong's musical recordings of the 1930s. Songs with Mississippi themes before 1936 include "Lazy River" (Nov. 3, 1931), "Mississippi Basin" (Apr. 24, 1933), and "Mighty River" (Apr. 26, 1933), and Armstrong continued to record such river songs after the publication of *Swing That Music*, for instance, "Shanty Boat on the Mississippi" (June 15, 1939) and "Lazy 'Sippi Steamer" (Mar. 14, 1940). His controversial "When It's Sleepy Time Down South" (Apr. 20, 1931) and similar titles—"That's My Home" (Dec. 8, 1932), "He's a Son of the South" (Jan. 26, 1933), and the minstrel compositions "The Old Folks at Home" and "Carry Me Back to Old Virginny" (recorded with the Mills Brothers on June 29, 1937 and Apr. 7, 1937, respectively)—were plantation songs that remained popular in the context of the Great Depression, when many yearned for a preindustrial pastoral ideal that was often associated with the American South. The lyrics depict crooning "darkies" and an "old mammy" ("When It's Sleepy Time Down South"), as well as places "where I labored so hard for old master" and "where the old darky's heart longs to go" ("Carry Me Back to Old Virginny").

As jazz historian David Stowe writes, the culture of American swing music included "not just the big bands, but their audiences, the writers who critiqued and promoted them, the media conglomerate that supported them."[58] Part of this media conglomerate were magazines such as *Esquire* and *Vanity Fair*, which contributed to the mediation of Armstrong's public image by tapping into the discourse of the benevolent South presented in *Swing That Music* and related sound recordings. In October of 1935, *Vanity Fair* featured a semifictional article by Hermann Deutsch that cast Armstrong's life story in a stereotypical black dialect that was very much unlike Armstrong's vernacular voice ("Hayah pappy! Hayah mammy! Hayah de gal chillen and de boy chillen all both!").[59] *Vanity Fair* ran an article a few months later that lauded Armstrong's achievements by pairing him with the classical violinist Fritz Kreisler in the form of an imaginary interview. In the context of the Southern discourse that would inform *Swing That Music* only a few months later, the minstrel language and imagery with which *Vanity Fair* identifies Armstrong are revealing: "Ah'll give yo' a job playin' fiddle in mah band."[60] The caricature of Armstrong and Kreisler by Miguel Covarrubias that accompanies the article heightens the minstrel element. Armstrong's shiny black face is beaded with sweat; he is rolling his eyes and flashing his teeth.[61] These mediations indicate the degree to which *Swing That Music* appeared as part of a larger conversation about the racial and cultural politics of swing, a conversation in which Armstrong frequently appeared as a phantom speaker whose words and visual profile were designed by others and whose limitations he would eventually overcome at least in part by publishing more self-controlled versions of his life story.

In the 1940s and 1950s, Armstrong made a concerted effort to publish a second version of this life story, one that would turn out to be substantially different from *Swing That Music*, not so much in terms of the basic storyline, but in terms of the text's ideological underpinning and discursive position. In 1944, he contacted the Belgian jazz critic Robert Goffin as a potential amanuensis for a second autobiography, and he also talked to Orson Welles about an (auto)biographical movie—"Orson Welles to Feature

Louis Armstrong in Film," Lawrence Lamar exclaimed in the *Chicago Defender* as early as 1941.[62] A six-page letter Armstrong sent to Welles in 1945 outlines the musician's life story from his time on the riverboats with Fate Marable and his work with King Oliver at the Lincoln Gardens in Chicago to his stint with Fletcher Henderson in New York and his appearance with the Erskine Tate Orchestra at the Vendome Theater in Chicago. Characteristically, the letter begins with a self-reflexive reference to Armstrong's writing activities: "Man, [. . .] I've been one of the busiest cats in the world since we had that chat backstage at the dressing room at the Orpheum. [. . .] I'm sorry about delaying my letter but they had me busy as a one-legged man doing the charleston. I couldn't even look at my typewriter, let alone beat out a few. . . ."[63] The movie, however, never came to pass; the 1947 film *New Orleans*, according to its opening credits, was based on an "original story" by Elliot Paul and Herbert J. Biberman, and the screenplay was written by Elliot Paul and Dick Irving Hyland. Paul had been one of the screenwriters for the Welles project, which explains the confluence of biographical elements and fictional content that characterizes *New Orleans* as a botched biopic.

Armstrong's correspondence with Goffin led to a series of "notebooks" that the musician sent as source material for an autobiography. Goffin, however, turned these writings into the biography *Horn of Plenty*, allegedly because he "was astonished by the high quality of the style" and by the fact that "Armstrong's text was so authentic and sincere that I did not dare to use it all for my book."[64] A comparative analysis of Armstrong's "The 'Goffin Notebooks'" and Goffin's *Horn of Plenty* illuminates the complicated transatlantic negotiation of biographical portraiture and autobiographical source text that came to be the only book-length English narrative about Armstrong in the 1940s.[65] Goffin essentially foiled the musician's attempt to produce a second autobiography, and *Horn of Plenty* is the text against which Armstrong's reinvigorated attempts to publish a more self-controlled work in the 1950s must be measured. In general, Goffin preserved the basic elements of the narrative, but his chronology and geography are frequently off. His account of Armstrong's life in New Orleans connects musicians and events ahistorically, for instance, when he writes that Armstrong regularly heard Buddy Bolden and Jelly Roll Morton perform. He also uses Armstrong's moniker "Satchmo" anachronistically; Armstrong received it in the early 1930s and did not use it in interviews and recordings before this time. The early years of Armstrong's life, which are not covered in the "Goffin Notebooks" (the narrative begins in 1918 and ends in 1931), had already been described in *Swing That Music* and in William Russell's chapter on Armstrong in *Jazzmen*, both of which provided additional sources for Goffin.[66]

Despite his later claim that he admired the quality and style of Armstrong's writing, Goffin makes no indication that Armstrong's idiosyncratic orthography and his colorful language have anything of importance to reveal about the musician and his music. Only once does he refer to Armstrong's penmanship, calling the letters he wrote to Joe Oliver "painfully scrawled replies."[67] He takes Armstrong's narrative as a point of departure but invents scenes and dialogue in order to flesh out the story, adding his own commentary about jazz by attributing it to Armstrong, whose mind he is seemingly able to read. Goffin's role in this particular version of Armstrong's life story thus recalls the editorial interventions of *Swing That Music*, but *Horn of Plenty* also adds new facets to the musician's life story by connecting him with a primitivist view of the black jazzman as a noble savage. Goffin's heavy-handed primitivism was not uncommon in 1940s revivalist criticism and can also be found in Mezz Mezzrow's *Really the Blues*, published just one year prior to *Horn of Plenty*.[68] The biography proposes a view "of the Negro's past" characterized by "the deep-voiced tomtoms rhythmically breaking the silence of the night, the wild jungle dances, and the awesome revelation of voodoo worship." Goffin further romanticizes life in Africa and American slavery when he depicts Armstrong's yearning "to mingle once more with those who—from the distant days of the torrid Congo, from father to son since—were writing in sweat and blood the heart-rending epic of his race." Apart from direct references to primitivism—"primitive hearts"; "the primitive cry of the New Orleans blacks"—an essentialist and even supremacist understanding of "the black man's soul" colors Goffin's account: "What magic powers did the music possess which slept in the souls of the blacks and raised them from their helpless state, yes, even as high as the esteem of the white man?"[69]

In addition to Goffin's primitivism, which also surfaces in connection with his invention of minstrel dialect, *Horn of Plenty* provides evidence of a fundamental difference in perspective between the performing musician and the jazz biographer.[70] In Armstrong's "Goffin Notebooks," musical performances on stage are seldom the object of narration. Armstrong's account of his success at the Vendome Theater with the Erskine Tate Symphony Orchestra in 1925 only includes statements such as "the 'opening night was sensational" and "I became quite a 'Figure at the 'Vendome.' Especially with the Gals."[71] Goffin's substantially longer version, however, gets much mileage out of depicting the performance itself: "Eyes closed, he felt himself borne to heaven on the wings of inspiration, and came down to earth only when a thunder of applause brought him back to reality. [. . .] Then time stood still once more. Louis shed all restraint and played. He was a pure musical spirit freed of all earthly ties."[72] This version of a racially grounded yet celestially pure spirituality sharply contrasts Armstrong's own account, which insists on the very earthly ties—the "Gals" in the audience—that Goffin denies. In an earlier chapter, Goffin writes about Armstrong's performance at the Lincoln Gardens with the Joe Oliver Band: "In a flash the young musician was blowing out his soul through the mouth of his trumpet. He blew so hard that the skin of his nape was stretched hard; he had closed his eyes, and seemed in a trance, out of the living world, completely possessed by unalloyed musical exaltation."[73] The passage contains many of the hallmarks of celebratory jazz fiction: the sexual suggestiveness of musical "blackness" (the "nape [. . .] stretched hard"), the romantic understanding of creative originality as a revelation of the self ("blowing out his soul"; "unalloyed musical exaltation"), and the trancelike effect that the music has on the listener and that is projected back onto the performing musician. A similar, though somewhat less unabashedly emphatic, discourse appears in later biographies, for instance in Jones and Chilton's *Louis* ("plays like a demon"; "satisfied feeling of a gladiator who had just taken care of the strongest lion in the country") and Teachout's *Pops* ("lifted up his horn to his deeply scarred lips to play a cadenza, gazing skyward as he floated up to a high note").[74] Yet it is very much unlike Armstrong's version in *Satchmo*, where the musician cites his familiarity with Oliver on and off the bandstand rather than heavenly inspiration or the unmitigated release of soulful expression as the reason for their musical rapport.

Remarkable, too, is Goffin's depiction of Armstrong's singing: "He wrenched out the word *baby* as if torn from the depths of his being. A shiver ran through his listeners. Everybody had stopped dancing. Louis finished the stanza and broke out at once into a toothy grin, wrapped his lips around the trumpet, shut his eyes, and climbed up and up." Claiming to be privy to Armstrong's inner life ("the depths of his being"), as well as to the perspective of the audience, Goffin continues: "The spectators were frozen into silence at the sight of this giant with the bulging neck, his nose flattened by the force of vibrancy, his left hand clutching a spotless handker-chief, who could stir up a whirlwind of strange music."[75] The musician's image on stage appears larger than life, and racial features are exaggerated in the process: "toothy grin," "bulging neck," "nose flattened." Goffin shuttles back and forth between Armstrong's supposed emotions ("felt himself borne to heaven on the wings of inspiration") and his own adula-tory gaze at the mysterious black genius beyond rational explanation ("trance"; "pure musical spirit freed of all earthly ties"; "strange music").

Armstrong attempted to revise such depictions, as becomes clear when we compare Goffin's version of the Saturday nights at Funky Butt Hall and Armstrong's recollection of these events (discussed in chapter 1). The "Goffin Notebooks" do not cover the dances at Funky Butt Hall, but Arm-strong's later versions can be understood as correctives to Goffin's primi-tivist portrait. In these revisionary stories, he depicts scenes of musicking and incorporates the participatory and vernacular dynamics of the jazz per-formance into the manner of his storytelling. In *Horn of Plenty*, however, Goffin misses the youngster's admiration for the dancers and musicians and substitutes Armstrong's earthy eroticism with racial caricature:

> A crowd pushed and jostled at the bar, with many a drunken and half-naked wench emptying her whisky glass at one gulp between puffs of smoke from a fat cigar. Louis hesitated; dared he go in? The jerky rhythm beat like his own pulse. A hulking Negro with shiny black face, white eyeballs, and glis-tening teeth, was hugging a "high yaller" who pretended to swoon as she crushed a camelia [*sic*] to distended nostrils.

Armstrong's proud portrait of black working-class styles is disfigured here by the references to the "half-naked wench," "hulking Negro," "shiny black face," "white eyeballs," and "glistening teeth," all of which evoke im-ages of blackface minstrelsy and related forms of racial representation.[76]

Moreover, Goffin interprets the vernacular evocation of "funkiness" and the erotic movement of body parts encapsulated by the name Funky Butt, which connects body odor with musical and physical exertion and views raunchy sweat as a sexually enticing scent, as a lack of refinement and culture: "To this day the denizens of Perdido have not forgotten that ill-smelling establishment. Its very name betrays a wanton etymology, graphi-cally characterizing the awful smell that always pervaded the air after the dances were over. They were totally unrestrained in their lewdness, and the black dancers' sweaty bodies heightened the general atmosphere of deprav-ity."[77] Here, Goffin's primitivist gaze motivates a moment of literal nose wrinkling. Expressions such as "ill-smelling," "awful smell," and "atmo-sphere of depravity" insinuate a racial difference that is coded in olfactory terms, and they distinguish between a culturally superior self that is inter-ested in the strange sonic productions of the primitive Other (the musical sounds emitted from black bodies) and a cultural outsider repulsed by the physical strangeness of that Other (black body odor). Armstrong's account of the same dances in a later piece in *Ebony*, by contrast, illustrates the pos-itive connotations of body odor. He recalls how he watched the dancers at Funky Butt Dance Hall through a window "and saw two or three hundred sweaty bodies grinding together as a shirt-sleeved trumpeter named Buddy Bolden urged them on, shouting: 'All right now, all the good gals is home to bed. Ain't none left but the stinkers. That's good, 'cause they living up to the name of this dance hall. Hey, any of y'all left your behinds at home? Hope not, 'cause you gonna have to shake 'em plenty to keep time with this stuff we 'bout to play.'"[78] It is enough for Armstrong and Charles L. Sanders to evoke this scene and let Buddy Bolden's sexual commentary stand on its own, including the reversal of conventional notions of propri-ety according to which badness and stink carry negative connotations.

Like *Swing That Music*, *Horn of Plenty* added to the larger aggregation of intermedial contexts within which Armstrong's life and music were re-ceived. The year in which it was published, 1947, marked a significant change in the musician's career. Armstrong was no longer the famed swing soloist and big-band leader, but became the front man of a smaller ensem-ble formation, the All Stars. This change is indicated by three versions of his life story in three different media: the biography *Horn of Plenty;* the loosely autobiographical film *New Orleans*, which plays up the Southern origins of jazz and dramatizes the famed closing of the Storyville district; and the appearance at the Town Hall in New York (May 17, 1947) of the first version of the All Stars, which signaled a return to New Orleans–style jazz after close to two decades of big band swing.[79] For many fans and crit-ics, this return meant a rejection of swing, especially its commercial objec-tives, and a simultaneous embrace of what was often romanticized as au-thentic New Orleans jazz. *Time* magazine, for instance, featured a short article titled "Satchmo Comes Back" in which the writer argued that "Louis Armstrong ha[s] forsaken the ways of Mammon and come back to jazz," while *Down Beat* announced that "Satchmo's Genius Still Lives." For

Armstrong, this return meant a renewed interest in the preservation of his life and music; he bought his first tape recorders and began to create an audio archive of his records, live performances, and personal reminiscences.[80]

In his controversial Armstrong biography, James Lincoln Collier makes an important observation about the media coverage preceding and surrounding the musician's role in the *New Orleans* movie. "In the ten or twelve months before the *New Orleans* premiere Louis Armstrong had received more media attention as a *jazz* musician than he ever had," he notes. "He was presented to the public by the press not as the minstrel man of the movies and radio, or the swing band leader of the records, but as a part of the growing jazz legend—the boy from the Colored Waif's Home, who had learned his jazz in the brothels of Storyville. It was good copy, and [. . .] the image of Louis Armstrong, the jazz genius from the slums of New Orleans, was building in the public mind."[81] The movie itself did not make any reference to Armstrong's time in the Waif's Home or to his experiences as a young boy, but it stirred up enough interest in his life to enable the promotion of his life story in different media, including an autobiographical reminiscence in *True* magazine ("Storyville—Where the Blues Were Born"), television appearances, and autobiographically inflected song titles and lyrics.[82]

This interest in Armstrong's life increased in the late 1940s and early 1950s. In 1949, the trumpeter was featured as the first jazz musician on the cover of *Time* magazine (in a drawing by Boris Artzybasheff); in 1950, *Down Beat* devoted the bulk of its July issue to his life and music, while the *New York Times Magazine* paid him tribute through a lengthy piece by Howard Taubman titled "Satchmo Wears His Crown Gaily." Such acknowledgments attested to the musician's elevated status at midcentury; they prompted efforts to publish a new version of his autobiography and led to a proliferation of narratives in the coming years. Armstrong began working on what would become *Satchmo: My Life in New Orleans* in 1950. This time, the public was aware of his efforts to author his life story since *Time* reported that he was "cashing in on his gift of gab by putting it onto paper" and "pecking away at an autobiography."[83] He also offered reminiscences about his Hot Five and Hot Seven recordings in the "Jazz on a High Note" essay for *Esquire* a year later and was able to promote it on Bing Crosby's radio show on November 28, 1951, where Crosby announced: "Louis, that's quite a write-up I saw about you. I was reading *Esquire* magazine this month; you're in there big, ain't you?"[84]

Throughout the 1950s, Armstrong's articles appeared both in the music press (*Down Beat, The Record Changer, Melody Maker*) and in mainstream magazines (*Esquire, Ebony*). In 1954, *Satchmo: My Life in New Orleans* was published as the first installment of a larger autobiographical project whose second installment never appeared and only survived in parts as "The Satchmo Story" (1959). And in 1957, Armstrong narrated his life story on *Satchmo: A Musical Autobiography*. These publications illustrate the degree to which new situations and new demands called for different versions of his life story, a difference that can be measured by the discrepancy between representations of Armstrong from the 1930s, for instance his characterization as a minstrel "darky" in *Vanity Fair* (Feb. 1936), and articles such as "Jazz: America's Own Music in Its Lusty Youth" in *Life* (Dec. 1958), which retains some of the racial and sexual stereotypes that had long been associated with jazz but also provides a more complex and more historically astute portrait of New Orleans as a multicultural and ethnically diverse space (including coverage of the jazz parades and other folk-urban rituals).[85] Publications such as this increased Armstrong's cultural capital and motivated a process of mainstreaming through which the musician secured a mass audience. He accomplished this by intervening in the public debate over bebop and by addressing his life story to an audience beyond the confines of jazz aficionados and musical experts.

In the decades after the Second World War, traditional forms of New Orleans and Dixieland jazz were embraced by many fans and critics as a countermovement to the radically new sounds of bebop. The debate built on the controversy that had pitted swing devotees against followers of the traditional, and supposedly authentic, jazz of black New Orleans (pointedly dubbed "moldy figs" in the jazz press) in the 1930s and 1940s. With the advent of bebop (and the self-styled "moderns" who advocated this music), a series of fault lines emerged that sought to establish more or less strict definitions of jazz and created enough media stir to keep the music in the public mind.[86] Not surprisingly, jazz musicians sought to position themselves in this debate. Armstrong, for instance, told George Simon of *Metronome*: "I'd never play this bebop because I don't like it. Don't get me wrong; I think some of them cats who play it play real good, like Dizzy, especially. But bebop is the easy way out. Instead of holding notes the way they should be held, they just play a lot of little notes. They sorta fake out of it."[87] Several pre-bop musicians also produced autobiographies, further competing with Armstrong for the attention of the American reading public. In 1939, Benny Goodman had already published *Kingdom of Swing;* in the 1940s, Mezz Mezzrow's *Really the Blues* (1946), Eddie Condon's *We Called It Music: A Generation of Jazz* (1947), and Wingy Manone's *Trumpet on the Wing* (1948) followed. By the 1960s, readers would also have been able to peruse Artie Shaw's *The Trouble with Cinderella: An Outline of Identity* (1952), Billie Holiday's *Lady Sings the Blues* (1956), Warren "Baby" Dodds's *The Baby Dodds Story* (1959), and Sidney Bechet's *Treat It Gentle* (1960), as well as Alan Lomax's edited book version of Jelly Roll Morton's oral autobiography, *Mister Jelly Roll* (1950).[88]

Armstrong's narratives of the 1950s never really acknowledge these autobiographies, but they adhere to the general principles of the revivalist position by connecting his life story with the mythological space of New Orleans as the cradle of jazz. Articles such as "Joe Oliver Is Still King," "Bunk Didn't Teach Me" (both in *The Record Changer*, July–Aug. 1950), and "Jazz on a High Note" were geared either toward a revivalist readership or toward an audience interested in jazz history more generally. All three are examples of Armstrong's public interventions in the debates over his life and music; they evidence a shift in perspective from star autobiography (*Swing That Music*) and primitivist biography (*Horn of Plenty*) toward a more self-assured and historically oriented consciousness. For example, Armstrong credits Joe Oliver as "my inspiration and my idol" and disassociates himself from Bunk Johnson, whom jazz revivalists had rediscovered and who claimed that he had given Armstrong cornet lessons: "Bunk didn't actually teach me anything"; "Bunk didn't show me nothing."[89] Or as he claimed in one of his taped conversations, he had never allowed anybody to play Joe Oliver "cheap right to the day when them ofay writers and all them cats, you know, wanna make money on the situation. They say: 'Didn't Bunk Johnson teach you?' I said: 'Bunk didn't teach me shit.' "[90]

The articles on Oliver and Johnson showcase their writer's new confidence. Armstrong ends "Joe Oliver Is Still King" with an anecdote about the Creole Jazz Band's studio work in the 1920s because he wants "[t]o show you how much stronger I was than Joe."[91] Moreover, as "Jazz on a High Note" illustrates, he was being called on to comment on recordings now considered classics, and he obviously embraced the opportunity to think back to these studio performances and give his readers a sense of the excitement that had accompanied them. The piece is filled with statements about the New Orleans origins of jazz but also pays tribute to musicking in the late 1910s and the Roaring Twenties: performing at the Pelican Dance

Hall during the First World War ("Potato Head Blues," May 10, 1927), playing at the Sunset Café ("Twelfth Street Rag," May 11, 1927), collaborating with musicians like Earl Hines ("Chicago Breakdown," May 9, 1927), experiencing mike fright in the Okeh studio ("Muskrat Ramble," Feb. 26, 1926; "Gut Bucket Blues," Nov. 12, 1925), writing jazz classics ("Struttin' with Some Barbecue," Dec. 9, 1927), and inventing scat singing ("Heebie Jeebies," Feb. 26, 1926).[92] Both "Joe Oliver Is Still King" and "Jazz on a High Note" attest to a wish to maintain narrative authority over early New Orleans jazz and its transition to a mass-mediated music in the 1920s and beyond. A figure like Bunk Johnson, whose playing in the 1940s was often said to revive authentic pre-1920s jazz, contested Armstrong's modernized playing, as well as his views on early jazz.

Apart from intervening in the debates over New Orleans jazz, Armstrong was eager to share his concerns about bebop. He referred to it as "that new-fangled shit" in one of his taped conversations and as "that whole modern malice" in a discussion with Mezz Mezzrow and Barney Bigard published in *Down Beat* in 1948, while the manuscript for *Satchmo* contrasts the "beautiful Dixieland Style" with "that "Bop Slop Music.""[93] Responding to Gillespie's 1952 recording "Pops' Confessin'," which poked fun at Armstrong's vocal mannerisms and trumpet style, he recorded a lush swing version of the "Whiffenpoof Song" (Apr. 13, 1954) that marked Gillespie's bebop scatting as a corruption of Armstrong's original scat delivery ("oodle-de-oooh, scoobie-dooo") and mocked the way in which the beboppers styled themselves (funny hats, being high). In the coming months, he performed this number at least four times, for instance at the Crescendo Club in Los Angeles on January 21, 1955, where he dedicated it to "Dizzy Gillespie and all the boys from the boppin' factory," and at the Hollywood Bowl as part of the *Colgate Comedy Hour* on September 19, 1954, where he wore a funny hat and gleefully intoned lines such as "they'll be passing and be forgotten" and "they are poor little sheep who have gone astray."[94] Armstrong's affectionate letter to Dizzy and Lorraine Gillespie from July 1, 1959, however, illustrates that the hatchet was buried in the late 1950s: "Thanks for the lovely wire [i.e., telegram]. But there's 'onething that you both should always remember—you can't kill a nigger ... Ha Ha Ha," he writes. But even after the musicians had engaged in a good-natured trumpet and scat cutting contest in a television performance of "Umbrella Man" for the *Timex All Star Show #4* hosted by Jackie Gleason (Jan. 7, 1959), Armstrong continued to claim authority as one of the originators of jazz, noting in the *Music Journal* in 1961 that bebop "has nothing to express, nothing to explain."[95]

Unlike some of his commentary on bebop, Armstrong's major publication of the 1950s, *Satchmo: My Life in New Orleans*, was clearly aimed at a general readership. Its garbled publication history foregrounds questions of narrative control and autobiographical politics. It is certainly true that the official text from 1954 mostly features his own voice and expresses his concerns far more openly than *Swing That Music* and *Horn of Plenty*. But apart from the fact that *Satchmo* was substantially shortened and edited, it is also striking that manager Glaser, who also acted as Armstrong's literary agent, did not immediately find an American publisher. *Satchmo* was first released in France as *Ma Vie: Ma Nouvelle Orléans* in 1952; Prentice Hall only picked it up two years later for publication in the United States. The French and English versions relied on the same manuscript, "The Armstrong Story." The French translator, Madeleine Gautier, apparently based her work on a photocopy of Armstrong's typed manuscript, and her editorial intrusions seem less drastic than those of the person or persons responsible for editing the English version of the book—perhaps an editor at Prentice Hall, perhaps one of Glaser's employees or even Glaser himself. Thomas Brothers speculates that Armstrong sent his manuscripts or photocopies of these manuscripts to Glaser, who then passed them on to the publisher. On the back of one of the few remaining photocopied manuscript pages, Armstrong wrote, "Dear Mr. Glaser, these are the two pages, you told me to send them back to you when I'm finished with them," which suggests that Armstrong had been doing some rewriting on the basis of an editor's comments.[96] Whatever the extent of this rewriting may have been, Armstrong's characteristic ellipses and punctuation were omitted in the French version as well—an editorial intrusion Armstrong does not seem to have resented since he pasted a photograph of himself chatting with Gautier and holding up the French paperback onto one of his scotch-taped reel covers.[97] In addition, many stories from *Horn of Plenty* reappear in both the French and the English versions of *Satchmo*, which underscores the notion that Armstrong had intended the collaboration with Goffin as an autobiographical project. *Satchmo*, then, is the autobiography that *Horn of Plenty* was not, and it revises—but neither fully rejects nor explicitly deconstructs—Goffin's narrative.

In terms of narrative content, there is significant overlap between *Horn of Plenty* and *Satchmo*. Both texts cover the setting of Armstrong's youth, musical ancestors like Buddy Bolden and Joe Oliver, neighborhood characters like Black Benny and the bouncer Slippers, Armstrong's arrest on New Year's Eve and his time in the Waif's Home, musical outfits (vocal quartet, blues combo, brass bands, the Fate Marable Orchestra), and Joe Oliver's famous telegram calling Armstrong to Chicago. More remarkable than these similarities, which are important because they guarantee a degree of narrative consistency that ensures that older narratives are never completely erased, but always complicated and extended, are the differences in language and narrative voice. These differences already announce themselves in the openings of each text. While Goffin's biography makes a universalist statement about "the starting point of a man's life and its peak," *Satchmo* could not be more concrete about the individuality of its subject: "When I was born in 1900, my father, Willie Armstrong, and my mother, May Ann—or Mayann as she was called—were living on a little street called James Alley [*sic*]."[98]

Satchmo reaffirms the autobiographer's narrative authority about his life, which Goffin's biography had usurped temporarily. Armstrong refers to the street in which he was born as "James Alley—not Jane Alley as some people call it."[99] Goffin was one of these people, and he was actually correct; for all we know, the street was indeed called Jane Alley, but the point is that Armstrong's statement claims ownership of his life story. Two brief examples document his conscious (but not explicit) rewriting of *Horn of Plenty*. When the young Armstrong first joins the Waif's Home orchestra, he is given the tambourine. "This was a wonderful beginning. Louis was overjoyed," Goffin writes. "Naturally, he would have preferred to blow on one of the shiny brass instruments—cornet, trumpet, or bugle—in imitation of his idol, Buddy Bolden, or even Bunk Johnson; but the newly-instilled discipline of the place had ingrained a certain degre[e] of philosophy in him."[100] In *Satchmo*, however, Armstrong's reaction is not one of joy: "I already pictured myself playing with all the power and endurance of a Bunk, Joe or Bolden. [. . .] To my surprise he [Mr. Davis] handed me a tambourine, the little thing you tap with your fingers like a miniature drum. So that was the end of my beautiful dream!"[101] While Goffin describes the boy's reaction as one of willing submission—a "philosophy" he may have assumed to be typical of a black Southerner who does not mind being handed the tambourine, an instrument often associated with the minstrel figure Tambo—Armstrong focuses on his ambitions and mentions musical qualities such as power and endurance. This difference appears again when

Goffin adds that Mr. Davis "cast a warm glance of approval on the boyish drummer" and that "Louis glowed with happy pride" when the teacher commended him for his playing. In *Satchmo*, the happy and glowing boy's passive reception of the teacher's judgment is substituted with an active sense of purpose: "His approval was all important for any boy who wanted a musical career."[102]

The second example comes later in Goffin's story. It depicts Armstrong's reaction to "the unknown wonders that awaited him in Chicago" and presents a thinly veiled sense of racial superiority: "He had escaped from the ghetto of his race, was no longer bound by the immemorial servitude that burdened his brethren in New Orleans, and he felt the uneasiness of a dog that has lost its master."[103] According to this assessment, Armstrong's escape from the shackles of Jim Crow may have afforded him with freedom from servitude, but his consciousness was yet to make the leap from dogged slave ancestor to master of his own life and career. Armstrong's version in *Satchmo*, on the contrary, presents a person fully (self-)conscious of the difficulties inherent in the relocation from South to North: "Anybody watching me closely could have easily seen that I was a country boy"; "I had a million thoughts as I looked at all those people."[104]

But the story goes on. Goffin describes Armstrong's initial reaction to hearing King Oliver's Creole Jazz Band at the Lincoln Gardens: "All the musicians were smiling at him and he grinned widely in response, his thick lips curled over gleaming ivory."[105] Compare this to Armstrong's version: "I was a little shaky about going inside. [. . .] I started wondering if I could hold my own with such a fine band. But I went in anyway. [. . .] The place was jammed with people and Joe and the boys did not see me until I was almost on the bandstand. Then all hell seemed to break loose. All those guys jumped up at the same time saying: 'Here he is! Here he is!' "[106] Goffin does not allow for Armstrong's self-doubts ("wondering if I could hold my own with such a fine band"), and he also falls back on minstrel imagery ("grinned widely"; "thick lips curled over gleaming ivory"). Such imagery stands in contrast to Armstrong's vernacular reference to himself as a "Real 'Country 'Sommitch'" and to his "little Country Boy Way[s]" in the "Goffin Notebooks." This contrast is vitally important because it points to an expressive economy within which biographical interpretations and autobiographical self-depictions compete for narrative and discursive authority.[107]

More generally, and apart from *Horn of Plenty*, the version of his life Armstrong gives in *Satchmo* is characterized by an insistence on New Orleans musicking culture as the source of early jazz. It is not merely a story about Armstrong but a story about the whole culture that made his music possible: his family; his neighborhood; older musicians; musical and non-musical peers; job opportunities; poverty; and musical venues/events such as the honky-tonk bars and cabarets, parades, and the Streckfus entertainment boats. Armstrong's insistence on heeding his mother's advice and the values he associates with his youth—ambition, honesty, respect, common sense, thrift—are compatible with the bourgeois values of the implied reader and indicate an awareness of his mainstream audience. It is remarkable, too, that there is no overt political commentary and no reflection of the social and political changes that were beginning to sweep the country by the early 1950s. It remains a matter of debate whether this absence is to be blamed on Armstrong or whether it resulted from his editors' and publishers' clever packaging of the text. The decision to end the narrative in 1922, when Armstrong arrived in Chicago, was apparently made by his editors, and the same was true for the marketing of the autobiography as a Horatio Alger–like memoir. But the shifts from the didactic focus expressed in the title of *Swing That Music* and the primitivist bacchanalia insinuated by the title of *Horn of Plenty* to the self-declarative *Satchmo: My Life in New Orleans* are noteworthy because they capture quite forcefully the different steps Armstrong had taken on his way to coming into his own as an autobiographer.

The publication of *Satchmo* heightened the public interest in Armstrong's life story. Together with his television appearances and live shows with the All Stars, it established him as a mainstream figure in American life. This move into the mainstream took place during the early stages of the civil rights movement, and it raised questions about his willingness to conjure up colorful anecdotes about life in segregated New Orleans and his apparent unwillingness to publicly support the struggle for civil rights. An essay Armstrong wrote for *Ebony* magazine in 1954 therefore made an effort to paint a distinctly black image of the musician for an African American middle-class readership. While not explicit about contemporary politics, it suggests Armstrong's continued relevance to black audiences and thus balances out, at least to an extent, his move into the white mainstream. Titled "Why I Like Dark Women," the essay carries the byline "Blacker the berry the sweeter the juice." In the piece itself, Armstrong repeatedly refers to the skin color of his wives: "I suppose I'm partial to brown and dark-skinned women [. . .] . None of my four wives was a light-colored woman"; "Daisy [Parker] was a pretty brown-skinned girl"; "Sure I like my women, beautiful, dark and tender."[108] It is possible to read such statements as Armstrong's attempt to appeal to a readership interested less in the specifics of jazz history than in the gossip factor of his life story. The fact that he portrays his four wives as distinct women indicates an appeal to a broad range of readers: Daisy "was a violent girl" and "had a mean streak in her"; Lil Hardin is "college-educated," as well as "cultured and sharp"; Alpha Smith is "young and polished," "modern," and "flashy"; and Lucille, Armstrong's present wife, is "a woman of poise and patience, good sense and understanding," as well as "almost an ideal type of woman" since she "doesn't get jealous."[109] Armstrong will stay black, passages such as these imply, despite being groomed for the white mainstream in other publications and media. What is more, the photograph on the magazine cover depicts Armstrong and Lucille as a respectably dressed black couple, but it also displays the musician's more devilish side: his trumpet extends from his groin to Lucille's bosom in an obviously phallic angle. Finally, Armstrong's celebration of Lucille's "deep-brown skin" and his criticism of "prevailing standards of Negro beauty" may be read as a recognition of the black-is-beautiful paradigm long before it became popular.[110]

In 1959, Armstrong wrote a sequel to *Satchmo*, posthumously published as "The Satchmo Story." This sequel indicates his intention to diversify his image and add previously unheard (or subdued) commentary on issues such as race relations and life as a black jazz musician in Chicago and New York. "The Satchmo Story" therefore marks a first substantial divergence from his more wholesome mainstream image. *Satchmo* had ended with his arrival in Chicago in 1922 and had preserved the rugged romanticism of the musician's youth, avoiding critical commentary about the entertainment industry and the exploitation of African American musicians. As biographer Laurence Bergreen explains, Armstrong wanted to call the sequel "*Gage*, his pet name for marijuana, but once his manager found out about the title and the subject of the work, he suppressed the manuscript, trying to protect Louis's reputation."[111] This is an effect of the autobiographical politics within which Armstrong was working, as well as an indication of the distribution of power in the field of jazz. The narrative begins with the words "The first time that I smoked Marijuana (or) Gage" and proceeds with a plea for legalizing the drug. With obvious glee, Armstrong refers to marijuana as "'Gage—'Muta—'Pot—or some of that *good shit*" and covers his drug arrest in Los Angeles in 1930, when he was caught smoking pot between sets with the white drummer Vic Burton. Armstrong had already celebrated marijuana on recordings such as "Muggles" (Dec. 7, 1928) and "Sweet Sue—Just You" (Apr. 26, 1933), "muggles" being a slang term for marijuana and "Sweet Sue" featuring a verse of drug-addled mumbling. His preference for "muggle-smoking" had been mentioned in *Time* magazine articles in the early 1930s, and he would preserve the story of the drug bust for posterity by telling it to his British biographers Max Jones and John Chilton in a letter (ca. 1970) and by speaking another account into his tape recorder.[112]

Besides celebrating his favorite recreational drug, Armstrong also brags about his sexual prowess and refers to blacks as "nigger[s]" and to whites as "Mr. Charlie." While he talks about music occasionally, it seems that he is less interested in outlining the high points of his musical career than in recollecting his personal observations in writing and celebrating his life as a successful musician and entertainer. One can only imagine how much editing would have been necessary to transform the following passage into straightforward autobiographical narration. Speaking of the drummers who inspired him throughout his career, Armstrong writes: "here's a few that used to gas me through my early years blowing my trumpet and who used to really make Ol' Dipper (that's me—then) get up and blow his ass off."[113] Overall, the writing seems unfocused and rambling. After a long rumination on pot smoking, he recalls a piece of advice from his mother about the ways of the world and then talks about African American hairstyles: "Konklines (hair do)."[114] This is followed by an extended New Orleans reminiscence that includes Joe Oliver, funerals, a sermon in Reverend Cozy's church, the Waif's Home, his boyhood crush on Wilhelmina Martin, a celebration of the black community, and more. Only after covering such a wide range of topics does Armstrong come back to the issue of drummers. He is obviously relishing the opportunity to present his story in the vernacular mode, as an autobiographical performance in which he can follow his inspiration wherever it takes him. Geneva Smitherman's notion of "narrative sequencing" as a storytelling technique of African American discourse that involves moments of spontaneous diversions and a meandering narrative style provides the proper framework for this autobiographical piece.[115]

With "The Satchmo Story," Armstrong sought to diverge from his mainstream image, but Glaser apparently kept the text under wraps. The text marks a transitional moment in which Armstrong was beginning to move toward a rather disgruntled stance that was becoming more and more prominent in the 1960s. One example in this regard is the interview with Richard Meryman for *Life* magazine (1966), in which he muses critically about the politics and economics of the entertainment business. A second example is "Louis Armstrong + the Jewish Family in New Orleans, La., the Year of 1907" (1969–70), in which he answers charges of racial accomodationism and political cowardice that had been leveled against him in the wake of the civil rights movement. Both texts show an autobiographer who is more interested in speaking frankly and holding nothing back than in maintaining good relations with his critics and audiences.

The interview with Meryman is remarkable for Armstrong's reflections on his role as a public performer and entertainer who negotiates a complicated interracial terrain. Armstrong speaks rather openly about what William Kenney calls his "tactics as an intercultural performer, a subject about which he had spoken only privately before."[116] Confessing that he "never did want to be no big star" and that he "never was carried away by anything in my whole career," Armstrong reveals a professional attitude toward his audience: "the main thing is to live for that audience" and "to please the people." Five years later, in Meryman's book version, he would turn on fellow musicians who had denounced him as an old-timer: "If I'm out of style now, I was a flying cat when I was in—so to hell with it now. If a son-of-a-bitch came to the conclusion, 'We don't ever want to see Louis Armstrong again'—Thank you! 'cause I can get in a corner, look at TV for days and take my shower, sleep, and let the maid come in, don't even look out the window for six months. I'll still be Satchmo."[117] This statement responds to the views of jazz modernists, who tended to speak of Armstrong as a figure of the past, but Armstrong also comments on the jazz press:

> What they say about the old days is corny. They form their own opinions, they got so many words for things and make everything soooo big—and it turns out a—what you call it—a fictitious story. And when these writers come up so great they know every goddam [*sic*] thing, telling you how you should blow your horn. That's when I want to shoot the son-of-a-bitch. Just because they went to Harvard or Yale, got to make the public realize how superior they are, so what they do to plain old jazz! Bring up terms, goddam, the people reading it got to have a dictionary.[118]

Obviously, Armstrong was under intense discursive pressure. His musical relevance was under fire ("If I'm out of style now"); the institutional powers of the new jazz criticism ("Harvard or Yale") over the rules of jazz ("telling you how you should blow your horn") and the elitism with which many critics interpreted the music and its history ("the people reading it got to have a dictionary") threatened to make his life narratives obsolete and weaken his status as a jazz historiographer.

Unlike the later book version, the *Life* interview begins with a long introductory paragraph by Meryman that sets the stage for the narrative. As in *Swing That Music*, this is an example of peritextual framing in which a white collaborator prepares the audience for what is to come and puts a specific spin on the musician's narrative. The byline on the inside of the pull-out cover advertises the interview in terms of the quintessential Armstrong myth while simultaneously stressing its novelty: "America's genius of jazz talks his warm, intimate story—from the golden boyhood days in New Orleans to the fame he *didn't* seek as Satchmo."[119] The interview can be seen as an attempt to come to terms with a potentially postmainstream Armstrong, a narrative that is also suggested by the photographs that accompany the magazine article. Philippe Halsman's portrait of Armstrong blowing his trumpet, reproduced on the pull-out cover, still caters to the Armstrong most audiences knew. Shot from above with a wide-angle lens, it captures the mixture of sophistication (the suit, shirt, bow tie, silver watch) and the kind of minstrel mugging (the popping eyes, the trademark handkerchief) of which Armstrong was increasingly accused in the 1950s and 1960s. Yet the photographs printed alongside the article document the diversification of Armstrong's autobiographics. One of the photographs, taken by John Loengard, shows a somber Armstrong in profile on his tour bus and presents the musician in a more self-reflexive, thoughtful, and potentially disillusioned state of mind than earlier photographs had done; another one shows an extreme close-up of Armstrong's scarred lips, connecting Armstrong's happy entertainer persona with an image of hard labor and physical pain.

If the Meryman interview had announced the musician's growing wariness about his status as a star musician, Armstrong's final version of his life story, "Louis Armstrong + the Jewish Family in New Orleans, La., the Year of 1907," took issue with the neighborhood people of his youth. The political criticism to which this account reacts is illustrated by Armstrong's insistence on the fact that he had "always done *great* things about *uplifting* my *race* (the Negroes, *of course*) but *wasn't appreciated.*" Rejecting accusations of being "a *White* Folks *Nigger*," he concludes: "I am just a *musician* and *still* remember the time, as a *American* Citizen I *Spoke* up for my people during a *big* Integration *Riot* in Little Rock (Remember?). I wrote Eisenhower."[120] It is important to note here that Armstrong's intervention in the Little Rock crisis in 1957, when he wrote a telegram to President Eisenhower to protest the racial segregation of an Arkansas high school and criticized Governor Orval Faubus in the daily press for his unwillingness to enforce federal antisegregation laws, anticipated his political comments in the 1960s. In that sense, his political commentary in "Jewish Family" did not reflect an entirely new stance. But it is equally significant that these initial steps away from Armstrong's mainstream image were presented in a telegram and in the daily press, and not in one of his autobiographical essays or manuscripts. With "Jewish Family," however, Armstrong voiced his grievances in a major autobiographical narrative, even though he was unable to see it published during his lifetime.

"Jewish Family" is Armstrong's most outspoken longer autobiographical statement. It ventures beyond the careful calibration of earlier narratives, providing harsh commentary on the black community of his youth (commentary that reversed much of what he had written in earlier versions of his life story) and revealing a complicated attitude toward questions of inter- and intraracial contact. This disillusioned narrative, which must be read in the context of the backlash against Armstrong's public image that followed his appearance as the King of the Zulus in the Mardi Gras parade of 1949 and as a reaction against the criticism leveled at him by civil rights activists, reverses the musician's preference for black audiences. Like all of Armstrong's earlier writings, it revisits the scenes of his childhood and youth, but it makes a critical statement by straying from the popular image of the smiling entertainer and complaining vociferously about laziness, enviousness, and intraracial hatred in the black community in a language unprecedented in its willingness to offend: "Negroes *never* did stick together and they *never* will"; "*Negroes* has always *connived* against each other' and they *still* do"; "he will be the *first* Negro who will *Rape* a *white* woman."[121]

One way to account for this new take on the culture of Armstrong's youth is to place it in its appropriate political contexts. Another way, which is compatible with a political reading but adds an intermedial dimension, is to connect "Jewish Family" with a performative ethos that suffuses all of Armstrong's expressions. Looking back over the many autobiographical versions Armstrong produced throughout his lifetime—from early letters to *Swing That Music* to "Jewish Family"—one is struck by the obvious intermedial interface between his writings and his music. After all, Armstrong also recorded countless versions of signature songs such as "When It's Sleepy Time Down South" and "Basin Street Blues," and there is good reason to wonder whether the similarity in his approaches to autobiography and music is not more than a simple coincidence, but rather the result of a shared performative disposition. In his study of Caribbean music, Dick Hebdige observes: "Sometimes a reggae record is released and literally hundreds of different versions of the same rhythm or melody will follow in its wake. Every time a version is released, the original tune will be slightly modified. A musician will play a different solo on a different instrument, use a different tempo, key or chord sequence. A singer will place the emphasis on different words or will add new ones." Hebdige further discerns a tendency to perform and record "parodic versions of other artists' songs and singing styles." Considering the proximity of New Orleans to the Caribbean and the "Spanish tinge" that Jelly Roll Morton and others have identified in jazz, it is not surprising that Hebdige concludes: "'Versioning' is at the heart not only of reggae but of *all* Afro-American and Caribbean musics."[122]

Versioning was especially prominent in the polyphonic ensemble playing of New Orleans jazz, for instance, on the recordings made by King Oliver's Creole Jazz Band, which follow an "ethic of variation" according to which "no note is played automatically" and where "[e]ven the most inconsequential motif is shaped, and any repetition is varied. It is this 'ethic' which [. . .] can make those paraphrases of Armstrong's which stick close to the melody—and which are therefore uninteresting to melodic and harmonic analysis—deeply satisfying to hear."[123] This "ethic of variation" can also be heard on recordings such as "Georgia on My Mind" (Nov. 5, 1931; at the beginning of his solo), and it appears in the subtle differentiations applied to the prominent three-note motifs in "Twelfth Street Rag" (May 11, 1927) and "Savoy Blues" (Dec. 13, 1927). Armstrong's chorus on a recording of "Shanghai Shuffle" (Nov. 7, 1924) with the Fletcher Henderson Orchestra further illustrates this musical practice. In the middle of the solo, he repeats a single note more than a dozen times. While the rhythmic figure consists of regular eighth notes placed on the first and third beats of the measures, "each of these notes is played differently from the one before it—given a different inflection or placed somewhat differently against the beat."[124] On "Shanghai Shuffle," Armstrong follows a rhythmic versioning impulse; he *places* notes on, in front of, and behind the beat. In his solo on "Potato Head Blues" (May 10, 1927), he *inflects* the same note in ways that cannot be properly scored and can only be heard in performance or on the recording.[125]

In addition to structuring Armstrong's placement and inflection of notes, the ethic of variation extends to the melodic content of his playing. Some of the more suggestive verbal descriptions of this variational ethic include "embroider[ing]" and "embellishing," as well as "melodic paraphrase."[126] Mezz Mezzrow refers to Armstrong's musical practices as variations rather than improvisations: "Sometimes the variations will be in the phrasing rather than the notes, but those solos are always changing, depending on the tempo, the atmosphere, or who's playing with him at the time."[127] Such observations are supported by Armstrong himself: "once you got a certain solo that fit in the tune, and that's it, you keep it. Only vary it two or three notes every time you play it. [. . .] There's always different people there every night, and they just want to be entertained."[128]

How, then, is this musical versioning ethic related to Armstrong's autobiographical writings? Perhaps we can say that each new autobiographical version stands in relation to previous statements and to basic biographical facts. Therefore, each new statement rephrases and recombines these facts by adapting them to the specific context of its telling. This is especially poignant in light of Armstrong's tendency to use consecutive improvisations to refine and polish ideas into fully crafted solos.[129] Lawrence Gushee speaks of Armstrong's "storehouse of licks and formulas" in his trumpet work; in autobiographical narrative, such storehouse elements may appear in the form of puns ("I'll never forget, as long as I'm colored"), pet phrases ("red beans and ricely yours"), and anecdotes (how he allegedly invented scat; how Black Benny had told him to always keep a mistress). This recalls Dan Morgenstern's understanding of Armstrong's autobiographical narratives as "tales that add up to fascinating variations on a theme": a series of variations that retain a basic narrative pattern and utilize a more or less fixed repertoire of narrative elements.[130] The question that remains to be answered is whether musical principles are transposed to writing or whether Armstrong's approach to self-expression in music and autobiography is rooted more deeply in a personal sensibility and in a specific cultural aesthetics.

One would be hard-pressed to argue that the tight structuring, melodic ingenuity, complex phrasing, and clear tone of Armstrong's trumpet solos find simple correlations in his autobiographical narratives (even though excessive vibrato, slurs, and blue notes would qualify in this regard). After all, Armstrong was a professional trumpet player whose work in the 1920s and 1930s stunned a whole generation of musicians, but he was only a self-professed hobby writer who made next to no impact on American letters. If there is a more direct influence between music and autobiography, it is his oral approach to both media: the vernacular influence in his jazz singing and trumpeting and his vernacular style of writing. But there seems to be an even deeper connection, one that can be described as a versioning impulse and that is related to what Paul Anderson theorizes as "social othering" and "musical othering." While social othering describes a process of transforming "groups into others—outsider groups misrecognized and rendered invisible by majority-constructed stereotypes"—musical othering "can respond to social invisibility and externally imposed 'fixed equations' with 'a slightly different sense of time' [. . .] and similar variations of mastery through artful discrepancy."[131] Examples of social othering appear in Gerlach's presentation of early jazz musicians as uneducated but natural improvisers, in Goffin's celebration of Armstrong as a primitive minstrel, and in the promotion of Armstrong's life as a development from slum boy to jazz king by the publishers of *Satchmo*. By creating discrepant versions of self in autobiography, for instance, the disillusioned entertainer in his interview with Richard Meryman for *Life* and the angry black elder persona in "Jewish Family," Armstrong countered such instances of social othering with a slightly different sense of self in the same manner in which he performed different versions of his signature tunes throughout his long career.

What is more, the musician's versioning practice results from a transmedial impulse: a cultural disposition that Henry Louis Gates perceives as a form of "signifying" in his vernacular theory of African American literature and criticism. This disposition is rooted in an aesthetics of "repetition and revision," and it privileges process over product in all media Armstrong utilized to disseminate his life story and perform public versions of his self.[132] It manifests itself in a "storytelling effect" that "runs consistently through Armstrong's music, writing, conversational manner, and photocollages." This effect, Jorge Daniel Veneciano has argued, is achieved through "an aesthetic that plays the contingent and the provisional against the archival and the museum standard."[133] In music, melodies are reinvented, lyrics are changed, song structures are modified, mock versions of other artists' songs and singing styles are presented, and spontaneous comments are added to mark specific moments of performance. As Armstrong confesses after a brief scat interlude on "I'm a Ding Dong Daddy (From Dumas)" (July 21, 1930): "I done forgot the words." Thus, instead of repeating the exact words of the original version, he uses them as the basis for a new and scatted version of the music. Forgetting the original lyrics paradoxically enables the kind of "black formal repetition [. . .] with a [. . .] black difference" that Gates locates at the center of African American expression.[134] In stage presentation, Armstrong adhered to this expressive mode when he impersonated and parodied stock characters such as comic black preachers and evoked echoes of nineteenth-century minstrelsy. In autobiographical narrative, he did so by continually revising earlier representations; retelling anecdotes; and investing his prose with a spontaneous, oral feel. And while Gates's notion of a black difference clearly comes across in Armstrong's vernacular performances, the deep structures of these productions are a central characteristic of all oral cultures. According to Walter Ong, "Narrative originality lodges not in making up new stories but in managing a particular interaction with this audience at this time—at every telling the story has to be introduced uniquely into a unique situation, for in oral cultures an audience must be brought to respond, often vigorously."[135]

In African American literature, the serial structure of versioning finds precedent in Frederick Douglass's multiple autobiographies and in the sermons of itinerant preachers such as Jarena Lee. As William Andrews maintains, "the dynamic principle [. . .] in the history of Afro-American autobiography is the *revising*, not the canonizing, of traditions, and even texts."[136] One of Armstrong's major achievements was to bring an interactive ethos to expressive media in which audiences were not directly present: sound recording, on which he frequently addressed his listeners directly as ladies and gentlemen (e.g., on "Chinatown, My Chinatown"; Nov. 3, 1931), and autobiographical narratives, which are filled with rhetorical questions, apostrophes to the reader, and deictic comments. The musician's popularity and the self-conscious promotion of his life story indicate that a vernacular impulse like versioning works exceedingly well in a mass-mediated and (inter)national culture. In fact, they show that the structures of intermedial communication increasingly came to fulfill the modern audience's thirst for the creative enunciations of racially and ethnically diverse entertainers and artists.

Apart from versioning, Armstrong employed a set of writing strategies that open up further interfaces between autobiography and music. The next chapter discusses his peculiar textual annotations, indexical markers, and jive linguistics as a form of musico-textual intermediality that points beyond the autobiographical text to musical and stage performance and vice versa. "As in his music, so in his writing, Armstrong's style was essential to his meaning; it was not what notes or words he chose but how he used them," William Kenney has claimed.[137] The next chapter investigates this claim.

CHAPTER 3

"Diddat Come Outa Mee?"

Writing Scat and Typing Swing

One of the most frequent claims about Louis Armstrong's speech and writing is that they resemble his trumpet playing and singing. An early reviewer of *Satchmo*, for instance, noted that the autobiography was "less a book than a literary jam session"; others have argued that Armstrong "used words like he strings notes together"; that he "tossed off letters and memoirs with the same abandon he tossed off riffs"; that his "thoughts tumble out in elliptical phrases, hinting at jazz riffs"; and that he was "pouring out letters in torrents of elliptical phrases, somewhat like swinging riffs." For many critics and admirers, Armstrong's "prose is delightfully musical," his written voice "every bit as distinctive as his musical voice"; his "prose style reflects structural and emotional aspects of his musical expression," and his writings constitute "word solos."[1] According to these statements, Armstrong's writing mimics his music either in terms of its interactive qualities (like a jam session), its style and structure (like notes and riffs), its improvisational effects (like word solos), its narrative voice (like his musical voice), or its expressivity (like his music's emotional suggestiveness). Even critics who vehemently oppose such interpretations tend to write in the same discourse. "The fact is that old Gates [Armstrong] did not make that typewriter sing like his horn. He did not write as masterfully as he sang or as he spoke, his instantly and universally infectious jive talk," as Albert Murray maintains.[2]

This chapter examines the ways in which Armstrong's language and writing practices simulate the moment of performance and seek to reproduce the immediacy of musical improvisation. The goal is to avoid a simplistic understanding of his language and writing as quasi-musical forms of expression but to recognize the existence of intricate interconnections among his verbal and musical expressions nonetheless. Especially his indexical markers and textual annotations—the dashes, ellipses, parentheses, single and multiple underscores, apostrophes, interjections, question marks, and capitalizations that clutter his writings—suggest expressive techniques and creative processes that establish an intermedial interface between musical performance and life narrative.[3] My first working assumption is that Armstrong's idiosyncratic orthography and typography as well as his frequent use of jive language create a sense of spontaneity that possesses close affinities with his musical practices and stage performances. A second assumption is that Armstrong's narratives are complex performative negotiations between an African American musician and his heterogeneous audiences that are best described as transmedial enunciations of a specific "scat aesthetics" (Brent Edwards's term), which constitutes a particularly powerful element of Armstrong's autobiographics. What can we learn about Armstrong as a storyteller, writer, and musician by looking closely at the linguistic practices that lie at the heart of his lifelong communication with editors, readers, interviewers, and his heterogeneous audiences?

Armstrong's penchant for wordplay and jive language is thematized in *Swing That Music*, which portrays swing musicians as having "a language of their own" and as living in "a world of their own that [. . .] most people have not understood." The narrator declares: "I hope this book will help to explain it [i.e., the jazz world] a little—it is the real reason I have tried to write it and kept on after I found out what hard-going writing was for a man who has lived all of his life mostly with a trumpet, not a pencil, in his hand."[4] While probably written by the ghostwriter, the passage is significant for its emphasis on a jazz language, as well as for its attempt to make sense of Armstrong's writing practices (pencil) in contradistinction to his musical practices (trumpet). It does not consider, or perhaps is not aware of, the fact that Armstrong had been writing letters for at least fourteen years at the time of the autobiography's publication. Yet in his letter to Hugues Panassié from the early 1930s, reprinted as a foreword to the French critic's *Hot Jazz* (the 1934 French version, as well as the English translation from 1936), Armstrong had similarly downplayed his writing abilities himself: "I won't add much. Writing articles—making speeches, or anything other than swinging the good ol' trumpet, I am really lost."[5] He would certainly overcome this initial humility in later years, when he freely professed his love of writing and unabashedly indulged in this hobby, but these early statements indicate an essential insecurity about his authorial abilities.

By mixing Standard English with black vernacular expressions and jazz jive, translating the latter two for his readers, Armstrong frequently employed what Werner Sollors calls the "possibilities of playfulness in establishing [an ethnic] voice." In this way, he was able to talk to "an actual or imagined double audience, composed of 'insiders' and of readers, listeners, or spectators who are not familiar with the writer's ethnic group."[6] Consider a letter he sent to his Swiss friend Madeleine Bérard on November 25, 1946. Since Bérard is not a native speaker, Armstrong addresses the issue of translation directly and explains neologisms and slang in parentheses: "I noticed in one of your letters where you asked the definitions of several little things I said—such as 'Tee Hee—'Savvy—'Wee Wee and Nightie. . . . Of course I've not paid any attention to the expressions to that extent . . . Using them all my life . . . But since you don't *Dig them*—Ahem—I'll do my very best to make you Latch on (I mean understand them. I've explained them—Tee hee—."[7] Here, verbal playfulness is created through sentence fragments ("Using them all my life"), speech pauses (signaled by the dashes), and extralinguistic expressions such as "Ahem" and "Tee hee," all of which create an oral feel—"Two Fingerly Speaking," as Armstrong referred to his typing activities in the "Forward" to his *Joke Book*.[8] In the Bérard letter, he explains the phrase "Latch on" but cannot resist the urge to engage in more linguistic play. He introduces the slang term "dig," meaning "understand" or "appreciate," as a playful versioning of "Latch on," and he communicates his momentary pleasure about his linguistic cunningness by surrounding the phrase with the spontaneous utterances "Ahem" and "Tee hee." Such playful translations of jazz lingo also occurred in oral speech, such as when Armstrong explained to Edward R. Murrow that "cool" means "a cat that's playing a trumpet and is too lazy to hit a high note."[9]

Armstrong further expressed his love of verbal play in a radio interview from the 1940s, where he displays an ability to switch language codes. According to the transcript, the interviewer taunts him with a scripted version of "jive," and Armstrong retorts: "I could always fall in the righteous groove with the rest of the cats, and either dig the jive or beef on back with the Duke [Ellington], the Cab [Calloway], the Coop or the other killer-dillers. But all that comes natural, and what I'm really proud of is my ability to speak and write straight English. [. . .] I'm a two-fingered blip on my portable typewriter."[10] This conversation encapsulates the intricate politics and poetics of jazz jive. First, there is the radio announcer, who is almost certainly white and definitely an outsider to the jazz scene. Nonetheless, he is aware of the specific language spoken by jazz musicians, which means that jive had already entered the cultural mainstream and become a popular signifier of jazz. An unnamed critic's assertion in the jazz magazine *Metronome*, "You should hear Benny Goodman and his men put on the flutter tongue when Benny reads a term like 'killer diller' from the typewriter of a radio script genius," indicates that Armstrong was responding to a common practice of scripted interviews on the radio.[11] Second, Armstrong's answer constitutes a rebuttal of the announcer's presumptuous use of an in-language. He comes back with a masterful jive retort that makes clear where the linguistic competence and authority over this language lie. But perhaps most important, Armstrong insists on the seriousness of his writing endeavors and resists the stereotype of the flamboyant, ignorant jazz musician. Unlike the announcer, he is able to speak and write jive *and* Standard English. He demonstrates his mastery of two linguistic registers common in black speech: "broad talk," which twists the "vernacular into stylized use, in the form of wit [or] repartee," and "formal talk," which centers on "eloquence and manners through the use of formal standard English."[12] Thus, Armstrong can decipher the script, but he also knows when and how to diverge from it. He uses this knowledge to utter spontaneous verbal statements that question the public persona prescribed by radio interviewers. As an article in *Time* noted in the early 1930s: "Radio [. . .] is a little wary of his improvisations. Several times he has been switched quickly off the air for getting profane or slipping in sly remarks about his friends' extra-marital escapades."[13] What we have here are signature moments in which a specific medium (radio) and genre (interview/live broadcast) propose conventions that run counter to the vernacular, spontaneous, and improvisatory aesthetics that characterizes Armstrong's approach to all forms of expression. Armstrong essentially projects a specific persona to his listeners, a persona that is characterized by spontaneity, humor, and a natural ebullience and that reinforces the image of the unmistakably individualistic solo musician, band leader, and entertainer. Two reel-tape covers from Armstrong's later years offer visual context for this jiving and the effects it would have had on interviewers. These covers depict scenes from the mid-1950s that show a grinning Armstrong and two interviewers obviously enthralled by whatever joke or jive retort the musician has just made.[14]

But how exactly does jive, this "African-American dialect cultivated especially by jazz musicians," work as a linguistic process?[15] Neil Leonard proposes a romantic view when he maintains, "Unable to convey his deepest emotions in the received idiom, the jazzman invented terms of his own" and "probed the unknown or unexpressed with metaphor, oxymoron, and synecdoche in ways puzzling to unattuned ears." Despite its romanticism, this view suggests an interesting connection between jazz jive and jazz music as expressions that "not only meant, [but] *created*."[16] In his autobiography, *to BE, or not . . . to BOP* (1979), Dizzy Gillespie connects this notion of musical and linguistic improvisation with his social and racial status as a black musician and emphasizes the search for alternative meanings: "as black people we just naturally spoke that way. [. . .] As we played with musical notes, bending them into new and different meanings that constantly changed, we played with words."[17] Music and jive language thus share a series of characteristics that serve as a reminder that these forms of expression take place in similar contexts and follow similar performative processes. Like jazz, jive is a fast-changing, eclectic, and simultaneously vernacular/hip expression, and like jazz, it is a coded, playful, and creative act of communication between an in-group (frequently black jazz musicians) and outsiders (usually heterogeneous audiences). And like jazz phrases, the meanings of jive words such as "crazy" and "bad" not only depend on contextual markers such as inflections, shadings, and other performative gestures; they also require an audience willing to appreciate the speaker's expressive elegance and verbal agility.[18]

Armstrong was a very prominent jive speaker among American jazz musicians. One of the first printed jive glossaries appeared toward the end of *Swing That Music* and featured translations of typical Armstrong expressions such as "cats," "mugging," and "licking their chops" along with a series of musical terms such as "gutbucket," "barrel-house," "lick," "break," and "jam session."[19] In 1938, Cab Calloway followed in the footsteps of *Swing That Music* when he published his "Hepster's Dictionary," a much longer listing of jive terms that included entries from Armstrong's first autobiography and thus attests to the text's lasting significance among jazz musicians and audiences. Calloway referenced his jive dictionary in his recording of "Jive (Page One of Hepster's Dictionary)" of the same year and included the sixth edition as an appendix to his autobiography *Of Minnie the Moocher and Me* (1976). In the 1940s, it was Mezz Mezzrow's ten-page glossary in *Really the Blues* that kept jive in the public ear.[20]

In Armstrong's case, it makes sense to understand jive as more than a series of coded jazz words and elements of a colorful musical language.

While these are essential elements of his jiving, the vernacular impulse inherent in jive's divergent linguistics ultimately leads to performative expletives such as "motherfucker" and ironic responses to racists such as "Yassuh," "No Suh Boss," "Shucks," and "Sho Nuff." It also leads to evocations of black folklore such as "rabbit in a briar patch" and the shortened "B'rer" as well as to mock expressions of religious sentiments ("Yass Lawd").[21] Moreover, it accounts for racial epithets—for instance, "spades," "darkies," "niggers"—that Armstrong sometimes used ironically, sometimes to criticize, sometimes as a means of expressing self-conscious pride. For whites, terms like "ofay," "cracker," and "Mr. Charlie" appear on occasion.[22] Armstrong's recollection of his time with the Fletcher Henderson band further indicates the significance of jive as the language of the underdog; retelling a scene from 1924, he reverts to expressions such as "Yassuh" and "Shucks" in order to illustrate his youthful and Southern ignorance as he is addressing the more educated and lighter-skinned Northern band leader.[23]

In Armstrong's music, jives appears in titles such as "Don't Jive Me" (June 28, 1928) and on recordings such as "You're Driving Me Crazy (What Did I Do?)" (Dec. 23, 1930), which begins with a jive exchange between Armstrong and drummer Lionel Hampton. During this exchange, Armstrong calls his band members "cats" and "boys," demands that they play more vigorously, and introduces slang expressions such as "we're gone." His response to Hampton's stuttered excuse ("we just muggin' lightly") is more confused stutter and the admission "you got me talkin' all that chop suey-like." In the second chorus of "Just a Gigolo" (Mar. 9, 1931), Armstrong substitutes the phrase "just another jig, I know" for "just another gigolo," thereby engaging in racial word play—"jig" being short for "jigaboo," a racial epithet with primitivist overtones. Buck Clayton remembers, "Louis changed the words a little bit at the end. It kind of stirred up some people, especially the NAACP. [. . .] Well, you know the word 'jig' often means a coloured person, which isn't too bad a word really; we use 'em, words like 'spook' and 'jig,' or at least we used them in those days, not so much now. But that's just the way Louis was; he put his own little version in there."[24] Versioning, this remembrance illustrates, is not limited to the wide dispersal of varied life narratives, but it also occurs on the level of lyrical adaptation.

As these examples show, Armstrong's creative adaptation and transformation of song lyrics follow a performative ethos—slipping in phrases coded with aberrant meaning—that also appears in his writings. While the editors of *Swing That Music* erased the fact that Armstrong's first wife, Daisy Parker, was a prostitute, they did not catch a jive reference to an extramarital affair with "a little colored girl," about which he recalls: "We sure fried some fish those two nights."[25] And in a letter to Mezz Mezzrow written from Birmingham, England, in 1932, Armstrong uses jive to make a veiled "proposition" that urges Mezzrow to supply him with marijuana: "So 'Mezz' I'd like very much for you to 'Cooperate with me on this 'Proposition. [. . .] I'd like for you to 'start 'right 'in and 'pack 'me enough 'orchestrations' to last me the "whole 'trip (TRIP) [. . .] ." At the end of the letter, Armstrong states: "What 'we want to keep in mind 'now' is the 'orchestrations in 'Paris." Under the word "orchestrations," he writes "MUTA" in block letters (his slang term for marijuana) in order to ensure that Mezzrow—but not any unauthorized person who might read the letter—will decode his jive.[26]

But jive is even more than a secret strategic language or a way of evoking a jazz world foreign to outsiders. It is also an expression of verbal black comedy that has substantial consequences for musical performance. In his autobiography *Hot Man* (1992), the pianist Art Hodes describes Armstrong backstage: "there'd be a lot of good feeling in the room. And somebody would say something funny, and that would give Louis an opening and you couldn't beat Louis at being funny. [. . .] And we'd laugh through the whole intermission, and then slowly walk Louis back to the stand. [. . .] Man, the guy could really blow then."[27] Humor and jive thus flourish between musical performances—they peak at the interstice between music and conversation—and even enhance these performances, allowing the musician to "really blow." They are also part of Armstrong's stage show: the mugging for which he was famous and that constitutes a central communicative strategy. Gillespie's statement about his own comedy indicates the workings of this strategy: "As a performer, when you're trying to establish audience control, the best thing is to make them laugh if you can. [. . .] A laugh relaxes your muscles [. . .] all over your body. When you get people relaxed, they're more receptive to what you're trying to get them to do."[28] In that sense, jive comedy and laughter can be seen as instruments with which Armstrong sought to control audiences, entertain fellow band members, and prepare the way for another high-energy performance.

Yet the playfulness and humor of these practices frequently served a serious function. In a letter to Frances Church from March 10, 1946, Armstrong relates how he and his band were harassed by "two old cracker sheriffs" on a tour in the South. The sheriffs had confiscated one of the trumpets they falsely believed to be Armstrong's. On the story level, Armstrong falls into the role of the subservient black minstrel figure and answers the sheriffs' questions with the submissive "Yassuh," "No, suh," and "Yassuh, boss." On the level of narrative discourse, however, the letter is ripe with jive expressions such as "that awful 'drag,'" "ofay promoter," and "hip'd to the jive," which allows Armstrong to convert a humiliating experience into a story of cunning subterfuge and thereby gain narrative compensation for socially enforced submission.[29] That such exchanges were relatively common can be seen when we turn to one of the most famous episodes of Armstrong's jiving, which took place in Memphis in 1932. The singer and his band were arrested because manager Johnny Collins's white wife was traveling with the African American musicians. Once bail was paid, the band went to the Palace, a Memphis theater where they were scheduled to play that night. According to several accounts, Armstrong dedicated "I'll Be Glad When You're Dead You Rascal You" to the Memphis police force, not a mean feat considering the fact that members of the police were in the audience and that the concert was broadcast over the radio. Eyewitnesses recall that the policemen did not catch on to the signifying jive of the singer wishing them dead.[30] Instead, they thanked Armstrong for the dedication: "You know, Mr. Armstrong, we have had a number of important jazz orchestras come through Memphis, people like Paul Whiteman and Jean Goldkette, but none of them ever thought enough of the Police Department to dedicate a song to us!" Armstrong's then-trombonist Preston Jackson further recalls the policemen's response: "We appreciate it, and we want you to know that at your next show we will be reserving the first several rows for ourselves and our wives."[31]

These examples reveal several specific functions of jive. It can be hilariously funny (entertaining musicians and audiences alike), self-consciously ironic (signaling superficial submission), potentially subversive (launching a coded attack), and conspicuously creative (playing with words and scripted music to generate new meanings). That these multiply functional jive practices were important to Armstrong is indicated by his frequent naming of these practices: "loudtalking," "signifying," "jive," and "telling lies."[32] Translating such vernacular terms into scholarly discourse, Geneva Smitherman lists rhetorical devices such as exaggerated language, mimicry, proverbial statements, punning, spontaneity, image making, broggadocio, indirection, and tonal semantics.[33] On that view, one of Armstrong's remarks about his virility—"Well I won't mention my sex sessions these days, because I hate to be called a *braggadosha*"—shows that we are dealing with a speaker who is more deeply versed in African American linguistic practices than his edited writings insinuate. Armstrong apparently enjoyed semantic play and was proud to claim that he had mastered several registers of language.[34] His repeated use of the term "S'language," a mixture of "slang" and "language," indicates his self-awareness as a writer and pride in his verbal mastery. Whether Armstrong coined this term cannot be said for certain; he uses it in a letter to Madeleine Bérard dated November 25, 1946, but it appears two years earlier in *Dan Burley's Original Handbook of Harlem Jive* from 1944, in which the author defines jive "as an auxiliary slanguage."[35]

This auxiliary s'language emerged within an expressive economy that Henry Louis Gates and others find paradigmatically represented in the verbal strategies described in, and enacted by, the signifying monkey tales that have their origin in Africa and were still prominent in the linguistic and musical practices of jazz musicians.[36] In these tales, the Monkey appears as a trickster figure; he "is a rhetorical genius" whose intent is to demystify the Lion as king of the jungle, and he does so by using his superior rhetorical powers to pit the Lion against the strongest animal of the jungle, the Elephant. According to Gates, the signifying tale "turns upon the free play of language itself, upon the displacement of meanings, precisely because it draws attention to its rhetorical structures and strategies and thereby draws attention to the force of the signifier."[37] Armstrong was aware of these tales; he wrote down several explicit verses of "The Signifying Monkey" in his *Joke Book* and also collected folk stories and toasts such as "Who's the King of the Jungle," "B'rer Rabbit + Mr Monkey + Mr Buzzard," and "The Elephant and the Muskeeter." In Armstrong's Memphis performance of "I'll Be Glad When You're Dead You Rascal You," the signifying deep structure underneath the lyrics was masked by the surface narrative about the black singer's anger at the adulterer's acts and his indignation at his wife's infidelity. The vernacular nature of lines such as "You just ain't no good, oh you dog!" suggests a black context that may have seemed quite remote to the lives of the white policemen, but since Armstrong impersonates the "I" of the lyrics when he enunciates it, he also implicitly addresses his actual audience, intoning that he would be "tickled to death" if they died and "left this earth." The meaning of this and other signifying performances is therefore never "definitive, given the ambiguity

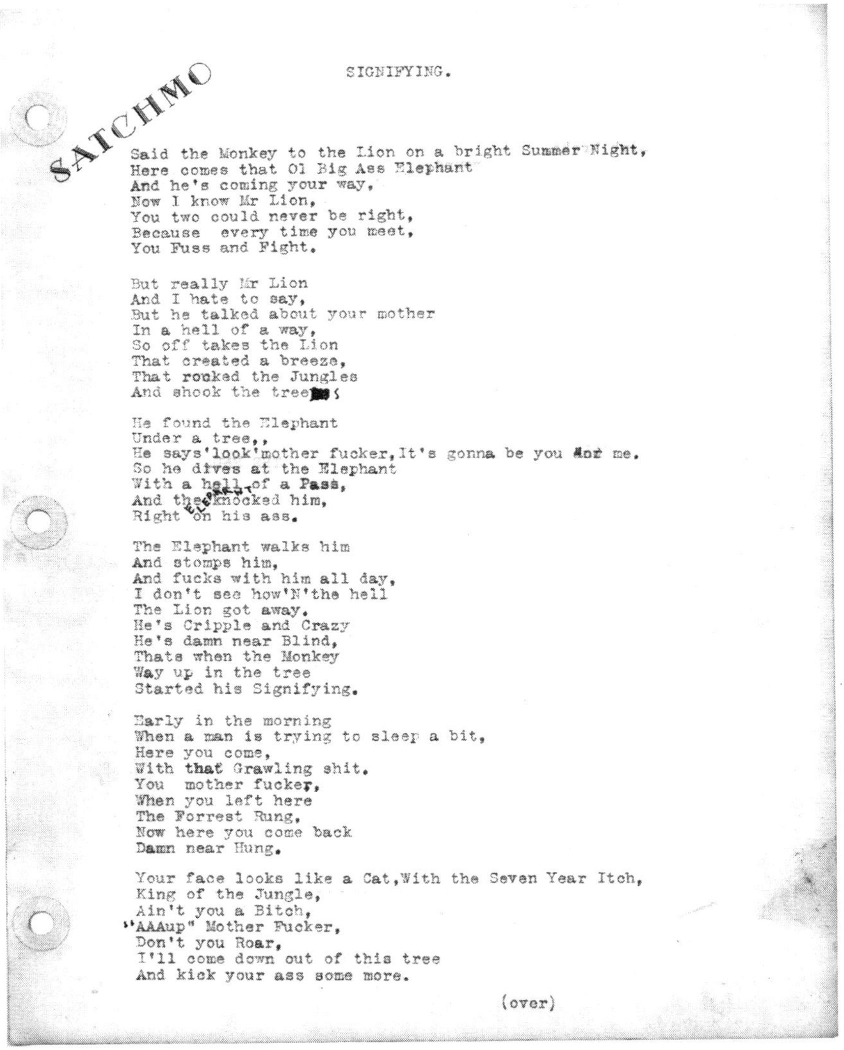

SIGNIFYING.

SATCHMO

Said the Monkey to the Lion on a bright Summer Night,
Here comes that Ol Big Ass Elephant
And he's coming your way,
Now I know Mr Lion,
You two could never be right,
Because every time you meet,
You Fuss and Fight.

But really Mr Lion
And I hate to say,
But he talked about your mother
In a hell of a way,
So off takes the Lion
That created a breeze,
That rocked the Jungles
And shook the trees

He found the Elephant
Under a tree,,
He says 'look' mother fucker, It's gonna be you Aor me.
So he dives at the Elephant
With a hell of a Pass,
And the knocked him,
Right on his ass.

The Elephant walks him
And stomps him,
And fucks with him all day,
I don't see how'N'the hell
The Lion got away.
He's Cripple and Crazy
He's damn near Blind,
Thats when the Monkey
Way up in the tree
Started his Signifying.

Early in the morning
When a man is trying to sleep a bit,
Here you come,
With that Grawling shit.
You mother fucker,
When you left here
The Forrest Rung,
Now here you come back
Damn near Hung.

Your face looks like a Cat, With the Seven Year Itch,
King of the Jungle,
Ain't you a Bitch,
"AAAup" Mother Fucker,
Don't you Roar,
I'll come down out of this tree
And kick your ass some more.

(over)

Fig. 5. Louis Armstrong, "Signifying," from *Joke Book*, undated. Courtesy of the Louis Armstrong House Museum.

at work in [their] rhetorical structures" and given their tendency toward "obscuring [. . .] apparent meaning."[38]

The full complexity of signifying only becomes graspable once signifying practices in various media are assessed as elements of Armstrong's intermedial autobiographics. The signifying monkey tales are examples of a form of "verbal dueling" that is based on the speaker's ability to encode messages and make a point through indirection.[39] Musically, the dueling process finds expression in the bucking and cutting contests of Armstrong's youth and in the rhythmic sensation of swing, which can be interpreted as a form of "signifying on the timeline."[40] If linguistic signifying makes use of metaphor, metonymy, hyperbole, chiasmus, and synecdoche, Armstrong's music uses quotations (advertising jingles, snatches of opera music, other solos by himself and others) as metaphor, while his flashy sound and high-note playing may be said to be expressions of hyperbole. Chiasmus appears as rhythmic inversion and melodic paraphrase, while a synecdochic principle may be found in the use of individual phrases taken from longer melodic statements.[41]

On a larger scale, Armstrong's musical signifying appears in two related forms. First, his s'language surrounds and infuses the music (backstage talk, onstage patter); it appears as part of the music (in the form of lyrics and vocal interjections) but also provides a stream of extramusical information that often obscures, rather than clarifies, meaning. Second, the linguistic process of jiving motivates the transgression of medial boundaries in the sense that humorous language invades musical sound production. Thus, rather than segregate jive talk and jazz music into independent medial categories, we may read both of them as the effects of a transmedial impulse, as expressions of spontaneity, playfulness, and creative contest that follow the same performative logic: "As we played with musical notes, [. . .] we played with words," to reiterate Gillespie's point; "Louis swings more telling a joke than most others do playing a horn," to cite tenor saxophonist Bud Freeman.[42]

In autobiographical writing, such a swinging linguistics is realized not only in the form of a special vocabulary of jive terms; it also infuses Armstrong's orthography and syntax. Dashes, for instance, tend to indicate caesura and enumeration. Talking about narcotics, Armstrong writes: "A dope addict, from what I noticed by watching a lot of different 'cats' whom I used to light up with but got so carried away—they felt that they could get a much bigger kick by *jugging* themselves in the ass with a needle—

Heroin—Cocaine—etc.—or some other unGodly shit . . ." In other in-stances, dashes signal the insertion of a spontaneous thought: "But to me—I being a great observer in life [. . .] ." Apostrophes and unusual capitaliza-tion frequently convey emphasis: "If you 'Kick my 'Ass' 'Once you can 'bet I won't come back if I can 'help it, so you can 'Kick it Again." Slang ex-pressions are written in italics (underlined in typed and handwritten man-uscripts): "Why I'd much rather shoot a nigger in his ass than to be caught with a stick of *shit* . . . The Judge would honestly respect you better. . . ." ("*Shit*," of course, is slang for marijuana). The ellipses in this quotation represent a habit of delivering punch lines after a short pause. Unusual spelling tends to show a playful engagement with language, as becomes ob-vious in a postcard in which Armstrong sends "a 'beeg keees for my wife."[43] Such linguistic devices do not altogether stray all that far from standard conventions. One could argue that they are "consistent enough that we may speak of an orthographic style," an "oral orthography," or even "an entire system of punctuation establishing a rhythm which made his texts lively."[44] The assumption, then, is that a functional reading of Armstrong's writing practices may indeed be possible and that these writing practices share essential characteristics with oral expression.

The recording of Armstrong's interview with Edward R. Murrow from 1955 gives weight to this assumption.[45] The interview touches on all of the topics Armstrong's autobiographical narratives in the 1950s routinely cov-ered—Joe Oliver, the musical styles of New Orleans, how he received the name Satchmo—and it showcases the musician's jive language. But it is even more telling in terms of its close resemblance to Armstrong's ap-proach to writing. It begins with a funny anecdote similar to many other anecdotes he wrote down (the Swiss waiter who misunderstands the jive term "solid" as an order for salad) and registers laughter, which would be represented as "tee hee" or "haw haw haw" in writing. It addresses Murrow directly and thereby elicits audience response: "you dig? [. . .] you dig, okay daddy." Letters by definition address a reader directly, but even in his es-says and longer narratives, Armstrong frequently asked questions that re-quire an immediate response as in conversation. Moreover, the interview features characteristic neologisms such as "passing facitasy" (probably a pun on "passing fancy/passing fantasy" directed at bebop) and "rhythemat-ical" (followed by the rhetorical question "Did that come outa me?"), and it offers idiosyncratic definitions of musical styles such as gutbucket (a "low and gutsural music, you know what I mean, raaaaawwww"). Finally, the way in which Armstrong raises his voice and inflects the names of classical composers and the popular songs in his repertoire suggests that those names and titles would be underscored in writing.

One of Armstrong's early letters, sent to the French jazz critic Hugues Panassié on April 14, 1936, aptly demonstrates how the musician transposed oral speech into writing, even though the underscores and excessive apostrophes were presumably omitted. Armstrong begins by ventriloquizing Panassié and then addresses the critic as if he were sitting across the room: "Well! Well! Well, If it ain't a letter from my old Pal, old Gate Mouth, Louis (Satchmo) Armstrong. . . . Well, what do you know about that? . . . One thing I've always had it in my mind to write you first chance I'd get and now's the time, 'Yessir' ee. . . . [. . .] I'll bet you, right now you're listening to some records. . . . Eh? . . . Yessir, I'll bet, you have your head real close by the Victrola, getting a good load of whatever Band's playing."[46] Geneva Smitherman's notion of "tonal semantics" comes to mind here: "In using the semantics of tone, the voice is employed like a musical instrument with improvisations, riffs, and all kinds of playing between the notes. This rhythmic pattern becomes a kind of acoustical phonetic alphabet and gives black speech its songified or musical quality."[47] The rhythmic pattern that underlies the repetitions in "Well! Well! Well," "letter," "Well," "get," "Yessir," "bet," "Yessir," "bet," "head," and "getting" is amplified by an acoustic pattern: "e-"sounds shape these expressions and reappear in phonetically isolated form in the exclamations "ee" and "Eh." Even though Panassié would not have heard Armstrong's actual voice when reading the letter, he could have relied on exclamation marks, ellipses, direct speech, and deictic information in his perusal of Armstrong's lines. Question marks mandate a raising of the vocal pitch, exclamation marks indicate an increase in volume, and the elongated "ee" vowel suggests a higher pitch (or a higher note, if one thinks in musical terms) than the "Eh" utterance that follows it. In addition, its length of enunciation would exceed that of the "Eh" sound, while ellipses of varying lengths may function as speech pauses. What is more, Armstrong had used the phrase "Well, what do you know about that?" on two takes of "Laughin' Louie" (both Apr. 24, 1933), which illustrates the transposition of oral expressions into writing. Being familiar with the recordings, Panassié would have been able to recall Armstrong's voice and intonation when reading the phrase in the letter.

As all of the examples cited thus far make clear, Armstrong's writings are performative self-referential statements rather than carefully revised works of literary autobiography—"'Just a little 'Scribblings,'" as he calls them elsewhere.[48] What we find in them is an effect created by "putting the provisional to work," an effect he achieves in his photo-collages by *fixing* elements *impermanently* (by using scotch tape) and by giving his works across media "a persistent and decidedly makeshift quality."[49] In writing, unconventional and flexible (i.e., not quite random, but not altogether systematic) orthography and typography foreground the spontaneous creation of autobiographical narrative. Even when dictating a telegram, Armstrong adhered to this provisional, spontaneous, and animated style. As Panassié recalls, "Instead of simply cabling: 'Will arrive such-and-such a date at such-and-such a time. Best Wishes, Louis Armstrong,' he would write: 'Dear old pal, it's Friday that I will swing again my good old Selmer trumpet in New York. . . . Ha, ha, ha . . . Red beans and ricely yours . . . Louis (Satchmo) Armstrong.'"[50] In music, this provisional quality is expressed through spontaneous vocal insertions that comment on the performance as it is in full swing.

But why did Armstrong adhere to such a provisional and spontaneous aesthetics? One possible answer is that annotations and indexical markers are a means through which he expressed self-conscious irony when dealing with racially charged encounters.[51] A letter he sent to Leonard Feather on September 18, 1941, shows such a self-consciousness at work. The performativity of the account illustrates a complex attitude toward the racism Armstrong encountered in Atlanta, Georgia: "We're getting ready to play a swell dance here tonight for the colored folks and the white folks are invited as spectators and I'm telling you Leonard you never seen such wonderful gatherings in all your life as they do" all down in these parts . . . Honest they get along down here at these dances just like one 'beeg family . . ."[52] What Armstrong does here is set up a contrast between his white fans, "spectators" who do not participate in the concert, and his love for the "colored folks," for whom he will "play a swell dance." It would be difficult to miss the irony inherent in a phrase like "they get along down here [. . .] just like one 'beeg family." Indeed, Armstrong's awareness of communicating with two audiences not only structures his musical performances. As can be seen in this example, it simultaneously emerges in his autobiographical poetics. He is not simply writing about the white spectators at his shows in the South; he is also writing to a white jazz critic who will report his experiences to a wider reading audience.

Translated into Standard English, as many of Armstrong's writings were, the letter to Feather would lose much of the ironic undertone created by the cacographic misspelling "big" as "beeg."[53] If the passage in the Feather letter were to read "get along [. . .] just like one big family," Armstrong's point would be lost. Standardizing the letter not only would have altered his style but would also have silenced the statement's inherent ambiguity. This ambiguity makes possible an accommodationist reading (the "darky" entertainer matches his toothy grin with the elongated and widened "ee" of "beeg") and a critical, if not necessarily subversive, reading that finds Armstrong and Feather shaking their heads at the hopelessly reactionary white Southern audience. The following passage, in which Armstrong writes about his experiences on the *Sydney* entertainment steamship, further underscores the importance of accounting for the orthographic and stylistic peculiarities of his writing as they are conserved in manuscript form and as they differ from the finished product (*Satchmo*, in this case):

> . . . at first, we ran into a lot of ugly moments while we were on the band stand. . . . Such as, 'come on 'thar—'black boy, etc, . . . We (most of us) were from the South anyway—and being used to that kind of jive—we'd—just keep on swinging just like 'nothing happened. And before the night was [obscured] ignored all of that mad jive they'd—layed' on us the first part of the evening, and beating out that fine music for them in fine fashion— hmmmm, They 'Love us, —'do you hear me????—they 'Loved us. . . . We couldn't turn for them singing our praises, etc. . . . Telling us to hurry up and come back. . . . Cute? . . .[54]

In this passage, an ironic, even sarcastic, view of the Southerners' patronizing "love" for the black musicians could be said to result from the repetition, capitalization, and use of apostrophes around " 'Love us" and " 'Loved us," phrases that are broken up by a direct question posed to the reader: " 'do you hear me????" "Hear" suggests an oral/aural dimension and thus a sympathetic listener, as well as performative immediacy (the question demands an affirmative "yes"); the quadruple question marks create a forceful, emphatic tone. The speech pauses indicated by the ellipses may imply discomfort with, and disbelief in, the bigotry of the steamship audience. The representation of Southern dialect in "thar" mocks the ignorance of those who exert social control over the performance, an ignorance that is undermined by the jazzy semantics of Armstrong's signifying after the fact: "mad jive," "swinging," "beating out [. . .] music," and so forth. Finally, the vocal insertion "hmmmm" evokes a knowing, morally superior response to his audience's double standards and adds to the oral feel of the passage.

The extent to which Armstrong's writings were tailored by editors and publishers for public consumption can be gauged when the manuscript is compared to the version that appeared in *Satchmo:* "The ofays were not used to seeing colored boys blowing horns and making fine music for them to dance by. At first we ran into some ugly experiences while we were on the bandstand, and we had to listen to plenty of nasty remarks. But most of us were from the South anyway. We were used to that kind of jive, and we would just keep on swinging as though nothing had happened. Before the evening was over they *loved* us."[55] The passage does convey the general idea of the original version: the white Southern audience looks down on the musicians, but once the black jazzmen play their stimulating music, the audience embraces them. The italicized *loved* carries a remnant of the irony expressed in the original, but without the interspersed expression of disbelief ("'do you hear me????"), the italics can be read as emphasizing the sincerity of the audience's loving attitude toward the black musicians. Therefore, what is missing from the edited passage is more than just the flavor of Armstrong's autobiographical voice caused by the absence of oral effects (no direct speech, no multiple question marks, no rhetorical question at the end, no insertions such as "hmmmm"). Indeed, the critical subtext of the passage is lost, and gross misreadings become not only possible, but likely. Missing are the fake Southern accent ("thar"), the offensive "'black boy," and the protest implied in the phrases "'Love us,—'do you hear me????" and "Cute?"

As significant as the argument about Armstrong's production of ironic distance and the observations about the orality of Armstrong's writings and their idiosyncratic orthography are, they do not fully account for the linguistic intricacies of the musician's autobiographical narratives. Speaking of a "syntax of scat" and a "scat semantics," Brent Edwards identifies a performative practice that recognizes both the communicative effects of Armstrong's music and writing and the fact that they cannot always be systematized.[56] Edwards understands scat not as improvised nonsense syllables, as it is most often described, but rather as the "excess of meaning, a shifting possibility of a multitude of meanings," that Armstrong achieves in music, stage acting, and autobiographical writing. Scat possesses a semantic flexibility that emerges from a "[d]eliberately 'false'" vocal production [. . .] supplementing the sayable."[57] This production recalls Armstrong's reference to his singing as "my *vocalizings*" and points to a communicative mode that includes *all* vocal expressions that venture beyond the scripted lyrics and melody of a song.[58]

In order to allocate a transmedial scat aesthetics in Armstrong's autobiographics, it is necessary to make sense of scat as a vocal practice first. The recording that made this practice famous, "Heebie Jeebies" by the Hot Five, is a first indicator of the "excess of stimulation" that Edwards finds in Armstrong's scat singing.[59] If we think back to Armstrong's anecdotal presentation of "Heebie Jeebies" as a spontaneous reaction to the alleged dropping of the lyric sheet, we should find it easy to agree with Edwards's observation that scat is presented "as a fall, as a literal dropping of the words—as an unexpected loss of the lyrics that finally proves enabling. [. . .] It is not exactly that the 'song' is separated from the 'script,' but more that the anecdote relies on an oral/written split to *figure* the way that Armstrong's voice peels gradually away from the iteration of the chorus, and from linguistic iteration altogether."[60] Or as the inimitably hyperbolic Mezzrow writes in his autobiography, this recording "almost drove the English language out of the Windy City for good."[61]

On "Heebie Jeebies," "Skid-Dat-De-Dat" (Nov. 16, 1926), and similar recordings, Armstrong's scat transformed the written lyrics and the melody of a song, thereby transfiguring lyrical loss into a new iterative form. This transformation is particularly prominent in his renditions of the Tin Pan Alley songs that make up the bulk of his repertoire in the 1930s and early 1940s. Three classic recordings, "Lazy River" (Nov. 3, 1931), "Chinatown, My Chinatown" (Nov. 3, 1931), and "Shine" (Mar. 9, 1931), are particularly prominent examples since they feature intricate scat passages and spoken patter that circulates around and in between the written words. They can be understood in terms of Mikhail Bakhtin's notions of "parodic stylization," where the "intentions of the representing discourse are at odds with the intentions of the represented discourse."[62] Applied to Armstrong's scat singing, the represent*ed* discourse relates to the content of the lyrics the singer delivers, while the represent*ing* discourse designates his rendition of—and additions to—these lyrics.

"Lazy River" begins with Armstrong's trumpet introduction, followed by the main melody played by the saxophonists in the band (Lester Boone, George James, Albert Washington). Armstrong enters into call-and-re-

sponse interaction with the saxophones, answering their melodic statements with the utterances "yeah," "aha," "sure," "uh-huh," and "way
down, way down." These utterances are made in his speaking voice,
whereas the lyrics of the first verse are rendered in a higher, singing register, suggesting a second voice and thereby adding a ventriloquizing effect.[63] Alfred Appel interprets the initial utterances as "mock exhortations
[. . .] in a lightly sarcastic tone" that suggest "a wry self-parody" and
counter the pastoral scenes sketched by Hoagy Carmichael and Sidney Arodin's lyrics: a man whose troubles simply melt away as he is taking a nap
in the beautiful midday sun under an old tree by the Mississippi River.[64]
These insertions distinguish precomposed musical material (Bakhtin's represented discourse) from Armstrong's improvised commentary (Bakhtin's
representing discourse), which is part of the music since it is *on* the recording but is also a reflection on the performance, a sort of metacritique inextricably implicated in the musical production. This is significant because
the lyrics of "Lazy River" reinforce stereotypical images of "blackness"
that confront the singer with a problem of rendition: either remain faithful
to the lyrics and pander to racial stereotype (resulting in self-negation),
openly confront racial injustices (risking ostracism), or trouble the lyrics by
transforming them in a highly individualized and creatively challenging
manner that draws on African American expressive practices such as signifying (expressing a degree of self-affirmation).

On "Lazy River," the segue to the lyrics proper—"way down, way
down"—announces both Armstrong's highly personalized rendering of
these lyrics and the scat improvisations to which he will subject the second
verse of the song. This segue establishes a gamut of musical, geographical,
sociocultural, and even sexual references and thus connects Armstrong's
verbal signifying practices on musical recordings with his autobiographical
narratives. On the one hand, the phrase "way down" conjures up images of
the segregated New Orleans of Armstrong's childhood (still segregated in
the early 1930s) and popular images of the Mississippi as the "lazy" river,
thereby mixing romanticized notions of the American South with images
of Jim Crow laws, racism, and lynching. It repeats the North-to-South
gaze of minstrel and postminstrel songs with titles such as "Way Down
South in the Alabama" (ca. 1840s or 1850s) and "Way Down Yonder in
New Orleans" (1922) and lines such as "way down upon de Swanee ribber"
in Stephen Foster's "The Old Folks at Home" of 1851. On the other hand,
getting "way down" alludes to the sexual stimulation and erotic dancing at

Funky Butt Hall, where the "chicks would get way down" when Buddy Bolden sang the raunchy "Don't Go 'Way Nobody" after he had signaled his band to play "way down low" so that he could hear the dragging of the listeners' feet.[65] In this sense, the phrase signals performer-audience inter-action and, in Armstrong's version of "Lazy River," calls his fellow musi-cians' and his audience's attention to the change from the introductory pat-ter to the mellow verse of the song.

In terms of Armstrong's enunciation of the lyrics, it is especially his unique voice but also the syncopated placement of individual syllables and the swinging sensibility with which they are set around the beats that add a personal dimension to the subject matter of the lyrics. By thus playing with the narrative proposed by the lyrics and by exhibiting irreverence toward the original words and vocal line, Armstrong is teasing out new meanings. However ambiguous and implied these meanings may be, the performance emerges from his creative transformation (*how* he sings the lyrics) of pre-determined material (*what* he sings). The vocal patter that introduces "Lazy River" is picked up after the scat verse with statements such as "boy am I riffin' this evenin'" and "oh you river, oh you dog! [. . .] Look out there, Charlie Alexander [the pianist about to take his solo], swing out there on them ivories there, boy." These exclamations reproduce the in-teractive dynamics of Armstrong's stage performances, something he had already introduced on the Hot Five recording "Gut Bucket Blues" (Nov. 12, 1925). They infuse the rendition of the tune with the energy and exu-berance that contemporary music critics frequently associated with Arm-strong's live shows. The singer is unable to confine himself to the written script and, as if powered by an overcharge of electric current, bursts out in spontaneous exclamations about his own and his fellow players' creativity. Not only do these exclamations counteract the "fixing" of the performance through the electric recording process—listeners are reminded that they witness on-the-spot invention—but they also add jazz jive and thus an African American element to the pastoral lyrics of the tune, which pro-duces narrative tension: "riffin'" for vocal delivery that follows the logic of instrumental improvisation; "ivories" for the keyboard of the piano. Such expressions indicate that a different language ("s'language") is needed to talk about music that diverges from established standards. Armstrong's ref-erences to himself as "dog" and Charlie Alexander as "boy" represent black Southern vernacular language ("dog" as a blues-inflected term for a scoundrel or unfaithful lover) and offer a jive take on the language of white supremacism ("boy"). These expressions signal to the listeners that Armstrong wants them to hear the music in two specific cultural contexts that were not originally present in the lyrics: African American blues culture and Southern Jim Crow racism.

The central piece of scatting in "Lazy River" is the second verse, in which Armstrong dispenses with the written lyrics and offers scat improvisation in their stead. The rendition comes across as sincere; musically, it is imaginative and demanding. How do we make sense of this passage, then? Perhaps we could argue that the scatting signifies on the preceding verse, creating a version of the song in which the jazz singer uses his *own* expressions and thereby allocates narrative control in the person of the performer. Thus, the pastoralism of the first verse is not exactly renounced, but counterstated by a decidedly different, personalized, and jazzified form of expression. Moreover, the wordlessness of scat provides a potential for divergent interpretations. It suggests parody and criticism of the preceding passage as much as it insinuates musical humor and plays into romanticized or racialized notions of black performative energy and exuberance. Armstrong's answer to his own improvisation—"boy am I riffin' this evenin'"— records mock surprise at his own eloquence and constitutes another form of call-and-response. Armstrong regularly expressed this kind of surprise in interviews and writing, where the phrase "did that come out of me?" caters to the racial stereotype of intellectual inferiority while simultaneously questioning it. Vocal scatting accomplishes the same effect: Armstrong is uneloquent—his scat is wordless—and eloquent—it is musically complex and masterful—at the same time.

"Chinatown, My Chinatown" differs from "Lazy River" in terms of mood, theme, and setting. Instead of Carmichael and Arodin's nostalgic blackface vision of the minstrel South, listeners encounter a Northern setting and urban yellowface narrative scripted by William Jerome (the song was published in 1910). The Chinatown of this song is inhabited by a "festive Chink" whose dreamy almond eyes and lazy sighing are the result of opium-induced dreams. Much of this narrative remains submerged since Armstrong sings only the chorus of the tune. By redirecting the listener's attention to his transformation of the material through his jiving, scatting, and trumpet improvisation, he recasts the material from a caricatured representation of the Chinese Other into the personalized and individualized sonic expression of a performative exuberance that certainly feeds on the long history of black stereotypes in American culture but nonetheless displays a very modern sense of artistry and entertainment according to which traditional categories of gender, ethnicity, and race are deessentialized.

In Armstrong's interpretation of "Chinatown, My Chinatown," we find a ventriloquist interplay between vocal patter and sung lyrics similar to "Lazy River." We further find a personification of instruments and a staging of musical interaction as conversation. Armstrong presents the song as an argument between his trumpet and the saxophone section, asking his own instrument, "Ain't that right, little trumpet?" The argument soon turns into an anthropomorphic chase, with the cats who play the saxophone parts running away and Armstrong's trumpet trying to catch them. Armstrong introduces every new segment of the chase verbally. After the first verse, which already contains snippets of vocal scatting and jiving (including commentary on his surprising musical eloquence: "you rascal, you"), he taunts the saxophones: "what's the matter with you?" Following the saxophone section, he introduces his own solo by acknowledging that the cats are getting away. "I'm ready, so help me, I'm ready," he states.[66] The trumpet solo is much less frantic than the dramatic frame of the song would suggest, which has led many a critic to conclude rather naively that the music is pure artistry and the patter is silly comedy. It combines a clear tone and systematic narrative construction (variations, tension, climax, call-and-response patterns) with trumpet techniques that were long considered nonstandard and "dirty" but had been popularized by Armstrong's success and the more general infatuation with "blackness" as racial Otherness: slurs, shakes, vibrato, and high-note effects.

The recording of "Chinatown, My Chinatown" self-consciously marks the music as an ethnically inflected stage act. At the end of the opening monologue, Armstrong tells his band members to "get your chops together boys, while we mug lightly, slightly, and politely." While "chops" refers to the lips that produce the music as well as to the musician's technical abilities, the vernacular term "mugging" describes excessive gestures and bits of stage hokum that are not necessarily needed to play the music but code the performance in an aura of "blackness" that is intended to transfix and amuse an audience expecting the light, slight, and polite entertainment of genteel society.[67] Performativity is further enhanced by the greeting at the very beginning of the song when Armstrong tells his listeners that the song they are about to hear will be a novelty. When Alfred Appel writes that "Armstrong wants his alive music to enter our living room" and that "Armstrong is [a] most *phonogenic* recording artist [. . . who] invented self-reflexive phonography," he captures the effect the direct address must have had on the home audience: "Armstrong asks the listeners at home to build on their visual and visceral sense of him, grinning or grimacing, and to eavesdrop on the bandstand as he talks comprehensible jive to the cats in the band."[68] The music becomes a vehicle for an extended self-performance that transforms the artificial boundaries of the musical medium, consciously violating the convention that vocal renditions of musical pieces stick to the precomposed material and that the singer of a song must not spoil a performance by talking and laughing into the microphone.[69]

Overall, the performative effects of such scat transformations are difficult to assess. It is, however, fair to say that through scat, Armstrong moves from mimetic realism to a nonmimetic mode of singing, as Stephen Casmier and Donald Matthews note: "A sense of the sublime occurs in the tension produced by our ability to conceive of, but not 'present,' an idea." In other words, nonmimetic discourse, if it is effective, "overcomes alienating conventions and human banality, undermines hegemonies, and invokes creativity, the sublime, presence and spirituality."[70] Armstrong's 1931 version of "Shine," a tune from a musical show with lyrics by Ford Dabney and Cecil Mack, makes the most of the nonmimetic potential of scat. At first, Armstrong remains faithful to the racially deprecating lyrics, describing his curly hair, pearly teeth, and fondness of fancy clothes and recounting his ability to counter trouble with a smile. But then the lyrics turn to the singer's skin color: "Just because my color's shady, different maybe / That's why they call me . . ." The missing word at the end of the last line is "shine," a racial slur. It is substituted in Armstrong's version with a scatted riff delivered furiously over an instrumental break. Here, Armstrong moves from the mimetic mode, which postulates a problematic image of blackness, to a mode on nonmimetic discourse that challenges, in a nonconfrontational and indirect manner, the racially coded lyrics by showcasing the musician's creative engagement with the material and by marking his resistance to singing the racist phrase: instead of a stereotypical "shine," we hear the unmistakably individual Louis Armstrong. This is an excellent example of what Nathaniel Mackey calls "the way a scat singer makes inarticulacy speak," and Armstrong does so in a doubly coded manner. Dabney and Mack were successful African American Broadway composers, so Armstrong's transformation of the lyrics resists both the white stereotype of blacks as "shines" and the black middle-class sensibilities proposed in the song through images that shuttle between self-demeaning iconography (curly hair, pearly teeth, shady skin) and a sense of urban sophistication (the singer is dressed in the latest style; the lyrics are written in Standard English).[71]

The politics of performance, however, are ultimately more restrictive and complicated than these conclusions imply. In the 1942 soundie for "Shine," the story of the happy-go-lucky shoeshine boy is visualized, adding another dimension to the stereotype. The chain of associations runs like this: shoeshine boy—black shoe polish—burnt cork or grease as black face paint—blackface performance. Here, then, Armstrong does *not* scat the title, and even if he is not directly involved in the skit that accompanies the musical delivery, he is nonetheless part of the overall production and its minstrel overtones.[72] And in the 1932 version of the song, performed as part of the film *Rhapsody in Black and Blue*, he delivers the song wearing a leopard cape and a wooly black wig topped with bushels of grass, an outfit that arguably takes popular culture's primitivist fantasies to the extreme. Again, he does not do any scatting—he does, however, point to his jungle outfit when he sings the line "Like to dress up in the latest style," thus subtly foregrounding the incongruities inherent in the lyrics, his attire, and his musical abilities. What we find here is a representational economy particular to the visual medium. Armstrong is granted greater leeway on musical recordings than on the movie screen, a discrepancy that illustrates the particular power of visual codes of racial representation.

The scat aesthetics that structures Armstrong's renditions of "Lazy River," "Chinatown, My Chinatown," and "Shine" variously expresses sarcasm and mockery, as well as comic and creative exuberance, while it also comments on prewritten material (in terms of both music and lyrics) that situates the singer within particular narratives of "blackness." Armstrong's scat creates ambiguity, sometimes through vocal patter, sometimes through wordless improvisation. While meaning is often elusive, scat is never meaningless. The vocal performances represent an effort to extend and enliven the medium of sound recording through statements aimed directly at fellow musicians and the audience. Scat further marks the performance as a performance, introducing an element of self-consciousness that opens itself up to many readings: it can be denied or interpreted as the spontaneous burst of natural musicality, but it can also be taken as the subversive deconstruction of racist lyrics.

The performative impulses and expressive structures that govern Armstrong's scat vocals can also be identified in his autobiographical writings, as one of his letters to manager Joe Glaser reveals. A central passage reads: "Something else Black Benny [said] to me, came true → He said (TO ME) "DiPPER'" as long as you live, no matter where you may be → always have a white man (WHO LiKE YOU) and Can + will Put his Hand on your shoulder and say—"THis is "'MY" NiGGER" and, Can't Nobody Harm' Ya.""[73] In the original text, Armstrong underlines the words "white man" once, "DiPPer," "THis," and "is" twice, "MY" five times, and "NiGGER" four times. The passage exemplifies the interaction of excess and lack as literary signifiers of "blackness." Passing off the advice as folk wisdom related to him by the notorious New Orleans gangster Black Benny (note the sprawling quotation marks and apostrophes around the most critical statement: ""THis is "'MY" NiGGER""), Armstrong shifts narrative agency away from himself and toward the uneducated Benny, whose remarks can be brushed off as vernacular banter. In addition, the emphatic use of capital letters in "WHO LiKE YOU" could be interpreted as Armstrong's recognition of Glaser's friendship or at least of his manager's professional sponsorship.

Yet other markers, for instance, several of the apostrophes, the "plus" symbol, and the arrows, cannot be easily explained in terms of a set orthographic system. It is more productive to read the passage as an excess of indexical signs that complicates the interpretation. The visual appearance of the text renders the words uneducated and unclean; trumpet techniques such as slurring and blue notes and the gravel tone of Armstrong's voice come to mind. Comparable to the "high density of 'sound effects'" that John Edgar Wideman detects in African American folk narratives and that include "narrative devices which lend themselves to performance as a tale is orally transmitted to an audience" (phatic phrases, rhetorical questions, call-and-response patterns, word repetition), Armstrong's use of indexical markers connotes a racial difference that can simultaneously signify deficiency (in a negative sense: lack of education and intellect) and deviance (in a positive sense: cunningness and subversion).[74] Larry King's description of Armstrong's handwriting as a series of "large, undisciplined letters" and Robert Goffin's reference to Armstrong's letters as "painfully scrawled replies" further indicate the confounding lack of discipline (negatively: a lack of civilization; positively: an act of conscious disobedience), as well as a troubling notion of racial inferiority on Armstrong's part, a presumed lacking on racial grounds that was one of the major justifications for slavery and the politics of Jim Crow.[75]

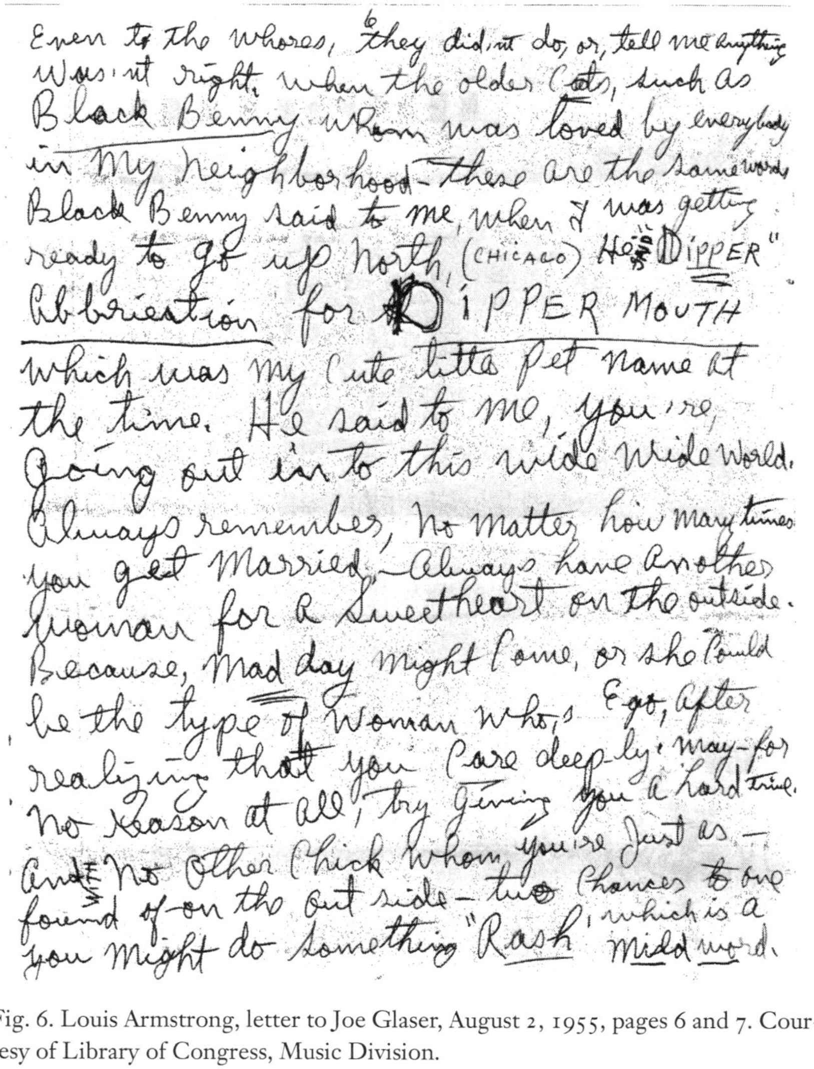

Even to the whores, they did'nt do, or, tell me anything Was'nt right. When the older Cats, such as Black Benny who was loved by everybody in My Neighborhood — these are the same words Black Benny said to me, when I was getting ready to go up North, (CHICAGO) He "DIPPER" Abbrieation for DIPPER MOUTH which was My Cute little pet name at the time. He said to me, you're, going out into this wide wide World. Always remember, No matter how Many times you get Married — Always have Another Woman for a Sweetheart on the outside. Because, Mad day might Come, or she could be the type of Woman who's Ego, after realizing that you Care deeply, may — for No Reason at all, try giving you a hard time. And No Other Chick whom you're Just as — found of on the outside — two Chances to one you might do something "Rash, which is a mild word.

Fig. 6. Louis Armstrong, letter to Joe Glaser, August 2, 1955, pages 6 and 7. Courtesy of Library of Congress, Music Division.

The indexical markers in the letter to Glaser certainly produce uncertainty. Is Armstrong simply jiving? Is he engaging in an act of ethnic self-dramatization that amplifies racial difference for personal gain?[76] Is he mocking the racism pervading American society as well as the music business? Is he dead serious, implicating Glaser in acts of exploitation by situating himself in the position of the black boy (the underlined and capital-

I find the advice Benny gave me turned out, to be very lodgical Because I can look back through all of my marriages with the comfort of my "horn & told all those "Bitches" whenever they'd start showing they "Asses" you can go to Hell. Because, I have my horn to keep me Worm. Something else Black Benny, to me, came true → He said (TO ME) "DIPPER" As long as you live, no matter where you may be → Always have a white Man (WHO LIKE YOU) And Can + will Put his Hand on your shoulder And say — "THIS is "MY" NIGGER" And, can't nobody Harm, ya" By, Sweets having that baby for me, gave Lucille one of best ass whippings IN, HER LIFE. As nice + sweet + as wonderful she is she still has a sense of "fire's" that I've never Particularly Cared for →

ized "NiGGER") in need of protection from the white man (a phrase also underlined and capitalized in the passage quoted above)? Most likely, he is doing all of these things at once because the markers engage in linguistic play and evade easy verification. Brent Edwards suggests that the "wealth of indices" and the "overflow of graphic marks and pointers" create the sense of a code but provide the reader with no access to this code, no reliable means of deciphering potential irony, multiple voices, and rules governing the generation of meaning. Instead of pointing the reader to the author's intention, they produce an *"excess* of signification."[77] As the result of a transmedial impulse, this excess also structures Armstrong's photo-collages, which involve "using a lot of scotch tape," as well as "pick[ing] out the different things during what I read and piece[ing] them together and making a little story of my own."[78] Not only is Armstrong using *a lot of* scotch tape to create the collages, but he is also using *a lot of* indexical markers to embroider his letters.

The visio-literary representations of excess and the resulting lack of stable meaning can be linked specifically to a double dimension of racial invisibility (being seen only as lacking) and racial hypervisibility (being seen as excessively Other). Being hypervisible and hyperaudible as an artist of color but invisible and inaudible as a black social being, Armstrong uses excessive self-presentation as a dramatic marker of difference that counters the notion of lack (of consciousness, intelligence, white skin color, and so forth) while heightening it at the same time. As Ralph Ellison's Invisible Man tells his readers, Armstrong "bends that military instrument into a beam of lyrical sound. Perhaps I like Louis Armstrong because he's made poetry out of being invisible."[79] The intensity of Ellison's synaesthetic metaphor also informs trumpeter Max Kaminsky's recollection of Armstrong's appearance with the Carroll Dickerson band at Chicago's Savoy Ballroom in 1928: "I felt as if I had stared into the sun's eye. All I could think of doing was to run away and hide till the blindness left me."[80] While the markers allude to a meaning behind the written words, the lack of a code to the excessive, blinding encryption testifies to the impossibility of pinning down one stable meaning. Armstrong's autobiographical narratives thus transpose the indeterminacy of scat to written form through the visual markers and annotations that decorate the page.

But indexical markers may have a purpose that has only been implied thus far. Apart from suggesting semantic flexibility and an excess of signification, they may also perform an ornamental function, following Zora Neale Hurston's "will to adorn" and the "urge to adorn" that allegedly characterize "Negro expression."[81] While Armstrong's page decorations do not necessarily come across as particularly artistic or even beautiful, they tend to follow the logic of his musical creations, of which "When You're Smiling (The Whole World Smiles with You)" (Sept. 11, 1929) is a fitting example. The piece contains typical elements of Armstrong's vocal practices—variations of syllable lengths and uncommon stresses that diverge substantially from the original melody, trumpet techniques (especially smears) applied to singing, and black dialect ("When *you* smiling"). The transitions between the individual lines illustrate the ornamental aspect of indexical marking. It is difficult to represent Armstrong's vocals in writing—after all, Armstrong himself employs techniques indigenous to writing by hand or typewriter—but for analytical purposes, Armstrong's diversions from the original lyrics may be placed in brackets in the following short transcript:

> The whole world smiles with you [ba-ba-ba-by]
> [oooh] when you laughing
> [baaaabe] when you laughing

Armstrong uses the space between the lines for ornamental fillings that surround and connect the words; he manages to squeeze in such fillings by using the rubato technique of shortening syllables.[82] In one of his letters, he similarly annotates the lyrics to "My Brazilian Beauty," a song he had performed with his vocal quartet in New Orleans, thus translating vocal declamation on the street to visual expression on the page:

> 'My—'Brazilian 'Beau-ty—
> Down on 'Ama'zone—
> 'That's where my 'Love is 'Gone' → Gone—'Gone"—Gone
> <u>"Babe Singers' Break</u>
>
> Ev-ry 'Night 'I'm 'Drea-min"
> '<u>Bout</u> '<u>My</u> '<u>Bra'Zilian</u> '<u>Beauty'</u>
> '<u>Down</u> '<u>on</u> <u>-the</u> '<u>Ama'zone</u>

Here, then, the transcribed lyrics look remarkably similar to Armstrong's prose writing, and the musician is clear about the effect he intends the markers and annotations to have: "You can almost 'feel the 'melody from the 'Lyrics. '*Huh?*'."[83]

Creative ornamentation and its emotive effects had already been observed in African American musical performances before jazz became a national sensation. In 1899, Jeannette Robinson Murphy noted about "Negro melodies" that "around every prominent note [the singer] must place a variety of small notes, called 'trimmings,'" and "must also intersperse his singing with peculiar humming sounds."[84] Roughly a quarter century later,

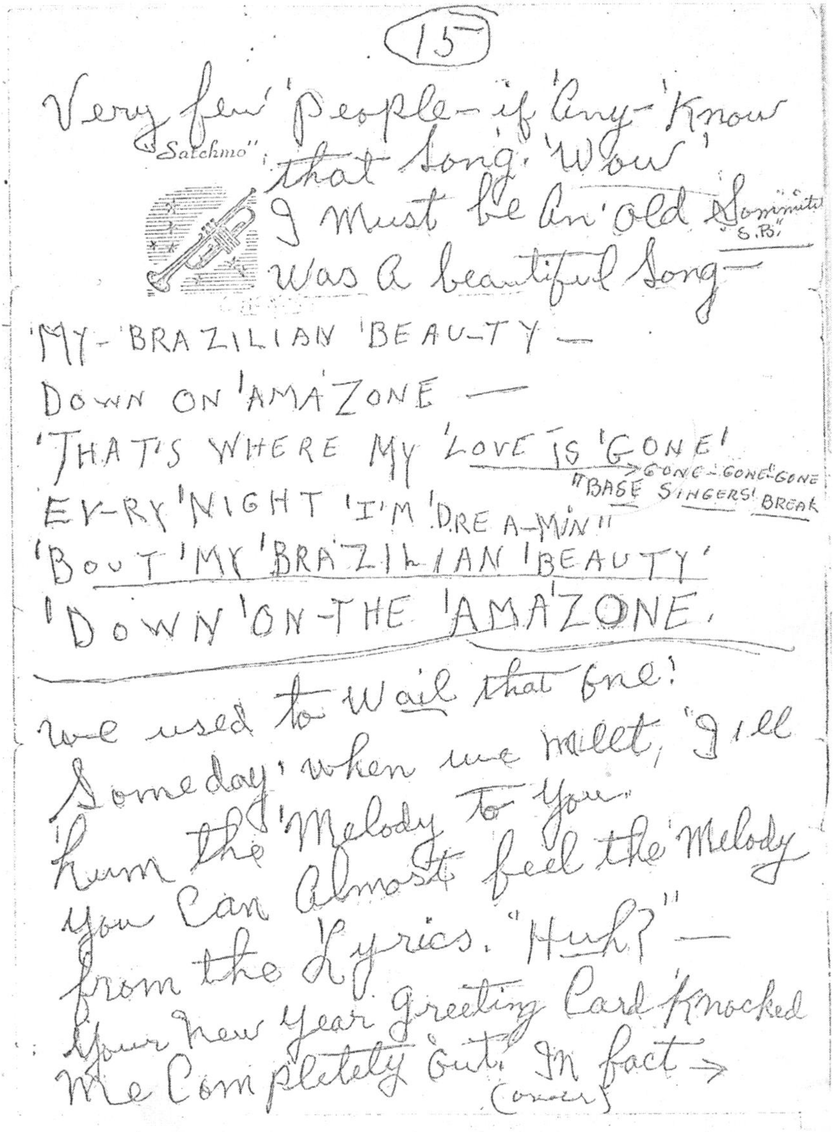

(15)

Very few people – if any – know
"Satchmo" that song. Wow
I must be an old Sommits
S.B.
Was a beautiful Song –

MY – BRAZILIAN BEAUTY –
DOWN ON AMAZONE —
'THAT'S WHERE MY LOVE IS GONE!
GONE-GONE-GONE-GONE
"BASE SINGERS' BREAK
EV-RY NIGHT I'M DREA-MIN'"
'BOUT MY BRAZILIAN BEAUTY'
'DOWN ON-THE AMAZONE.

we used to Wail that one!
Some day when we meet, I'll
hum the Melody to you.
You Can almost feel the Melody
from the Lyrics. "Huh?" –
Your New Year Greeting Card Knocked
Me Completely out. In fact →
(over)

Fig. 7. Louis Armstrong, letter to Slim Evans, September 31, 1967, page 15. Courtesy of the Louis Armstrong House Museum, Jack Bradley Collection.

Abbe Niles elaborated on this idea in his introduction to W. C. Handy's *Blues: An Anthology* (1926). In most blues performances, he wrote, "each line of the words occupies considerably less than its allotted four bars, leaving a long wait before the next sentence and phrase begin. [. . .] It affords to the improviser [. . .] a space in which his next idea may go through its period of gestation. [. . .] But [. . .] he can utilize this space, not as a hold, but as a *play-ground* in which his voice or instrument may be allowed to wander in such fantastical musical paths as he pleases."[85] Apart from Armstrong's creation of new melodic content—based on, but very much different from, the original content—it is this creative utilization of space between vocal lines, a playing around on the playground between scripted vocal lines, that characterizes his rendition of "When You're Smiling" and many other songs. Such vocal interpolations and insertions are central to African American music; here, the call-and-response interaction of different singers is incorporated into the delivery of a single performer. In a similar manner, though in a different medium and by utilizing the particular mechanics of this medium, Armstrong fills the space between written words and lines with ornaments: apostrophes, underscores, arrows, plus signs, and so forth. When asked by Ralph Gleason whether his trumpet accompaniment of classic blues singers like Ma Rainey and Bessie Smith in the early 1920s demanded a different kind of approach than his ensemble and solo work with the Fletcher Henderson orchestra, he stated: "No, just play the blues and fill in them gaps."[86] Adding a quasi-functional dimension to these gap-filling ornaments, the second "laughing" on "When You're Smiling" is sung with a slight but melodically enticing variation. The second syllable briefly slides up before falling back to the original pitch. Thus, the word "laughing" is enunciated differently each time it is pronounced, and when such variations occur in writing, indexical markers are one way to indicate such differences.

Armstrong's scat writing achieves additional complexity when it is perceived as part of his overarching autobiographics. Gary Giddins has noted that the trumpeter's facial expressions on stage are "so much a part of his vocal performances that it is impossible for anyone who has seen him to listen to his records without imagining his facial contortions."[87] As the concert Armstrong and his band recorded on a sound stage in Copenhagen in 1933 demonstrates, visual impulses have a major impact on the delivery and reception of the music.[88] As the band is playing the opening riff of "Dinah," Armstrong is bending forward. He is facing the band; his back is to the imaginary audience. His shoulders are accenting the time, his head is nodding rhythmically, and his foot is tapping the beat. He then turns to the microphone and the camera. Singing the first verse, he keeps his eyes closed. Moments before the first chorus begins, he opens them in an exaggerated fashion. All the while, his mouth has been in motion, overly articulating every note it is producing. The closing/opening eyes, the raised eyebrows, and the exaggerated lip movements create visual effects that are amplified by his vocal interjections ("babe," "ohhhh," and fragments of scat), as well as his charismatic grinning. But these facial expressions "don't correspond to any discernible development in the production of sound," as Brent Edwards notes. They invest the music with a visual strain that, while indelibly connecting the performer's body with the product of its labors, is ultimately confounding. Trying to make sense of the performance, then, viewers "confront a swinging incommensurability—an untamable, prancing set of contradictory indices that seem to be saying all too much at once."[89] In fact, they did so far beyond the Copenhagen concert or similar performances of the 1930s. Even though Armstrong was less animated in his appearances with the All Stars, the few full concert videos that exist—of shows in Belgium (1959), Sweden (1962), and Australia (1964)—capture many of the same facial expressions and body movements.

The singing and acting on these and other performances indicate that "blackness" is a partially conscious and partially unconscious intermedial spectacle. On the one hand, it evolves from a conscious playing with established performative and theatrical codes of operatic or classical music. In the Copenhagen appearance, Armstrong parodies the stiff decorum of operatic and classical music performances when he bows and greets his imaginary audience with an excessively demure "Good evening, ladies and gentlemen."[90] On the other hand, as Dan Morgenstern has observed about Armstrong's work in the recording studio, the musician "delivered all his vocals with the gestures and expressions we know from his public performances—proof positive that this was his natural way of getting into his material, not an act or affectation."[91] As a structural effect so central to Armstrong's performative practices that it emerges even when no audience is present, scat aesthetics works in writing as it does in other media: "Scat works the 'accompaniments of the utterance' in a given medium: in song, the vocal play that liquefies words; in performance, the excessive, oblique physicality of mugging; in writing, the overgrowth of punctuation, self-interruptions, asides, that exceed the purposes of emphasis, intonation, and citation."[92] In photo-collage, the creative reassembling of materials mirrors Armstrong's treatment of words in scat singing; the images he created for his scrapbooks and reel-to-reel tape covers play with media representations of his life (headlines, photographs, advertisements) and defamiliarize popular narratives by first fragmenting and then reassembling them in novel combinations.[93] In writing, scat aesthetics appears in the form of indexical markers and annotations, as well as eclectic narratives that include puns, jokes, anecdotes, reminiscences, gossip, and off-color stories, all of which contribute to the creation of a "swing" or "groove" approach to life writing. In order to make his readers feel "the New Orleans groove," as he labels it in "Jazz on a High Note," Armstrong produces what Charles Keil has called the "participatory discrepancies" of music: elements such as "inflection," "articulation," "creative tensions," "groove," "swing," and "timbre," which diverge from standard forms of enunciation and delivery and establish a sympathetic connection between performer and audience: "when I get a letter or even a 'Card from you, I feel 'Just like—I am 'right there sitting 'next to you,'" Armstrong wrote to the clarinetist Slim Evans, and he must have expected his own writing to have the same effect.[94]

Syncopation and swing release both lyric and melody from the strictness of musical script and free up energy constrained by the rules and structures of European classical music. Conversely, Armstrong's autobiographical writings are freed in some sense from the soundless and static nature of written text through the proliferation of indexical stimuli that evoke his aural and visual presence. Maybe this is what Armstrong meant in his letter to Glaser when he commented onomatopoetically about his broken typewriter, which had fallen out of his luggage the previous day: "Tch, Tch, isn't it a Drag? And I wanted so badly to swing a lot of *Type Writing*."[95] The verb "swing," as it is used in this sentence, indicates a personalized, nonstandard approach to typewriting, including not just aberrant content (Armstrong's unusual life story) and idiosyncratic orthography and style, but also the act of punching letters onto the page via the mechanical medium of the typewriter: hands swinging rhythmically over the typewriter's keys, moving to the music emanating from the record or tape player, and extending Armstrong's thoughts to the page. Dan Morgenstern implies such a dimension: Armstrong's "approach to language, spelling, and syntax—even his *touch* on the typewriter—is inimitable, and as distinctive as his handwriting."[96] Since the material conditions of the typewriter make it difficult to translate this *touch* onto the page—a manipulation of letters can only be achieved by hitting the keys with different degrees of strength—Armstrong uses jive language and signifying techniques as well as spelling, syntax, indexical markers, and annotations to achieve in writing what is achieved more easily in music: the rhythmic drive of swing and the semantic flexibilities of scat.[97]

In his early study of jazz, Sidney Finkelstein draws attention to the differences between nineteenth-century classical music and twentieth-century jazz: "The tendency of nineteenth century classical music was to erase from the listener's mind all consciousness of the medium of expression, and instead to arouse in the mind a sense of pictorial color or shifting psychological mood."[98] While classical musicians underwent years of training to eliminate any unwanted sonic traces of their instruments, for instance, scratches, harshness, and slurs, jazz musicians inflected their playing with quasi-vocal qualities and percussive elements that draw attention to both the musician (the mind and body operating the instrument) and the instrument that mediates personal expression. This difference in musical approach forcefully illustrates the shift from the European tradition of classical music, where the notated score of the composer generally represents the supreme work of art and where solo musicians and orchestras bring the composition to life, to the modern and substantially African American ethos of the performing musician as the originator of new, and frequently improvised, sonic creations. Yet once the performances of jazz musicians were captured on sound recordings, the result was "a schism between sound and source, between sound and environment," a splitting off of the performer's physical body and all its cultural connotations from the sonic channel of communication.[99]

Armstrong's creative response to this schism was twofold. He soon learned to capitalize on the peculiar sound of his voice and developed a series of unique vocal mannerisms that allowed him, through scat delivery and jive commentary, to break apart the unity of singer and vocal line and foreground the body and consciousness of a singer who is able to use his source material as a vehicle for self-performance. By investing original vocal lines with grunts, moans, and other vocal utterances beyond the enunciation of the scripted notes, he heightened the physicality of his voice and emphasized the music-producing body to which this voice always inevitably points. Roland Barthes has called this phenomenon "le grain de la voix" (the grain of the voice) and has argued that a singer's voice does not so much reflect a singer's personality, but rather reflects his or her specific body and the ways in which this body produces sound. Significantly, however, the physiognomy of the human voice is determined by a complicated mixture of physical factors (the shape of the oral cavity, tongue muscles, teeth); learned techniques (enunciation); and the cultural contexts in which it is honed, presented, and received. It is especially the heterogeneous reception of Armstrong's singing as the product of a racially charged black male body but also as a signifier of a modern black consciousness and masculinity that provided the discursive field that Armstrong would eventually enter by speaking and writing about his body and soul.[100] His turn to jazz autobiography, then, can be seen as an attempt to reconnect sound and source of recorded musical performance through self-referential narratives that reinscribe sonic production with personal meaning and claim authority over the interpretation of his life and music. Yet a similar schism between sound and source appears in the context of autobiographical writing, where the printed letters truncate the sounds of oral speech and where multisensory experiences are reduced to the monosensory experience of reading silent text.

Armstrong's writings therefore seek to reconnect the physical body of the writer and the sonic sensations of the music with the spoken word. In the culture of Armstrong's formative years, music and language were equal parts of an "oral, mobile, warm, personally interactive lifeworld," as Walter Ong has noted about oral cultures, while the print and media culture of the North, represented by the typewriter, "isolated [written words] from the fuller context in which spoken words came into being. [. . .] Spoken utterance is addressed by a real, living person to another real, living person or real, living persons, at a specific time in a real setting which includes always much more than mere words."[101] In Armstrong's writings, indexical markers, annotations, and insertions strive to overcome the erasure of the creator and his audience from his work by infusing the printed words on the page with the voice and body of the performer. On the level of content, the frequent anecdotes about physical needs and desires—eating, digesting, and sex—reinstitute the bodily functions and physical presence of the writer in the reader's mind. The "somatic excess of th[e] body" that Edwards finds in Armstrong's stage performances is recuperated, or at least s(t)imulated, in writing through these markers, annotations, and insertions.[102]

What is more, the root of "scat" is "scatology": the obsession with excretory functions and the study of fecal matter. In this sense, Armstrong is not only a master of vocal and written scat; he is also a master scatologist and literal bullshitter. Take his lifelong obsession with herbal laxatives, which manifested itself in countless references to Pluto Water and Swiss Kriss and even resulted in a privately produced but publicly circulated postcard depicting him on the toilet with his pants down: "Satchmo Slogan—Leave It All Behind Ya."[103] In "Jewish Family," Armstrong explicitly connects excretion with music: "I *made* it to the *Throne* in time. And All of a *Sudden*, music came—Riffs—*Arpeggios—Biff notes—etc*. Sounded just like ("Applause") Sousa's Band playing "Stars and Stripes Forever," returning to the *Channel* of the Song—*Three Times*. Wonderful." In his letter to L/Cpl. Villec, he establishes a similar connection when he talks about listening to his own recorded music: "And when I am 'Shaving or 'Sitting on the 'Throne with 'Swiss Kriss' in me—*That* Music 'sure 'brings out those 'Riffs 'Right Along with 'Swiss Kriss." Elsewhere, he speaks of "the Swinging Actions of dear old Swiss Kriss," and in one of his taped monologues, he declares: "As long as I can hit that john every morning from Swiss Kriss and hit them biff notes, I'm straight."[104]

Brent Edwards finds in passages like this "[a]n ethics of discard ('Leave It All Behind Ya') that also provides the foundation for a poetics."[105] In this sense, the variously spelled phrase "Did that come out of me?"/"Diddat Come Outa Me?" takes on a double meaning. Armstrong used this phrase many times to record mock surprise about his own eloquence: "Thats why I explained everything *thoroughly* . . . ump . . . Didthat come outa mee??"; "I just hadn't had the time to go over to Rudy Muck's place, and 'Intercede . . . 'Ump—"Diddat Come Outa Mee?"; "And if you get a little time drop 'Ol Satch a line or two . . . 'T,would, be most' 'APPRECIATABLE. . . . 'ump,—Did dat come Outa Mee?"; "A letter from you would be most "appreciateable." Ump. Did that come outa me?" To Glaser, he wrote in a telegram: "We are put here on this earth for humanitarily purpose. (Hmp.) Did that come out of me?"[106] Chatting with journalist Gilbert Millstein, he remarked about his trumpet playing: "Did you hear what came out of that horn?"[107] Films and photographs have captured this expression of surprise. When Armstrong and his orchestra performed "I Can't Give You Anything But Love" in *Jam Session* (dir. Charles Barton, 1944), movie viewers saw him listening attentively to the saxophone and clarinet solos, cupping his ear and turning it toward the instruments; a promotional photo from the early 1930s shows him looking into the bell of his own trumpet, with his face registering pleasant surprise.[108] Such visual depictions not only recall Whitney Balliett's characterization of jazz as the "sound of surprise" but also capture Armstrong's transmedial self-understanding.[109] Everything he produces is connected not just through the creative mind that conceives of his productions, but also through the body that physically brings forth music, words, semen, and excrement. Armstrong cements this connection by employing the same word, "wailin'," for music making, love-making, and visiting the throne. In "Satchmo Story," for instance, he moves from his mother's explanation of friends' premature deaths ("They didn't *shit enough*") to his musical and sexual prowess: "I am blowing better and twice as strong [in 1959] as I was when I was in my twenties . . . Well I won't mention my sex sessions these days, because I hate to be called a braggadosha. . . . Wow . . . Did that come *outa Mee.* . . ."[110] Armstrong's favorite topics therefore illustrate the extent to which "[e]ach man has his own music *bubbling up inside* him and—quite *naturally*—different ones will *let it out* in various ways.'"[111]

That Armstrong's crude bathroom humor, his love of sexually explicit jokes, his haphazardly taped photo-collages, and his heavily indexed and annotated writings seem to stand in stark contrast with the brilliant sound and structural coherence of his trumpet playing is one of the central mysteries of Armstrong's autobiographics. Despite his devotion to Joe Oliver, he did not invest his trumpet playing with any kind of freak effects or the growling for which his mentor had become famous and that would have enabled him to translate fecal humor into musical expression. One explanation may be that Armstrong's love of opera and the sweet sounds of the Guy Lombardo orchestra influenced his musical aesthetics in ways that simply found no equivalent in terms of a social ideal according to which bathroom activities would have been off-limits for polite conversation and formal autobiographical expression.[112] At least according to his writings and public statements, Armstrong was much more eager to cross musical boundaries and incorporate a vast array of influences from other styles and cultures than he was interested in transcending his social background and racial heritage by embracing an ethos of upward mobility. Another explanation would be that the interfaces among autobiographical speech and writing, photo-collage, and musical performance seldom emerge from the direct translation of material from one medium to another but more often reside within a larger expressive economy, Armstrong's autobiographics, in which trumpet playing has a privileged role but is always reintegrated with other forms of expression, including verbal production in the recording studio and on stage.

Whatever we think of Armstrong's trumpet creations, it is obvious that the trumpet was more than just a musical instrument for him. One of his German biographers observed: "As he cared for his body, he cared for his trumpet by rinsing it daily with hot water, then drying and oiling it. The mouthpieces he stored carefully in a leather pouch in order to protect them from dirt, hazardous bacteria, and flying insects. He handled the instrument like a part of his body and his body like an instrument."[113] The trumpet, the typewriter, and even the scotch tape with which he created his photo-collages were instruments that became his "second nature, a psychological part of himself," in Walter Ong's terms; or, as Armstrong himself explained: "When I'm blowing, it's like me and my horn are the same thing."[114] That he is rarely depicted without his trumpet on photos or on film and that he referred to his instrument in anthropomorphic terms as a living being—"ain't that right, little trumpet?" he asks on one recording, and he christened his trumpet "Satchmo"—suggests an understanding of the trumpet as a medial extension in Marshall McLuhan's sense of the term: a means through which Armstrong extended his self to his audiences and sought, to quote Ralph Ellison, "to make life swing."[115] Speaking metaphorically, one could say that by making his life swing in the public sphere, Armstrong created a series of powerful resonances and reverberations. He positioned himself within a cultural poetics that shaped the public reception of his life and music in significant and often unacknowledged ways. The next chapter analyzes the productive ambiguities that emerged from this poetics.

CHAPTER 4

"A happy go lucky
sort of type of fellow"

The Productive Ambiguities of Minstrel Sounding

The Louis Armstrong House Museum owns an anonymous watercolor caricature that depicts Armstrong with his Jewish manager Joe Glaser (ca. 1950). Armstrong is grinning somewhat uneasily, flashing a row of white teeth, holding his trumpet and clutching in his hands the white handkerchief with which he routinely wiped the sweat off his face during live performances. Behind him, with his right hand placed firmly on his shoulder, stands Glaser, who is hovering over his protégé and is urging him toward an imaginary stage and audience.[1] On August 2, 1955, Armstrong described a similar scene in a letter to Glaser, recalling the New Orleans drummer Black Benny Williams's advice to "always have a white man (WHO LiKE YOU) and Can + will Put his Hand on your shoulder and say—"THis is "'MY" NiGGER" and, Can't Nobody Harm' Ya.""[2]

Another version of this anecdote appears in Richard Meryman's interview for *Life* magazine: "And then he [this time it is Slippers, a honky-tonk bouncer] said, 'Always keep a white man behind you that'll put his hand on you and say, "That's my nigger."' Years later I told that to Joe Glaser, my ofay manager, and he said, 'You're nuts.'"[3] Armstrong related the anecdote yet another time in a letter to his biographer Max Jones:

> Slippers was a bad M-F (Mother for you) but dropped everything when he learned I was leaving them [the black people of Armstrong's New Orleans neighborhood] and the Honky Tonk [where Armstrong played music and where Slippers worked]. He came right over to me and said "When you go up north, Dipper, be sure and get yourself a white man that will put his hand on your shoulder and say 'This is my nigger.'" Those were his exact words. He was a crude sonofabitch but he loved me and my music. And he was right then because the white man was Joe Glaser. Dig, Gate?[4]

On the story level of this anecdote, Armstrong is saying that his relationship with Glaser is a professional necessity. He had learned early in his life that a black man needs a white boss to protect and promote him. In return, the boss, who may be said to own the black man (the possessive pronoun that prefixes the racial epithet in "*my* nigger" leaves little doubt about that), reaps much of the profits of his work. This situation strongly resembles the argument advanced by nineteenth-century apologists of slavery like George Fitzhugh, whose *Cannibals All! or, Slaves without Masters* (1857) defines the slave master's role as one of "superintend[ing] and provid[ing] for the slave in sickness, in health, infancy and old age" and predicts that "if he will feed and clothe, and house him properly, guard his morals, and treat him kindly and humanely, he will make his slaves happy and profitable."[5] The benevolent and fatherlike slave master justifies his legal ownership of the slave by offering him protection as his property: "Joe Glaser [. . .] protected me and I got along with the white folk all right," Armstrong is quoted by Jones and Chilton.[6] On the level of narrative discourse, the anecdote raises questions about performative context: why is Armstrong recalling this anecdote, to whom does he address it, and why does he tell it so many times and in these specific ways? In the letter to Glaser, he attributes the advice to Black Benny, making sure that Glaser is not explicitly associated with the white patron of the tale. In the Meryman interview, he connects the "ofay" Glaser with the "white man" by proxy; Glaser's reaction—"You're nuts"—indicates that the manager suspects that he might be the real addressee of Armstrong's signifying. Finally, in the letter to Jones, which Armstrong wrote late in his life when Glaser had already passed away, the connection with Glaser is made explicit: "the white man was Joe Glaser."[7]

Yet the watercolor drawing and the various versions of the anecdote are only two of many verbal and visual depictions of Armstrong's relationship with his white managers. One photograph from 1949 shows Glaser as he is actually placing his right hand on Armstrong's shoulder. A second photograph, taken much earlier, indicates that the visual narrative that accompanies the Slippers/Black Benny anecdote is not confined to Glaser. The shot from the early 1930s depicts Armstrong's then-manager Johnny Collins standing next to his protégé and holding on to his arm in a gesture that recalls the statement about the white man's hand on his shoulder that the musician reiterated so frequently. As Michael Cogswell notes, "Curiously, in almost every snapshot Collins is touching Louis, e.g., a hand on the elbow or an arm around him."[8]

Apparently, Armstrong found nothing wrong with the power Joe Glaser wielded over his career (he was less fond of Collins). Tape box #86 from his reel collection, for instance, features the heads of a smiling Armstrong and a friendly-looking Glaser. Underneath their heads, Armstrong pasted a cut-out photograph of a trumpet, his fingers nestling around the valves.[9] It is difficult to read this and similar photo-collages with a great deal of precision, but the image seems to illustrate a lasting gratitude to his manager. Furthermore, "Jewish Family" is dedicated to the ailing Glaser, who would pass away soon: "I dedicate this book / to my manager and pal / Mr. Joe Glaser / The best Friend / That I've ever had / May the Lord Bless Him / And 'Keep Him Always." Armstrong wrote this statement when Glaser was in the hospital; after Glaser's death, he crossed out the final line, added the words "Watch Over Him Always," and signed this dedication with the words "His Boy + disciple who <u>loved</u> him <u>dearily</u>."[10] These and similar statements express a good amount of gratitude that Armstrong must have felt for Glaser's managing skills. In his letter to Slim Evans from September 31, 1967, and in his interview with Richard Meryman, he happily recalls how Glaser featured him as a star attraction with Carroll Dickerson's Orchestra in the 1920s, putting his name on the marquee and announcing him as "The World's Greatest Trumpeter." In a letter to Little Brother Montgomery, he expresses his love for Glaser ("I love that man") and acknowledges that "[h]e was the greatest for me and all the spades that he handled." In the "Goffin Notebooks," he justifies his selection of Glaser as his manager by stating that he "just *impressed* me different than the other Bosses I've worked for. He seemed to understand Colored people so much."[11]

Commentary about the white boss/black worker relationship also appears regularly in Armstrong's correspondence: "I'm supposed to do a concert, so Mr. Glaser and Leonard Feather sez. They're the bosses"; "I'll have to check up on it and talk it over with the big Magaffy (Mr. Glaser)"; "With me, Joe's words were law"; "First I must write my Bossman, Mr. Glaser."[12] As a writer versed in the intricacies of jive, Armstrong routinely used verbal play to cloud his intentions. The only dialect word in the first sentence quoted above, "sez," is a self-conscious dialectal inflection that introduces a sense of ironic self-awareness, and "the big Magaffy" is a humorous phrase that deflates Glaser's position of power, leaving unresolved the question of whether Armstrong is simply enjoying the verbal play for its own sake or whether he is couching criticism in humorous terms. Such

Fig. 8. Louis Armstrong, "Louis Armstrong + the Jewish Family in New Orleans, La., the Year of 1907," March 31, 1969–70, page 3. Courtesy of the Louis Armstrong House Museum.

generally playful depictions of the relationship with Glaser, however, are accompanied by less benign statements. In a later letter, Armstrong wrote angrily: "Dear Mr Glaser" please don't ignore this letter. I just don't like to be ignored. I think that I am *entitled* a little bit *some* what *as* sort of being treated like a man instead just a god dam child all the time. *That* we can forget."[13] Talking to Meryman, he praised his manager first—"I've always known my manager Joe Glaser is the only cat that dug Louis Armstrong"—but ended the sentence on a more dubious note: "like a baby or a little dog always knows the one who ain't slapping him on the rear all the time. So I go all out to do everything I possibly can to keep him satisfied."[14] Through Armstrong's aural-oral narrative technique, the noun "cat" introduces the semantic field of pets, which is picked up later in the sentence by the phrase "little dog," while the verb "dug" sonically prefigures Armstrong's self-characterization as a "dog." The statement recalls an essay by Zora Neale Hurston in which she criticizes white patronage and control over African American cultural production. The piece, titled "The 'Pet' Negro System," is written in the style of a black sermon ("Brothers and Sisters, I take my text this morning from the Book of Dixie"). It was published in the *American Mercury* in 1943 and identifies the logic behind interracial relationships between white mentors and black protégés similar to that of Armstrong and Glaser as part of a system of racial subjugation and submission that had determined the literary productions of black writers from the very beginning and that was still operative, at least to an extent, in the 1940s.[15]

In the letter cited above (Aug. 2, 1955), Armstrong makes a series of demands, mostly payments for his mistress and friends, which Glaser must fulfill if the trumpeter is to go on an overseas tour. In order to keep Glaser satisfied, Armstrong addresses him as *"ol Man,"* "daddy," "Pops," and "Boss," the first three of which are jive terms that pay tribute to Glaser's nominal power over the musician (they are also terms of familial endearment in Armstrong's vocabulary) and the last of which alludes to the racial semantics of the Southern Jim Crow regime.[16] The closing statement of the letter, however, indicates that Armstrong must have seen his relationship to Glaser as a collaboration mediated through a form of class- and race-conscious role-play that resonated with the cultural discourses and racial stereotypes of their times: ""HM . . . It has been such a real Pleasure writing to you, Boss. Hope, I didn't bore you. Just wanted to let you know. As long as I am Slated to blow this Trumpet don't spare the Horses. I love the instrument. *Then too*—the *loot* looks good in my pocket." Armstrong demands remuneration for his trumpet work ("don't spare the Horses"), while the performativity of the letter is amplified by the noun "loot," a slang term for money that also suggests an act of appropriating goods from the economically and politically powerful.[17]

The musician's relationship with Glaser represents a microscopic version of a larger racial discourse. Armstrong's letters, autobiographies, and spoken statements about Glaser, as well as the visual narrative of their relationship, recognize the power of a particular form of racial interaction, one in which a grinning and subservient black musician strives to satisfy his benevolent but stern white owner, who acts as a father figure to the black man-child and is "<u>loved dearly</u>" in return. The historical dimension of Glaser's paternal role as manager and patron and the quasi-filial adoration it produces is illustrated by a painting the manager put up in his office, which depicted a Southern plantation scene complete with black slave musicians expressing gratitude to their white master.[18] Armstrong's designated part in this Southern plantation play is clearly indicated by Glaser's admonition that he "sing and make faces and smile. Smile, goddamn it. Give it to them [the audience]." This is not to say that Glaser did not respect, or even admire, Armstrong—he signed one of his letters to the musician "Your great admirer and pal"—but the fact that *Time* magazine's cover story on Armstrong picked up on the slavery discourse in 1949, when it interpreted the fact that Armstrong called his manager "'Mister' Glaser" as "a kind of plantation politeness," underscores the volatility and pervasiveness of this discourse of black submissiveness.[19]

One should note here that white patronage of black writers and artists had a long history in American culture, reaching back to the tutoring that the slave poetess Phillis Wheatley received from her mistress Susanna Wheatley, as well as to Frederick Douglass's indebtedness to William Lloyd Garrison, and resurfacing in the twentieth century in the form of Carl Van Vechten's sponsoring of the black arts during the Harlem Renaissance. In the fields of literature and ethnographic research, Langston Hughes and Zora Neale Hurston depended on white patrons, while musicians such as Count Basie and Billie Holiday were promoted by the Vanderbilt heir John Hammond. Armstrong's strategic responses to Glaser's patronage were not unprecedented either. Signing her letters to her philanthropist patron, Charlotte Osgood Mason, with "Your Pickaninny, Zora," Hurston showed her awareness of the troubled history of paternalism (here: maternalism) and patronage. Like Hurston, who played the stereotypical black child to Mason's "mistress," Armstrong sometimes played the "darky boy" to Glaser's "boss," confessing once that "[a]sking me about Joe is like askin' a chile 'bout its daddy."[20]

Armstrong's communication with and about Glaser reveals a simultaneity of contradictory messages that unfold their meanings within an intermedial cultural poetics of blackface minstrelsy. This poetics includes actual and figurative forms of blackface, and it fundamentally shaped the ways in which Armstrong devised his public self-presentation. What is more, it is part of the medial glue that holds together the musical, textual, and visual components of his autobiographics. While often recognized by his critics, it is hardly ever unpacked in terms of its power over the construction and reception of jazz and the intermedial Satchmo persona in particular. James Lincoln Collier, one of Armstrong's more notorious biographers, offers a pseudo-psychological explanation for Armstrong's use of minstrel-related material when he finds a "paradox in Armstrong's nature": an affliction of insecurity and a "relentless, sickening, interior assault on his self-respect" that could be alleviated "temporarily [. . .] by performing, standing up there before those dozens or thousands or millions of people and playing and singing and smiling and mugging and soaking up the healing applause."[21] According to this interpretation, the musician recorded and performed postminstrel songs such as "Shine," "Snowball," and "Shoe Shine Boy" because "he seems to have *liked* to sing them. It was a way of ingratiating himself with whites, who, increasingly through the 1930s, became his major audience. He was once again the black man looking for the white to put his hand on his shoulder and say, 'This is my nigger.'"[22] In his recent reassessment of Armstrong, Terry Teachout is much more cautious about the musician's personal motivations, but when he concludes that Armstrong possessed "a streak of shy passivity" and an "unwillingness to take charge of the direction of his professional life [that] was in part the result of his having been born at a time when it was taken for granted by most whites that blacks were inferiors," he points to the psychological legacies of slavery and institutionalized racism but stops short of delving into the cultural complexities of blackface minstrelsy, which transmitted these legacies into the realm of popular entertainment and back.[23]

Reconstructing the specific cultural locations and historical moments in which Armstrong operated and in which his work was received can reveal the more devious interconnections between twentieth-century constructions of popular black selfhood and the restraints and possibilities that shaped such constructions. After all, as William Mahar has argued, blackface minstrelsy and the urban culture industry emerged at the same time, in the early 1830s, and "[b]lackface minstrelsy was one of the primary paradigms for the whole enterprise recognized now as the popular culture industry."[24] Armstrong's stage performances, musical recordings, and especially his autobiographical narratives are self-reflexive engagements with racial stereotypes, and to make sense of their tendency to point to blackface minstrelsy's sounds, sights, and narratives also means to account for the genealogy of figures like the Sambo, as well as for Armstrong's modern reinterpretation of this figure as Satchmo. This chapter does so by tracing the Satchmo figure back to nineteenth- and early twentieth-century depictions of the minstrel Sambo and its "coon" descendants; by looking at the contexts in which Armstrong would have encountered and even evoked the minstrel poetics; and by analyzing musical, visual, and verbal references in his oeuvre that create linkages to various types of minstrel representation.

Midway in *Satchmo*, Armstrong reminisces about America's entry into the First World War and about the effects the fighting in Europe was having on the lives and careers of New Orleans musicians. He begins by noting that the New Orleans authorities pursued a "work or fight" policy that was problematic for musicians because dance halls, honky-tonks, and theaters had been shut down and had left few work opportunities for those who wanted to avoid the draft. Without his regular musical engagements, Armstrong was struggling to make ends meet, and joining the armed forces entered his mind: "I was perfectly willing to go into the Army, but they were only drafting from the age of twenty-one to twenty-five and I was only seventeen." The Navy was his next choice: "I tried to get into the Navy, but they checked up on my birth certificate and threw me out. I kept up my hope and at one enlistment office a soldier told me to come back in a year. He said that if the war was still going on I could capture the Kaiser and win a great, big prize. 'Wouldn't that be swell,' I thought. 'Capturing the Kaiser and win the war.' Believe me, I lived to see that day."[25]

This is all Armstrong has to say about the issue. When we consider the significance of the war experience for African Americans fighting in Europe, including the boost of self-confidence that the sight of returning black war heroes instilled among the people back home and the violence the black soldiers' return spawned in many Southern communities, Armstrong's anecdote appears strangely comical, oblivious to the weight of its subject. This is bolstered by the fact that the well-known African American band leader James Reese Europe had fought with a regiment of colored soldiers. Returning victoriously from France, he and his orchestra, the 369th U.S. Infantry "Hell Fighters" Band, were celebrated and paraded around New York City in 1919. Armstrong was certainly aware of the Hell Fighters since he mentions them on one of his many tape recordings.[26] Moreover, in the postwar climate of the early 1950s, when he told the anecdote, the "Double V" campaign (double victory: abroad against Nazi Germany and at home against racial segregation and discrimination) and the racial integration of the armed forces were still present in the minds of many African Americans.[27] So why does Armstrong present this historical moment without the political verve one could expect him to muster?

James Lincoln Collier offers an insufficient interpretation: "Although in *Satchmo* Armstrong maunders on piously about wanting to fight the Kaiser, in fact he was determined to avoid being drafted."[28] By misreading the tone of the anecdote, which is largely humorous, perhaps self-mocking, but certainly not pious or maundering, and by reading the anecdote as an indication of Armstrong's character rather than an autobiographical performance, Collier misses its larger point. This point is the treatment the young Armstrong received from the undoubtedly white soldier at the enlistment office and the lack of explicit critical commentary offered by the autobiographer more than thirty years after the event. Comic depictions of ignorant black soldiers had been popular since the Civil War, and it is only logical that the soldier at the enlistment office adhered to the cultural stereotypes inherent in such depictions. During the Civil War, slaves had fled from the Confederate territory, and some of them had joined the Union army. Minstrels discovered in these soldiers a fitting object of ridicule, casting them as cowards and fools in uniform. In the "Black Brigade" (1860s), for example, a black soldier vowed to fight for the Union army "by word ob [*sic*] mouth," but not for "death and glory"; the popular farce "Raw Recruits" (1862) showed black soldiers jumping into a lake when they were ordered to "Fall In" and answering an officer's command "Eyes Right" with "I'se right too."[29] Especially poignant is the title of Charles White's minstrel play *The Recruiting Office, an Ethiopian Sketch in Two Scenes* (1874), which describes a setting similar to the one in which Armstrong meets the soldier at the enlistment office. When the soldier says that Armstrong "could capture the Kaiser and win a great, big prize," he is obviously poking fun at the supposed naiveté of the youngster by drawing on deeply entrenched minstrel material. The German "Reich" becomes "the Kaiser" in a process of synecdochic simplification, suggesting that a black boy from the American South could singlehandedly win a world war, and the boy is promised a prize if he entertains his white master (for whom the white soldier stands in). But why is this narrative affirmed by the autobiographer's reaction long after the event had occurred? " 'Wouldn't that be swell,' " Armstrong had allegedly thought. " 'Capturing the Kaiser and win the war.' "

The answer to this question lies at the center of this chapter: Armstrong's account generates productive ambiguities through a process of minstrel sounding that takes place within, and receives its energy from, a specific cultural intermediality. The practice of "minstrel sounding" connotes what Houston A. Baker has called "speaking (or *sounding*) 'modern' in Afro-America" in his analysis of Booker T. Washington and Charles Chesnutt. Minstrel sounding means communicating on two levels at once: conjuring up the sounds and sights of blackface minstrelsy while indicating, often indirectly and implicitly, an awareness of one's speaking position within this discourse.[30] In the passage from *Satchmo*, ambiguities are produced by the evocation of minstrel sounds and images (the soldier's remarks) and the autobiographer's unresolved stance toward these sounds and images. Armstrong not only presents the soldier's remarks but also describes his reaction to them, and this reaction follows the minstrel gaze (the young Armstrong thinks the idea is a swell one) while simultaneously questioning it: the reference to the "great, big prize" is dropped, and the comment "Believe me, I lived to see that day" is added, making room for an ironic tone that may have been more pronounced in the lost part of the manuscript, where apostrophes, underscores, rhetorical questions, and insertions probably complicated narrative signification. Later in *Satchmo*, Armstrong makes reference to "[t]he Kaiser's monkey business" and describes the Armistice as "the day the United States and the rest of the Allies cut the German Kaiser and his army a brand 'noo one," which adds a moment of vernacular jiving to the minstrel codes evoked earlier in the text.[31] Instead of believing that Armstrong's account reveals his disposition toward World War I or identifies his allegedly cowardly character, as Collier does when he underestimates both the musician's social position in the late 1910s, when the encounter took place, and the performativity of the autobiographical memory, which mobilizes the minstrel poetics and a sense of black jiving in the mid-1950s, it is more productive to read this account in Houston A. Baker's terms as evidence of Armstrong's "mastery of the minstrel mask" and of his "primary move in Afro-American discursive modernism": his ability to satisfy minstrel expectations and, at the same time, to signal—however slightly—that there is more to the story than such expectations may suggest.[32]

The ability to detect these and similar moments of minstrel sounding in Armstrong's performances depends on a historical awareness of the Sambo stereotype. Sambo was one of the most prominent racial fantasies of the nineteenth century. "Sambo was found everywhere, in every nook and cranny of the popular culture," Joseph Boskin notes; he was the "first truly American entertainer" and can be taken as a master code for various intermedial and multigeneric codifications of comic "blackness."[33] An early reference appeared in Frederick Reynolds's theatrical comedy *Laugh When You Can* (1799), which featured a character named Sambo (a freed slave, servant, and musician), as well as the theatrical device of blacking up: Sambo is played by a white actor wearing black makeup. Sambo also appeared as a title character in *Sambo and Toney: A Dialogue in Three Parts* (1808) and as a character in two English dramas that played in New York, Isaac Jackman's *The Divorce* (1781) and John Murdock's *The Triumph of Love; or, Happy Reconciliation* (1795). Dale Cockrell estimates that between 1751 and 1843 more than twenty thousand theatrical productions featuring blackface could be seen on American stages, many of which would have included Sambos or Samboesque characters.[34]

The kind of racial cross-dressing performed by white actors such as Thomas D. Rice or Dan Emmett, who slipped into the role of the black slave or ex-slave and offered comic simulations of a perceived "blackness," was commercially successful in the minstrel shows of the nineteenth century, but it went beyond the historical context of the Jacksonian era and the plantation South. In fact, it determined popular representations of "blackness" until well into the twentieth century and shaped stage codes for generations of postbellum and post-Reconstruction black actors and musicians. And while "blackness" certainly was not always the most important issue in the minstrel shows, the blackened faces of the actors constituted an expressive code through which the frolicking black body of the singing, dancing, joking, laughing, and music-making slave and "darky" entertainer was universally marked.[35]

The depiction of blacks as servants and musicians soon became a staple of the American stage. In the late 1820s and throughout the 1830s, the period in which blackface entertainment underwent a process of Americanization, the English black servant became the slave of the American South, and the black characters of the "legitimate" stage morphed into the caricatured physique of the blackfaced minstrel.[36] Blackface Sambos appeared in skits and songs with titles such as "Sambos 'Dress to be Bred 'run" (early 1830s), "The Jolly Sambo" (1840s), "Sambo's Lamentation or Dinah Mae" (1852), "Sambo's Right to Be Killt" (1864), "Sambo's Invitation" (1869), and "Sambo and His Banjo" (1890s). Outside of the theater, the Sambo figure became associated with the role of the "performing slave," who entertained master and mistress by singing, dancing, and joking and who familiarized whites with the slave's "Samboisms," as the English comedian John Bernard called them.[37] Variations of this figure can be found in many cultures and historical periods, but in the years in which Armstrong made his entry onto the national stage, it was Al Jolson's blackface alter ego Gus from Broadway musicals such as *Sinbad* (1918), *Bombo* (1921), and *Big Boy* (1925) who embodied the submissive but witty servant figure most famously. Significantly, Jolson in blackface sings minstrel and neominstrel tunes such as "Swanee" and "My Mammy" and anticipates Armstrong's film role in the 1938 venture *Going Places*; in *Big Boy*, Jolson plays a jockey, while in *Going Places*, Armstrong is a stable boy taming a famous racehorse with his music.

Popular nineteenth-century depictions of the Sambo as an essentially funny and frolicsome character tended to deny the strategic uses to which slaves and slave performers put their knowledge of their masters' behavioral expectations by "laughing at the man."[38] The wish to give credence to this denial and the increasing need to justify slavery produced a literature filled with references to the Sambo, who soon became a ubiquitous character in Southern letters.[39] In combination with theatrical presentations, musical compositions, and graphic illustrations, these literary depictions forcefully established a series of Sambo codes: "Indolent, faithful, humorous, loyal, dishonest, superstitious, improvident, and musical, Sambo was indelibly a clown and congenitally docile. Characteristically a house servant, Sambo had so much love and affection for his master that he was almost filio-pietistic; his loyalty was all-consuming and self-immolating."[40] Sambo's language and music, as well as his nappy hair, thick lips, bulging eyes, and exaggerated gestures, expressed racial codes that not only assigned intellectual inferiority, speech deficiencies, and other derogatory attributes to African Americans but also constituted the discursive terrain on which Americans (and Europeans as well) discussed and understood the meanings, sounds, and sights of "blackness." These racial codes were long-lived, widespread, and intermedial. They functioned as "the extender of Sambo in both high and low culture"; they "welded the image of the black male to the material culture [and] laid the foundation for its entry into the electronic media of the following century."[41]

Satchmo, Armstrong's popular nickname, evokes these codes in ways that illuminate what Robert O'Meally has described as "Armstrong's complicated place in American cultural iconography."[42] In "Jewish Family," Armstrong explains how he received this name:

> New Orleans always was a town where Nick Names Originates. Even in my young days I accumulated several Nick Names, Given by your little pals and people who likes you. [. . .] I have Originated Several Names for my playmates, and others as I grew up through the years. And they're *all* in good Faith. In fact—some of those names strikes me *funny*. [. . .] Of course "Satchmo" is here to stay. According to my Fans, all over the world. And I love it. Sort of a trade mark. [. . .] The *Dipper Mouth* is still around whenever I go to New Orleans and Run into some of the Old timers. [. . .] Here's some Nick Names that very few fans, I doubt ever heard of. Such as—*Boat Nose*—Hammock Face—*Rhythm Jaws*—Satchelmouth—like a Dr's valise. In fact, I think that's how the name *Satchmo* was Originated. An Englishman who met me at the 'Boat in 1932, when I first went to England [. . .]—he shook my hand Saying "Hello *Satchmo*"—*Man* I flipped. That was *my* first time hearing this name. I shook his hand saying *watcha* say *Gate*? [. . .] I had to talk to my Trombone player [. . .]—I said to him, "The Editor of the Melody Maker Magazine just Shook my hand and called me *Satchmo* when my name was *Satchelmouth* before I came over here, why?" [. . .] He said to me, "Because the man *thinks* you've got *Mo Mouth*." Hmm. So *that's* how it happened. And I've been *Satchmo* ever since. You see how one can acquire a name that sticks.[43]

Like many of his favorite anecdotes, Armstrong told this one many times, for instance to the jazz aficionado Joachim-Ernst Behrendt in an interview that accompanied the screening of the All Stars' 1962 Goodyear Tire concert performance on German television.[44] But apart from being an example of his versioning approach to life narrative, this anecdote is particularly revealing because the name Satchmo simultaneously evokes minstrel codes (the stories, sounds, and images associated with the Sambo), black vernacular culture (New Orleans nicknaming practices), and Armstrong's self-conscious performative modernism (recognizing the popular potential of a nickname that sticks and disseminating it widely). The nicknames of his youth were "[g]iven by your little pals and people who likes you," and "they're *all* in good Faith," whereas Satchmo is a "trade mark," a public name that Armstrong strategically embodies. Consider the distribution of agency: Armstrong contrasts his active involvement in the coining of New Orleans nicknames ("I *accumulated* several Nick Names"; "*I have Originated* Several Names") with his passive role in the invention of the Satchmo name ("*Satchmo was Originated*"). It is the autobiographical narrative itself that finally enables Armstrong's participation in the public construction of his Satchmo image. It overcomes the initial passivity of the nickname by legitimizing it retroactively. As an article on Armstrong in *Ebony* reported in 1964, the musician regarded "Satchmo" as an integral part of his name, which is supported by the fact that Armstrong's stationery had been carrying the moniker at least since the early 1940s.[45]

Satchmo is part vernacular nickname, part commercial trademark. As such, it advertizes Armstrong to a worldwide audience—that the musician was christened Satchmo by an English journalist underscores its transnational appeal—but also carries traces of his grounding in the black working-class community of New Orleans, where jocular language battles were common and where nicknames signified one's place in the communal structure. As Ralph Ellison wrote in his *Saturday Review* essay on Charlie "Bird" Parker, "nicknames are indicative of a change from a given to an achieved identity." They "tell us something of the nicknamed individual's interaction with his fellows."[46] For black New Orleanians, references to Armstrong's big mouth, his "*Rhythm Jaws*" and "Satchelmouth," would most likely have connoted comedic talents and musical prowess: he is a big-mouthed joker, and his jaws produce jazz rhythms. Satchmo, by contrast, is both a malapropism and a sonic reference to the Sambo. The British reporter Percy Brooks thinks that the black Armstrong has a bigger mouth—"*Mo*[re] *Mouth*"—than the average white man, perhaps because he was so stunned by Armstrong's trumpet and vocal delivery that he imagined a racially based physical difference as the source of all that jazz.[47]

In the American context, images of black oral magnitude had a long tradition. *The Yankee Pedlar; or, Old Times in Virginia* (1834), for instance, spoke of a slave whose "mouth was so big that he had to get it made smaller for fear he'd swaller his own head."[48] The topos of the gaping black mouth soon became one of the most widely known comic elements of the minstrel stage, and it shaped the postbellum work of black minstrels such as Billy Kersands, who combined athletic dancing with facial contortions that included the swallowing of two billiard balls to display the stunning capacity of his oversized mouth. The "coon" songs that followed the failure of Reconstruction translated the minstrel poetics into more aggressive depictions of African Americans by adding further images of the black mouth as an all-consuming orifice to the fray of racial misrepresentations. The sheer number of such songs—more than six hundred were published in the 1890s alone—and their unprecedented success—some sold over three million copies in sheet music—indicate their cultural and economic power.[49] Compositions such as Malcolm Williams's "My Watermelon Boy" (1899) and Elmer Bowman's "I've Got Chicken on the Brain" (1899) depicted the black "coon" as a voracious eater of racially coded food (watermelon and chicken), and this discourse was visualized on countless postcards that depicted black children grinning over watermelons and on sheet-music covers such as Bert Williams and George Walker's "The Phrenologist Coon," which features six black faces with thick lips and oversized mouths.[50] Some of these turn-of-the century expressions reimagined the more benevolent Sambo of Southern plantation fiction and the minstrel shows as the violent and potentially threatening "coon" and depicted blacks "as not only ignorant and indolent, but also devoid of honesty or personal honor, given to drunkenness and gambling, utterly without ambition, sensuous, libidinous, even lascivious."[51]

The exaggerated black mouth of the minstrel shows, "coon" songs, and visual depictions of African Americans represents a locus from which black cultural production emanated, and it came to signify a complex mélange of character traits and expressions, among them greed, lust, and gluttony, but also laughter, jive language, and scat vocalization. The black mouth metonymically expressed both racial anxieties (being devoured by an African American population deemed to be physically aggressive and denounced as prone to lying, drinking, gambling, and razor fighting), as well as racial fantasies (the black mouth as producer of beautiful melodies, comedy, and laughter). In this context, it is highly significant that Armstrong's autobiographics is filled with references to the black mouth. Indeed, his smile became so prominent and so widely acknowledged that one advertisement showed only his mouth and teeth. The situations in which Armstrong made reference to his mouth, lips, and smile are various, and they foreground the wide dispersal and signifying power of these racially resonant facial features. He once anticipated lip problems after playing a gig in New Orleans by stating, "I'll have lips like a toilet bowl"; the Hot Five recorded a composition titled "Jazz Lips" (Nov. 16, 1926); the lyrics to "Shine" speak of the black dandy's pearly teeth; on "I'll Be Glad When You're Dead You Rascal You" (Nov. 16, 1941), Armstrong refers to an adulterer who "asked my wife for some cabbage, and [. . .] ate just like a savage, ha ha ha"; he frequently used the slang expression "chops" to refer to both a musician's mouth and his or her musical skills.[52] It should be no surprise, then, that a white musician like Hoagy Carmichael, not unlike the British reporter Percy Brooks, sought to process Armstrong's spectacular performances on stage and in the recording studio by seeing and hearing them as racially different, as products of "big lips" that produced a music that was both enticing and threatening to the ears of white listeners: "blubbering strange cannibalistic sounds."[53]

In 1949, when Armstrong participated in a radio broadcast of the *Bing Crosby Show*, a (probably prescripted) joke about the trumpeter's mouth revived the minstrel and "coon" stereotype in a good-natured manner in order to entertain the radio audience: "I wish you could see the grin on the man's face, folks. When you smile, Louie, you look like the Grand Canyon with teeth," Crosby jokes, and Armstrong responds: "I'm probably the only trumpet man in the world who can blow from either end of the horn."[54] This response certainly conjures up Billy Kersands's magnificent mouth and the black minstrel's billiard ball swallowing. Yet at the time when Kersands was performing, images of voracious "coons" were not just a more or less funny throwback to an earlier time; they were so widespread and so deeply woven into the cultural fabric that it is fair to say that the "coon" phenomenon represented "a complex code of signification central to the entire racial discourse of late nineteenth-century America."[55] This code pointed to one of the social functions of popular representations of black Americans, which was to provide an outlet for the growing anxieties of a population faced with an increasingly multiethnic demographics. These anxieties were alleviated in part by casting the "coon" as a potentially violent but ultimately funny, or at least grotesquely funny, figure, and they were accompanied by a fascination with the music and culture produced by ex-slaves and the first generation of blacks born after the end of slavery. The fascination with black culture, especially music and dance, opened up the field for black performers, who began to insert themselves and their performances into the "codified cluster of signs" generated by the "coon" representations of their time.[56]

The degree to which these performances were intended to change stereotypical representations of "blackness" cast in the Sambo code remains a matter of debate. The depiction of the "coon" figure in the black minstrel Sam Lucas's "Coon's Salvation Army" (1884), for instance, is not substantially different from the lyrics of "coon" songs by white composers: "De melon patch am safe today / No coons am dar in sight / De chickens dey may roost in peace / Wid in der coops tonight." One of the most famous "coon" songs, "All Coons Look Alike to Me" (1896), was composed by the African American Ernest Hogan, and it, too, did not diverge from the stereotypical formula (neither did the sheet music cover).[57] And even Bert Williams and George Walker, who billed themselves as "Two Real Coons" from 1896 onward and rank among the most significant black performers of the transitional era between the minstrel shows and Harlem Renaissance musical theater, produced songs such as "The Coon's Trade Mark" (1898), whose lyrics proclaim: "As certain and sure as Holy Writ, / And not a coon's exempt from it, / Four things you'll always find together, / / Regardless of condition of sun and moon— / A watermelon, a razor, a chicken, and a coon!"[58]

Armstrong admired Bert Williams, and in the 1960s, he would even pun on the title of Hogan's composition: "All you white folks look alike to me, Pops."[59] As part of his autobiographics, this is more than an innocent pun because it emphasizes the transition from the minstrel and "coon" eras, where African Americans could be caricatured as all looking alike, to the Harlem, or New Negro, Renaissance and later the civil rights movement. During the Harlem Renaissance, which had its roots in the final decades of the nineteenth century and lasted well into the twentieth, "[b]lack Americans sought to re-present their public selves in order to reconstruct their public, reproducible images," as Henry Louis Gates has argued, and they often turned to the powers of music to create a usable past and imagine the future of black American culture. This representation and reconstruction followed from a wish "to 'turn' the new century's image of the black away from the stereotypes scattered throughout plantation fictions, blackface minstrelsy, vaudeville, racist pseudo-science, and vulgar Social Darwinism."[60] Armstrong's Satchmo thus appears as an ambiguous figure, as a modern response to the lovably docile Sambo and his more vicious "coon" offspring. It benefited from the fact that these blackface figures had themselves been invested with a considerable degree of ambiguity by the people who invented them for the stage—who loved what they took to be the images and sounds of "blackness" enough to appropriate them as source material for popular comedy—and by the mass audience that consumed blackface performances across a variety of genres and media for decades if not centuries.[61]

While Armstrong's musical originality and his performative techniques frequently questioned the validity of the Sambo code, they never fully erased it. Armstrong simultaneously evoked and undermined this code, and he therefore occupied a middle position between the two cultural constructs Gates discerns as antipodes in the struggle over the images and sounds of modern(ist) "blackness": "the 'New Negro' [. . .] and the white figure of the black as Sambo," with the New Negro functioning "as a sign of plentitude" and "reconstructed *presence*" and the Sambo "as a sign of lack" and "negated *absence*." Instead of an "antithetical relation" and "relation of reversal" between the New Negro and the Sambo, Armstrong's performances suggest elements of the New Negro's self-determination, as well as moments in which the black performer appears as, or could be conceived as, racial stereotype.[62] The coexistence of Sambo and New Negro resonances in the Satchmo persona (with a heavy dose of New Orleans working-class ethics thrown into the mix) created productive ambiguities that secured the performer's widespread appeal and his double status as master musician and grinning entertainer. This appeal built on the complicated cross-racial dynamics inscribed into American popular culture through the minstrel shows and offshoots like "coon" productions.[63] In other words, Armstrong's performances fed on the racial ambiguities of the minstrel poetics, and to analyze these ambiguities is to reveal their cultural productivity as part of what Berndt Ostendorf has described as black culture's longstanding significance as "a hidden dynamo of American popular culture."[64]

Even though Armstrong never appeared in a minstrel show and never wore minstrel makeup, he was certainly familiar with blackface minstrelsy and the cross-racial dynamics of white borrowings of black musical styles. He certainly did not hesitate to use this familiarity for humorous purposes. There is a moment at the beginning of an All Stars live performance of "Now You Has Jazz" in Australia when he wipes his face with his white handkerchief and says, "my makeup's coming off again."[65] In this instance, the racial implications of skin color and the politics of racial cross-dressing through blackface are playfully acknowledged, but not explicitly criticized. A few years earlier, Armstrong had actually worn a particular kind of blackface as part of his 1949 appearance as Zulu King during the New Orleans Mardi Gras festivities. Parading around New Orleans with a Zulu King at the helm was a black working-class practice that had been a staple of Mardi Gras for many decades and that required the person elected as Zulu King to wear black face paint and white makeup around the eyes.

Apart from leaving a substantial textual, visual, and musical record of his complexly mediated and highly controversial Zulu King appearance, Armstrong included a tidbit of information in "Jewish Family" about what must have been a "whiteface" contest ("I won an amateur contest—dip face in flower"), which black New Orleanians may have staged as a way of mimicking a similar event, a "blackface" contest perhaps, organized by the city's white population.[66] Reversing the cultural logic of blackface masking, if that is what the amateur contest did, followed the logic of signifying, and it might have been indebted to the whitefacing practices that were part of the John Kooner (or John Canoe) festivities during which slaves impersonated slave owners by wearing white face paint. Armstrong's familiarity with such practices of ethnic play-acting and racial masquerade thus resulted at least partly from his folk-rural roots and his involvement with the folk-urban culture of New Orleans.[67]

That minstrelsy, in various forms and media, was an integral part of the cultural environment into which Armstrong was born and not just the entertainment world of the North to which he moved is illustrated by a New Orleans magazine called *The Mascot*, which ran from 1887 to 1891 and routinely featured "coon" caricatures of African Americans dancing, playing music, and gambling.[68] Two decades later, in the 1910s, minstrelsy was still common; the New Orleans police force, for instance, put on an annual minstrel show, and sound recordings, films, and (by the 1920s) radio ensured the ready availability of minstrel-related material.[69] Black musicians understandably have had little to say in their autobiographies and oral histories about the minstrel conventions of their youths. Among the exceptions are blues composer W. C. Handy's acknowledgment that the postbellum minstrel shows absorbed the best black composers, singers, musicians, and performers, as well as clarinetist and saxophonist Garvin Bushell's stories about providing minstrel entertainment with the Sells-Flo circus in 1916.[70] The few accounts of New Orleans musicians that do exist point to a substantial presence of minstrel-related performances in their home-town. Oscar "Chicken" Henry, for instance, describes his encounters with minstrel music in New Orleans in the early decades of the twentieth cen-tury: "those bands we heard and second-lined to, was minstrel bands. Like Primrose and West; Primrose and Dockstader. The Dirtz Dixie Min-strels—R. G. Fields, Lew Dockstader. When I was a kid, I heard and saw every band that come to the city of New Orleans. [. . .] I used to go to the Orpheum Theatre [. . .] and watch the men in the orchestra pits rehearsin' Sophie Tucker." Armstrong also mentions the Jewish "coon" shouter So-phie Tucker and the white minstrel producer Lew Dockstader, whose troupe performed at the Orpheum Theater in New Orleans in front of seg-regated audiences. He further recalls having "to sit in the Buzzard Roof to dig em," meaning that he was forced to sit in a segregated section of the au-dience usually called the "peanut gallery."[71]

Minstrelsy obviously played a significant role in the cultural environ-ment of early New Orleans jazz, and it may have impacted the selection of songs Armstrong would record in later years. Fellow New Orleanian mu-sician Lawrence Duhé accounts for the historical nexus among minstrel material, plantation-style proto jazz, and their urban continuations in New Orleans. Living on a plantation near LaPlace, Louisiana, Duhé and others ragged many different tunes, including the minstrel ditty "Turkey in the Straw."[72] As a child, Armstrong occasionally went to his mother's home-town, the rural Boutte, where he may have heard such music. As a teenager, he would intone "[m]any of the old plantation songs and the popular tunes of the day" with his vocal quartet, the "singin' fools," for instance as part of amateur contests staged at Bill and Mary Mack's tent show, where he "was singing tenor" and where the quartet was a big success on at least one oc-casion, as Zutty Singleton remembered.[73] In the 1910s, these tunes would have included modernized versions of Stephen Foster's minstrel evergreen "The Old Folks at Home" (1851; also known as "Swanee River"), as well as older minstrel compositions such as "Jump Jim Crow" (late 1820s or early 1830s).[74] Armstrong must have appreciated this material, perhaps because it reminded him of his youth and the people he remembered fondly. He recorded "The Old Folks at Home" with the Mills Brothers (June 29, 1937) and cited its theme in his solo on the up-tempo version of "St. Louis Blues" he performed during his hiatus in France (Nov. 7, 1934); he played another one of Foster's compositions, "My Old Kentucky Home" (1853), with the All Stars for the *Satchmo Plays King Oliver* album (Sept. 30–Oct.

1–2, 1959). He also recorded "Carry Me Back to Old Virginny" (1878), a minstrel song composed by the so-called Negro Stephen Foster, James Bland (also with the Mills Brothers; Apr. 7, 1937).

It is important to remember here that Armstrong was certainly not unique in recording and performing such material. While he recorded similarly minstrel-inflected tunes with the Fletcher Henderson Orchestra ("Go 'Long, Mule," Oct. 7, 1924) and the Hot Five ("Big Fat Ma and Skinny Pa," June 23, 1926), it was Duke Ellington, the self-declared "primitive pedestrian minstrel," who associated himself more explicitly with a primitivist variant of the minstrel poetics with his Cotton Club floorshows and with compositions titled "Jungle Nights in Harlem" (1930), "Dinah's in a Jam" (1938), "Watermelon Man" (1938), and "Happy Go Lucky Local" (1946).[75] It is equally significant to keep in mind that minstrel and pseudo-minstrel songs make up a culturally significant but nonetheless relatively slim sample of Armstrong's recording portfolio. The recording session with the Mills Brothers, for instance, also produced a version of "Darling Nellie Gray" (Apr. 7, 1937), an abolitionist composition by Benjamin R. Hanby from 1856 that depicts the sadness of a slave over the loss of a lover who was sold to a new master. This recording complicates any easy association of Armstrong with the minstrel narratives of "The Old Folks at Home" and "Carry Me Back to Old Virginny" and should prevent simplistic assumptions about his enthrallment with minstrel material as an indicator of willful racial submission.

The transplantation of Armstrong's performances from New Orleans honky-tonks to the entertainment venues of Chicago, New York, and other urban centers in the North represented a momentous rift, a sea change from a more or less vernacular and localized phenomenon of live music to a nationwide as well as mass-mediated phenomenon of popular entertainment—"catapult[ing] the vernacular into a national rage," in Kathy Ogren's memorable formulation.[76] For many black jazz musicians, the new situation offered an unprecedented amount of cultural capital, and they used this capital to reshape the public image of the black musician from the dancing "coon" to a more complex and also more modern figure. Armstrong began to wear fancy clothes and proudly dressed in the latest fashions as a way of communicating his new status as a musical star. Many photos from these years offer visual documentation of his newfound fashion sense, and he recalls wearing "real new Vines" (i.e., a new suit), trying to look "real sharp," and adapting to the urban modernity of Chicago: "No more 'Boisterous—'Barrel house 'stuff. Am trying to 'Cultivate Myself.'"[77] Yet the value system of his youth prevented him from fully embracing notions of bourgeois respectability and modern elegance. Despite his admiration for new fashion styles, which he proudly displayed on publicity photos, he repeatedly disassociated himself from any feelings of class-conscious superiority, rejecting behavior he considered "Blaa'zay" and referring to band leader Fletcher Henderson's personal conduct as "that society shit."[78]

But the performance venues of the 1920s also thrived on the prevailing minstrel mode. They provided "marginal zones" and a new "physical landscape" by adding a visual dimension to musical performances and placing musicians and customers in "worlds geographically separate" and "culturally unfamiliar to many whites."[79] Places in Chicago's South Side ("The Stroll") and Harlem's entertainment section ("Jungle Alley") sported names that referred to the mythical antebellum South: Sunset Café (managed by Armstrong's manager-to-be, Joe Glaser), Plantation Club, Club Alabam, Cotton Club, and Club Swanee. The Plantation Club featured "log cabins, Negro mammies, picket fences around the dance floor, a twinkling summer sky, and a watermelon moon."[80] At least one musician anachronistically recalls a plantation scene that included the "replica of a Southern mansion with weeping willows and slave quarters [. . . and] created a *Gone with the Wind* atmosphere."[81]

When it came to booking artists and entertainers for their shows, nightclub and dance hall owners were often guided by a lingering plantation mentality that privileged lighter-skinned blacks over darker-skinned musicians. Armstrong, for instance, was not allowed to play at the Cotton Club until after it reopened in the late 1930s; he was considered "[t]oo Negro" by the club's owner, Owney Madden. He did, however, play at Frank Sebastian's New Cotton Club in Los Angeles in 1930 and called his band the Sebastian New Cotton Club Orchestra on recordings.[82] In the 1920s, he performed at the Plantation Club and places like the Sunset Café and must have been aware of shows like the one that took place at the Plantation Club on November 9, 1926, which featured "the Season's Current Hit 'Minstrel Days'" in combination with "A Real Old-Time Minstrel First Part."[83] His involvement with musical theater—especially *Great Day* (1929) and *Swingin' the Dream* (1939)—connected his persona with the minstrel mode apart from the nightclub and dance hall environment. Vincent Youmans's *Great Day* was set on an antebellum plantation, as was

Swingin' the Dream, an adaptation of Shakespeare's *Midsummer Night's Dream* that featured a minstrel caricature of Armstrong by Al Hirschfeld on the playbill. Finally, at least two cartoons from around the same time, *Clean Pastures* (Warner Brothers, 1937) and *Swing Wedding/Minnie the Moocher's Wedding Day* (MGM, 1937), associated Armstrong with minstrel iconography by depicting him (as well as Fats Waller and Cab Calloway) with stereotypically bulging eyes and thick lips.[84] What we can gather from the intermedial dispersal of such representations is that minstrel resonances appeared not just as isolated instances and not just in Armstrong's engagements with his audiences, but constituted a whole set of widely acknowledged and deeply ingrained codes and contexts that shaped the reception of American jazz in the first half of the twentieth century.

Judging from Armstrong's Hot Five and Hot Seven recordings, which at times explicitly evoke the setting of the nightclub or dance hall ("Sunset Cafe Stomp," Nov. 16, 1926; "Savoy Blues," Dec. 13, 1927) and which frequently contain a structure of comic bantering audiences would have known from the minstrel interlocutor's communication with his endmen, Armstrong's nightclub performances must have been ripe with minstrel-inflected humor.[85] Yet these performances certainly ventured beyond minstrel comedy. They updated minstrel material by adding moments of vernacular jiving in which audiences could recognize humorous impersonations of established comic figures. And they did more: they confronted jazz writers and journalists with a musical spectacle of "hot jazz" that was revolutionary in its musical originality and explosive in its social and sexual implications, the latter of which being illustrated by several jokes Armstrong would later tell.[86] One of these jokes refers to the white actor Raymond Massey, "who played *Abe Lincoln in Illinois* on Broadway [. . . and] got so carried away [that] after his last performance he went up [to] Harlem and freed the Cotton Club girls." Another joke was scripted for a short comedy routine Armstrong did with Bing Crosby on Crosby's radio show; here, Armstrong recalls performing at Frank Sebastian's Cotton Club in 1930 while Crosby was playing at the nearby Coconut Grove. Crosby, the punch line goes, went to the Cotton Club to hear Armstrong more often than he showed up for his job at the Coconut Grove.[87]

The notion of black culture as a hidden dynamo of American popular culture is clearly apparent in these jokes. In order to tone down the volatility of the new music and performance styles that jokers like Armstrong embodied, the music industry frequently reverted to the minstrel poetics. It was as if a safeguard was needed against what was perceived as the revolutionary potential of the music and the social powers it could afford its performers. An advertisement for one of Armstrong's most melancholy recordings, "St. James Infirmary" (Dec. 12, 1928), a touching tribute to a dead lover and a thoughtful piece about poverty and mortality, is a case in point. Reaching a mass audience through the medium of sound recording proved vital for Armstrong and his musicians. But buying a recording and listening to it at home constituted an experience very much different from being in a nightclub, where one entered an unfamiliar, exoticized world and encountered the musicians in person. For buyers of Okeh race records like "St. James Infirmary," an additional set of codes therefore mediated the musical experience, as an advertisement in the *Chicago Defender* illustrates. Rather than visualize the folk roots of the tune, which was also known as "Gambler's Blues," the ad depicts a dandy figure in blackface and exclaims: *"Yeah! It's. . . .* 'St. James Infirmary' / See dis Strutter! He's Jess like that. Jess like that. And he don't give a doggone whut you say 'bout his clothes." The strutter's dandyish clothes cannot hide his "darky" nature, as the minstrel dialect ("dis"; "Jess"; "doggone whut") ensures.[88] Here, then, Armstrong is associated with the urban minstrel dandy, and not with its country counterpart, Jim Crow.[89]

Stock characters like the Sambo, the plantation slave Jim Crow, and the urban dandy Zip Coon exerted cultural power beyond the immediate context of the minstrel shows, not merely because of their ubiquity and comic appeal but also because they "reinforced northerners' sense of difference and distance from the colonized, backwards ex-Confederacy, as well as their own sense of white supremacy."[90] Thus, it is not surprising that the "darky strutter" who serves as a stand-in for Armstrong in the Okey advertisement mutes the musician's modern, self-conscious, and professional artistry. What was new, however, was that black musicians played a music that attracted unprecedented numbers of white listeners who went on slumming trips to urban black neighborhoods, not so much because they wanted to see blacks ridiculed by white actors in blackface, but because they wanted to soak up what promised to be a colorful atmosphere of licentiousness, eroticism, and musical extravagance.

Looking back on Armstrong's personal experience, it is reasonable to speak of an intermedial minstrel poetics with which he came into contact as a youngster in New Orleans and that he also confronted, in a modernized and more complexly mediated form, when he moved first to Chicago and then to New York. What remains to be determined is the extent to which he integrated this poetics into his autobiographics and how he influenced the ways in which it shaped his popular reception. It is, after all, one thing to be depicted as a strutting "darky" in a newspaper advertisement and quite another thing to actively suggest, or even promote, such interpretations. To what extent, then, did Armstrong connect his music and life story with the minstrel poetics? And how exactly is this poetics reflected in the music he recorded, in the films in which he starred, and in the stories he told about his life?

Armstrong recorded few actual minstrel songs, but he recorded a series of neominstrel titles with Southern themes, among them "magnolia-theme" and "carry-me-back" songs such as "Rockin' Chair" (Dec. 13, 1929), "Dear Old Southland" (Apr. 5, 1930), "Dinah" (May 4, 1930), "When It's Sleepy Time Down South" (Apr. 20, 1931), "That's My Home" (Dec. 8, 1932), "He's a Son of the South" (Jan. 26, 1933), and "There's a Cabin in the Pines" (Apr. 26, 1933), as well as songs about the Mississippi River as a blissful Southern setting, including "Lazy River" (Nov. 3, 1931), "Dusky Stevedore" (Apr. 24, 1933), "Mississippi Basin" (Apr. 24, 1933), "Shanty Boat on the Mississippi" (June 15, 1939), and "Lazy 'Sippi Steamer" (Mar. 14, 1940).[91] "Rockin' Chair" features bantering similar to the minstrel exchange between a white interlocutor and a blackfaced endman, who argue about drinking gin, remember "dear old Aunt Harriet" in heaven, and spend their days in a cabin in the South. "Dinah," a song from a musical theater show of the same title from 1923, revives the minstrel figure "Dinah from Carolina." The river song "Dusky Stevedore" depicts a "shufflin'" black dockworker "on the Swanee shore workin' and singin' a song," while "Mississippi Basin" presents a displaced Southerner who yearns for the "dear folks" of the Mississippi basin and plans to "cross the Mason-Dixon [to] that Mississippi basin back home." "Shanty Boat on the Mississippi" revels in fantasies of "work[ing] no more," while "Lazy 'Sippi Steamer" references the minstrel South most explicitly: the "[l]azy sun is shining"; the speaker is drowsy and wants to take a nap while traveling homeward on the Mississippi steamer. From the late-afternoon setting (snowy white cotton fields, sweet air, lazy breeze) to blacks "hummin' in the bayou" and "singin' on the shore," the lyrics paint a picture of an idyllic South (the black man's "homeland") listeners would have known from *Swing That Music* and from countless literary, musical, and visual representations of the nineteenth and twentieth centuries.

But in Armstrong's case, it is not primarily the material he recorded that matters; it is also how he transformed this material and integrated it into his overarching autobiographics. In general, the loving attitude toward the South in Armstrong's performances of "Lazy 'Sippi Steamer" and similar songs seems genuine—at least, this is insinuated by the seriousness of his vocals and the quality of the trumpet solos. It is Foster-like sentiments of nostalgia, and not the burlesque exuberance of the dancing Jim Crow, that structure Armstrong's rendition of these tunes. The 1932 recording of "That's My Home" even contains an explicit reference to Foster's pastoral river setting—"Where the Swanee river flow [sic]."⁹² "That's My Home" and other neominstrel tunes and river songs that Armstrong recorded in the 1930s are delivered in a mostly serious mood and contain little scat or jiving. While the lyrics frequently trigger a series of "coon" echoes—"though your eyes are black as coal your little soul is white as snow to me" in "Little Joe" (Apr. 28, 1931); "your hand and feet [are] just as black as tar" in "Snow Ball" (Jan. 28, 1933)—the degree of productive ambiguity is relatively low and creeps into these performances only occasionally, such as when Armstrong calls the "coon" baby on "Little Joe" little Satchelmouth Joe and little Gatemouth Joe. Instead of simply reinforcing black stereotypes, these songs can be just as productively heard as tributes to a lost home and as emotional engagements with a personal past irretrievably gone.

The fact that Armstrong recorded such tunes does not necessarily prove the prominence of a minstrel poetics that influences the production and reception of his public image. But apart from recording minstrel and neominstrel tunes, Armstrong frequently connected blackface minstrelsy and his own persona in speech and writing, and he played film roles that further supported the minstrel continuum. "You see, I've always been a happy go lucky sort of type of fellow," he writes in "The Satchmo Story." He makes this comment in a passage that deals with his arrest for possession of marijuana in 1930, where he ponders the jealousies of others (he alleges that he and drummer Vic Burton were set up by someone who disliked them for their success) and his own benevolence toward people in general. The sentiment comes across as heartfelt—a few lines down he refers to drummer Zutty Singleton as a "[h]umorist good natured guy"—but one wonders about Armstrong's choice of words: "happy go lucky" is a phrase charged with echoes of the plantation Sambo and the "coon" figures played by actors Bill "Bojangles" Robinson and Lincoln Perry ("Stepin

Fetchit").[93] For James Weldon Johnson, the phrase forcefully suggests a "tradition of the Negro as only an irresponsible, happy-go-lucky, wide-grinning, loud-laughing, shuffling, banjo-playing, singing, dancing sort of being," and a writer for the *New York Herald Tribune* directly connected black jazz with the Sambo code via this particular phrase: "the average white New Yorker [. . .] thinks of [Harlem] as a region of prosperous night clubs; of happy-go-lucky Negroes dancing all night to jazz music."[94]

Armstrong used the phrase "happy-go-lucky" a second time on one of his tape recordings, where he talks about the filming of *High Society* and says about his character and the "boys" in his band: "we're all so happy-go-lucky." This reference is to the roles he and the members of his band play in the movie, but additional recollections indicate that Armstrong is focusing on the acting performance, and not on the final outcome. Noting that the players in his band "can ham up a thing," he adds: "you know, they're all tryin' to steal that scene. Trummy Young mugged so much, folks, I'm tellin' ya, even when the director was explaining the scene, he was muggin', listenin'." Rather than being too concerned with the product of the performance, Armstrong must have relished the performance itself, and rather than urging the director to present the musicians in nonstereotypical fashion, he and his bandmates milked the engagement for what it was worth. They are perpetually grinning and, except for Armstrong, never appear as anything more than happy jazz players.[95] Dealing with such stereotypical roles, we can gather from these remarks, was the musicians' daily fare, and it would not have been feasible to reject such roles all too openly.

The in-group humor that must have accompanied the shooting of *High Society* surely relied on the language of jive and on practices of signifying. There is no question that jiving created a lexicon that may have included the ironic usage of a phrase like "happy-go-lucky," perhaps as a response to its appearance in places as prominent as the *Time* cover story from February 21, 1949, which speaks of "that happy-go-lucky Louis Armstrong." But many of Armstrong's film rolls amplify the verbal references to minstrelsy and cater to an intermedial discourse beyond Armstrong's jiving. *Pennies from Heaven*, for example, features a notorious "coon" joke about the Negro's love of chicken. The simple-minded musician Henry (Armstrong) promises the owner of the Haunted House Café (Bill Crosby) that he will procure all the chicken needed for the café's grand opening. For those viewers unable or unwilling to decode this plot element and Armstrong's grin as gestures toward the stereotypical chicken-loving "darky" figure, the filmmakers have the musicians run away as the police shows up looking for the chicken thieves. In another scene, Henry asks his boss for a better percentage of the proceeds. He wants 7 instead of 10 percent because the band has seven members and none of them can divide 10 percent by seven. Armstrong's performance of the musical skit "Skeleton in the Closet," however, is much more complex in its relation to the long history of minstrel-inflected ghost stories in American literature and culture—think of Harriet Beecher Stowe's "Authentic Ghost Story" in *Uncle Tom's Cabin* (1851–52), Mark Twain's blackface depiction of slave Jim's superstitions in *Adventures of Huckleberry Finn*, and animated short films such as George Pal's *Jasper and the Haunted House* (1942). On the one hand, it depicts the stereotypical black man's fear of ghosts and features the bulging eyes and other stage signifiers of minstrel "blackness" (the band members wear black clothes and white eye masks). On the other hand, Armstrong's singing and trumpet playing show a self-confident and highly skilled musician who is not at all afraid of the skeleton dancer and finally blows him out of the room, thereby suggesting that the frame story is only a theatrical setup for a masterful performance (much like Bert Williams's "You Can't Do Nothing Till Martin Gets Here" comedy routine, which was delivered in blackface but used the haunted house scenario as the starting point for an African American folk story about a black preacher). Armstrong himself never resolved these seeming incongruities; he calls his scenes with Bing Crosby "Classics" and a ""GUSSUH" personified" in an undated letter, expressing fondness rather than indignation for the minstrel humor that is inscribed in them and that competes for public attention with the vernacular practices that can also be seen and heard in his movie performance.[96]

Complicating matters, Armstrong's writings include several instances of actual minstrel speech, which points to an even deeper meaning behind his relationship with the minstrel poetics than selected jokes or movie performances may suggest. These instances appear almost exclusively as responses to figures of authority or as exclamatory statements. In *Swing That Music*, Armstrong tells the reader: "*No Suh!* My mother, Mary-Ann, always would say to me and my sister, Mamma Lucy, never to steal from anybody." A few pages later, he boasts: "We had the hottest band for a bunch of youngsters just starting out that there was. *Yes, suh!*" About his preparations for his first job on the Streckfus entertainment boats, he remembers: "I had bought myself a fine new instrument just before starting out, but even that wasn't shiny enough for *this* trip. *No, suh!*"[97] Similar exclamations occur in

"Jazz on a High Note," as does a variation of them: "Every note that I blew in this recording ['Potato Head Blues'], I thought of Papa Joe . . . "Yass Lawd" . . ."[98] The expression "Yass Lawd" suggests comedic depictions of black spirituality, as well as the sermons of the Sanctified Church, where the excited believer recognizes the power of the Lord. These expressions are also represented in direct speech when Armstrong recounts conversations from the past. In *Satchmo*, his response to the black musician Sam Dutrey's command to get off the stage is a repeated "Yassuh." He extends the same response to Fletcher Henderson's musical directions in 1924: "I said, 'Yassuh,' and went on up there" on the bandstand. When a few years later he and his band members are stranded with a broken-down car in New York after the long drive from Chicago and a white policeman thinks that they may be gangsters, Armstrong responds to the policeman's question, "Hey there have you boys any 'Shot Guns in that Car?" with a submissive "No Suh Boss." Coupled with the occasional "shucks," these expressions constitute more than throwaway comments.[99] They connect Armstrong's writings with minstrel and postminstrel representations of comic "blackness" and establish the discursive threads that connect these writings with the musician's larger intermedial autobiographics.

On occasion, minstrel speech appears even more forcefully, for instance, when Armstrong represents his and Zutty Singleton's excuse for discontinuing a basketball game: "'*AH'M*' So 'tired'"; ""AH'M' Too""; when he recalls a fellow Waif's Home inmate's excuse for running away: "Ah wasn't gwine no whars"; and when he is asked by an employee of the Okeh company, for which he was under exclusive contract, whether he knew who the anonymous singer was on a recording for another company (it was Armstrong himself, earning some extra cash and violating his contract) and answered, "I don't know. But I won't do it again."[100] All three examples reenact the master-slave relationship in coded form. The first example shows two African American speakers using the minstrel code humorously. Addressing other African Americans, Armstrong and Singleton mimic the stereotypical lazy slave/"coon" who is always too tired to carry out the master's/boss's orders. In the second example, the code is used strategically. The inmate feigns ignorance and hopes to escape punishment by acting like a submissive boy who uses "darky" dialect to affirm the racial ideology of the boss. The final example is even more complicated. Sambo's lack of intellect obviously causes him to acknowledge his guilt ("*I* won't do it *again*"), but the overall intention may have been to manipulate the Okeh employee into believing that the naive and childish figure must be forgiven because he knows no better.

Beyond the realm of Armstrong's musical recordings, film roles, and verbal utterances, minstrel references crop up in the statements of fellow musicians. At least two of these musicians have described Armstrong's physical appearance in minstrel terms: "He be sittin' down in his underwear with a towel around his lap, one around his shoulders an' that white handkerchief on his head, and he'd put that grease around his lips. Look like a minstrel man, ya know," guitar player Danny Barker recalled about Armstrong's backstage looks.[101] The grease was a special lip ointment from a German company with which Armstrong treated his bruised lips after performing, but the visual effect was startling enough to warrant Barker's comment. Thinking back to Armstrong's ragged country clothes worn for his first shows with Fate Marable on the Streckfus entertainment ships, Baby Dodds remembered: "He used to wear jumpers, starched and ironed. It had been washed and faded so bad that it wasn't blue anymore. And it was stiff with starch. [. . .] He just sat there [on stage] looking like the end man in a minstrel show."[102]

No photographs exist that would directly illustrate Dodds's recollections. The few photographs of Armstrong's tenure with Marable that do exist show the musicians dressed up for the occasion.[103] But several other photographs support Barker's remark about Armstrong's backstage looks and thus establish an intermedial interface among musical, verbal, and visual representations of Armstrong as a figure reminiscent of minstrelsy. These photographs produce a multiplicity of meanings in which minstrel imagery mingles with other visual narratives. Two such photographs were taken by Weegee (Arthur Fellig) around 1955 at Bop City in New York. They show Armstrong in his underwear, chatting with admirers and clowning for the camera with a white towel on his head.[104] Here, viewers get an uncensored look at Armstrong's backstage persona, a look that does not necessarily depend on any notion of blackface representation but that nonetheless casts Armstrong's in a subject position very much different—as black, funny, uninhibited—from what one would expect of, say, a composer, conductor, or performer of European classical music. There is also a very intriguing photograph in a *Life* magazine article about Armstrong's trip to Buenos Aires in 1957, where he is shown next to singer Velma Middleton and where his black skin blends in almost entirely with the black background. This black background accentuates Armstrong's white teeth and his popping eyeballs, and the resemblance to the Jewish singer and actor Al Jolson in blackface is striking.[105] While this resemblance may be a coincidence, it is nonetheless significant because it establishes a connection between Armstrong's physical appearance and Jolson's blackened face that cannot be easily erased from the public record.

That this public record included a whole reservoir of minstrel personas can be seen in the photograph that is printed in *Ebony* alongside Armstrong's essay on black women. It shows the musician aboard a train; his aged face, the handkerchief tied at the front, and the polka-dot bathrobe he is wearing strongly evoke popular depictions of the stereotypical slave mammy and later advertising icon Aunt Jemima.[106] And there is yet another photograph that Armstrong used as material for a tape cover and that shows him in his bathrobe with the handkerchief, but this time not so much as the matronly Jemima figure but rather as a rascally figure flanked by two young white female admirers and grinning slyly.[107] Lest we interpret all of this photographic material as documents of cunning and calculated public performances by a strategic master signifier who changes from a private person to a public actor whenever he is in the limelight, we should consider Dennis Stock's backstage photographs from the late 1950s and *New York Times Magazine* journalist Howard Taubman's account of his 1950 visit to Armstrong's home in Queens. Taubman was greeted by someone who was "not self-conscious about his get-up" and wore the "brilliantly striped pajamas" and the "white towel [. . .] wrapped around his head to protect his recently shampooed hair."[108]

A more plausible interpretation can be derived from a photograph that shows Armstrong backstage as he is standing in front of a mirror, wearing a white handkerchief and putting on his tie. On the white space of the handkerchief, he wrote in longhand: "WiTCH HAZEL AN COTTON ON SATCHMO'S CHOPS." He also drew a squiggly arrow from these words to his whitened lips and dedicated the photo to a Jimmy Morgan, to whom he might have sent or given it. The larger significance of this personally inscribed photograph, however, is that the handkerchief and lip balm could signify many things at once: minstrel makeup as well as witch hazel; the big mouth of the minstrels and "coons" as well as the battered chops of the master musician.[109] In addition to these and the many other photographs that depict Armstrong with a white handkerchief on his head (Dennis Stock's works from 1958 show a concentrating pre-show musician as well as an entertainer in post-show relaxation), these portraits illustrate

Fig. 9. Louis Armstrong backstage. Photograph by Dennis Stock, 1958. Courtesy of Agentur Focus/Magnum Photos.

Fig. 10. Louis Armstrong backstage. Photograph by Dennis Stock, 1958. Courtesy of Agentur Focus/Magnum Photos.

why Barker would have thought of Armstrong as a "minstrel man" and why Larry King would write in the mid-1960s that Armstrong sometimes "resembled Aunt Jemimah [*sic*]."[110]

The discrepancy between Armstrong's visual evocation of the "minstrel man" and the Aunt Jemima image and his apparent unselfconsciousness about his looks is amplified by the role that handkerchiefs play in his writings. In fact, tracing the various meanings associated with handkerchiefs prevents us from pinning down any single stable meaning and allows us to grasp the multiplicity of significances that shape Armstrong's engagements with his environment. In his tribute to Joe Oliver for *The Record Changer*, he depicts his childhood experiences of second lining in the New Orleans parades and soaking up Oliver's performances: "Joe would have a handkerchief on his head and put his cap on top of it, with the handkerchief covering the back of his neck to keep the sun off him while he's blowing."[111] Here, the handkerchief performs a utilitarian function. Following in the footsteps of his idol, Armstrong would go through dozens of white handkerchiefs during his shows to wipe the sweat off his face. Marshall Stearns's recollection of Armstrong's use of handkerchiefs in the recording studio, where no audience was present, underscores this interpretation.[112] In *Satchmo*, however, Armstrong describes how Freddie Keppard would put a handkerchief over his fingers when playing in a parade "so that the other cornet players wouldn't catch his stuff."[113] This indicates how widespread the use of handkerchiefs must have been among New Orleans cornetists, and it suggests that Armstrong's use of them was a way of paying tribute to musical elders like Keppard. Moreover, sporting white handkerchiefs for dramatic effect was also common among the Sanctified clergy. Perhaps Armstrong had learned not only his singing tactics but also a thing or two about showmanship in the sermons he had attended in his youth.[114] Furthermore, he also attributed his use of handkerchiefs to his third wife, Alpha, who taught him "how to keep plenty of handkerchiefs (one of the smiley main things), and also took good care of these fine vines."[115] In this case, it is both class-conscious fashionable refinement (handkerchief and suits—or "vines"—as status symbols) and showmanship ("smiley main things") that explain the significance of the handkerchief.[116] Ultimately, however, the ambiguity inherent in this accessory is not resolvable, and this is exactly what makes for its cultural power and belies the common assumption that it merely expresses an overly theatrical form of self-deprecating mugging. It enables different, even conflicting, readings that are all the more productive because they are so widely mediated.

Could we argue, then, that Armstrong willingly and consciously cast himself in the role of the Sambo? The answer is as simple as it is intriguing: Armstrong cast himself in the role of Satchmo. That is to say, he certainly demonstrated a self-reflexive awareness of the sway of minstrel codes in American culture, and he included a good deal of minstrel references in his written, musical, and visual work in order to keep the intermedial poetics of blackface minstrelsy in the audience's mind as a larger frame of reference. This frame of reference was essential for Armstrong's success as a popular figure in American life, and it was also productive because it provided fodder for biographical rewritings such as Robert Goffin's *Horn of Plenty*. This first Armstrong biography illustrates how easily the singing and dancing Satchmo could be embraced as a Samboesque figure. Goffin describes a scene from Armstrong's youth that connects the musician's dancing with the minstrel mode by revisiting "Ethiopian Delineator" Thomas D. Rice's story of the origins of "Jump Jim Crow." According to Robert Toll, Rice claimed that he had met an "old Negro" in 1828 "whose right shoulder [was] deformed and drawn up high, his left leg gnarled with rheumatism, stiff and crooked at the knee, doing an odd-looking dance while singing: 'Weel about and turn about and do jus so; / Ebery time I weel about, I jump Jim Crow.'"[117] Rice allegedly memorized the words and song and even bought the dancer's clothes as stage attire. The changes he made, adding verses as well as "quicken[ing] and slightly chang[ing] the air [i.e., tune]," were said to have preserved the original flavor of the performance while turning it into a presentable form for white audiences. It is telling that the origins of American popular culture are constructed as black, disabled, and strangely anonymous.[118]

Goffin's depiction of Armstrong as a young dancer is indebted to Rice's tale: "Louis knew only one kind of dance. He would buckwing his way into the center of the group of kids, and imitate a hunchback or a lame man, then straighten up abruptly and dance a lively jig."[119] Here, black dancing derives its expressive powers from a disabling of conventions that draws audiences into the performance by way of participatory discrepancies. The liveliness of the jig and buckwing emerge from a funny mimicking of black Otherness coded, as in Rice's tale, as physical disability. The hunched back and lameness of the black slave who appeared in plantation romances and minstrel representations as the Old Uncle are translated into a New Orleans jazz context. In a way, Goffin's biography strained to accomplish for Armstrong what the souvenir program of *The Jazz Singer* (dir. Alan Crosland, 1927) had intended to do for Al Jolson two decades earlier: secure the safe passage of older blackface minstrel material into the hands of more modern performers and thereby "update [. . .] tales of minstrelsy's origin for a postbellum, postslavery, postmigration, black Renaissance-infused, urban America."[120] The souvenir program included an essay titled "Al Jolson's Own Story: The Jazz Singer in Real Life," which not only repeated Rice's gesture toward self-legitimization and the black origins of his Jim Crow song-and-dance routine and thus prefigured Goffin's account but also staged its plea for racial authentication as a biographical narrative.

The surviving portions of Armstrong's "Goffin Notebooks" do not include the buckwing and jig dancing imagined in *Horn of Plenty*, but banjo player and Armstrong's contemporary Johnny St. Cyr remembers a somewhat similar event. Setting the performance at Pete Lala's Cabaret in New Orleans, St. Cyr explains: "old man Lala had a limp and he would come across the floor, limping and shaking his finger at Louis . . . After he had turned his back, Louis would go into a little dance which would end up with him taking a few steps with a limp and shaking his finger just like the old man. This of course would bring the house down."[121] Like Rice's Jim Crow, Lala is an old man, and he is limping as well. More remarkable about this performance, however, is that St. Cyr situates the dance within an African American context (the originator and the appropriator are black men; the performance takes place in a black New Orleans honky-tonk) and wrestles performative power away from blackface minstrelsy, albeit without erasing minstrel resonances. Armstrong, the soon-to-be jazz king, uses Lala's funny walk, not a version of Rice's Jim Crow, as the raw material for his act. The messy history of cultural borrowings marks the complexity of such assessments. It is ultimately impossible to know in which way exactly the Jim Crow influences had traveled: whether Rice had copied a black folk dance that would survive into the 1910s, when Armstrong used it to ridicule Lala; whether Armstrong was familiar with Jim Crow–based minstrel dances or with dances derived from the performances of the black minstrel performer "Juba" (William Henry Lane) in the 1840s and 1850s; or whether Goffin and St. Cyr simply channeled their recollections through the minstrel lens.

What we do know is that Armstrong's own recollections of his comedic dancing and funny skits revise Goffin's account and contrast Jolson's indebtedness to the old Southern "darky" who legitimizes his blackface act by telling him, "Mistah Jolson, yo' is just as funny as me."[122] Armstrong describes a dance contest at the Sunset in Chicago that climaxed in an ultra-fast version of the Charleston, a dance that had been popular since the Broadway show *Runnin' Wild* (1923). The retrospective telling emphasizes the comic physique of Armstrong and three of his band members, and the sight of black dancers moving their bodies to the rhythms of a jazz tune is certainly compatible with minstrel comedy: "There was Earl Hines, as tall as he is; Tubby Hall, as fat as he was; little Joe Walker, as short as he is; and myself, as fat as I was at the time. We would stretch out across that [dance] floor doing the Charleston as fast as the music would play it. Boy, oh boy, you talking about four cats picking them up and laying them down—that was us." But Armstrong notes elsewhere: "All the white people, all the nightlifers, the rich people from Sheridan Road and the big hotels would come out there on the South Side. [. . .] I'd sing songs through a megaphone and four of us [in the band] would close the show doing the Charleston."[123] In this version of the story, the minstrel resonances are complicated by other sounds and images. The dancing must have been rather acrobatic, especially considering the speed of the musical accompaniment.[124] What is more, the performance was obviously meant to entertain a white audience, and not just any white audience, but "the rich people from Sheridan Road and the big hotels" who were willing and able to spend money on black entertainment and thereby supplied the musicians' salaries. In "Jewish Family," Armstrong wrote knowingly about the economic and emotive relationship between black musicians and their white audiences: "White Audiences [. . .] seem to *love all* the *Negroes* that has *Music* in their *Souls—Operas, Spirituals, etc.*"[125]

Armstrong further mentions a specialty number he performed with drummer Zutty Singleton at the Metropolitan Theatre. Even though he gives no indication of the stage setting and club decor, the elements of the show alone must have conjured up the minstrel mode. The number follows in the footsteps of the cross-dressing "wench" routines of the minstrel shows, for instance, the "Lucy Long" impressions from the 1840s and 1850s; the female impersonations of Rollin Howard and Patrick Francis Glassey as Francis Leon from the 1850s to the 1880s; and the work of figures like Earl Gillihan, who was billed by 1892 as "Vaudeville's Greatest Wench." The comic dancing described in the following passage further recalls Jim Crow's jerky jumping, while the comedy invests the music with a minstrel aura that contemporary audiences would have seen as typical of black entertainment in Harlem: "Zutty [. . .] would dress up as one of those real loud and rough gals, with a short skirt, and a pillow in back of him. I was dressed in old rags, the beak of my cap turned around like a tough guy, and he, or she (Zutty) was my gal. As he would come down the aisle, interrupting my song, the people would just scream with laughter."[126] Again, Armstrong describes a minstrel comedy scene (the raggedy clothes of the Sambo, Zutty's cross-dressing) first but ends his account with his and Zutty's effective handling of their screaming audience, which reinstates the performers' masculinity by substituting the childlike Sambo and the emasculated black "wench" with an image of two skilled entertainers and comedians.

Goffin's depiction of a similar dance act by Armstrong's vocal quartet in New Orleans, on the contrary, fully embraces the Sambo: "the quartet's big hit was a side-splitting scene in which Louis Armstrong made passionate love to Redhead Happy," the account alleges. "While the three others were blowing a discreet accompaniment [. . .] Louis declared his love in passionate terms and rolled his eyes in a simulation of desire. [. . .] Louis would break forth in his low voice, his lips drawn back to show the pearliest set of teeth in Dixie, and sing his biggest hit: '*Everybodys* [sic] *gal is my gal, and your gal is my gal too!*'" Whether Goffin invented this scene or not is unclear, but the fact that he and his translator made the Sambo code explicit through the wording of this passage ("rolled his eyes"; "pearliest set of teeth in Dixie") foregrounds the inherent ambiguities produced by Armstrong's intermedial performances. While Armstrong presents himself as Satchmo, a critic like Goffin sees and hears the Sambo.[127] Of course, Goffin was not all too familiar with the sociocultural environment of Armstrong's youth. Those who came from the same environment, like Armstrong's music teacher Peter Davis, saw the comedic dancing as an integral part of Armstrong's musical act and as a habit he had cultivated long before he became a national sensation: "I remember Louis used to walk funny with his feet pointing out and at the first note of music he'd break into comedy dances," Davis told the *New Orleans Times-Picayune* in 1962.[128] The next chapter elaborates on these and similar productive ambiguities and argues that these ambiguities depended both on habitual practices of self-presentation and on the many cultural resonances that oscillated among New Orleans folk sources, minstrel codes, and enunciations of modern "blackness."

CHAPTER 5

"He didn't need black face—
to be funny"

The Double Resonance of Postcolonial Performance

In the opening paragraphs of *Satchmo: My Life in New Orleans*, Louis Armstrong portrays his social surroundings as well as the characters that inhabit these surroundings: "James Alley [. . .] lies in the very heart of what is called The Battlefield because the toughest characters in town used to live there [. . .] . There were churchpeople, gamblers, hustlers, cheap pimps, thieves, prostitutes and lots of children. There were bars, honky-tonks and saloons, and lots of women walking the streets for tricks."[1] Several of these characters attain the status of quasi-mythical figures in Armstrong's hometown litany: Black Benny Williams, Nicodemus, and Slippers, in addition to his musical idol Joe Oliver. Nicodemus, for instance, "was [. . .] one of the best dancers the honky-tonks had ever seen. He was a homely, liver-lipped sort of guy with a peculiar jazzy way of dancing and mugging that would send the gang in the tonk at Gravier and Franklin absolutely wild. [. . . H]e would grab the sharpest chick standing by and would go into his two-step routine, swinging all around the place." Nicodemus is a snazzy dancer whose movements may have inspired Armstrong's own dancing style. He is a favorite with the black working-class patrons of the honky-tonks and represents an image of proud masculinity. As Armstrong further recalls, "After midnight judges, lawyers and cops would make a beeline over to see Nicodemus dance," which suggests that the dancer was equally liked by white audiences, who "always threw him a lot of money."[2] The presence of this double, black and white, audience, sections of which would have possessed very different expectations of, and ideas about, black working-class modes of performance, makes itself heard in Armstrong's account. Nicodemus is described as a "liver-lipped sort of guy" whose jazzy dancing is accompanied by a series of mugging antics. Thus, both the performance and its translation into autobiographical narrative generate meanings that can be enjoyed by different audiences on different levels. Nicodemus is a liver-lipped mugger *and* a swinging jazz dancer; he recalls the "coon" figure's thick lips and clowning (minstrel poetics), *as well as* the rhythmic elegance of an African American dance master (black vernacular culture).

Yet Nicodemus is not merely a performer; he also "had an awful temper and he would fight at the drop of a hat. He was jet black, a good man with the big knife called the chib, and most of the hustlers were afraid of him—except Black Benny." Black Benny, in turn, is "one of the best all-around drummers that ever paraded in that city," and he is "always ready to come to the aid of the underdog." Benny's bouts have legendary status. He defeats Nicodemus in a fight without "dirty work," a violent encounter that those involved, "sticking together," hide from the police.[3] In a later reminiscence, Armstrong calls Benny "[o]ne of the greatest characters I ever know" and describes his death as follows: "He was going with one of those bad whores and he whipped her up in a honky-tonk one night and she shot him. He lived for a whole week with a bullet in his heart. He was good with his dukes, always had a pistol, but the church people liked him, everybody liked him. He was devilish."[4] According to this account, Benny is one of the greatest characters Armstrong "ever know," not "ever knew" or has "ever known," the phrase evoking a timeless aura. He is both "devilish" and liked by the "church people," and he has almost superhuman powers ("lived for a whole week with a bullet in his heart").

Armstrong's portrayal of his New Orleans ancestors in these and other narratives is significant because it reinforces Ralph Ellison's distinction between stereotypes as "malicious reductions of human complexity" and archetypes as "embodiments of abiding patterns of human existence which underlie racial, cultural and religious differences."[5] On the one hand, Nicodemus, Black Benny, and Slippers are portrayed as archetypical father surrogates and role models. They protect the young Armstrong because they see his musical talents and want him to become successful. Slippers encourages him to keep up his playing: "Just listen to that little son-of-a-bitch blow that quail!" he would praise Armstrong, who calls him "as nice a fellow as God ever made" and "loved him just as though he had been my father."[6] Armstrong's biological father, William, had left the family when Louis and his sister, Beatrice (nicknamed Mama Lucy), were very young; "Mama Lucy + I were bastards from the Start," as Armstrong wrote toward the end of his life.[7] William was succeeded by a series of "stepfathers," none of whom ever married his mother, Mayann, but some of whom provided at least a semblance of a father figure for the young boy: "Mayann had enough 'stepfathers' to furnish me with plenty of trousers. All I had to do was turn my back and a new 'pappy' would appear. Some of them were fine guys, but others were low lives."[8] When Armstrong left New Orleans, he lost touch with these ersatz fathers, and he only rarely went back to his hometown after his initial trip to Chicago in 1922 because it remained racially segregated for most of his life. In order to compensate for this loss, he would praise his mother's ingenuity and common sense in almost all of his written and spoken recollections and would cling to Joe Oliver, whom he sometimes called "Dad."[9]

On the other hand, Armstrong's depiction of his New Orleans years produces echoes of "coon" images as well. In "Jewish Family," his most explicit statement in this regard, he writes: "Many Kids *suffered* with *hunger* because their Fathers could have done some honest work for a change. *No*, they would *not* do that. It would be *too* much like *Right*. They'd rather lazy around + gamble, etc."[10] What is more, frequent references to knives, razors, free-for-all fighting, plus pimps and prostitutes in this and other autobiographical narratives evoke a panoply of minstrel and "coon" images without ever fully or clearly legitimizing them. Historically, gambling, and especially rolling dice and playing cards, had become popular as an essential trait of the "coon," and it was carried over into a twentieth-century context by Bert Williams's famous "Darktown Poker Club" routine, which he recorded in 1914 and whose sheet music included a vivid illustration of "coons" with razors playing cards.[11] As a kid, Armstrong tells his readers, he and other neighborhood runts "were always shootin' dice and fighting," and as teenagers, he and his friends "shot dice for pennies or played a little coon can or blackjack."[12] In both scenes, however, the "coon" codes are, if not revoked, then at least complicated. In the first instance, Armstrong notes that "my mother would try to talk to me and make me better," and he indicates that the new jazz music soon interested him more than gambling. In the second instance, the young boy "got to be a pretty slick player and [. . . on s]ome nights [. . .] would come home with my pockets loaded with pennies, nickels, dimes and even quarters." From the proceeds of the gambling sessions, "Mother, sister I would have enough money to go shopping. Now and then I even bought mother a new dress, and occasionally I got myself a pair of short pants."[13] Thus, the money is put to good use; it is used to alleviate the family's poverty.

Toni Morrison provides a lens through which the importance of Southern characters like Nicodemus, Benny, and Slippers for Armstrong's life up
North can be discerned. Writing about the significance of neighborhoods
in black literature, she notes: "What is missing [. . .] is the ancestor. The
advising, benevolent, protective, wise Black ancestor." For Morrison, ancestors are "timeless people whose relationships to [other] characters are
benevolent, instructive, and protective, and they provide a certain kind of
wisdom."[14] Armstrong, for instance, celebrated his mother's cooking and
her common sense throughout his life, and he relied on advice from Black
Benny when he sought the protection of white managers such as Tommy
Rockwell, Johnny Collins, and Joe Glaser. Losing contact with these ancestral figures when he left New Orleans, Armstrong purchased a typewriter. While letter writing was one important way to remain in contact
with family members, hometown friends, and fellow musicians, playing
with other New Orleans transplants in King Oliver's Creole Jazz Band and
then his own bands and recording New Orleans–based music were equally
significant in linking the Southern past with the Northern present.[15] But
Armstrong did more than write letters back and forth with the people he
had known in New Orleans. By the 1930s and 1940s, he began to negotiate the complicated confluences of minstrel stereotypes and black archetypes in his autobiographical writings. What emerges from these writings
are the voices and stories of a postcolonial performer who intervenes in the
public construction of his life, his music, and his culture.

As the recent literature on postcolonialism suggests, "[t]he point of
postcolonial intervention [. . .] does not consist in replacing a 'bad' stereotype with a 'good truth,' but in understanding this productive ambivalence."[16] In other words, marginalized authors are often embroiled in "a
struggle for agency, an imbalance of power, and a need, a desire, for release."[17] Armstrong was a marginalized and postcolonial performer in
many ways; as a writer, he employed the autobiographical form as one of
the most effective modes of postcolonial expression.[18] Slavery had ended
less than two generations before he was born, releasing the Southern black
folk from their status as a colonized people on American soil into a state of
second-class citizenship. Moreover, as part of the minstrel shows, blackface
performances "Americanized" cultural models from Europe; converted immigrant performers to the status of Americans; and directed the public gaze
at the absent yet present*ed* black body and its sonic productions, thereby
enabling "America's cultural declaration of independence from Europe half

a century after the revolution."[19] Since the "double vision" expressed in these types of postcolonial performance often produced an essential "cultural ambiguity" among those who witnessed the performance, it is crucial that we also listen for the double resonances generated by Armstrong's impersonations of the intermedial Satchmo.[20] This chapter therefore pays particular attention to the incongruities, indeterminacies, and ambiguities that are produced by the "elastic polarity" of ethnic humor, and it does so by taking seriously the power of autobiography to function as "a medium of expression for writers under assail."[21] The three major subject areas in which the assailed black autobiographer asserts narrative agency are the mixing of black comedy with autobiographical storytelling, the use of the migration narrative as a narrative pattern that also enables minstrel readings, and Mardi Gras practices of cross-racial burlesque and signifying.

In *Satchmo*, Armstrong writes about his early work experience in New Orleans: "Handling and selling charcoal was certainly a dirty job. My face and hands were always black, and most of the time I looked like Al Jolson when he used to get down on his knees and sing *Mammy*."[22] Connecting this childhood memory with the image of Jolson in blackface, Armstrong comments on Tin Pan Alley, Broadway, and Hollywood representations of "blackness" that were popular with audiences in the 1920s and well into the 1950s. While employed primarily for comic effect, this memory also emphasizes Armstrong's knowledge of, and commentary on, blackface entertainment. Yet this commentary goes beyond a single reference to Jolson's appearance in *The Jazz Singer* and occurs more elaborately in written tributes to the black comedians Bill "Bojangles" Robinson and Bert Williams. These tributes suggest that the sources of Armstrong's comedic performances were filtered through the work of African American performers and comedians. And unlike Duke Ellington's instrumental compositions "Bojangles" and "A Portrait of Bert Williams" (both 1940), they offer verbal assessments of the influence these two entertainers wielded over the musician's construction of his modern black public persona.

Among Armstrong's favorite entertainers was Bill "Bojangles" Robinson, a famous tap dancer who starred in several Hollywood films and a man whom Armstrong calls "a funny 'sommitch'" and "my boy 'Bo" in the "Forward" to his *Joke Book*. About Bojangles and Lincoln Perry, the latter of whom popularized the lazy "coon" figure Stepin Fetchit in films such as *Hearts in Dixie* (dir. Paul Sloane, 1929) and *Judge Priest* (dir. John Ford, 1934), Armstrong noted: "Bill Robinson and Stepin Fetchit are my Two

Choice 'Spade "Actors.""[23] It is especially Robinson's style that enthralled
Armstrong and his fourth wife, Lucille: "She + I still think that Bill Robinson is the greatest showman that we've ever had in our Race. [. . .] He was
the sharpest Negro Man on stage that I *personally* ever seen in my life."[24]
Armstrong assessed Robinson's performances twice toward the end of his
life, and both assessments reveal much about his relationship with blackface entertainment, stage performance, and theatrical stock characters. After noting that he "had *heard* and *read*" much about Robinson before he left
New Orleans, he describes the effect Robinson's act had on him when he
saw it for the first time in Chicago. "I am sitting in my seat in the theater'
very anxious to see this man. And sure enough' the great one appeared,"
the account begins. It continues:

> As he came out of the *wing* on stage' the first thing that hit him was the
> *Flashlight. Sharp—Lord* know" *that man*' was *so Sharp* he was *Bleeding*" (our
> expression when we mention someone that's well dressed). Anyway he had
> on a sharp light tan Gabardine summer suit, Brown Derby and the usual
> expensive thick soul shoes in which he taps in.
>
> It was a long time before Bojangles could open his mouth. That's how
> popular he was and well liked by all who understood his greatness as a
> dancer and showman. He waited after the Thunderous Applause had
> finished—And looked up into the booth and said to the man who con-
> trolled the lights—Bill said to him "*Give* me a *light my color.*" And *all* the
> lights *all* over the house "*went out.*" And *me* sitting there when *this* hap-
> pened' with the whole audience just Roaring with Laughter' When I real-
> ized it—I was Laughing so Loud' until Bill Johnson whom I was with 'was
> on a verge of taking me out of there. I hadn't heard anything like that be-
> fore or witnessed it either. Then Bojangles went into his act. His every
> move was a beautiful picture. I am sitting in my seat in thrilled ecstasy' and
> delight, even in a trance. He imitated a *Trombone* with his walking cane to
> his mouth, blowing out of the side of his mouth making the buzzing sound
> of a trombone [. . .] . He told a lot of Funny jokes, which everybody enjoyed
> immensely. Then he went into his dance and finished by skating off of the
> stage with a silent sound and tempo. *Wow* what an artist. I was sold on him
> ever since.[25]

This account is remarkable for a number of reasons. First, there is Robinson's act. Robinson tap dances—with "thick *soul* shoes," not "thick-*soled*

shoes"—and does musical comedy by mimicking the trombone with his voice, evoking the sounds of black preachers Armstrong would have known from his youth.[26] His opening gag, the joke about skin color, stands in a long line of skits that date back to the minstrel shows and survived through "coon" shows and vaudeville routines. Armstrong occasionally made similar jokes about skin color. In his "Goffin Notebooks," for instance, he wrote that he once had promised his mother after a youthful indiscretion, "*Mother* I will never do that again—As long as I'm 'Colored.'"[27] He may have inherited this type of pun from Joe Oliver, who often joked about dark skin color in minstrel terms, as trombonist Clyde Bernhardt reports: "When he see somebody real dark he strike a match and whisper: 'Who dat out dare? What dat movin'?'"[28] Second, there is Armstrong's emphasis on style and artistry, on Robinson's sharp looks and masterful performance. Robinson's command of his body is "a beautiful picture." It is so impressive, in fact, that it suggests "silent sound." Third, Armstrong's description of his own reaction to the act provides a rare glimpse of him as an onlooker, as a member of the audience. When he portrays himself as being "in thrilled ecstasy' and delight, even in a trance," he positions himself in a discourse readers would have known from Goffin's *Horn of Plenty*.

A year earlier, Armstrong had already penned a lengthy autobiographical manuscript in which he celebrated Robinson's talent and style. In this manuscript, he offers a joke Robinson had told him and connects this joke with a New Orleans funeral that Robinson had allegedly attended. Armstrong presents the joke as one of Robinson's autobiographical recollections:

> Bill Robinson, who was a Southern boy himself [. . .] , knew all about the *Wakes* where everyone can Review the Body. People who lined up for the last look at the Dead Body, had their different comments. When Bojangles reached in the coffin, touched the man's *forehead*, he immediately went into the *kitchen* where the *Dead* man's *wife* was *Crying*. Bill Robinson *said* to his *wife*, he *said* to *her*, "I *touched* your *Husband's Forehead* and he seemed a little *warm* to *me*." His wife *raised* up from her crying and said to Bojangles— "*Hot* or *Cold*—he *goes out* of *here tomorrow*."—Take's *only Bill* Robinson to tell that one. To me he was the greatest comedian + dancer in my race.[29]

This anecdote illustrates Armstrong's fascination with black New Orleans, where funerals were communal events in which musicians were frequently involved by providing music. Armstrong paid tribute to the funerals on recordings such as "New Orleans Function" and "St. James Infirmary," and one of his remembrances of a jazz funeral even made it into Langston Hughes's *Book of Negro Humor* (1966).[30] The anecdote further documents his love of vernacular comedy and its blues-inflected attitude toward human failures. The woman cries publicly over her husband's death, but when she hears that he may not be dead after all, she wants to hear nothing of it.

The funeral's New Orleans setting and Robinson's joke fit nicely into the corpus of stories Armstrong told about his hometown, including an anecdote attributed to him in Max Jones and John Chilton's biography that almost exactly follows Robinson's joke. Jones and Chilton do not name their source, so it is not certain where exactly they picked up this anecdote. It is, however, attributed directly to Armstrong and told in his voice, which makes it likely that the biographers are citing from one of the musician's many unpublished oral or written recollections, perhaps a letter he had sent them:

> You got a lot of humour at some of them wakes, you know. When the body's laid out in the front room, and you all go in the house, you lead off with a hymn and then walk right back to where they got coffee, ham and cheese sandwiches and plenty liquor. So this fellow, who was a brother in the Elks club one time, was viewing the body of brother Jones. He touched the dead man on his forehead, and it seemed to him to be warm. So he went to the kitchen and told the widow: "Mrs Jones, I just touched Brother Jones's forehead and he seemed a little warm to me." Now she's crying, and all of a sudden she wipes her eyes and looks right at him, and says: "Hot or cold, he's going out of here tomorrow."[31]

The story remains close to Robinson's version, but it is personalized (the Elks club, Brother Jones) and presented as an autobiographical reminiscence that echoes Armstrong's earlier depictions of funerals. Maybe Armstrong internalized jokes and routines when he typed them into one of the many versions of his *Joke Book* and from thereon thought of them as his own. Robinson's name appears repeatedly in Armstrong's "Forward" to the *Joke Book*, and an off-color minstrel joke about "Church Goers" might very well have been supplied by him: "'Whom Am Dat Distinguished Pusson Urinating up and down the Aisle?' 'Suh! not so loud—'dat am de Rectum of 'Dis yer Constipation.'""[32] At any rate, the funeral anecdote connects minstrel images as well as overly sentimental depictions of black suffering and deprivation with a story about how poor African Americans dealt with the experience of death: by turning wakes into celebrations ("a lot of humour"; "coffee, ham and cheese sandwiches and plenty liquor") and by transforming personal pain into communal pleasure.

Armstrong's admiration for Robinson's comic material and delivery suggests that the image of the black funnyman was not at all bothersome to him as long as the comedy was genuine and the style of performance masterful. This becomes most obvious when he compares Robinson with Bert Williams, who had appeared in blackface throughout his career and had billed himself, together with his partner George Walker, as the "Two Real Coons" in the 1890s and 1900s. Unlike Williams, however, Robinson "didn't need black face—to be *funny*. Better than Bert Williams. I personally Admired Bill Robinson because he was *immaculately dressed*—you could see the Quality in his Clothes even from the *stage*. *Stopped every show*. He did not wear old *Raggedy Top Hat* and *Tails* with the *Pants cut* off—*Black Cork* with *thick white lips*, etc. But the Audiences *loved* him very much. He was *funny* from the first time he *opened* his *mouth* til he finished. So to *me* that's what *counted*. His *material* is what *counted*."[33] The dash in the first sentence of this passage is essential because it authorizes a double reading. On the one hand, Robinson "didn't need black face to be funny"; he is such a skilled performer that he does not have to rely on the comic makeup to be funny. On the other hand, while he appeared in important all-black movies such as *Harlem Is Heaven* (1932, dir. Irwin Franklyn) and *Stormy Weather* (1943, dir. Andrew L. Stone), he played minstrel-type figures, albeit not in blackface, in movies such as *The Little Colonel* and *The Littlest Rebel* (both 1935, dir. David Butler), walking the thin line between black stylishness and racial self-caricature. In this sense, the pregnant pause suggested by the dash implies that Robinson may not have needed blackface to be funny, but that he may have needed to adhere to its codes in order to be successful as an actor and entertainer. After all, when Fred Astaire saluted Robinson's tap dancing in the "Bojangles of Harlem" feature in *Swing Time* (1936, dir. George Stevens), he did so in blackface. Telling the story in this way, Armstrong may be acknowledging indirectly that he himself relied on minstrel resonances, or was at least aware of their discursive power, in order to achieve and sustain mainstream popularity.

The passages about Robinson and Williams represent two of the very few instances in which Armstrong spoke directly about African American entertainers and their involvement with blackface performance. What he describes is essentially a difference in style; Robinson's "sharp light tan Gabardine summer suit, Brown Derby and the usual expensive thick soul shoes" stand in opposition to Williams's "old *Raggedy Top Hat* and *Tails* with the *Pants cut* off—*Black Cork* with *thick white lips.*" This opposition signals a change from Williams's minstrel costume and makeup to Robinson's, and also Armstrong's, more modern and stylish clothes, a change that also signaled a shift in public attitudes toward black stage comedy and musical performance but did not preclude Armstrong from paying tribute to both Robinson's *and* Williams's style of comedy. It seems that he acknowledged Robinson as a fellow contemporary artist and Williams as one of the black ancestral figures whose entertainment skills and comedic talent had an influence on his own performative practices despite the blackface makeup and stage attire.

Obviously, Armstrong had no lasting objections to Williams's comic material. As early as the mid-1920s, he performed a preacher act that was most likely inspired by Williams's skits and recordings. Laurence Bergreen describes an Armstrong performance that presumably took place in 1923: "He loved taking the audience into his world, and introducing them to a repertoire of imaginary characters based on stock minstrel figures and his memories of New Orleans. One of his favorite creations was the Preacher. How Louis loved to imitate preachers, and satirize their avarice and lechery. He'd shout, he'd jump, he'd deliver mock sermons."[34] It is difficult to verify the accuracy of such depictions since there is little documentation beyond Armstrong's own and his fellow musicians' recollections, often presented decades after the fact. Taken together, however, the stories and anecdotes that have accumulated about these performances paint a fairly detailed picture of Armstrong's preacher routine, a picture that, while certainly not comprehensive, is richly suggestive. William Russell's account situates the preacher act in the context of Armstrong's appearances with Erskine Tate's Little Symphony Orchestra at the Vendome Theater in Chicago in 1925. "He donned a frock coat and identified himself as the Reverend Satchelmouth," Russell wrote in the late 1930s. "He proceeded with throaty stuttering to announce his text. [. . .] While he exhorted his flock, he thrust his chin out, looking for some response from the brothers and sisters. [. . .] Then his voice went really low [. . .] and when the congregation was ready for the light he whipped out the little cornet, and gave it to them."[35] While several biographers trace Armstrong's comedic talent to his New Orleans childhood and youth in general terms, Goffin actually sets the preacher routine in New Orleans, which implies that it had its origins in folk theatricals and not in the commercialized world of ethnic comedy and vaudeville. Goffin's habit of putting words into Armstrong's mouth is irritating, for sure, but his depiction connects Armstrong's routine with the spirit of Mardi Gras, the most prominent New Orleans folk theatrical. According to Goffin, Armstrong once announced "Basin Street Blues" by saying: "An' now, [. . .] here's the Reverend Satchmo' who's gonna preach a Lenten sermon. Oh, yea! I wants everybody to bow down and repent. Reverend Satchmo' is gonna to lead us into Paradise—yea, men, the Paradise o' Basin Street!"[36] In combination with Goffin's reference to the Lenten season and thus to Mardi Gras, Erskine Tate's recollection that Armstrong wore the clothes of a preacher at the Vendome theater, did "a satire on something called *Preaching Blues*," and sang "a kind of ring-chant tune [. . .] making calls like a Baptist preacher while the audience made the responses," suggests a triple matrix of folk theatrical, black vernacular comedy, and a modern minstrel mélange.[37]

According to these varied accounts, the Reverend Satchelmouth figure appeared with relative frequency in Armstrong's performances. In order to understand the cultural poetics within which these performances unfolded, we must recognize the intermedial significance of mock sermons and representations of the black preacher in minstrelsy, vaudeville, and other forms of popular culture as well as in African American folk theatricals. In other words, Armstrong's commentary on, and performances of, preachers and scenes from church life derive much of their expressive energy from the productive ambiguities that result from the mixture of popular comedy with autobiographical recollections and from the intermedial web of significances activated by this mixture. The question is: which ambiguities do Armstrong's references to preachers and his incantations of mock sermons produce when we move from autobiography, that is, from Armstrong's references to preachers in his writings, to autobiographics, that is, to his personification of preachers and parodies of sermons in other media?

Armstrong recorded two of Bert Williams's famous Elder Eatmore routines, "Elder Eatmore's Sermon on Generosity" and "Elder Eatmore's Sermon on Throwing Stones" (both Aug. 11, 1938).[38] In addition, he recorded numerous songs that showcase the Reverend Satchelmouth persona, for instance, "The Lonesome Road" (Nov. 6, 1931) and "When the Saints Go Marchin' In" (May 13, 1938, Jan. 21, 1955). "The Lonesome

Road" is Armstrong's first recorded example of the preacher figure. He introduces himself with what would become a signature line ("Sisters and brothers, this is Reverend Satchelmouth Armstrong") and refers to the band members as Brother Jack Randolph, Brother Preston, and so on, something he repeats on the religiously themed "Bye and Bye (Dec. 18, 1939) and on television during the jam session that closes off the *Timex All Star Show* #2 with a performance of "St. Louis Blues" (Apr. 30, 1958).[39] An opening similar to "Lonesome Road" can be found on the version of "When the Saints Go Marchin' In" from 1938, where Armstrong combines jazz jargon with biblical exegesis: "this is Reverend Satchmo gettin' ready to beat out this mellow sermon for you. My text this evening is 'When the saints go marchin' in.'" This is very much in line with Ralph Ellison's memories of his youth in Oklahoma, and it indicates that Armstrong and Ellison, while of vastly different educational backgrounds, drew on very similar personal and cultural source materials: "'Now, that's the Right Reverend Jimmy Rushing preaching now, man,' someone would say. And rising to the cue another would answer, 'Yeah, and that's old Elder "Hot Lips" signifying along with him, urging him on, man.' [. . .] And we might go on to name all the members of the band as though they were the Biblical four- and-twenty elders, while laughing at the impious wit of applying church titles to a form of music which all the preachers assured us was the devil's potent tool."[40]

"The Lonesome Road" revolves around a deacon named "little Satchelmouth Joe Lindsay" (the bass player of the orchestra) who initiates a collection for the benefit of Reverend Armstrong. Taking his cues from Williams's "Eatmore" sermons, which expose hypocritical church elders, Reverend Armstrong warns Deacon Lindsay to hand the money over to him: "don't put it in your pocket, will ya?" At the end of the performance, he complains to the church members that the collection did not exactly meet his expectations (he would have needed two additional dollars to retrieve his shoes from the pawn shop), but that he loved them anyway. Mocking the spiritual intensity of the sermon, the performance features one of the band members as a screaming woman, followed by Armstrong's laconic response, "Hold that sister, but get offa my foot." The choir at the beginning and ending of the song establishes a sonic reference to gospel music, to the genre of the minstrel pseudo-spiritual, as well as to graphic representations of black preachers and wailing congregations, and one is tempted to wonder, as Armstrong does in the middle of the performance, "What kind of church is this?"

Comical preacher impersonations and funny evocations of not quite pious church sermons were two approaches Armstrong took to his performances of religious material. In his liner notes for the reissued *Louis and the Good Book* album (originally released on Decca in 1958), Krin Gabbard suggests a third, more straightforwardly autobiographical approach when he interprets Armstrong's recording of the slave spiritual "Nobody Knows the Trouble I've Seen" (June 14, 1938) as a response to the death of his mentor Joe Oliver, who had passed away shortly before the recording was made. The elegiac spirit of this recording is retained on the later version of the tune that the All Stars did for *Louis and the Good Book*, but it may also be heard as a lament about the abundance of trouble caused by American civil rights injustices: "Seems like everybody's sick, sick, sick. And I'm right in there with them. Well, there's one thing that's for sure, ain't no use crying. [. . .] Sometimes you need help, that's when you look up." The seriousness with which Armstrong and the All Stars perform the song for the Goodyear Tire Company concert in 1962 further legitimates this interpretation. When Armstrong sings "nobody knows but Jesus," his bittersweet smile and the sad look in his eyes suggest a weariness that differs so substantially from his usual comic exuberance that it takes on political meanings at a moment in American history when racial tensions were growing and the civil rights movement was entering one of its most intense phases.

These meanings compete with the racial comedy Armstrong inherited from Bert Williams. One of Williams's most famous impersonations was that of the black deacon, elder, or preacher figure. This stock figure had been popularized by the Englishman Charles Mathews in the 1820s and had, in the following decades, become a staple of the minstrel show's olio segment, along with the lecture parody and the mock political oration. Mathews collected mock sermons and preacher jests when he visited the United States in 1822–23 and published them in *A Trip to America* (1824), with the goal of becoming "rich in black fun."[41] In minstrel shows and other nineteenth-century representations of black spirituality, religious caricature was a way of making sense, mostly through ridicule, of the seemingly strange beliefs and rituals of the slaves. Building on this tradition, as well as on the sermons recorded by actual Baptist and Sanctified clergy during the Great Migration, when storefront churches increasingly brought black Southern religious practices to the attention of the Northern population and when preachers addressed record buyers beyond their immediate congregations, mock sermons and preacher jests persisted until well into the twentieth century. Louis Jordan's several recordings of "Deacon Jones" of the 1940s and his performance of the tune with His Tympany Five in the film *Meet Miss Bobby Sox* (dir. Glenn Tryon, 1944) made use of this comic tradition, as did stand-up comedians like Pigmeat Markham, Richard Pryor, and, more recently, Martin Lawrence.[42]

Bert Williams also performed material from Will E. Skidmore and Marshall Walker's "Deacon Series," including "It's Nobody's Business but My Own" (1919) and "Save a Little Dram for Me" (1920).[43] In 1919, he recorded two sermons featuring "Elder Eatmore." These sermons were released by Columbia records, and Armstrong re-recorded them in 1938. The Eatmore sermons are significant because they may have shaped Armstrong's Reverend Satchelmouth routine in ways that have rarely been acknowledged. Laurence Bergreen believes that Armstrong meant them to express his anger toward Adam Clayton Powell Jr., whose overly moralizing sermon at Joe Oliver's funeral had allegedly angered Armstrong. "Never fond of the clergy, Louis considered ministers to be con artists and bullies who used the prestige of the pulpit to fleece their followers," Bergreen writes, while Krin Gabbard thinks that the Eatmore "sermons may be the most extreme manifestation of Armstrong's ambivalence about religion."[44] They *may* very well express the musician's attitude toward the clergy, and they *may* be a manifestation of his ambivalence about religion. But the fidelity with which Armstrong narrates the sermons is striking. The similarity in stresses, pauses, inflections, intentional mispronunciations, and delivery suggests that he had really studied the Williams 78s he owned. It also suggests that the inspiration for his renditions of these sermons was at least in part theatrical, rather than exclusively autobiographical. In other words, he must have analyzed Williams's vocal practices and was most likely influenced by his enunciation and oral approach to his material.[45]

"Elder Eatmore's Sermon on Throwing Stones" shows the Elder in bad humor and features as its exegetical text "eleventh of Ecclesiasteles." The Elder is disgruntled because a member of the congregation has seen him steal a turkey and has spread the news around the neighborhood. When the Elder exhorts the sinner, revealing that the informant himself had been stealing a chicken and had told on the Elder because he was jealous of the turkey, he draws hypocritically on the biblical passage stated at the beginning of the sermon: "He that is amongst you without sin, let him throw the first rock. [. . .] But I ain't takin' no chances on you all misunderstanding me." The attempt to shame the informant into submission fails when this man (spoken by Harry Mills) leads the final prayer and, in a classic example of signifying, intones: "Elder Eatmore sure is acting crazy; on last Thursday night, who was it that I had to almost tote home, that I almost had to carry home bodily? Yes, he who was so full of apple jack [. . .] and who was it, Lord, that stole the largest money and lost it playing five-up [. . .] ?" This comic routine, in both Williams's and Armstrong's versions, reproduces a series of minstrel codes, such as malapropisms, poultry theft ("procured the main article for his Thanksgiving dinner"), drinking, greed, gambling, and hypocrisy, that audiences would have known from movie shorts such as *How Rastus Got His Turkey* (dir. Theodore Wharton, 1910) and *How Rastus Got His Chicken* (1911). But since it also includes the signifying response, it potentially undermines these very codes by presenting an instance of linguistic tricksterism.[46]

Neither Elder Eatmore nor Reverend Satchelmouth appears in Armstrong's autobiographical narratives, which seems to indicate that the stock figure was part of his popular comedy and not one of the many New Orleans characters he frequently portrayed in his writings. But matters are more complicated, as Armstrong's use of Robinson's funeral joke for autobiographical purposes suggests. On *Louis and the Good Book*, he does not slip into the role of Reverend Satchelmouth but evokes the "wailing" New Orleans congregations of his youth when he adds a snippet of spontaneous jive at the end of "Ezekiel Saw the Wheel" (Feb. 7, 1958; "Old Zeke was wailin' that time"). He also delivers the verses (especially the first one) of "Jonah and the Whale" (Feb. 4, 1958) in a rhythm and intonation that recall the signifying monkey verses, and he presents the spiritual "Sometimes I Feel Like a Motherless Child" (Feb. 7, 1958) as a lamentation of the loss of home he experienced when he left segregated New Orleans for a musical career in the North. New Orleans church recollections, the Reverend Satchelmouth impersonations, the Elder Eatmore recordings, and the performances on *Louis and the Good Book* thus reveal an intermedial framework within which autobiographical reminiscences and presentations of popular materials are inextricably linked. Public performances and personal narratives cannot be easily separated but inform and influence each other, suggesting potential interconnections between comedic performances and autobiographical depictions of clergymen.

A fitting example in this context is a letter Armstrong sent to L/Cpl. Villec (1967), a marine who was stationed in Vietnam. Here, he describes his experiences as a young boy in Elder Cozy's New Orleans church:

> My Mother used to take me to 'Church with her, and the Reverend ('Preacher that is') used to 'lead off one' of those 'good ol good 'Hymns. And before you realized it—the 'whole 'Congregation would be "Wailing— 'Singing like 'mad and 'sound so 'beautiful. 'I 'being a little boy that would "Dig" 'Everything and 'everybody, I'd have myself a 'Ball in 'Church, especially when those 'Sisters 'would get 'So 'Carried away while "Rev" (the preacher) would be 'right in the 'Middle of his 'Sermon. 'Man those 'Church 'Sisters would 'begin 'Shouting 'So—until their 'petticoats would 'fall off. Of course 'one of the 'Deacons would 'rush over to her and 'grab her—'hold her in his 'Arms (a sorta 'free 'feel) and 'fan her until 'she'd 'Come 'to.[47]

This is followed by a second anecdote:

> Then there were those "Baptisms—that's when someone wants to be converted by Joining the 'Church and get 'religion. So they have to be 'Baptized. 'Dig this—I remember 'one Sunday the 'Church had a 'great big Guy they had to 'Baptize. So these 'Deacons all 'Standing in this 'River—in 'Water up to their waist in their 'white 'Robes. They had 'Baptized 'several 'women and a few 'Men—'saved their 'Souls. When in 'Walks' a 'Great 'big' 'burly 'Sinner' [. . .] . So—'these 'Deacons whom were 'very 'strong 'themselves, they grabbed 'hold of this 'Cat and said to him as they 'ducked him down into the water, as they let him up they asked him—"Brother 'do you 'Believe?" The guy didn't say 'anything—Just looked at them. So they 'Ducked him down into that 'River again, 'only they 'held him down there a 'few minutes 'Longer. So when the 'Deacons looked in the guy's eye and said to him—"Do you 'Believe?" This Guy finally 'answered—he said "Yes—I Believe you 'Son of Bitches trying to 'drown me."[48]

Both anecdotes paint a picture of the Sanctified Church that is both serious and comical. In the first anecdote, the preacher's call-and-response interaction with the congregation—he leads off a hymn; the congregation answers—as well as the intensity of the singing make an impression on the young Armstrong, who ""Dig[s . . .] 'Everything and 'everybody." Readers are essentially presented with an image of musicking here, of a communal performance that expresses religious and social messages through the music and lyrics of the hymn. The musicking is so intense that some of the female members of the congregation begin to swoon and lose consciousness. This mostly serious memory is followed by a funny ending that glances knowingly beyond the professed piety of the Sunday sermon at the lechery of the male deacons ("a sorta 'free 'feel"). The second anecdote reads even more like a comedy skit, but it, too, is presented as an autobiographical reminiscence. While Armstrong again produces information about specific religious practices such as river baptisms, he also signals his awareness of these practices as sources of popular comedy that could function as an expression of black vernacular punning as much as they could serve as reminders of the minstrel poetics, which had ridiculed African American religious practices for more than a century.[49]

Apart from recording preacher skits and depicting black clergy in ways that suggest both vernacular comedy and minstrel humor, Armstrong embraced a narrative trajectory for his life story that centers on the major politico-geographical fault line of nineteenth- and twentieth-century America, the Mason-Dixon line, which demarcates the conflict between the Southern and Northern states over slavery and the movement, after Reconstruction, of Southerners to the North as part of the Great Migration. It was also the line of scrimmage for civil rights activists who ventured into the South as part of the Freedom Rides in 1961. In Armstrong's case, the story involves a Southern childhood, often depicted in nostalgic terms; the journey from South to North, where the newcomer is overwhelmed by an almost entirely new world; and the struggles of this newcomer to make it in this world, which lead to moments of serious hardship, as well as humorous misunderstandings and misapprehensions. Farah Jasmine Griffin's conceptionalization of musical, visual, and literary migration narratives provides a useful handle on Armstrong's autobiographical narratives and performances. Migration narratives were the prime mode through which African American migrants made sense of, and communicated, their experience of dislocation from a provincial to a cosmopolitan setting that affected massive changes in the demographics of Northern cities. The number of Chicago's blacks quintupled in the 1910s and 1920s, and at least 10 percent of the black population shifted from South to North in the same period.[50] Armstrong certainly used the structure of the migration narrative to present his life story, but he did so by implicitly referencing a variety of racial stock figures that had served as popular representatives of the Northern gaze across the Mason-Dixon line: the country bumpkin Jim Crow and the citified dandy Zip Coon, both public emblems of the "half million darkies from Dixie" that "swarm to the North," according to one headline in a Chicago newspaper.[51] In Armstrong's autobiographics, both migration resonances *and* minstrel echoes shape the intermedial figure of the Satchmo.[52]

Armstrong's version of the country boy on his way up North follows the New Negro movement's celebration of the leap from South to North, provincial to cosmopolitan, "medieval America to modern."[53] At the same time, this story derives meaning from comic depictions of the citified minstrel dandy, who aspires to be fashionable and therefore deserves ridicule, and, more forcefully, from the sights and sounds of the backwoods country boy, who is ill-equipped to understand life in the North and whose foolishness is a source of comedy. It is no coincidence that the most popular radio show of the late 1920s and 1930s was *Amos 'n' Andy*, an example of verbal minstrelsy, or sonic blackface, in which the white ex-minstrels Freeman F. Gosden and Charles J. Correll appeared as the blackfaced, or rather black-voiced, characters Amos and Andy.[54] The show began as *Sam 'n' Henry* on January 12, 1926, shortly before Armstrong would score his first big hit with "Heebie Jeebies," and it depicted the experiences of two Southerners relocating from Birmingham, Alabama, to Chicago, Illinois. Broadcast in a new format as *Amos 'n' Andy* on March 19, 1928, and featuring "white America's favorite 'southern colored boys,'" who moved from Georgia to Chicago first and later to Harlem, the radio show could be heard nationwide and eventually reached an audience of up to forty million listeners six times a week.[55]

Amos 'n' Andy was set in a simulated all-black world, an illusion that worked on the radio, where the speakers mimicked and caricatured black speech, but had its difficulties on film and television. When the Duke Ellington Band appeared in *Check and Double Check* (dir. Melville Brown, 1930), Gosden and Correll's film version of *Amos 'n' Andy*, two light-skinned members of the band (Juan Tizol and Barney Bigard) were forced to wear blackface to avoid any suggestion of racial integration, and when a television version was introduced in 1951, it was quickly forced off the air by 1953 due to protests by the NAACP and other civil rights organizations. Like some of Armstrong's stories, *Amos 'n' Andy* derived much of its humor from "the characters' ignorance and the contrast of caricatured minstrel and black Southern folkways with the demands of urban living."[56] Amos was a modernized Jim Crow character, and Andy performed the role of a modern-day Zip Coon.

Armstrong recalls several episodes from his life story with which audiences would have been familiar, if not in fact, then at least in sentiment, from the *Amos 'n' Andy* shows. The account of a train trip to St. Louis in *Satchmo*, for instance, clearly presents a comic duo reminiscent of *Amos 'n' Andy*, with Armstrong performing as an Amos-like figure and his colleague David Jones playing an Andy-like character. It provides a glimpse at two "southern colored boys" taking the train up North. When the conductor tells people to change trains, Armstrong acts in a slow-witted and clumsy manner: "my ears pricked up like a jackass. When I grabbed all my things I was so excited that I loosened the top of my olive bottle, but somehow I managed to reach the platform with my arms full." Once people rush to board the new train, "somebody bumped into me and knocked the olives out of my arm. The jar broke into a hundred pieces and the olives rolled all over the platform. [. . .] I felt pretty bad about those good olives, but when I finally got on the train I was still holding my fish sandwich. Yes sir, I at least managed to keep that."[57]

Ten years prior to this account, Armstrong had already described the same train trip in his "Goffin Notebooks." The basic story line is identical, while the way it is told and some of the specific people and places involved are different: "We left New Orleans 'by "Train and by me not traveling to any place before, I did not know what [to] do as far as Lunch was concerned," he writes. And he continues:

> So I went to "PRATS 'RESTAURANT and Bought myself a Big "Fish Loaf—I think it was trout. I also Bought myself a Big Bottle of "Olives' I had it and the Fish Wrapped up in a Paper Sack. We had to change trains at a little town called GAILSBURG ILL. The Station was Crowded with people Changing Trains for All Directions. Our Train Arrived and by me rushing along to catch the train with David Jones (mellophone player)—I Dropped the "Fish Sandwich on the ground the '*Olives Dropped*' also and the Olives Bottle Broke and "Olives were running all over the place. The Fish Sandwich Bag Busted and the Fish fell all over the ground. "Oh Boy" was I Embarrassed—I thought sure, David Jones would help me pick up those things—But "*SHUCKS* He only walked away Embarrassed also.[58]

In his interview with Larry King, Armstrong connected the same incident with his journey to Chicago in 1922, thus displaying a flexible approach to autobiographical recollection while rejoicing in the opportunity to tell a good anecdote to a receptive listener: "I was carrying my horn, a little dab of clothes, and a brown bag of trout sandwiches my mother, Mayann, had made me up. Had on long underwear beneath my wide-legged pants—in July."[59] Robert Toll's description of the stage attire worn by the Virginia Minstrels—"baggy, mismatched patchwork clothes and huge shoes"— comes to mind in passages like this, as does Bert Williams's costume.[60] In the Meryman interview for *Life* a year earlier, Armstrong had already presented the anecdote, and while the basic storyline does not differ substantially from previous accounts, the punch line adds a self-conscious twist about Armstrong's country stylishness: "For the train ride up to Chicago Mayann fixed me a big trout sandwich. And I had on my long underwear 'cause she didn't want me to catch cold. I had me a little suitcase—didn't have but a few clothes—and a little case for my cornet. I traveled in style, you know, in my way."[61]

The different versions of the event relate to the minstrel poetics in various ways. In *Satchmo*, Armstrong is clumsy, bent on eating, and talking to himself ("Yes sir, I at least managed to keep that"). In conjunction with his exaggerated, animalistic physicality ("ears pricked up like a jackass") and the long underwear mentioned in the two interviews (King and Meryman), this evokes the comic physique, simple-minded nature, and raggedy clothing of the Sambo. David Jones's reaction to the accident—"*SHUCKS*"— may be interpreted as a self-conscious minstrel reference. But then again, the various versions of this anecdote can also be read as humorous pieces of vernacular storytelling in which a mature and urbane narrator looks back on his younger years and delights in connecting backward images of "blackness" with reminiscences of a doting mother who wanted to make sure that her beloved son would neither starve nor freeze on the daunting trip to an unknown world. As was so often the case, Goffin opted for the Sambo version in *Horn of Plenty*, changing the tone of Armstrong's anecdote from humor to fear, altering the cause of the accident from the overcrowded platform to Armstrong's clumsiness, introducing a racial dimension (he imagines a *white* trainman who is cursing the *black* klutz), and omitting Armstrong's assessment of this experience as a moment of bonding: "David Jones and I *'laugh* about that situation every time we run into each other."[62] The comic ambiguities that follow from these various depictions produce performativity. They extend Armstrong's versioned recollections into the realm of popular culture, where Satchmo's physical traits, behavior, and clothes resonate with Sambo representations and simultaneously reference specific cultural moments and media environments of the 1920s and 1930s, including *Amos 'n' Andy*.

These recollections of the train trip and the overall scope of Armstrong's narratives follow Griffin's four-stage pattern of the migration narrative: "an event that propels the action northward," "a detailed representation of the initial confrontation with the urban landscape," "an illustration of the migrant's attempt to negotiate that landscape," and "a vision of the possibilities or limitations of the Northern [. . .] or Midwestern city."[63] The event that propels Armstrong's action northward is the telegram he received from Joe Oliver on August 8, 1922 (first stage). The initial confrontation with the urban landscape occurs when Armstrong narrates his arrival in St. Louis or Chicago, depending on which version of the story he is telling (second stage). He confesses that he was confused by the tall buildings he saw in St. Louis. "There was nothing like that in my home town, and I could not imagine what they were all for," he writes. "I wanted to ask somebody badly, but I was afraid I would be kidded for being so dumb." When he finally musters up the courage to ask the more educated and experienced Fate Marable, "What are all those tall buildings? Colleges?" the answer is, "Aw boy, [. . .] don't be so damn dumb." As was the case with the fish-sandwich incident, Armstrong later remembered Chicago (and thus a somewhat later date) as the city in which this had happened: "I'd never seen a city that big. All those tall buildings. I thought they were universities."[64] Accounts of the train trip itself are situated between steps one and two. This additional narrative space is particularly interesting because it articulates a transitional moment in which minstrel comedy competes with an experience of personal and cultural affirmation. As Armstrong explains: "There was no place for colored people to eat on the trains in those days, especially down in Galilee (the South). Colored persons going North crammed their baskets full of everything but the kitchen stove." On the train, he meets a black woman he had known in New Orleans; she offers him "some of that good and pretty fried chicken," and he "lived and ate like a king during the whole trip."[65]

Moving on to the third stage of the migration-narrative pattern, Armstrong describes his initial confrontation with life in the North/Midwest— the cabarets of Chicago's South Side district in 1922 and 1923. He writes in "The Armstrong Story" that "I had just come up from the South," an expression that is repeated almost verbatim in "The Satchmo Story."[66] Armstrong recalled on many instances how his country clothes and behavior caused mocking commentary from his colleagues. Joe Oliver allegedly called him a "country so and so," as well as a "*Country Son of a Bitch*," and he further commented on the young cornetist's "*Sloe* Foot self," while Armstrong describes himself as a "Real 'Country 'Sommitch'" and mentions his "little Country Boy Way[s]" in the "Goffin Notebooks."[67] The musicians with whom Armstrong played in his first years in Chicago and New York all remembered his country looks. Arranger Don Redman, for instance, noted: "He was big and fat and wore high-top shoes with hooks in them, and long underwear down to his socks"; Kaiser Marshall recalled a man who "came walking across the floor, clump-clump, and grinned and said hello to all the boys"; Fletcher Henderson thought of him as "pretty much a down-home boy in the big city." Armstrong's future wife Lil Hardin "wasn't impressed at all [. . .]. I was very disappointed. 226 pounds, I didn't like anything about him. I didn't like the way he dressed; I didn't like the way he talked; and I just didn't like him. I was very disgusted."[68] But Armstrong soon found devoted followers: "I tried to walk like him, talk like him. I bought shoes and a suit like the 'Great One' wore," Rex Stewart reports, and Buck Clayton's account of meeting Armstrong for a rehearsal at Frank Sebastian's Cotton Club in Culver City in 1930 indicates that the musician eventually became a stylish entertainer: "He had just come out of the hotel and looked awfully sharp. His hair looked nice and shiny and he had on a pretty gray suit. He wore a tie that looked like an ascot tie with an extra-big knot in it. Pops was the first one to bring that style of knot to Los Angeles. Soon all the hip cats were wearing big knots in their ties. We called them Louis Armstrong knots."[69]

Armstrong quickly tried to adapt to the urbanity of his fellow musicians. A humorous passage in "The Armstrong Story" details how the new arrival sought to negotiate the urban landscape and its social codes. Only weeks after Armstrong had arrived in Chicago in order to appear with King Oliver's Creole Jazz Band at the Lincoln Gardens, the "'Country 'Sommitch'" attempted to change his "little Country Boy Way[s]":

> One night I came to work smelling real sweet and Bud Red [the manager of the Lincoln Gardens] gave me the devil about it—saying, "Where the so and so did you get that cheap stuff you are wearing?" I did not dare to tell

him that one of the roomers gave me that perfume—it came from the Stock Yards in a big bottle. Bud made such an issue of it, and laughed so hard at me, just when I thought I was dressed to kill, I just had to stop wearing it on my clothes to stop all of those cats from ragging me. Before I made up my mind fully to lay off that perfume, it started to smell like lineament. I got up enough nerve to ask the man what it was made of—he told me they made it from fertilizer. That really ended the smelling session.[70]

This passage presents an experience that hundreds of thousands of uprooted African Americans had shared—the intricacies of life up North, captured on song titles such as "Stock Yard Strut" by Freddie Keppard and His Jazz Cardinals (1926). It extends a nod to the "citified dandy" figure of the minstrel show and "coon" era. Armstrong had impersonated this figure on various recordings of "Shine," and it was also featured on the Okeh race records advertisement for "St. James Infirmary." The minstrel dandy fails at being "civilized" and "high class"; his exaggerated style and dress are ridiculous because they identify him as a clumsy imitator of allegedly superior white models. In Armstrong's case, the humorous discrepancy lies between the modern ways of the North and the new arrival's unfamiliarity with these ways. This discrepancy simultaneously suggests a minstrel dandy who wants to show class by wearing perfume but ends up smelling like fertilizer and a transplanted Southerner who has not yet mastered the demands of modern living. Undermining the country boy and dandy images by emphasizing a modern sense of musical excellence, Armstrong then recalls his and Oliver's technical innovations and the legendary solo breaks they were taking in the early 1920s, noting how they "developed a little system whereby we didn't have to write down the duet breaks" and whereby Armstrong "could take second to his lead in a split second. [. . .] No one could understand how we did it, but it was easy and we kept it that way the whole evening."[71] Here, Armstrong is the musical master again, superior to other musicians and dazzling his audiences with his playing and his miraculous rapport with Oliver. Passages like this signal his awareness of his audience's understanding of jazz as the music of socially inferior blacks (thus the Sambo resonances) whose offerings are especially fascinating because they seem natural and untutored. This, then, constitutes the fourth stage of the migration narrative: the migrant's experience with the possibilities and limitations that shape his life in the North, as well as the musician's attempts to recover a sense of home by surrounding himself with New Orleanians like Oliver. Writing about the migration experience and incorporating it into the referential space of his autobiographics constituted a fifth step beyond Griffin's model. It enabled Armstrong to inscribe his personal migration story into American cultural history.

The loss of the Southern home constituted a central rupture in Armstrong's life. Even though he eventually found a permanent home in Corona, New York, where he lived with his wife Lucille from 1943 until his death, he remained enthralled with the New Orleans of his youth. Ralph Ellison once noted that the movement to the North affected the "entire psychosomatic structure" of America's black citizens.[72] It is only logical, then, that Armstrong sought to work through the psychosomatic effects of his Southern exodus in his music as well as in his writings. He celebrated his Southern roots and his newfound popularity as an entertainer in the North on his recording of "Big Butter and Egg Man from the West" (Nov. 16, 1926), a song composed by the Sunset Café's show producer Percy Venable. In the middle of the recorded version from the same year, Armstrong ad-libs a passage in which he brags about his Southern roots ("I'm from way down in the South") and about his financial and musical prowess ("buy you all the pretty things that you think you need"; "I'll even hit high C's"). The singer proudly displays his Southernness because it brings him financial rewards and elevates him to the social status of a successful musician, but he also offers a vision of success to black migrants and would-be migrants.

Musical evocations of the South as home were indeed significant, as a statement Armstrong made about the reception of songs such as "Twelfth Street Rag" illustrates: "Everybody seems to have a good time—they jive— it makes them feel at home."[73] Being invited into the communal space created by the musicians on stage, the audience is to become part of their loving memories of New Orleans and to share their sentiments and joys. Thus, a song like "That's My Home" (Dec. 8, 1932), which creates a nostalgic scene where friendly "folks" welcome the singer at his "home, sweet home," where "mammy's love is true," and where the "Swanee river flow[s]," derives its popular appeal from its productively ambiguous evocation of a nostalgic minstrel South *and* a blues-inflected space determined by Armstrong's love of his mother (signified by the "mammy's love") and hometown (signified by the "home" and the Swanee River as a stand-in for the Mississippi). Furthermore, Armstrong's charismatic rendition (including his interpolation of "Satchmo" and the vernacular inflection in "where the Swanee river *flow*"), his lyrical solo, and the specific context in which the tune was recorded (in the studio with a group of mostly non-Southern musicians) do much to personalize the performance, and they substitute the minstrel South with images and sounds of early twentieth-century New Orleans and early 1930s studio musicking.

This is also true of the minstrel tunes Armstrong recorded with the Mills Brothers in 1937, "The Old Folks at Home" and "Carry Me Back to Old Virginny," which certainly revive the sounds and sights of the minstrel shows. Armstrong's singing on "Carry Me Back to Old Virginny," however, comes across as intentionally dignified, suggesting that he sought to countermand the reactionary lyrics through a beautiful rendition of the melody. He sings the tune masterfully, announcing himself with a soft and sensitive scat line that captures the nostalgic sentiments of the lyrics, and he intones the melody in a laid-back, crooning style. What is more, while the Mills Brothers retain the original phrase "dear ol' massa" in their portion of the verse, Armstrong sings "dear old master"; he also changes the deictic and self-referential "this old darky's heart" to the more distanced "the old darky's heart." His solo, too, displays a taste for subtle melodic variations entirely suited to the mood of the song and thus emphasizes Armstrong's genuine interest in the material and its Southern theme. Choosing a different kind of delivery, Armstrong mostly narrates "The Old Folks at Home." He turns himself into a type of black storyteller whom audiences might have known from Joel Chandler Harris's *Uncle Remus* stories and whom they would meet again in Disney television shows such as *Disneyland after Dark* (dir. Hamilton S. Luske and William Beaudine, 1962) and movies such as *Song of the South* (dir. Harve Foster and Wilfred Jackson, 1946). Armstrong recorded the theme song of *Song of the South* in 1968 for the album *Disney Songs the Satchmo Way* (the scat-influenced "Zip-A-Dee-Doo-Dah," May 16, 1968), and he ends "The Old Folks at Home" with a brief interlude that recasts the lyrics as an expression of the transplanted Southerner's longing for his home: "Well, look-a-here, we are far away from home." The version of another Foster tune, "My Old Kentucky Home," recorded with the All Stars for the *Satchmo Plays King Oliver* album, makes the same argument musically. It reshapes the song into a New Orleans classic, thereby exchanging the minstrel message for a personal setting and a specific historical context.

Armstrong was often faulted for keeping neominstrel songs like "When It's Sleepy Time Down South" in his repertoire throughout his career. It is important to note, however, that he eventually changed the racially offensive "*darkies* are crooning" to "*people* are crooning," thus toning down the minstrel echoes to a certain extent, but also that he saw little use in this change. Barney Bigard recalls Armstrong's reaction on the day after he had been urged to sing the new lyrics in the recording studio for the first time: "What do you want me to call those black sons-of-bitches this morning?"[74] Thus, there seems to have been a willingness to support nostalgic visions of the South, including minstrelized material, but these visions were usually coupled with a vernacular approach that personalized performances and drew them into the space of Armstrong's autobiographics, veering back and forth between moments of personal significance, show-business tactics, and cultural politics. In one of his final interviews caught on camera, he calls the song "my lifelong number [. . .] that lives with me," then sings a full version of it, and finally remarks, "the show is on, daddy." During the rehearsals for his birthday concert in 1970, he refers to the melodramatic ending he devised for the tune—an ending that contains the intricate scat line he had perfected over the years—as "my hustle," thus foregrounding its effectiveness as a concert opener and adding commercial considerations to the song's significance. A few years earlier, he had already acknowledged the discrepancy between the song's benevolent lyrics and the political changes that were sweeping the country: "I know that lots of things haven't been sleeping, they've been progressing."[75]

The spoken skit that introduces the first recorded version of "When It's Sleepy Time Down South" (Apr. 20, 1931) is a case in point because it anchors the performance within the experience of the Great Migration. The dialogue that prefigures the song introduces Armstrong's piano player Charlie Alexander as an old New Orleans acquaintance. When Armstrong asks how long Alexander had been living in the North, the pianist replies that he has been there for roughly a year and a half. Armstrong's response is crucial: "A year and a half? Man, I been up here a long time myself. I'm goin' back home. [. . .] Get some of them red beans and pig ears. You remember them sleepin' back there, daddy? [. . .] This is why I'm goin' back." Prefaced by this little skit, the neominstrel song actually laments the loss of the communal spirit of black New Orleans. The skit follows the logic of Sam Dennison's "carry-me-back" songs, but as a coded reference to Armstrong's hometown, it also foregrounds the larger autobiographics involved in this recorded performance. The song was written for Armstrong by the black actor Clarence Muse and two Creoles from Louisiana, Leon and Otis

René, and the phrase "red beans and pig ears" connects the skit not only with Armstrong's favorite food—food coded as poor, black, and Southern—but also with his letters and autobiographical writings, in which he frequently extended culinary greetings to his readers. A second coded reference, the jive term "daddy," links the skit with Armstrong's penchant for linguistic play. It reinforces the performative nature of skit and song and sanctions contrasting notions of performative exuberance as minstrel abandon and/or black soulfulness. Adding his speaking voice to the recording, he signals that he is not to be constrained by the lyrics of the song, and he triggers—via the workings of scat aesthetics—a visual/physical dimension of himself/his black body in performance.[76] Furthermore, besides the minstrel South described in the lyrics, another, more discrete South is conjured up by Armstrong's and Alexander's exchange: the South of the black working class as it had existed in the speakers' past below the Mason-Dixon line and as it existed, in adapted form, above this line as "[t]he South in the City."[77] One of the major achievements of the Great Migration was that those who ventured to the Northern metropolis took many of their cultural practices with them and managed to overcome "the noisy lostness" of places like Chicago and New York by adapting their musical ways to the new situation and by investing their performances with signifiers of their Southern home.[78]

The importance of Southern signifiers is illustrated by the soundie of "When It's Sleepy Time Down South" (1942).[79] The lyrics speak of crooning "darkies" whose life in the South is one of ease. These "darkies" prance around all day and sing dreamy songs that lure the singer "back there where I belong / right here in mammy's arms." The power of visual minstrel codes is demonstrated by the studio scenery, which includes bales of cotton and sacks of rice on which lazy black stevedores stretch out and slumber. A boy is fishing in the Mississippi River, while Armstrong is placed among a family that includes the boy, a stereotypical mammy (she is rotund, smiles, wears an apron and a bandana, but is not "old," as the lyrics proclaim), a pickaninny girl seated at her feet, and a no-good country husband (played by Nick "Nicodemus" Stewart) asleep to Armstrong's right. Throughout the performance, people are yawning and stretching, emphasizing the "sleepy time" of the lyrics and supporting the slow, languid music. When Armstrong sings of the "old mammy," the camera turns to the mammy figure (played by singer Velma Middleton), and when he sings of the prancing "darkies," the two children perform a slow-motion dance that could be interpreted as lazy but also as a highly stylized, slow-motion version of an African American folk dance. During Armstrong's solo, the husband, finally awoken by the smell and sight of the chicken drumstick the mammy has pulled out of her basket, performs his own version of the dance while munching on the tasty food. The connection to minstrel/"coon" codes—slow dancing, sleeping, chicken, the mammy—is obvious.

Apart from occasional insertions of "oh babe," Armstrong renders the lyrics faithfully—no scat, jive, or spoken patter spoils the serenity of the performance. But what about his trumpet playing? Does it affirm, question, or subvert the lyrical and visual tribute to the minstrel South? Or does it do something else entirely? This is difficult to say since musical meaning is always coproduced by visual and discursive signifiers.[80] Armstrong is dressed in country garb (checkered shirt, farmer's hat) and is sitting on bales of cotton; he remains static throughout the performance; he does not do any dancing, grinning, or any other form of mugging. Both his singing and playing are certainly of high quality; there seems to be no doubt that this is a professional musician who has mastered his instrument. It remains a matter of conjecture, however, whether Armstrong's artistry clearly undermined the minstrel code in the eyes and ears of contemporary audiences. The most reasonable assumption is that it produced ambiguities that resonated with depictions of the South in Armstrong's writings, sound recordings, and film appearances, but also with the larger poetics of minstrel and postminstrel performances of "blackness." On the film footage for the Goodyear Tire Company in 1962, for instance, Armstrong pops his eyes while he sings the verses of the song (especially during the line "when old mammy falls on her knees") but focuses his eyes inward—and thus away from the narrative of the song into a more personal and private space—as he is playing his solo.

The soundie and similar performances situate Armstrong at the fault line between the folk-rural America of the Sambo and the "New Negro" modern urbanity of his jazz ensembles. Depicting his departure from the culture of the crescent city, the train ride from New Orleans to St. Louis/Chicago, and his physical entry into modern America, Armstrong literally carries Southern food (from the fish sandwich to chicken drumsticks) and the cornet (the precursor of the trumpet), the instrument with which he would change the course of twentieth-century music, across the Mason-Dixon line. When Alain Locke in his introduction to *The New Negro* (1925) envisions the movement of African Americans from South to

North, country to city, and old stereotypes to new cultural self-determina-tion, as "a deliberate flight [. . .] from medieval America to modern," he grants the transformation from Sambo to Satchmo a central position in the modern cultural imagination even though he does not mention Armstrong in this piece.[81] The fish sandwich and the cornet are the true emblems of Sambo and the "New Negro" each, and they culminate in the productive ambiguities of Armstrong's intermedial autobiographics: the public sounds, images, and stories of Satchmo.

The cover of *Ambassador Satch* (1956), an album of live performances from a concert tour through Europe, affirms the emblematic power of this intermedial figure beyond the 1920s and 1930s. The photograph depicts a grinning Armstrong in his midfifties, still carrying the suitcase in one hand and the trumpet in the other more than three decades after his initial trip to the North. As Terry Teachout reports, the trumpeter probably had a generous load of marijuana in the suitcase, which reinforces the idea that single images and performances may carry different messages to different people—pot and politics, in this case—at the same time.[82] But in the post-war decades, Armstrong's significance as an icon of black modernity—a crosser of racial boundaries and restrictions—was seldom at the forefront of people's minds. He became more and more associated with a backward image of an overly accommodationist entertainer, as the reception of his appearance as King Zulu in the 1949 Mardi Gras parade indicates. This ap-pearance garnered widespread critique and caused confusion over his role as an African American artist and entertainer. As photographs of his ap-pearance document, he wore the traditional costume, including a black wig, a crown, a gown and grass skirt, and blackface makeup that accentu-ated the whiteness of his eyes and the blackness of his skin.

The public reaction to this event was divided, but its overall effect was stunning: "Armstrong's image as a regressive, plantation-style minstrel—an image that, from the start in New Orleans, had been used for spirit-lift-ing subversion—was now firmly imprinted on the national consciousness." Especially among many African Americans, the reaction to the Zulu ap-pearance was brutal. The Chicago attorney George C. Adams accused Armstrong of "stoop[ing] to such foolishness and thus disgrac[ing] all Ne-groes," while the New Orleans radio host O. C. W. Taylor held that Arm-strong "was always contented to return a grinning, ape-like Sambo and help keep the Negro in his 'Uncle Tom' status."[83] *Time* magazine published a lead article a few days before the event. "Among Negro intellectuals, the

Fig. 11. Louis Armstrong as King of the Zulus. Photograph by Edmond "Doc" Souchon, 1949. Courtesy of Louisiana State Museum, Jazz Collection.

Zulus and all their doings are considered offensive vestiges of the minstrel-show, Sambo-type Negro," the magazine writers observed. "To Armstrong such touchiness seems absurd, and no one who knows easygoing, nonintellectual Louis will doubt his sincerity. To Jazz King Armstrong, lording it over the Zulu Parade (a broad, dark satire on the expensive white goings-on in another part of town) will be the sentimental culmination of his spectacular career, and a bang-up good time besides."[84] This passage is particularly rich in implications because it is trying to rescue Armstrong from allegations of being a "minstrel-show, Sambo-type Negro" by stressing the satirical nature of the performance, but it simultaneously celebrates a minstrel image of the "easygoing" and "nonintellectual" entertainer who is having a "bang-up good time."

Leonard Feather's eyewitness account of the Mardi Gras events underscores the complex array of meanings the performance triggered:

Throughout my visit I saw Louis looking at me from the cover of *Time* on every white newsstand in town. I saw front-page stories in every local newspaper about Louis, the Zulus, and the parade; but I also saw black citizens wearing the "Zulu King" lapel button on which was caricatured a Negro face so grotesque that there would have been an uproar if whites had distributed it. I was refused a ride late at night by a frightened Negro cab driver who said "he couldn't drive white folk"; yet in broad daylight I followed the Zulus' parade with Lucille Armstrong and a mixed group of friends in an open car, and nobody said a word.[85]

In order to make sense of this account, the social and racial origins of the Zulu parades and the discursive history of the term "Zulus" must be considered. In linguistic terms, " 'Zulu' was a common racial slur, used right alongside 'nigger,' 'darky,' 'coon,' and 'monkey.' "[86] As a social practice, the Zulu parade was a working-class performance of "coal cart drivers, bar tenders—waiters, Hustlers, etc., people of all walks of life."[87] It was organized by the Zulu Social Aid and Pleasure Club, founded in 1909 by the black New Orleanian John L. Metoyer and a group of workers who called themselves "The Tramps." The Zulu Social Aid and Pleasure Club stands in the tradition of fraternal organizations in New Orleans that began as aid societies in the antebellum era and became more influential after Reconstruction. These organizations created a medical infrastructure and support system in order to compensate for the effects of racial segregation and extensive poverty.[88] But there is more to the story, since Metoyer and his group were inspired by a vaudeville troupe called Smart Set that had performed at the Pythian Temple Theater in New Orleans. Different incarnations of this troupe were organized by the white producer Gus Hill, as well as by Sherman H. Dudley and the Whitney & Tutt brothers; they included black dancers and comedians such as Ernest Hogan and Tom McIntosh. One of the comedy-and-dance skits the troupe did in their New Orleans show was called "There Never Was and Never Will Be a King Like Me." The performers were dressed up as faux African Zulus, and they wore grass skirts as well as blackface makeup. In other words, the Zulu Social Aid and Pleasure Club emerged at a moment in American cultural history in which Southern black working-class traditions in the form of fraternal organizations and the vaudeville styles of blackface entertainment comingled. As such, it delivered the impetus for a New Orleans social ritual, the Zulu parade, which offered the city's racially segregated and socially disadvantaged African Americans a chance to parody the white official version of Mardi Gras.[89]

Feeding the visual imagination, all members of the Zulu Aid and Plea-sure Club, including Armstrong's father in past parades, wear a "big white monkey suit" and throw coconuts from their floats. The King has "his face painted black" and wears "a 'grass skirt' along with a crown, sceptre and other paraphernalia."[90] The Zulu parade thus engages with white repre-sentations of Zulu "blackness" but does so through the filters of black vaudeville entertainment and vernacular forms of play-acting and signify-ing that climax in a "double-edged symbolism."[91] King Zulu and his fol-lowers ridicule the concept of Lent, including the idea of frugality and fast-ing, about which the black working poor obviously had different opinions than the more affluent whites. But they also do so by wearing outfits and makeup that carried the minstrel poetics into the twentieth century, even if its performers might have attempted, as many black performers at the time did, to develop a more nuanced and stylish black entertainment within the minstrel format.

This double-edged symbolism is reflected in the differences between the popular reception of the event and Armstrong's own testimony about it. These differences suggest that the ways in which the Zulu Parade was mediated to its audiences and the meanings of Zulu song and imagery in American popular culture had a bearing on the event's cultural effects. The preevent coverage by the *New Orleans Times-Picayune* indicates why African American intellectuals and middle-class audiences may have found the parade offensive. Titled "Head Hunters on the Loose," the article an-nounced: "The most ferocious assemblage of African bushmen ever to set sail from the Dark Continent will invade New Orleans for the annual Zulu Parade on Mardi Gras. [. . .] Reports are that the tribesmen, whose king is to be Louis 'Satchmo' Armstrong, intend to 'kill a few' along the line of the march." The newspaper piece is certainly written in the spirit of Mardi Gras. One could argue that it does in writing what the Zulus do in march-ing: playing with popular images of Africa. However, phrases such as "Dark Continent," "African bushmen," and "most ferocious" suggest racist notions of savagery and cannibalism and add substance to the accusations of backwardness and racial self-deprecation that black audiences were hurling at Armstrong.[92] It is not surprising, then, that the double-edged symbolism of Armstrong's Zulu appearance was received critically by many African Americans at midcentury.[93]

The majority of these African Americans as well as the public at large were probably unaware of the fact that the poster that announced Armstrong's live appearance at the Zulu Social Aid and Pleasure Club on February 27 relied on a very different discourse of suave entertainment.[94] It prints "King Zulu" in bold letters and displays a promotional photograph of a younger and elegantly dressed Armstrong minus the Zulu wig, costume, and makeup. In addition, his ensemble is listed as "Louis Armstrong and his Esquire All Star Band," which foregrounds Armstrong's elevated status as band leader and jazz soloist as well as his success as an artist. He and the members of the band had won the *Esquire* magazine jazz poll (initiated by Leonard Feather) and thus enjoyed a degree of public prestige that stood in stark contrast to the musician's lowly New Orleans origins. What emerges here is a difference of perspective between the mainstream press, which frequently did not recognize Armstrong as a self-conscious performer who had no qualms about dabbling with the vernacular practices of his hometown, and the black New Orleanians involved in the parade, who delighted in the spectacular possibilities of his appearance and celebrated him as a master performer and cultural hero. These New Orleanians welcomed their prodigal son, who had returned to the place of his birth and through his mere presence signaled that social mobility and personal success were possible even for the poorest of blacks.

But what is so particular about the Zulu imagery presented by the parades, amplified by the *New Orleans Times-Picayune* article and countered by the dapper Armstrong on the poster? And why is it relevant to discuss this imagery in connection with the cultural intermediality of Armstrong's work? For one, the Mardi Gras parade resonates with a long history of Zulu images in American culture, including the Smart Set vaudeville troupe; P. T. Barnum's presentation of "Two Real African Zulus" at Madison Square Garden in 1888; Williams and Walker's performance of "My Little Zulu Babe" in the musical show *The Sons of Ham* (1900); The Black Patti Troubadours' renditions of "In Zululand" in *A Trip to Africa* (1910); and short movies such as David Wark Griffith's *The Zulu's Heart* (1908), Arthur Hotaling's *Rastus in Zululand* (1910), and Hotaling's *Rastus among the Zulus* (1913). Williams and Walker recorded "My Little Zulu Babe" in 1901, and the original sheet music cover sports a photograph of a male and female dancer, both wearing skirts and looking comically "African." The man's nose is pierced by a giant ring, and the photograph is surrounded by a drawing of simianlike Africans with exaggerated lips, popping eyes, and leopard-skin dress.[95]

Moreover, the Mardi Gras appearance of 1949 was not the first time

Armstrong had evoked Zulu imagery. In 1926, he had recorded "The King of the Zulu's (At a Chit' Lin' Rag)" with his Hot Five (June 23, 1926).[96] The piece contains comic banter and uses the dialect of West Indian immigrants to create ethnic humor. A man with a fake Jamaican accent (spoken by Clarence Babcock) interrupts the song, exclaiming: "one of me countrymon tell me there's a chitlin' rag going on heah. Madam, fix me one out of those thing you call chitlin' but I call 'em inner tube, and I play one of me native jazz tunes!" Laurence Bergreen understands this skit as "reviving an old minstrel show routine," and he certainly has a point. But it actually does a lot more.[97] First, it points back to the very vaudeville origins of the Zulu Social Aid and Pleasure Club, the Smart Set Zulu skit that had inspired Metoyer and his friends, and thus to an important formative influence of Armstrong's youth in New Orleans. Second, it constitutes another moment of racial play-acting, an instance of comic masking (Babcock is a pretend Jamaican) that reveals the Zulu King spectacle as an expression of the carnivalesque spirit and pokes fun at West Indian immigrants. The performance does not, in fact, present a Zulu King at all, but rather a fake one, and it includes an element of jiving when the black vernacular term for pig intestines, "chitlin'," is substituted by the faux Jamaican term "inner tube." Third, it displays an element of strategic signifying. While the Jamaican is an immigrant and shares no direct cultural affiliation with the African Americans he encounters, he is confident that the color of his skin entitles him to some culinary freeloading. Like Armstrong, he hustles his music—which he offers to his audience as an authentic folk expression: "one of me native jazz tunes!"—in exchange for remuneration (here: food).

Both the Zulu jungle theme and the strategy of ethnic self-dramatization became associated further with Armstrong's public persona in two of his early appearances on film, Max Fleischer's *Betty Boop* cartoon and the movie short *Rhapsody in Black and Blue* (both 1932). The cartoon mixes animated scenes with live shots of Armstrong's band in performance. It begins with a version of "High Society," suggesting the imagined space of Western civilization, against which the ensuing images of the jungle, savages, and a steaming cauldron are placed (the cauldron will eventually hold Betty's friends Bimbo the Dog and Koko the Clown, and the soup will be stirred by drummer Alfred "Tubby" Hall). This journey into jungle darkness provides the frame for a series of primitivist staples. Betty is taken prisoner by the black natives, and Bimbo and Koko are chased by an evil-looking native with thick lips whose disembodied head eventually morphs into Armstrong's actual face as he is singing the cartoon's title number, "I'll Be Glad When You're Dead You Rascal You." Intriguingly, all characters in the cartoon are revealed as ethnic performers, and their identities are depicted as fluid: Armstrong morphs from animated cartoon character to a filmic representation of himself; Koko is revealed as a Jewish blackface entertainer when he loses his black clown suit and shows white skin underneath as he is running away from Armstrong and as his speed is measured in Hebrew script; Betty's racial heritage is ambiguous (white, Jewish, black). The cartoon's many affinities with the format of the vaudeville show (episodic skits, music, comedy) suggest the influence of, and commentary on, the prominence of Jewish vaudeville entertainers in blackface (Al Jolson, Eddie Cantor, Sophie Tucker), but they also initiate an understanding of ethnic masking and the playful engagement with racial identities as a fundamental element of modern American popular culture: the Mardi Gras spirit as the source of an amalgamated and modern popular form of performance; the jungle cauldron as Ellison's "melting pot [that] did indeed melt."[98]

Rhapsody in Black and Blue (dir. Aubrey Scotto) involves a happy-go-lucky husband who keeps ignoring his wife's order to sweep the floor because he wants to sing and drum along to an Armstrong recording. When the wife is fed up with her husband's Samboesque indolence, she socks him over the head with her broom, knocking him unconscious. Entering a land of dreams, the husband imagines that he is the Emperor of Jazzmania (a kind of Zulu King) and has Armstrong's band at his disposal. He appreciates his newfound powers and asks the musicians to play "Shine" and "I'll Be Glad When You're Dead You Rascal You." Armstrong is dressed in a leopard-skin outfit and wears a grass-topped hat—the jungle theme in film code. Add to this the minstrel-inflected song lyrics of "Shine" (which he introduces with the self-referential phrase "oh chocolate drop that's me" and which includes lines about his curly hair, pearly teeth, and shady skin color) and "I'll Be Glad" ("When you're lying six feet deep, no more chicken will you eat"), and the primitivist scene is complete. Several critics have argued about this film that Armstrong transcends the minstrel primitivism through his charismatic singing, artistic trumpeting, and the virility of the performance—for Terry Teachout, for instance, "Armstrong comes on less like Uncle Tom than Superman."[99] It is more plausible, however, to argue that audiences were again confronted with productive ambiguities, with a performance that allowed (and still allows!) Armstrong's more enthusiastic admirers to focus on its transcendent aspects while it enabled others to indulge in its minstrel echoes. These ambiguities were amplified by the fact that Armstrong as jungle king appears in a dream sequence and therefore performs in a piece of fantasy and by the fact that folk elements also mark the performance as a carnivalesque spectacle. Fellow musician Wingy Manone maintains that Armstrong "stuck his thumb under the lapel of that tiger skin [sic] and started to strut" as he would have during a New Orleans parade, and his fellow players spur him on toward a vigorous high-note finish that evokes the heated atmosphere of late-night dance hall performance.[100] Here, then, we encounter the full scope of productive ambiguities: Armstrong emerges simultaneously as a primitivist stock figure, vernacular signifier, and musical master.

As these examples indicate, elements of the Mardi Gras parade and the debate over its cultural resonances were reflected in, and did indeed build upon, various forms of racial representation. It is difficult to assess the extent to which audiences were aware of the cultural resonances of the multigeneric and intermedial Zulu code. But the complicated nature of the Zulu imagery—ethnographic term, minstrel mockery, black vernacular working-class expression—and its wide dissemination across cultural spaces and media—stage acting, song lyrics, sheet music covers, film appearances, the Mardi Gras parade itself—indicate the cultural horizon against which Armstrong's performances unfolded. This imagery also made a substantial impact on his autobiographics. The Zulu appearance and its repercussions are covered in several autobiographical narratives; Armstrong informed friends and music journalists about it in letters (Betty Jane Holder, Leonard Feather), narrated the event as an introduction to his re-recording of "King of the Zulus" on *A Musical Autobiography*, and pasted reports of it into one of his scrapbooks.

The photo-collage in the scrapbook is an interesting example of Armstrong's engagement with the public repercussions of the Zulu spectacle. While he was heavily criticized for his Mardi Gras masking, he himself focused on his personal achievements and his pleasurable memories of the event. In the photo-collage, a promotional photograph of him without makeup is pasted into the center of the page, and it is crowned by the headline "Hail King Zulu." This headline expresses love and respect for the King by his loyal subjects and thereby allows Armstrong to claim his regional roots: the people of his hometown revere him. Moreover, the photograph is surrounded by Armstrong's membership card for the Zulu Social Aid and Pleasure Club (which authenticates his standing as an

"Honorary Life Time Member" and thus attests to his cultural integrity), by a newspaper listing of the route that the parade was about to take (which gives the event local specificity), and by a roll call of former and later Zulu Kings and Queens (which reunites Armstrong with other black New Orleans luminaries).[101]

Yet three years after the Mardi Gras parade, Armstrong registered unease about his appearance. "No sooner that I had fallen asleep, when I felt something crawling all around my chops (my mouth)—etc . . . It was a member of the Zulu Club, whom the President had sent to my hotel to— 'make me up," he wrote to Betty Jane Holder in a letter dated February 9, 1952: "Put all of the white stuff around my lips,—eyes, in fact, everywhere he could *swerve a brush*. . . . As much as I was not accustomed to this sort of, creepy feeling, I did remember my step father—having the same stuff, put on his face, some 20 years before I was the King. . . . So, after I realized, what was happening, I stretched out and went fast asleep, while he still swung the brush . . ." The creepy feeling of something crawling onto his face and his being asleep while the makeup was applied introduce a note of self-justification, even apology, but they are offset by lengthy and detailed recollections of the cultural rituals represented by the Zulu Parades of his childhood years. Nonetheless, the account is ambiguous. When pianist Earl Hines sees Armstrong "with all of this jive on my face, Earl's eyes got as big as saucers."[102] It is not clear whether Armstrong was aware of this, but the one with eyes big as saucers was certainly he himself; photographs show huge white spots of makeup around his eyes. Since he used the phrase "eyes as big as saucers" elsewhere, it is perhaps not too far-fetched to find in this vernacular expression a microscopic representation of the double codification of Armstrong's cultural resonances.[103] Exaggerated physical features, popping eyes included, belong to the stage repertoire of blackface minstrelsy (Al Jolson being the most prominent twentieth-century representative), but they are also reappropriated in Armstrong's vernacular and anecdotal recollections, where they serve as funny expressions of shock and express a jive sensibility toward racial stereotypes and stock figures.

Armstrong expressed uncertainty about the reception of his Zulu appearance in his letters but did not do so in his published celebrations of the event. *Satchmo*, for instance, features a photograph of the musician in Zulu garb and makeup, and Armstrong writes: "It had been my life-long dream to be the King of the Zulus, as it was the dream of every kid in my neighborhood." This statement historicizes his Zulu masking, and Armstrong

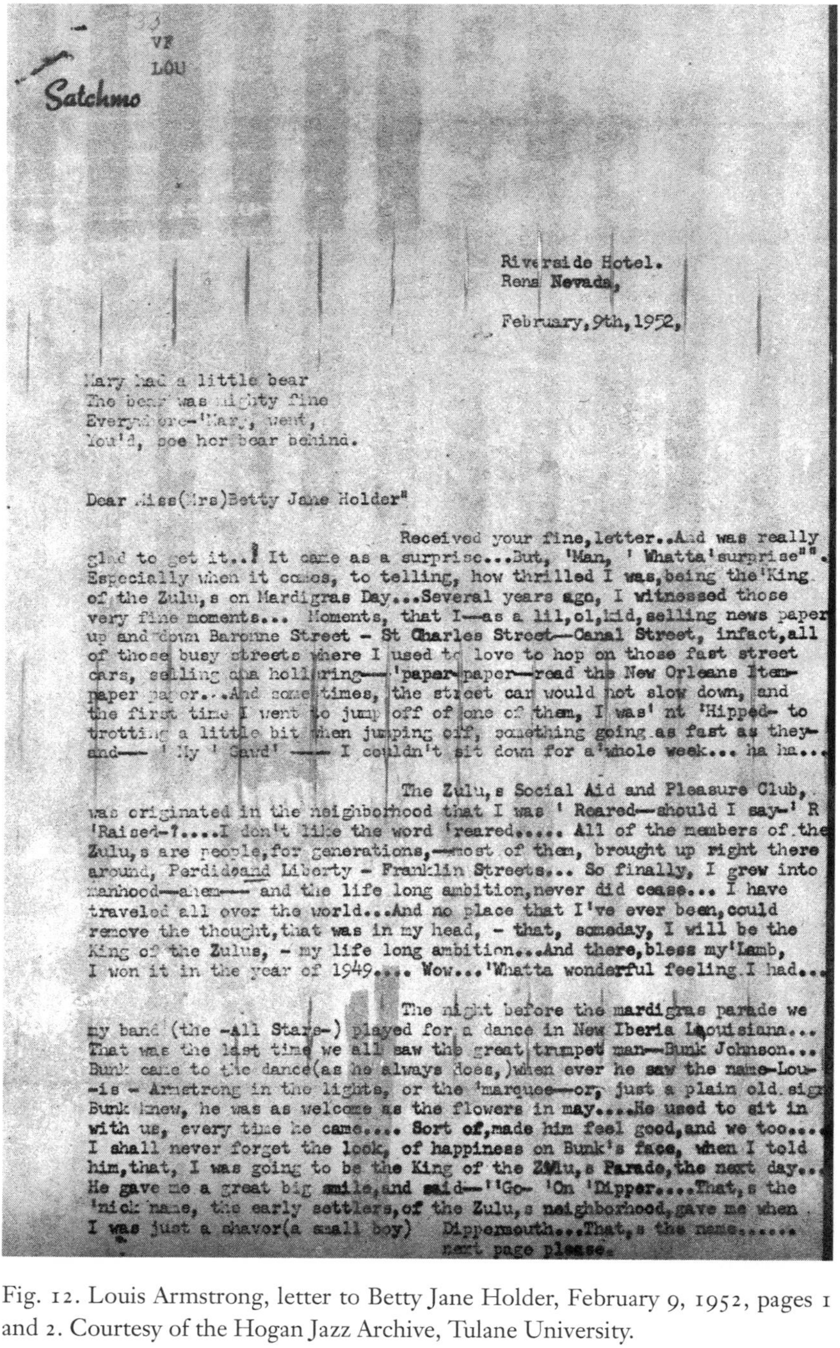

VF
LOU

Satchmo

Riverside Hotel.
Rens Nevada,

February, 9th, 1952,

Mary had a little bear
The bear was mighty fine
Everywhere—'Mary, went,
You'd, see her bear behind.

Dear Miss(Mrs)Betty Jane Holder"

Received your fine, letter..And was really
glad to get it..I It came as a surprise...But, 'Man, ' Whatta'surprise""
Especially when it comes, to telling, how thrilled I was, being the 'King
of the Zulu,s on Mardigras Day...Several years ago, I witnessed those
very fine moments... Moments, that I—as a lil,ol,kid, selling news paper
up and down Baronne Street – St Charles Street—Canal Street, infact, all
of those busy streets where I used to love to hop on those fast street
cars, selling cha hollering—'paper—paper—read the New Orleans Item—
paper papor..And some times, the street car would not slow down, and
the first time I went to jump off of one of them, I was' nt 'Hipped— to
trotting a little bit when jumping off, something going as fast as they—
and— ' My ' Gawd' — I couldn't sit down for a 'whole week... ha ha...

The Zulu,s Social Aid and Pleasure Club,
was originated in the neighborhood that I was ' Reared—should I say—' R
'Raised—?....I don't like the word 'reared..... All of the members of the
Zulu,s are people,for generations,—most of them, brought up right there
around, Perdidoand Liberty – Franklin Streets... So finally, I grew into
manhood—ahem—— and the life long ambition,never did cease... I have
traveled all over the world...And no place that I've ever been, could
remove the thought, that was in my head, – that, someday, I will be the
King of the Zulus, – my life long ambition...And there, bless my'Lamb,
I won it in the year of 1949.... Wow...'Whatta wonderful feeling I had...

The night before the mardigras parade we
my band (the –All Stars–) played for, a dance in New Iberia Laouisiana...
That was the last time we all saw the great trumpet man—Bunk Johnson...
Bunk came to the dance(as he always does,)when ever he saw the name—Lou
–is – Armstrong in the lights, or the 'marquee—or, just a plain old sign
Bunk knew, he was as welcome as the flowers in may....He used to sit in
with us, every time he came.... Sort of,made him feel good, and we too....
I shall never forget the look, of happiness on Bunk's face, when I told
him, that, I was going to be the King of the Zulu,s Parade, the next day..
He gave me a great big smile, and said—''Go– 'On 'Dipper....That,s the
'nick name, the early settlers,of the Zulu,s neighborhood,gave me when
I was just a shaver(a small boy) Dippermouth...That,s the name......
next page please.

Fig. 12. Louis Armstrong, letter to Betty Jane Holder, February 9, 1952, pages 1
and 2. Courtesy of the Hogan Jazz Archive, Tulane University.

Bunk said, he wouldn't miss the mardigras for the world...And he didn't
either.... We finished playing in New Iberia,around two o,clock,in the
morning...And by the time we had a bite to eat(which every bands does
after a hard night of swinging)—by then, it was three -A"M...Then we
tore out for New Orleans, by bus...Our chartred bus...We reached home
(at the hotel where we were staying—the wife Lucille and I) it was— six
o,clock—a,m, —— so I thought I'd stretch the.old frame - my body, for
an hour or so.... No sooner that I had fallen asleep, when I felt somethi
crawling around my chops*(my mouth)—etc... It was a member of the Zulu
Club, whom the President had sent to my hotel to - 'make me up.. You' no
put all of the white stuff around my lips, - eyes, infact, everywhere he
could swirve a brush .....

As much as I was not accustomed to this sort of,creepy feeling,I did
remember my step father -having the same stuff,put on his face, some 20,
years before I was the King....So, after I realized,what was happening,
I stretched out and went fast asleep, while he still swung the brush...
What amused me most about the whole thing at my hotel that morning, was
when Earl Father Hines—who was playing the piano with my All Stars at
the time, he and his wife Janie, came into my room looking for me to tak
a picture with his camera.... And when Lucille pointed towards me,with
all of this jive on my face, Earl,s eyes.got as big as saucers, saying
"WHAT THA HELL IS THAT—?.......... He said it so loud, he awakened me..

It was time for me to get up and get dress for the grand parade, and to
meet the Barg, which Mr Janckie - the great gravel man, loaned us each
year we had our parade.... Lucille, had a cute little secretary working
for her at the time....Her name was Selma Heralda...And Selma lived next
door from us,in Corona Long Island, where we have our home...Everybody
were trying to help me,get in to my Costume, etc, which was really a gem.
The very best and finest material... Everything went down and fit perfect
except for the hat...And for that reason, - all day long, I had trouble
trying to keep that hat on my head... Wondering to myself—Hrm-there must
be'some way,to keep this, so'N'so, hat on my big head.... Anyway we had
a real time, all over the city, throwing coconuts to the people,and sayin
hello,and waving to the old friends, etc....

Just think——twenty thousand coconuts, which each member on my float thre
threw to the crowd.... I happened to look up on a porch where a young man
was justa yelling to me, ' Come on Satchmo(meaning no) 'thru one of the o
fine coconuts up here... And I taken a real good aim, and threw one at
him,with all of my might...The guy waited until the coconut reached him
and the coconut hit the tip of his finger,and fell down on a bran new
Cadillac....... 'Ge eee.... I just turned my head to the direction in
front of me, just a nothin happened.... Wow...Close shave, - huh?....
I shall never forget the incident, when our float reached Dumain and
Claiborne Streets, and as high as I was sitting, I see straight down
Claiborne street, for miles,seemingly, and the whole street were blocked
with people waiting for the parade to come down their way...But instead—
the float,turned the other direction....And - all of those people made
one grand charge at once,towards the float....

The real surprise of the day,was———when the float that I was on turned
the corner, my eyes looked direct in to Hugues Panassie's...He's the
President of the Hot Club de France...Paris France...His secretary Miss
Madeleine Gautier was standing—eagerly waving with him....

reveals one of its most significant functions when he describes the activities of the Zulu Social Aid and Pleasure Club as "burlesquing some famous person." The spectacle of dressing up enabled the Zulus to poke fun at authority figures without having to fear serious repercussions because all was done in the spectacular spirit of Mardi Gras. Armstrong's comments about a character named Papa Gar show the critical potential of racial communication through ridicule: "Garfield Carter—or Papa Gar as we called him— was the proudest stepper in the whole parade, and he had the nerve to parody Captain Jackson. He paraded disguised as the captain of the Zulu Police Force. The crowd used to go wild when Papa Gar strutted by with his face blackened and with big white lips." Captain Jackson, the reader knows from an episode related directly before the depiction of the Mardi Gras performance, is "the meanest guy on the police force" and had arrested Armstrong only a few days earlier. New Orleanians like Armstrong and Papa Gar, the account in *Satchmo* tells us, voice their critique and vent their anger indirectly, in the form of racial burlesque rather than open resistance.[104]

This indirect critique and displaced venting of anger by members of the black New Orleans working poor was a way of addressing social and racial imbalances, as Mikhail Bakhtin's work on the carnival indicates. "Ritual spectacles" and "comic verbal compositions" are modes of ridiculing dominant hierarchies and critiquing oppressive social structures. In New Orleans, the spirit of Mardi Gras allows its black participants to ridicule "white" notions of decency and morality.[105] But the Zulu King's mocking of Rex, the white Mardi Gras King, does more than simply revive European carnival traditions. It "is a classic example of carnivalesque release of class tensions with the special twist of African-American signifying" and, as such, incorporates into its structure a parodic element that is characteristic of black vernacular culture.[106] Reid Mitchell therefore sees the Zulu Parade as an expression of racial parody, with the Zulu King mimicking and mocking Rex: "Zulu did everything that Rex did. If Rex traveled by water, coming up the Mississippi with an escort from the U.S. Navy, Zulu came down the New Basin Canal on a tugboat. If Rex held a scepter, Zulu held a ham bone. If Rex had the city police marching before him, Zulu had the Zulu police. [. . .] All that Zulu did caricatured Rex; a black lord of misrule upsetting the reign of the white lord, a mocker of a mocker."[107] Seen from this perspective, Armstrong's performance of "I'll Be Glad When You're Dead You Rascal You" for the British King George V in 1932 takes on a special dimension. As Armstrong recalls in his interview with *U.S. News & World Report*: "I hollered, 'This one's for you, Rex'—that's what I called him, 'Rex.'"[108] Here, Armstrong displays the full potential of social and racial signifying, an expressive practice that originated in black folk culture but found fertile ground in the antimonarchism of American mainstream culture in the 1920s and 1930s.[109] First, he verbally associates the British king with the white Mardi Gras king and thereby indicates his linguistic grasp of the situation ("Rex" meaning "king," of course). Second, he recognizes parallels between his weak social position in the American Jim Crow South and his socially and racially inferior status vis-à-vis the British royal. Third, he demonstrates his ability to deal with his social and racial status productively by directing his comical performance at the king, calling him a rascal and playfully suggesting delight in his demise. The British king is essentially reduced to a carnival figure, while Armstrong elevates himself to the powerful Zulu King, who gets away with burlesquing royalty: "There has never been and will never be another king like me," the Zulu royal traditionally proclaims.

Armstrong's Zulu Parade appearance looms so large in the critical evaluation of his career because it carries at its center rituals of masking and mimicry as means of dealing with socially pervasive racial stereotypes that had a long and troubled history in American culture. It is important to note here that the Zulu King had paraded without blackface in the years between 1915 and 1938 because of the negative reactions the theatrical makeup had caused among audiences who had regarded it as a throwback to a time in which black vaudeville performers had been forced to use the blackface makeup of white minstrels to establish themselves in the entertainment business. In 1980, when Woody Herman became the first white Zulu King, the racial poetics and politics inherent in this social ritual could be relegated to a bygone age, but when Armstrong became King of the Zulus in 1949, the makeup still carried an explosive edge.[110] Even if it might have been different from the way Al Jolson blackened his face on stage and the movie screen, it nonetheless constituted an exaggeration of something already expressed by Armstrong's grinning, flashing of the teeth, and popping of the eyes: his ability to conjure up images of the Sambo figure and all of the racial implications this figure transported. More important, carnival festivities and minstrel show performances shared both ritual functions and celebratory spirit. Appearing at around the same time in American culture (1820s to 1840s), Mardi Gras and minstrel show, as folk theatrical and popular culture, shared practices of masking, a fascination with physical excess, and a prevalence for ribald humor that pokes fun at those in power. The Mardi Gras techniques of masking and signifying therefore point to the existence of an overarching cultural poetics. Armstrong's performative interventions in this cultural poetics emerge from his ability to code his intermedial autobiographics ambiguously: Armstrong's Zulu King as an early twentieth-century version of the Samboesque entertainer versus Satchmo's signifying and burlesquing.

Ralph Ellison frequently sought to think through the very same ambiguities and complexities that marked Armstrong's Zulu King appearance. For Ellison, the Samboesque "'darky' entertainer" was an Anglo-Saxon construct that played an important symbolic role in American culture: "The [minstrel] mask was an inseparable part of the national iconography" because it held together an otherwise deeply segregated society: "the 'darky' act makes brothers of us all."[111] Especially in pluralistic societies, one of the major roles and functions of popular culture is to provide symbols through which social, economic, religious, and racial differences can be publicly negotiated and through which animosities and grievances can be articulated. In a country like the United States, where everybody "is a member of some minority group," masking is more than a means of superficial assimilation, willing submission, or cunning subversion. It is, in fact, "a play upon possibility" that is both socially necessary and culturally productive.[112] Ellison singles out Armstrong as a popular figure capable of mediating between the "whiteness" of the black mask (i.e., the mask as a mirror of white fantasies of race and cross-racial play) and the "clownish license and intoxicating powers" that it also affords.[113] According to this perspective, the ambiguities of the minstrel mask allowed Armstrong a degree of personal and expressive freedom he would not have otherwise had. Clownish license is productive because it motivates contradictory statements and signifying gestures and feeds on the dissonances sounded by feats of mugging, the voicing of serious critique, and the display of musical virtuosity.

In Ellison's reading, Armstrong stood in the tradition of the Elizabethan jester in performing the "*make-believe* role of clown."[114] Instead of becoming one with the role of blackface minstrel, who uses racial masquerade for commercial gain at the expense of others, or casting himself as a black folk hero, who liberates himself from any social constraints, Armstrong played upon the possibilities that the popular fascination with black cultural production offered him. He did so by tapping into the productive ambiguities that emerged from the deeply rooted and convoluted mixture of black vernacular culture and blackface minstrelsy in American history and by intervening in its dissemination across media and fields of cultural production. Armstrong obviously wanted to be understood as a serious musician and skilled performer, but he was also sensitive to the historical precedents of his performance antics and the racially coded expectations of his audiences. Speaking frankly to Richard Meryman about his performances of "Hello Dolly," he acknowledged: "And all my little gestures—coming out all chesty, making faces, the jive with the audience clapping—aw, it's all in the fun. People expect it from me; they know I'm there in the cause of happiness." But Armstrong does not equate these little gestures, his making of faces, and his jiving with the audience with clowning. Discussing fellow New Orleans cornetist Freddie Keppard, he clearly rejected notions of clowning: "His Ego when he was a young man and Clowning that he did must have been rather amusing for laughs, to get the recognition he achieved. But he sure did not play the cornet seriously at any time. Just Clowned all the way. Good for those Idiots' fans' who did not care whether he played correct, or they did not know good music, or cared less." Elsewhere, he maintained: "Critics in England say I was a clown, but a clown, that's hard. If you can make people chuckle a little; it's happiness to me to see people happy, and most of the people who criticize don't know one note from another."[115] Here, then, we encounter a musician's wish to entertain his audiences through techniques of showmanship that reach back to early twentieth-century New Orleans practices like parading and second lining and that reinforce, rather than burlesque or even deflate, the evocative power and social meanings of his music.

There is no easy way out of the contradictions that the role of make-believe clown produced in Armstrong's autobiographics and in American culture at large. It simply does not make sense to interpret Armstrong's performances solely as the work of a sly subversive genius. Their allegiance with the minstrel poetics renders such an interpretation implausible. Neither does it make sense to assume that Armstrong consciously bought into minstrel poetics to achieve fame and fortune. There is no reason to doubt the veracity of one of his most frequently quoted statements, "Man, you don't pose, never!"[116] Rather, he must have regarded mugging and joking as integral elements of his performances, as essential parts of his act. These gestures and facial expressions visualized the behavioral codes he had acquired as a child, and they continued to determine his understanding of race relations in the sense of what the French sociologist Pierre Bourdieu has theorized as the habitus: socially and culturally determined dispositions that involve partially conscious and partially unconscious behavioral patterns. If "the habitus is the result of a long process of inculcation, beginning in early childhood, which becomes a 'second sense' or a second nature," then Armstrong's childhood experience of living in a racially segregated working-class environment explains why he did not simply get rid of his performative antics.[117] As part of his habitus, they could not be easily discarded because they were based on dispositions that were not entirely conscious. In terms of African American cultural criticism, Bourdieu's "second sense" oscillates between a Du Boisian notion of a "double self" and "double-consciousness," according to which a figure like Armstrong would possess "no true self-consciousness" but would only "see himself through the revelation of the other [i.e., white] world," and an Ellisonian understanding of the "second self" as a series of "trickster's masks."[118]

All in all, Armstrong's minstrel sounding is an example of what may be labeled cultural intermediality because it employs intermedial codes that establish a connection between his autobiographics and the minstrel poetics. While Armstrong never refers to the *Amos 'n' Andy* shows directly, his depictions of life up North evolve against and mobilize the cultural horizon—the Great Migration, ethnic disguise and play-acting, racial comedy as popular culture—that also frames *Amos 'n' Andy*. Accordingly, the central performative technique of the postcolonial black entertainer is the creation of ambiguous humor that connects a single reference to the voracious "coon" or the dancing minstrel to an array of sights, sounds, and narratives: the minstrel preacher versus vernacular depictions of African American clergymen, the ignorant darky dandy versus the befuddled black migrant, the blackface Sambo versus the signifying Zulu King.

Since minstrel sounding shuttles between an affirmation of racially deprecating stereotypes and moments of "rebellious laughter" (Joseph Boskin's term), we may ask whether the laughter produced by Armstrong's performances "actually makes a difference to the incongruity from which it arises, or whether it in fact ultimately buttresses and thereby upholds the power imbalance." The next chapter therefore raises "the question whether laughter—in postcolonial cultural production—lends agency or whether it, in fact, prevents opposition and dissent by relieving some of the tension."[119] Furthermore, it considers whether the "deliberate ambiguity of humour" and the minstrel echoes it encoded prevented Armstrong from intervening in the struggle for civil rights during the last two decades of his life.[120]

CHAPTER 6

"My mission is music"

Armstrong's Cultural Politics

For many, Armstrong's King Zulu appearance of 1949 signaled the end of his relevance as a figure of modern racial identification. If a mass audience was able to see him in minstrel terms as a reassuring figure of the past, he was clearly out of step with the growing unrest among African Americans in the postwar era. As early as 1946, *Crisis* magazine's Phil Carter had written that Armstrong "doing the kind of 'mugging' for the camera [. . .] is becoming very unpopular with Negro movie-goers," and the Zulu appearance had substantially intensified this impression. A few years later, reviewer Wilfred Lowe went even farther when he referred to Armstrong's stage antics as "blackface buffoonery."[1] For Armstrong's career, however, the Mardi Gras appearance and films such as *Going Places*, in which he is addressed as Uncle Tom in one scene and responds with a submissive "yessuh, Ah knows, sir," created cultural and economic capital. They popularized his good-natured, down-home persona, enabled him to suggest a benevolent alternative to the militancy of the beboppers, and allowed him to present himself as an All-American icon rather than a spokesperson for the black civil rights movement. As Krin Gabbard points out: "We can only speculate about how much of Armstrong's success was related to the reassurances he gave to white audiences who wanted to believe that his grinning visage was more typical of black people than were the menacing faces of young African Americans that regularly showed up on the nightly news."[2]

The growing number of African Americans who protested publicly against civil rights abuses saw Armstrong as a highly problematic figure. "He's a good, happy black boy. He hasn't played to a black audience in ten years," Julius Hobson noted sarcastically in the mid-1960s.[3] Not only did activists like Hobson fault Armstrong, but several jazz musicians attacked the minstrel resonances which his performances produced. "I criticized Louis for [. . .] his 'plantation image.' We didn't appreciate that about Louis Armstrong, and if anybody asked me about a certain public image of him, handkerchief over his head, grinning in the face of white racism, I never hesitated to say I didn't like it. I didn't want the white man to expect me to allow the same things Louis Armstrong did," Dizzy Gillespie remembered years after the fact.[4] At the time of the controversy, he had voiced his criticism of Armstrong in *Esquire* by announcing in no uncertain terms: "I violently disagree with [Louis Armstrong] because of his Uncle Tom–like subservience—nowadays no cat should be a Tom."[5]

Trumpeter Rex Stewart painted a more affectionate picture: some musicians "consciously resent Louis' antebellum Uncle Tomism. The youngsters object to his ever-present grin, which they interpret as Tomming. This I feel is a misunderstanding. No matter where Louis had been brought up, his natural ebullience and warmth would have emerged just as creative and strong. This is not to say that even today, in an unguarded moment, a trace of the old environment, a fleeting lapse into the jargon of his youth will make some people cringe with embarrassment."[6] Unlike Gillespie, Stewart was of Armstrong's generation (Gillespie was born in 1917, Stewart in 1907). He had known Armstrong in the 1920s, when the cornetist from New Orleans became a national sensation, and he was willing to acknowledge the power of the minstrel poetics over black performance styles. While acknowledging this poetics ("antebellum Uncle Tomism"; "ever-present grin"; "jargon of his youth"), he nonetheless felt compelled to downplay it in hindsight: minstrel echoes come in "unguarded" moments; they are not evoked on purpose ("lapse"); they are essentially elusive, "a trace" and "fleeting"; and they are the result of both Armstrong's nature ("natural ebullience and warmth") and the racism that was endemic in the musician's formative years ("the old environment").

The discrepancy between Gillespie's and Stewart's views points to a generational divide among African Americans at midcentury. James Baldwin's short story "Sonny's Blues" (1965) fictionalizes this divide. When Sonny tells his brother that he wants to be a jazz player, the brother asks: "You mean—like Louis Armstrong?" Sonny's fascination with Charlie Parker and bebop determines his answer: "No, I'm not talking about none of that old-time, down home crap."[7] A similar, though less strongly voiced, sentiment comes across in the movie *A Man Called Adam* (dir. Leo Penn, 1966), which showcases the All Stars as they perform a ribald version of

"Back o' Town Blues" (including stage banter and comedy) but ultimately associates Armstrong, who plays "Sweet Daddy" Willie Ferguson, with the pre–civil rights era and a jazz ethos that is based on a willingness to entertain rather than on an artistic urge for self-realization.[8] The younger generation, as the personal struggles of Adam Johnson (Sammy Davis Jr.) in *A Man Called Adam* and Miles Davis's explicit endorsement of the beboppers' focus on artistic expression and black pride indicate, sought to project a wholly new self-understanding: "I didn't look at myself as an entertainer like [Armstrong] did. I wasn't going to do it just so that some non-playing, racist, white motherfucker could write some nice things about me."[9]

Armstrong, by contrast, recalled the advice of a black New Orleanian as late as 1966—"As the oldtimer told me when I left New Orleans, he say, 'Stay before them people'"—and explained that his mother and schoolteacher had taught him to "[b]e honest and keep smiling."[10] It is true that such advice went very much against the grain of black politics in the 1960s, but Armstrong connected this piece of advice with the horrors of life in the postbellum South: "I come out of a part of the South where it ain't no way in the world you can forget you're colored. My own mother went through hell down there. My Grandma used to have tears in her eyes when she'd talk about the lynchings and all that crap. Even myself I've seen things that would make my flesh crawl. But it wasn't a damn thing I could do about it . . . and keep on breathing." His grandmother, who obviously was a follower of Booker T. Washington rather than W. E. B. Du Bois, told him further: "Them that kicks over the traces too quick forgets that I seen the days when we was sold on the hoof like dumb cattle. Them that goes too fast gets nowhere. Them that shines and makes a lot of fuss is goners."[11] This is a particularly powerful statement, especially when we consider Armstrong's development from an aspiring trumpet player in the black neighborhoods of New Orleans to a nationally and internationally acclaimed entertainer, whose career in the 1920s did take off extremely fast and whose public appearances in front of increasingly white audiences arguably "shined" and "made a lot of fuss." Armstrong's insistence on pleasing the public and his ever-smiling face might therefore be understood as parts of his habitus: habitual mechanisms through which he cushioned his potentially revolting impact on his audiences.

It is, furthermore, crucial to understand how the generational divide between old-timers like Armstrong and the younger beboppers came about and what it entailed. When bebop arrived in the 1940s, it constituted "a revolution in culture," as Ralph Ellison put it.[12] Beginning with this arrival, a series of profound musical changes, along with new social and political messages audiences expected from the music, fundamentally altered the image of the jazz musician, and they threatened to make New Orleans players like Armstrong obsolete. Armstrong was aware of the criticism directed at him even though, according to Larry King, "He was not eager to talk civil rights." He explained in 1961: "Some have even accused me of being an Uncle Tom, of not being 'aggressive.' How can they say that? I've pioneered in breaking the color line in many Southern states (Georgia, Mississippi, Texas) with mixed bands—Negro and white."[13] He further told King that his tactic of achieving popular success first and worrying about social equality later had paid off: "I had it put in my contracts that I wouldn't *play* no place I couldn't *stay*. I was the first Negro in the business to crack them big white hotels."[14] Under increasing political pressure, Armstrong eventually talked about his role in the civil rights movement, acknowledging that people expected him to participate in the marches. But he resisted these expectations for fear of getting hurt and having to end his career: "if I'd be out somewhere marching with a sign and some cat hits me in my chops, I'm finished." One of his solutions to this dilemma was to provide financial support; another one was to take part in the "Jazz Supports the Freedom Riders" fund-raising concert organized by the Congress of Racial Equality (CORE) on June 28, 1961. Yet his final verdict was unusually blunt: "If my people don't dig me the way I am, I'm sorry."[15]

It would be too easy, then, to argue that Armstrong's comments about his political achievements were made purely from a position of defensiveness. Rather, his balancing act of minstrel sounding underwent a process of reevaluation in the 1950s and 1960s—by himself as well as by his fans, critics, and colleagues—because many of his performative practices were essentially tied to a pre–civil rights poetics of black entertainment. Now, he was being perceived variously as a submissive Uncle Tom figure or as the more outspoken Ambassador Satch, as a smiling black entertainer whose music and performances allowed audiences to ignore the more violent aspects of the civil rights movement or as a Cold War icon who sometimes spoke rather openly about the racial injustices he was encountering at home and abroad. This chapter proposes that hearing, seeing, and reading Armstrong's live performances, recordings, film and television appearances, spoken statements, and autobiographical writings as part of his overarching autobiographics can reveal the difficult cultural positions that popular entertainers inhabited during the civil rights era and can thus deepen our understanding of the political seismology of the postwar decades. After all, these decades fall within an era Manning Marable has labeled "the second reconstruction in black America," and they "marked a sea change in American and international race relations."[16] The aim of this chapter, therefore, is to shed light on the historical contingencies of the Uncle Tom and Ambassador Satch roles and to unearth important subtexts in Armstrong's autobiographics. These subtexts include the musician's continued reliance on the everyday practices of black working-class politics (through so-called hidden transcripts); an understanding of political engagement that is strongly tied to the moral lessons he had learned as a youngster in New Orleans; and a strong belief in music's ability to transcend boundaries of race, ideology, and nation.

In the mid-1950s, Armstrong became known as Ambassador Satch, a public figure that afforded him a new political platform. The primary function of jazz ambassadors was to present themselves and their music on international tours sponsored by the State Department with the objective of exporting a democratic image of America into regions of the world in which the Soviet Union sought political influence. The jazz tours were meant to tap into jazz's international appeal and its widespread significance as a music associated with individual freedom and social equality. The musicians who toured for the State Department—Armstrong, Dizzy Gillespie, Duke Ellington, and Dave Brubeck, among others—had traveled abroad earlier in their careers (Armstrong as early as 1932, to Europe) and had built an international following before they were recruited as jazz ambassadors.[17] Moreover, a bare three weeks before the first official jazz tour (featuring Gillespie) commenced, Armstrong was already celebrated in the national press as America's goodwill ambassador. Enthralled by Armstrong's successful concert tour through Europe, Felix Belair wrote in his front-page article for the *New York Times* on November 6, 1955: "America's secret weapon is a blue note in a minor key. Right now its most effective ambassador is Louis (Satchmo) Armstrong."[18] The musician's new political role was captured a year later on the cover of *Ambassador Satch*, the LP that promoted his musical ambassadorship most visibly and audibly. The cover features a grinning Armstrong dressed as a roving diplomat, whose personal achievements as a goodwill ambassador and popularity as Cold War icon are further celebrated in George Avakian's liner notes.

In order to come to terms with the political implications of Armstrong's new role as Ambassador Satch, one has to take into account that jazz was increasingly being sold to audiences abroad as part of a concerted effort to promote American democracy and pave the way for American consumer culture. The tours played a substantial part in this promotion, along with radio programs such as the *Voice of America*, which frequently aired Armstrong's music and for which Armstrong posed in photographs. Jazz in the 1950s and 1960s was seen as a "valuable exportable U.S. commodity" (*Time*), as "structurally parallel to the American political system," and as "a musical reflection of the way things happen in America," according to VOA deejay Willis Conover. Jazz, Conover proclaimed, "corrects the fiction that America is racist."[19] The jazz musicians' job was to advertise an idealist notion of American-style democracy and connect the political yearning for personal freedom and the musical experience of pleasure with a desire to purchase American consumer products.

Through his involvement with the international tours and his commentary about his experiences, Armstrong was able to carve out a space from which he could offer his audiences abroad and at home his own, carefully negotiated understanding of American race relations and democracy. And while the prevalence of the color line in the American South barred him from bringing his integrated band to New Orleans, he managed to cross another line that shaped the twentieth century: the Iron Curtain. As Armstrong's bass player Arvell Shaw recalls, Armstrong and his band were able to cross into West Berlin after a concert in East Berlin in 1955:

> We got to the East German side, and the Russian soldiers and East German police had their guns out. One of the guards looked at us and said "Louis Armstrong." He called out all the guards, got Louis' autograph and waved us all on. And when we got to the American side, a [. . .] sergeant from Texas [. . .] said, "How'd you get through here? Where are your papers?" And he got out handcuffs. Sergeant looks and says, "Satchmo—this is Satchmo!" He called the guards and they got autographs and waved us on. Every night we went back and forth. When the American ambassador heard, he said: "How'd you do that? I can't do that!"[20]

This reminiscence is completed by Armstrong's statements about Russian fans crossing the Iron Curtain to hear their favorite musician in person: "When I played Berlin," he told a *Newsweek* reporter, "a lot of them Russian cats jumped the Iron Fence to hear Satchmo, which goes to prove that music is stronger than nations."[21]

The complex issues surrounding the State Department tours can be unpacked through an analysis of Armstrong's first trip to Africa in 1956, which was organized by television producer and newscaster Edward R. Murrow (who broadcast them on television as part of his *Satchmo the Great* documentary), and his second trip to the continent in 1960–61, which was sponsored by the State Department. On the first trip, which lasted only two days, Armstrong received a glorious welcome in the British Gold Coast colony, which was on its way to becoming an independent Ghana. Much has been made of Armstrong's celebrated afternoon performance for a crowd of one hundred thousand people, the musician's symbolic significance for the African independence movements, and the television images Murrow brought back to the United States. Pushing a civil rights agenda, these images showed Africans dancing to New Orleans jazz and included reverse shots of Ghana's prime minister Kwame Nkrumah tearing up as Armstrong and his band performed "(What Did I Do to Be So) Black and Blue?" Most important in terms of Armstrong's autobiographics, however, was the musician's public recognition of his connection with Africa: "I came from here, way back. At least my people did. Now I know this is my country too. After all, my ancestors came from here and I still have African blood in me." This recognition of his African roots, in terms of both racial background and musical heritage, was visualized in a photograph that shows Armstrong and his band playing for an old African dancer who is wearing the traditional garb of his tribe. Armstrong pasted another photograph of himself and Trummy Young playing for dancing Africans onto one of his tape covers.[22]

When Armstrong returned to Africa in 1960, his allegiance with its peoples and places was even more pronounced: "I feel at home in Africa—more so now since I've been all through the place. I'm African-descended down to the bone, and I dig the friendly ways these people go about things. I lived the same way in New Orleans and they get my message here. I got quite a bit of African blood in me from my grandmammy on my mammy's side and from my grandpappy on my pappy's side."[23] Not only does Armstrong feel at home in Africa, a place that resembles his New Orleans neighborhood and differs decidedly from the primitivist Congo sketched in Goffin's *Horn of Plenty,* and not only does he embrace Africa as an ancestral birthplace; he also uses the media attention his trip to the region was generating to make a statement about race relations in the United States. He claims an African racial heritage ("I'm African-descended down to the bone") but, ever so slightly, acknowledges a history of racial mixing: "I got *quite a bit* of African blood in me from my grandmammy on my mammy's side and from my grandpappy on my pappy's side." This sentence points to a genealogical complexity that cannot be easily resolved. It could suggest that Armstrong thought of his maternal grandmother and paternal grandfather as Africans ("African blood"), even though they could not have been brought into the country as part of the international slave trade, which was abolished long before they were born. They were, however, born into slavery, and it is interesting that Armstrong may have conceived of his slave ancestors as Africans. The statement may also imply that there had been interracial sexual contact among his ancestors (since he is not a full-blooded African), even though it carefully softens the assumption that this contact could have occurred on unequal terms—it was a common practice among white slaveholders to rape their black female slaves—by alluding to these ancestral relationships through a vaguely minstrel-related terminology: "grandmammy" and "mammy," as well as "grandpappy" and "pappy."

Armstrong's personal affirmation of his African roots was accompanied by aggressive efforts of American companies to sell their products on the African continent. As Robert Alden reported in the *New York Times* (Oct. 14, 1960), "Louis Armstrong and his trumpet arrived in Ghana [. . .] to take up a battle position in Africa's ice-cold war. [. . .] The war is between Coca-Cola and Pepsi-Cola. The prize is the African market. Mr. Armstrong, familiarly known as Satchmo, is Pepsi-Cola's latest weapon."[24] Pepsi-Cola sponsored the African tour, and its advertising campaign utilized the evocative power of Armstrong's wide smile on posters and concert tickets. Pepsi's advertisement people cunningly connected their product with Armstrong's benevolent image, codified by his grin, and they chose a catchy syllogism as their slogan: "You like Satchmo. Pepsi brings you Satchmo. Therefore, you like Pepsi."[25] The political logic implied in the slogan is particularly revealing about the attempt to use Armstrong's fame for both political and commercial purposes: You like Satchmo. America brings you Satchmo. Therefore, you like America. Armstrong did not explicitly question this particular logic in any of his public statements about the tour, a fact that implicates him in the aggressive Cold War politics of the U.S. administration and complicates his significance as a figure of racial identification for many Africans.²⁶

Yet apart from producing advertisements of a grinning Satchmo, the tour of 1960–61 generated a number of photographs and film clips that resonate intriguingly with earlier visual representations of Armstrong. One of these photos shows Armstrong playing his trumpet amid a large group of cheering children and adolescents at a health center in Cairo. The scene evokes images and sounds of second lining and parading in New Orleans and thereby establishes a continuum from Armstrong's American youth in poverty to his present status as an internationally respected and financially successful musician. Another photograph depicts him instructing a young African student on how to hold and play the trumpet, contradicting notions of untutored musicianship and also suggesting the community-based musical education Armstrong received in New Orleans. In both of these images, Armstrong exports communal cultural practices instead of American soft drinks to Africa, practices that, in fact, were tied to the confluence of African, Caribbean, and European social and cultural traditions that had made the New Orleans of his formative years such a cosmopolitan city. A film clip of the trip to Africa revises Armstrong's earlier role of Mardi Gras king in Zulu makeup. Here, he is shown sitting on a thronelike chair (without makeup and costume) as he is being carried through the Congolese town of Leopoldville by a group of traditionally dressed Africans. He is no longer a Zulu King whose aim it is to overcome his status as a socially powerless person through racial mockery of the white king, but he is revered and celebrated as a race leader and culture hero.²⁷

While the *New York Times* recognized Armstrong's newfound cultural power—the headline proclaimed "Satchmo Plays for Congo's Cats: Trumpeter Arrives on Red Throne and Crew of Bearers"—and while the author of this piece, Paul Hofmann, cites an African official who claims Armstrong as the "son of our African race," echoes of the minstrel poetics intrude nonetheless. As Armstrong was being carried around on the red throne, Hoffman writes, "He wiped his brow and elicited a roar of laughter by saying, in atrociously accented French, 'Merci beaucoup, beaucoup.'"²⁸ The reference to the "roar of laughter" evokes both the comic Sambo and the primitivist jungle savage, as does the comment about Armstrong's animated physicality ("wiped his brow"), while the comment about his "atrociously accented French" triggers the sounds of minstrel malapropisms, as well as a strange mixture of geopolitical associations that include francophone New Orleans and the Congo's Belgian colonial history. The postcolonial parallels are indeed intriguing. The minstrel Sambo as a postcolonial figure in nineteenth-century America meets Satchmo as an emblem of national self-determination for his African fans. What we find here are attempts to tone down the powerful sounds and sights generated by Armstrong's second African tour, which added to the visual and verbal complexity of his autobiographics, with coded references to the cultural poetics of blackface minstrelsy and its primitivist offshoots.

In keeping with his generally amenable position on race relations and in order to steer the public reception away from overly politicized interpretations of the photographic and filmic images his second African tour provided, Armstrong used the forum of the press conference to emphasize a seemingly apolitical position. As he was quoted by Leonard Ingalls in the *New York Times:* "'I don't know anything about [politics]; I'm just a trumpet player,' he said with a laugh in his gravelly voice. 'The reason I don't bother with politics is the words is so big. By the time they break them down to my size, the joke is over.'" Despite the self-deprecating humor, as Penny Von Eschen argues, this statement may have also "expressed cynicism and frustration in suggesting that politics was a 'joke.'"[29] This humor was, of course, of the minstrel type, an example of the "reassuring *sounds* from the black quarters" that frequently fueled the musician's productive ambiguities and inscribe this statement with both a subversive (politics as a joke) and an affirmative ("I don't know anything about [politics]") element.[30] Favoring an affirmative reading—Armstrong as an Uncle Tom— the reporter makes sure that this message is not lost on his readers: "laugh" conjures up Armstrong's wide grin, while the "gravelly voice" foregrounds the physicality of his performances and his mugging, all of which tend to downplay Armstrong's new powers as a political figure. Facing such interpretations by the mainstream press, Armstrong informed his audiences that Ambassador Satch was just one of many roles he was capable of playing in the public arena: "Ambassador Satch? Well, it's kicks, it's amusing to me, that the way I look at it. Not serious," he told Millstein, and he added a comment about the vernacular origins of role-playing and nicknaming: "We used [to] call one another that when we was broke and hungry. That where the Duke got his name—Duke Ellington—and the Count—Count Basie."[31]

In the 1920s, 1930s, and 1940s, Armstrong had kept the veil mostly in place when it came to political issues.[32] In the 1950s and 1960s, however, the veil came off more frequently. In the late 1960s, he would even refer to the New Orleans of his youth as "Disgustingly Segregated and Prejudiced," would admit that "we were all well aware of the *Congo* Square—*Slavery—Lynching* and *all* of that *stuff,*" and would speak of the white citizens of New Orleans who terrorized the black population with their "Nigger Hunting" as "those Old *Fat Belly Stinking* very *Smelly Dirty* White Folks."[33] But in 1957, when the civil rights movement was picking up steam (Emmett Till had been murdered, and Rosa Parks had already sparked off the Montgomery bus boycott in 1955), he uttered his most vocal protest against Southern segregation and racial discrimination. Orval Faubus, the governor of Arkansas, had been unwilling to integrate public schools despite the 1954 U.S. Supreme Court ruling in *Brown v. Board of Education of Topeka.* Stranded in a North Dakota hotel room after a concert, Armstrong was enraged by the television images of men and women threatening and screaming at a group of black children, the "Little Rock Nine," who wanted to be admitted to Central High School. When he was interviewed by the young reporter Larry Lubenow for the *Grand Forks Herald* on September 17, he expressed his anger openly: "The way they are treating my people in the South, the government can go to hell," he exclaimed. He further accused President Dwight D. Eisenhower of being "two-faced" and having "no guts" and added, "It's getting almost so bad a colored man hasn't got any country."[34] About Governor Faubus, the *New York Times* quoted Armstrong as saying that he was an "uneducated plow boy," but Lubenow recalls that this was a euphemism he suggested because Armstrong's "double-barreled hyphenated expletive" was unprintable. As Terry Teachout reports, Lubenow recently revealed that Armstrong had called Faubus a "no-good motherfucker" and Secretary of State John Foster Dulles "another motherfucker." As deliberate public statements, these are as bold as anything Americans would have heard from an African American entertainer in the 1950s, including the politically much more active and much more outspoken Paul Robeson, whose passport had been confiscated in 1950 and who was forced to sing his music to a London audience via telephone from New York in 1957.[35]

In the aftermath of this explosive interview, Armstrong explained his position to the *Pittsburgh Courier* on September 28:

> I've had a beautiful life over 40 years in music, but I feel the downtrodden situation the same as any other Negro. My parents and family suffered

through all of that old South [. . .] . My people—the Negroes—are not looking for anything—we just want a square shake. But when I see on television and read about a crowd spitting on and cursing at a little colored girl—I think I have a right to get sore and say something about it. Do you dig me when I still say I have a right to blow my top over injustice?[36]

He told another reporter: "They've been ignoring the Constitution, although they're taught it in school, but when they go home, their parents tell them different—say 'You don't have to abide by it, because we've been getting away with it for a hundred years.'"[37] It is significant that Armstrong made these statements to the daily press, and not in one of his autobiographical essays or books. Without the control of the coaxers and coachers who sought to manage his public image, he spoke with unfamiliar plainness. Yet his denunciation of Eisenhower and Faubus was not merely the result of a spontaneous outburst. Because the Associated Press would not put Lubenow's story on the national wire without proof of its authenticity, the reporter went back to Armstrong's hotel the morning after the interview in order to have the statements verified. According to Lubenow, Armstrong confirmed: "That's just what I said, and I still say," and he signed the printed version of the story with his name and the word "solid."[38] Armstrong's road manager, Pierre Tallerie, apparently tried to control the situation by telling the press the day after the statement had appeared in the news that Armstrong "was sorry he spouted off" and that "Louie isn't mad at anybody," but Armstrong refused to take back what he had said and fired Tallerie (but rehired him later).[39]

On September 24, Armstrong wired a personal appeal to President Eisenhower:

DADDY IF AND WHEN YOU DECIDE TO TAKE THOSE LITTLE NEGRO CHILDREN PERSONALLY INTO CENTRAL HIGH SCHOOL ALONG WITH YOUR MARVELOUS TROOPS PLEASE TAKE ME ALONG "O GOD IT WOULD BE SUCH A GREAT PLEASURE I ASSURE YOU.[40]

The telegram addresses Eisenhower in jive terms as "daddy," and a somewhat sarcastic note creeps into the statement through phrases such as "your marvelous troops" and "O God it would be such a great pleasure." Armstrong ends the telegram in the same manner in which he had ended his letter to Glaser from August 2, 1955: with a goodwill gesture of praise, his charismatic smile cast in words: "AND MAY GOD BLESS YOU PRESIDENT" YOU HAVE A GOOD HEART." The telegram further reveals Armstrong's views on taking political action. He wants Eisenhower to intervene personally, to show "guts," and he wants to be present when that happens. Political action means personal involvement on a grassroots level, not big politics; it means a reliance on personal integrity, not on political institutions. Actual political change in this sense requires the interracial collaboration of good-hearted rather than "two-faced" people, here represented by Eisenhower and Armstrong. As Armstrong remarked elsewhere: "Passing all them laws to open everything up—fine, okay, lovely! But it ain't gonna change everybody's hearts."[41]

One may doubt the effectiveness of this understanding, but it is crucial to realize that personal involvement and compassion are values Armstrong had learned from his mother as well as from the people of New Orleans and that interracial collaboration was something he had practiced on many levels throughout his career. The integrated status of his All Stars and his long musical partnership with the white Texan trombonist Jack Teagarden, which is documented on recordings, in concert footage, on television shows, and in films such as *The Strip* (dir. Leslie Kardos, 1951), are examples of such interracial collaboration. About his relationship with Teagarden, Armstrong said to Larry King: "I'm a spade and you an ofay. We got the same soul—so let's blow." And in contradistinction to the rhetoric of 1960s black nationalism, he defended this position until the end of his life. "Race-conscious jazz musicians? Nobody could be who really knew their horns and loved the music," he wrote to Jones and Chilton. "Those people who make the restrictions, they don't know nothing about music, it's no crime for cats of any colour to get together and blow."[42]

Significantly, Armstrong's telegram to Eisenhower stands in sharp contrast to the stance taken by *Time* magazine: "Policy is Policy. Implementing its 1954 school-desegregation decision, the U.S. Supreme Court called for 'all deliberate speed' in integration, and it named the judges of the federal district courts as its agents for seeing that the order was carried out," the writers for *Time* opined on September 30, 1957. "It was in line with the policy set forth by the Supreme Court that the Administration fought its battle in the courtroom, and not with such grandstand stunts as having President Eisenhower fly to Little Rock and lead Negro children by the hand through the National Guard lines."[43] Unwilling to acknowledge that the phrase "with all deliberate speed" resulted from a legal compromise that had enraged many civil rights advocates because it catered to the sensibilities of Southern defenders of the Jim Crow system, the *Time* article is especially interesting because its understanding of politics is diametrically opposed to, and much less progressive than, Armstrong's cultural politics. Its trust in political institutions and its disavowal of Eisenhower's personal involvement as "grandstand stunts" clash with Armstrong's direct appeal to the president "to take those little Negro children personally into Central High School," and they are further contradicted by Armstrong's assessment, made only a few years later, that the controversy went beyond the particular circumstances of Little Rock. Rather than present Little Rock as an isolated incident, Armstrong recalls "a bad spirit" throughout the South; Southern blacks frequently faced physical abuse, he explains, and they armed themselves in response.[44]

The central significance of Armstrong's discursive intervention in the Little Rock crisis lies in the fact that it not only seriously endangered his career but hit very close to home in terms of American domestic and foreign politics. Since Eisenhower met with black political leaders only once during his presidency (in June 1958, and for just forty-five minutes), and since the single African American member of the White House staff, Frederic Morrow, was advised to refrain from bringing up the issues of race relations and civil rights in his talks with Eisenhower, Armstrong's telegram and his comments in the daily press were perhaps the only ways in which the president could be reached.[45] Eisenhower had even tried to sway the opinion of Chief Justice Earl Warren in the *Brown v. Board of Education of Topeka* case by arguing that Southerners "are not bad people" and only wanted to ensure "that their sweet little girls are not required to sit in school alongside some big overgrown Negroes."[46] The wording of this sentence betrays a racist ideology that American moviegoers would have encountered most forcefully in 1915, when David Wark Griffith had popularized it in the melodramatic *The Birth of a Nation*, and that characterized black men as evil "coons" lusting after innocent white girls. Armstrong, by contrast, rejected this ideology openly, questioning the constitutionality of Jim Crow ("They've been ignoring the Constitution"), linking Little Rock historically to the institution of slavery and its violent aftermath ("that old South"; "getting away with it for a hundred years'"), and suggesting that he was having trouble feeling at home in the United States ("getting almost so bad a colored man hasn't got any country").

The *Chicago Defender* even connected Armstrong directly with Eisenhower's final intervention in the Little Rock crisis: "His words had both the timing and the explosive effect of an H-bomb. They reverberated around the world. It wasn't long after he had dropped the verbal explosives that swift military action brought on a change in the Little Rock drama." The *Defender* further recommended Armstrong for the NAACP's Springarn medal because of his "courage, sincerity, and vision": "While our high-powered leaders recoiled into their shells, Old Satchmo stepped into the breach to battle the enemy."[47] Statements such as this brought war rhetoric, which had been used most prominently in the context of international politics, into the realm of internal political conflict. The battle, it seemed, was now taking place at home as well, and its casus belli was the violent segregation of the races in the American South.

Little Rock did not just incense Armstrong; it "quickly became the foremost international symbol of American racism" at a time when Ghana had just declared independence (March 1957). When Thomas Borstelmann speaks of "[t]hose twin struggles for racial equality, the American civil rights movement and the African quest for independence," he indicates the potentially global significance of American jazz, a music that was used by the federal administration to propagate American freedom but that inadvertently served to foreground the discrepancies between political ideals and political reality both in the American South and on a global scale.[48] Many in the United States and abroad were critical of the administration's wish to export a rhetoric of freedom and democracy at a time when the Jim Crow regime still reigned supreme in many Southern states and when the federal government remained unwilling to support the African freedom struggle. It is indicative of Armstrong's political presence—but not necessarily of a conscious orchestration of his political convictions or even a concerted political program—that he was involved in the American struggle against Jim Crow (through his comments on Little Rock) and in the quest for independence of African nations (through his African tours).

Significantly, too, Armstrong backed up his words with action. While Sonny Rollins recorded "The Freedom Suite" as a musical response to Little Rock in 1958 and while Charles Mingus attacked Governor Faubus with his "Original Faubus Fables" composition in 1960, Armstrong canceled his upcoming State Department tour to the Soviet Union, endured the ostracism and criticism of several African American celebrities (Sammy

Davis Jr. and Adam Clayton Powell, among others), and faced boycotts of his records and concerts.[49] When reporters inquired about his unwillingness to travel abroad as an official cultural ambassador, he answered: "The people over there ask me what's wrong with my country, what am I supposed to say? If I ever go to Russia, I'll go on my own."[50] The State Department publicly hoped that Armstrong "would not let the segregation issue keep him from making a musical mission to Moscow," but he stuck to his cancellation of the tour and declared that he would nonetheless prefer playing in the Soviet Union over playing in Arkansas because "Faubus might hear a couple of notes—and he don't deserve that."[51]

Reading over these statements, one wonders why Armstrong would frequently backpedal from this position and why he would claim an apolitical stance on so many occasions. After canceling the tour, Armstrong waited several years before he finally agreed to return to Africa. In the meantime, he softened his stance toward American race relations: "the situation in general for Negroes is far better than it used to be, despite what happened at Little Rock," he informed South American reporters in late 1957.[52] In an interview for *Ebony*, he put his views on American politics into further perspective. While he is an honorary life member of the NAACP, he explains, he is "not a political person"; "I don't get involved, otherwise, I'd always be in trouble." His condemnations of Faubus and Eisenhower were not made "from a political standpoint. I was just hot." In 1955, he had already etched out an apolitical position of retreat for himself, informing the public that "All I know is the horn, not politics," and he reclaimed that position after the Little Rock controversy had died down.[53] Armstrong would repeat claims about his disinterest in politics for the rest of his life—in "Satchmo Says," for instance, he proclaimed: "I don't dive into politics, haven't voted since I've lived in New York, ain't no use messing with something you don't know anything about"[54]—and it seems that this professed disinterest in, and disengagement from, the political system went back to a deep distrust of "white" institutions that he had most likely acquired as part of his habitus during his formative years in early twentieth-century New Orleans. What is more, Armstrong's apolitical declarations must be weighed against other, more defiant and self-assertive pronouncements. After all, a powerful statement like "I come along with my trumpet, I defend my race and my music" fundamentally undermines his apolitical stance, and it suggests that the musician possessed an understanding of political engagement that was closely tied to his role as a popular musician and entertainer.[55]

Three interventions in the racial conflicts and discourses of his time apart from the Little Rock controversy illuminate the obvious discrepancy between Armstrong's apolitical statements and his political commentary. The first of these interventions is a musical revue composed by Dave and Iola Brubeck, which featured him in the lead role and celebrated him, as the title announces, as one of *The Real Ambassadors* (1962), those jazz musicians who went abroad to play their music in front of foreign audiences as part of the State Department tours. The show was conceived as a tribute to Armstrong and was intended specifically to reestablish his political significance. Some of the more confrontational lyrics include remarks about "what *we* need is a goodwill tour of Mississippi" and "Forget Moscow—when do we play in New Orleans?" They also include Armstrong's interruption of the female narrator, whose assumption that the protagonist has the "ability to keep his opinions to himself" is overridden by the musician's declaration "Lady, if you could read my mind, your head would bust wide open." On "King for a Day" (Sept. 19, 1961), whose title evokes Armstrong's Mardi Gras appearance of 1949 as well as the film footage of his Leopoldville reception, the lyrics attack the gradualist stance of segregationist apologists and suggest that a jam session led by Armstrong could solve the most pressing problems in international politics. More credibly, the lyrics foreground the music's greatest political potential, its ability to move people along in sympathetic understanding of a shared groove: if the trumpeter were allowed to organize world politics, "this world would be a swingin' place!"; everybody would "fall right in a swinging groove / And all the isms gonna move." Armstrong did not write these lyrics, but they may have been based on a comment he had made in 1960 during his second African tour: "one day I'd like to slip behind the Iron Curtain! The summit meetings they have with all those ministers don't seem to be getting anywhere much. Perhaps old Satchmo could achieve something with his trumpet at a little conference in the basement."[56] Fearful of the revue's potential political impact, however, Joe Glaser apparently prevented television cameras from filming the only live performance of *The Real Ambassadors* at the Monterey Jazz Festival in 1962, precluding an overly politicized reception and thus ensuring that Armstrong's image as a benevolent entertainer remained largely unharmed. In a television interview with Joachim-Ernst Behrendt, Armstrong says a few months before the Monterey concert that it "might be on TV," but he casts a wary off-camera glance, perhaps to his road manager, Pierre Tallerie, which suggests that there might have been some controversy about whether the concert should be broadcast on television or not.

A second performative intervention took place only a few years later, in 1964. Charles L. Sanders's article in *Ebony*, "Louis Armstrong—The Reluctant Millionaire," showed him posing with a copy of LeRoi Jones/Amiri Baraka's *Blues People*, which had been published a year earlier. For Penny Von Eschen, this photograph signals Armstrong's identification with Baraka's Afrocentric interpretation of jazz history and "marks an endorsement of a specific moment in black cultural production linked explicitly to politics and the black freedom movement."[57] One cannot be certain whether Armstrong himself chose to display the book or whether the photographer coaxed him into making this gesture. If he was indeed responsible, he probably selected the book not so much for its association with Baraka's political outlook than for the fact that a radical black critic like Baraka had publicly recognized his enduring cultural centrality past the bebop era and had turned him from a racial stereotype (Sambo, Uncle Tom) into a cultural archetype: "Armstrong was, in terms of emotional archetypes, an honored priest of his culture—one of the most impressive products of his society," Baraka had written in *Blues People*. "Armstrong was not *rebelling* against anything with his music. In fact, his music was one of the most beautiful refinements of Afro-American musical tradition."[58] In the same interview, however, the trumpeter indicated that regardless of the advances of the civil rights movement, he was always conscious of the fact that he was "still Louis Armstrong—colored."[59]

The third performative intervention was an interview with David Dachs for *Ebony* magazine, which was printed as an as-told-to autobiographical narration in the May 1961 issue. Here, Armstrong prefigures much of the explicitly political commentary he would voice three years later in "Louis Armstrong—The Reluctant Millionaire." This commentary includes an account of life in the 1930s, when he sold out fancy nightclubs but could not rent a room in downtown Los Angeles and had to spend his nights in hotels for black guests on Central Avenue. Armstrong also refutes the Aunt Jemima stereotype directly when he recalls that the limited number of Hollywood parties he attended "left a sour taste in my mouth" because "[s]omebody would always come up [. . .] and say, 'Y'know,

I once had a colored mammy,'" which caused him to "explode inside." In addition, he was always acutely aware of his social status as a colored man, feeling that "they wouldn't want you in their kitchens or in their pools." Thus, while these white Hollywood celebrities "are friendly to Negroes, [. . .] we aren't social." These observations make up a substantial part of the interview; they trouble the euphemistic byline of the piece about the "vast improvement" in the ways in which black musicians are treated and con-textualize the many photographs of himself with several white celebrities that accompany the article (among them Grace Kelly, Bing Crosby, and Richard Nixon).[60]

Armstrong's superficial disengagement from political action—his pro-fessed unwillingness to dive into politics—is counteracted further by the stories he repeatedly told about his experiences with racial segregation, which usually end with an affirmation of his music's power to reach across the racial divide. In the Dachs interview, he recalls the events surround-ing a show he was scheduled to play at the fancy Suburban Gardens nightclub in 1931 and that was broadcast over the radio. This was the first time a black band was allowed to play in this club, and the show attracted many representatives of the white New Orleans upper class. "They had a mike in front of the bandstand, which used to broadcast only for white bands," Armstrong notes, and the audience was huge: "50,000 colored people were on the levees, close to radios. At the last minute, the South-ern radio announcer said: 'I can't announce that nigger man.' [. . .] I turned to the boys on the bandstand and said: 'Give me a chord.' I got an ear-splitting chord and announced the show myself. It was the first time a Negro *spoke* on the radio down there." Later in the interview, Arm-strong notes that the sexual codes of the segregationist South had turned for the better but adds a stinging remark about the cruel irony of being the recipient of the key to the city and having a playground dedicated to him but being unable to play in his hometown because "[t]here's a state law that doesn't allow mixing of Negro and white musicians. They want me to leave the two white boys in my band home. But I say, 'That wouldn't be my band.' So I don't go."[61] These complaints reveal the de-gree to which Armstrong was willing to speak his mind in the 1960s. In his letter to Myra Menville from December 23, 1956, he had still couched his refusal to play a concert in New Orleans in decidedly more ambigu-ous terms: "I Sho'd" like to Come back home And blow Some *fine Jive* for my home folks. But, Since the AXE has *hit* All *bands* with 'Ofays +

'Spades' together "MMM". Anyway' maybe later."[62] Here, the Sambo code was still clearly visible and audible.

As these political interventions show, Armstrong did speak out about race relations and American politics, sometimes in very explicit terms and with unmistakable force. Yet he frequently presented his criticisms indirectly, as a more or less veiled critique that usually confined itself to personal observation and seldom led to confrontational political statements. A seemingly casual anecdotal reminiscence about his "first experience with Jim Crow" in *Satchmo* bears this out. When he was five years old, he recalls, he went riding on the segregated New Orleans streetcars for the first time in his life: "I walked right up to the front of the car without noticing the signs on the backs of the seats on both sides, which read: FOR COLORED PASSENGERS ONLY." When he remains oblivious to the signs, a black lady from the neighborhood yells at him to move to the back of the bus. Young Armstrong, however,

> thought she was kidding me so I stayed where I was, sort of acting cute. What did I care where she sat? Shucks, that woman came up to me and jerked me out of the seat. Quick as a flash she dragged me to the back of the car and pushed me into the rear seats. Then I saw the signs on the backs of the seats saying: FOR COLORED PASSENGERS ONLY.
> "What do those signs say?" I asked.
> "Don't ask so many questions! Shut your mouth, you little fool."[63]

Typical of his narrative strategy in *Satchmo*, Armstrong adds a speck of minstrel sounding ("Shucks") to an otherwise serious presentation. Instead of lambasting the injustices of racial segregation, which some readers may have expected from a text written in the early 1950s, he continues his story with a brief description of momentary triumph over the separate but allegedly equal system: "There is something funny about those signs on the street cars in New Orleans," he observes. "We colored folks used to get real kicks out of them when we got on a car at the picnic grounds or at Canal Street on a Sunday evening when we outnumbered the white folks. Automatically we took the whole car over, sitting as far up front as we wanted to. It felt good to sit up there once in a while. We felt a little more important than usual. I can't explain why exactly, but maybe it was because we weren't supposed to be up there."[64] This allusive account of temporarily overcoming the systematic racial segregation on public transportation that the U.S. Supreme Court had legitimized with its "separate but equal" ruling in *Plessy v. Ferguson* (1896) is indicative of Armstrong's carefully calibrated commentary on race relations ("something funny"; "I can't explain why exactly"; "maybe"). Robin D. G. Kelley's study of black working-class behavior in the segregated South emphasizes the social implications inherent in the musician's portrayal of the spontaneous integration of busses. Kelley observes that "these young men and women who rode public transportation in groups were emboldened by a sense of social solidarity rooted in a shared culture, common friends, generational identity, not to mention a level of naiveté as to the possible consequences of 'acting up' in white-dominated public space."[65] Social solidarity and a shared culture surface in Armstrong's account through the frequency of the plural pronoun "we," which appears seven times in the short passage.

Furthermore, the passage exemplifies two crucial ways in which African Americans in the South, especially those of the working class, dealt with their position as social underdogs. As a first mechanism, Armstrong and the people of his neighborhood reverted to something that Earl Lewis describes as a process of turning segregation into congregation: congregation "symbolized an act of free will, whereas segregation represented the imposition of another's will."[66] On an overcrowded bus, the segregated seating that codified the color line in the public sphere is quickly, though only temporarily, erased and turned into a form of pleasurable congregation ("get real kicks"; "felt good"; "felt a little more important"). Characteristically, Armstrong's recollection both downplays and emphasizes the fact that this congregation signified an act of free will. While the transgression of seating regulations is said to have happened "[a]utomatically" and only because the bus was overcrowded, its black occupants actually *"took the whole car over"* and sat "as far up front as we *wanted* to."

The second mechanism through which the black working class in the segregated South engaged in what Kelley calls the "politics of the everyday" was to develop social and cultural modes of community beyond the eyes and ears of those who determined their social status and policed their adherence to the Jim Crow laws. Kelley's reading of James C. Scott's "hidden transcripts" is particularly useful in this context: "despite appearances of consent," he summarizes, "oppressed groups challenge those in power by constructing a 'hidden transcript,' a dissident political culture that manifests itself in daily conversations, folklore, jokes, songs, and other cultural practices." In other words, "The veiled social and cultural worlds of oppressed people frequently surface in everyday forms of resistance"; these forms not only express "the pleasures and politics of black communities under segregation" but can also be deployed, according to Scott, as "weapons of the weak."[67] These weapons constitute the means through which oppressed subjects manage their status of oppression and through which they exert a degree of agency. They do so by constructing their own space free of the oppressor's control and by engaging in forms of resistance that are not immediately recognizable as such. The perceived clumsiness, laziness, and intellectual inferiority of the Sambo, for instance, secured the slave a limited degree of power on an everyday basis. He could bungle work assigned by the master and thus hamper the speed of production without being accused of sabotage; he could work slowly and thereby protect himself from physical exhaustion without appearing to be willfully unproductive; he could manipulate master and mistress by feigning ignorance and hiding his actual intentions.

In general terms, Armstrong's politics of the everyday surfaces in his choice of narrative genres and his peculiar choice of subject matters. Instead of offering one grand narrative of racial uplift and musical geniality (a definitive autobiography), he supplies scattered snippets of bathroom humor; stories about pot-smoking and sex sessions; and a seemingly endless string of working-class anecdotes about New Orleans prostitutes, pimps, razor fights, and folk medicine. The daily conversations, jokes, and songs that constitute a major part of the hidden transcript appear in various forms. Many daily conversations are inscribed directly into the epistolary record (Armstrong chatting with his letters' recipients), while others are either recalled in autobiographical narrative (take Black Benny's advice about white patrons and mistresses), transmitted onto the grooves of sound recording (through studio chatter and scat aesthetics), or captured on private tape recordings. That Armstrong had acquired much of his folk knowledge and linguistic strategies such as jiving and signifying from the "churchpeople, gamblers, hustlers, cheap pimps, thieves, [and] prostitutes" of his neighborhood, and that he was schooled in the "bars, honky-tonks and saloons" of New Orleans, signals his versedness in the hidden transcripts of black working-class New Orleans: "the people who loved us and spoke our language" in cultural spaces in which the nominally powerless, according to Earl Lewis, "gather their cultural bearings, to mold the urban setting."[68]

One prominent space in which Armstrong gathered his cultural bear-

ings was the barbershop. Indicative of his loyalty to New Orleans customs
and mores, he devoted a separate essay, titled "Barber Shops," to his favorite barbershops in Corona, New York. "In my neighborhood [. . .] I
have (2) Barber Shops," he writes:

> I can get my Hair when ever I want to. The <u>Soul</u> Barber Shop closes on
> <u>Mondays</u> (rain or shine). My <u>Spanishes</u> Barber Shop <u>never</u> closes, except,
> only on <u>Sundays</u>. Sometimes, if I just have a <u>Hair Cut</u> on a <u>Monday</u>, and
> just can't wait until the next day, I will make a <u>bee</u> line to the <u>Spanish one</u>,
> and they are just as glad to have me, anyway. It's just that I'll give ole <u>Soulee</u>
> the Benefit of the doubt anyway. And we <u>Soulees</u> speak the same <u>lan-
> guages</u>,—<u>slanguages</u>—the usual B.S.—talk <u>loud</u>—etc.[69]

The hidden transcript is clearly referenced here. The black barbershop,
which Michael Cogswell has identified as "Joe's Artistic Barber Shop," is
called a "<u>Soul</u> Barber Shop." Operated by Joe, the "ole <u>Soulee</u>," it is filled
with the daily conversations, folklore, jokes, and other cultural practices
that constituted the hidden transcripts of black Southern communities under segregation.[70] As the essay illustrates, the relocated Southerners of the
Great Migration held on to these transcripts in the new urban context.
Armstrong names the language practices that signify the existence of an
African American discursive community behind the doors of the shop
("<u>slanguages</u>—the usual B.S.—talk <u>loud</u>"), and while he appreciates the
services and company of the Spanish barber, he "give[s] ole <u>Soulee</u> the
Benefit of the doubt." What is more, he taped two photographs of himself,
his barber, and several customers into one of his many scrapbooks. This
way, he documented spaces and transcript without fully unveiling them. In
the essay, he does not recount "the usual B.S." he exchanged with his soul
barber in their regular loud-talking sessions; the photographs only hint at
this transcript because of their status as a nonverbal medium. A photograph taken by John Loengard gives a more expansive view of the shop and
a better sense of the conversations that must have accompanied the scene.
It depicts several customers of various ages as they move around the shop
and interact with each other both verbally and nonverbally, but it, too, can
only suggest what they may have been saying to each other.[71]

Moving from the inner space of the black barbershop to the public display of particular hairstyles, the political subtext of Armstrong's recollections of the so-called conk, or "Konklines (hair do)," is worth a moment of

consideration.[72] In "The Satchmo Story," Armstrong describes the precarious process of hair straightening as follows: "Konks were the thing in those days [the 1920s]. [. . .] Most of the show people and musicians who used to konk their hair, were too lazy to keep it up . . . Because when your hair is konked—[. . .] the barber had to use real lye—mixed up with some kind of stuff looked like putty." He then points to the disadvantages of this process, punning in his characteristic manner: "And if he put this stuff into your hair and if he's a split second late getting to the wash bowl [. . .] , 'Man—that lye is *liable* to burn all of your hair out of your head and make a gang of great big fester bump Sores—head sores that is. . . . So you had to be real hipped and *be sharp—feel sharp—and stay sharp.*"[73]

Yet in the late 1950s, when Armstrong wrote "The Satchmo Story," the conk had not only fallen out of fashion but was also sending out the wrong political message. In his autobiography, published a few years after this piece, Malcolm X makes much of the hair straightening he underwent as the hipster Malcolm Little, referring to his conk as his "first really big step toward self-degradation [. . .] , literally burning my flesh with lye, in order [. . .] to have it look like a white man's hair. I had joined that multitude of Negro men and women in America who are brainwashed into believing that the black people are 'inferior.'"[74] Unlike Malcolm X, however, who uses his commentary to formulate a political ideology, Armstrong treats the conk like a snapshot, a brief flash of memory unearthed in the course of the autobiographical performance devoted to the theme of haircuts (Armstrong had stopped straightening his hair by 1930).[75] Nonetheless, his words about the "konkline" attain a political dimension once they are situated within the shifting constitution of the minstrel poetics. Ayana D. Byrd and Lori L. Tharps argue that the conk originally signified more than a pandering to white conceptions of beauty because it was associated with an aura of stylishness and hipness.[76] Armstrong's memories of the 1920s therefore indicate that, for an earlier generation, the conk had meant a move away from the "nappy" or "kinky" hair ridiculed in countless minstrel and "coon" representations.[77] For Armstrong and fellow musicians, the conk represented artistic achievement and public self-respect: "you had to be real hipped and *be sharp—feel sharp—and stay sharp.*" This means that this hairstyle could signify different things to different people: a break with Sambo's wooly head for fashion-conscious African American musicians in the 1920s and a reactionary sight for civil rights–conscious observers and black revolutionaries in the 1960s.

The autobiographical treatment of barbershops and the brief celebration of the conk as an emblem of show-business success point to a deeply anchored politics according to which Armstrong engaged his audiences not by pronouncing radical slogans, but by creating a sense of communal understanding and interpersonal connection between performer and listener. This type of politics was the result of the New Orleans culture that, as far as can be gleaned from his autobiographics, shaped much of Armstrong's outlook on life. According to this outlook, audiences "want to be entertained" rather than politically instructed.[78] At a time when the civil rights struggle was entering its most violent phase, this position was difficult to justify. As the church bombing in Birmingham, Alabama, on September 15, 1963 (which left four young black girls killed and inspired John Coltrane's "Alabama," recorded that same year); the beatings of non-violent protestors in Selma on March 7, 1965 (known as "Bloody Sunday"); and the urban riots in Watts, Newark, and Detroit were riveting the nation, Armstrong counterbalanced his more political statements with a repeated retreat to an apolitical stance: "It's all show business," he stated. "And I don't think I'd want to be one of them serious kind." He did, however, make a few critical comments about the Selma protests: "They would beat me on the mouth if I marched. [. . .] [T]hey would beat Jesus if he was black and marched," he told the *New York Times*, and he revealed to a writer for *Down Beat* that he "became physically ill after watching a television news program showing Selma Police action against civil rights marchers in the Alabama city."[79] He further acknowledged that Martin Luther King "is a magnificent man" but also insisted that "my mission is music" and made sure that "(What Did I Do to Be So) Black and Blue?"—the song that had introduced him to Broadway in 1929 and had figured so prominently in Ellison's *Invisible Man*—would not become an emblem of political protest: "It's a serious thing, and I used to sing it serious—like shame on you for this and that. But I don't want to do nothing that would ask people to look at the song and be depressed and thinking about marching and equal rights. [. . .] Way I sing it now with a little chuckle, get a *big* reaction."[80]

The remarks about "(What Did I Do to Be So) Black and Blue?" are explicit about Armstrong's unwillingness to be associated with the civil rights movement: people should not have to think about "marching and equal rights" when they attend one of his concerts.[81] By emphasizing his role as an entertainer and by striving to keep his music free from the ugly political violence of the times—that his audiences are predominantly white remains implicit—he retreated to a position in which minstrel sounding and Sambo resonances were still possible. If his persona thrived on people's affectionate response ("a *big* reaction") and if his performative strategies depended on his ability to produce resonances of the chuckling Sambo (however faint), then associating himself too obviously with strategies of civil disobedience and passive resistance, not to speak of more aggressive forms of protest, would have threatened the very foundation on which his personal success story rested. Yet his words do not exclusively pander to the depoliticizing gaze of his mainstream audience. In fact, Armstrong acknowledges that the theme of the song, commonly taken to be the singer's lament over racial discrimination and most problematically expressed in the lines "I'm white inside but that don't help my case / 'cause I can't hide what is in my face," is "a serious thing."[81] Some of his readers would have been familiar with his performance of the tune on Murrow's *Satchmo the Great*, including the filmic narrative of Nkrumah's emotional reaction to its sentiment and of the struggle for African independence for which the song, only a decade earlier, could stand. And in the magazine version of the interview, Armstrong told Meryman that all the songs in his repertoire "display my life somewhat."[83] This, then, signals the return to his own politics, which thrive on the notion of personal engagement against racial segregation and the wish to create moments of collective happiness through beautiful music and the communication of a meaningful life story.

Moreover, Armstrong frequently insisted on his music's ability to transcend boundaries of race, caste, and nation, as the stories about jumping the Iron Fence cited earlier indicate. "You see that horn? That horn ain't prejudiced," trombonist Trummy Young recalls him telling interviewers in the Middle East. "Music's the same everywhere," Armstrong stated at a press conference during his second African tour, and he exclaimed about his encounters with fans in Eastern Europe: "We met on common ground: music. We came to liven up the situation—not to depress anybody." He further said to Gilbert Millstein: "They get their soul lifted because they got the same soul I have the minute I hit a note."[84] Such soul-lifting was politically significant in a culture in which interracial communication and interaction were troubled by racial prejudices, antagonisms, and misconceptions. Particularly in places dominated by Jim Crow, Armstrong and his white admirers would have found it difficult to meet on equal terms in the social realm, but they would have had better chances at entering an interpersonal connection in the potentially liminal moment of live performance. In 1961, Armstrong informed *Ebony* about the people who attend his concerts: "These same society people may go around the corner and lynch a Negro. But while they're listening to our music, they don't think about trouble. What's more they're watching Negro and white musicians play side by side [in the All Stars]. And we bring contentment and pleasure. I always say, 'Look at the nice taste we leave. It's bound to mean something. That's what music is for.'"[85]

Armstrong's argument about his cultural politics is that music can further political achievements indirectly, that it has a harmonizing potential whose political effectiveness is difficult to measure but must not be underestimated. In 1959, he boasted accordingly: "Unify Germany? Why, man, we've already unified it. We came through Germany playing this ol' happy music, and if them Germans wasn't unified, this ain't ol' Satchmo talking."[86] This statement certainly points to Armstrong's wishful thinking about the Cold War and to his interest in promoting his image as a jazz ambassador, but it also gestures toward the multicultural musical world of New Orleans. The social and musical organization of New Orleans jazz—call-and-response interaction, funeral parades, the second line, and the heterophonic singing of the Sanctified Church that had shaped life in what was arguably "the most globalized city in the world" in the late nineteenth and early twentieth centuries—underscores the fundamentally democratic ethos that infused Armstrong's cultural politics, even though its actual political efficacy is debatable.[87] Many of these practices were retained in the All Stars performances from the 1950s and 1960s. As such, they appeared as more than musical elements from an old or even outdated kind of jazz, but as integral parts of a specific worldview. The All Stars end their Australian performance of "When the Saints Go Marchin' In" from 1964 by parading across the stage, inviting the audience to participate in the marching activities and thus become part of the music. On the version of the tune they did for the 1962 Goodyear Tire concert, which was recorded in the studio with no audience present, Armstrong tells his imaginary listeners that they "can all sing with us" and that they "all sing pretty out there." In both versions and the many others the All Stars performed and recorded throughout the years, call-and-response interaction among the members of the interracial band further amplifies the democratic, participatory, and harmonizing potential of the music. These performances extend an invitation to their respective audiences to engage with the worldview expressed in the music, but as prime examples of popular commercial entertainment, they certainly also offer apolitical ways of enjoyment and pleasure.

This potential can also be detected in the Mardi Gras festivities, which were fundamental to the development of jazz's interracial appeal, including practices of masking and signifying. As Reid Mitchell puts it, "I see in Mardi Gras much [of] what I hear in a really good jazz band: a model for the just society" and "a model for community where individual expression is the basis for social harmony."[88] And as Berndt Ostendorf suggests, "the role playing of Louis Armstrong may hide deeper secrets" because masking and play-acting often "indicate a political credo, namely an anti-imperialistic and anti-colonist willingness to begin to understand the other, though it be in stereotype or in unavoidable initial prejudice."[89] Thus, Armstrong's desire that music would "change everybody's hearts" and his wish to "bring contentment and pleasure" and leave a "nice taste" with his audience constitute the purpose of his music: "what music is for." This seemingly harmless message is radicalized by the environment in which it is presented: in front of the Southern "society people" who attend his concerts and who, outside of the space of the dance hall, "may go around the corner and lynch a Negro." Members of the White Citizens Council of Knoxville, Tennessee, did, in fact, throw a stick of dynamite at the auditorium in which the All Stars were performing in 1957, and few years earlier, a bomb had exploded only hours after Armstrong and his band had finished their performance at the Towne Casino in Cleveland.[90]

In many ways, the particular power of music—its entertainment value but also its ability to infuse the consciousness of the listener—was a primary weapon of the socially weak yet prominently exposed black musician. In that sense, Armstrong's views on the purpose of music are not merely the result of naive musings. Rather, they point to a process in which, as musicologist Lawrence Kramer has noted, an audience's "pleasure in listening [. . .] becomes a vehicle of acculturation: musical pleasure, like all pleasure, invites legitimation both of its sources and of the subject position its sources address. [. . .] To some degree, the act of personifying the musical subject situates the listener within that subject's cultural order."[91] In Armstrong's case, the music was personified by the performing musician, while the cultural order within which his performances situated black and white listeners alike—at least for the duration of the performance—was one of harmonious interracial collaboration. "When we hit Savannah we played

'You'll Never Walk Alone,'" Armstrong told David Halberstam about a show in Georgia in 1957. "[T]he whole house—all Negroes—started singing with us on their own. We ran through two choruses and they kept with us and later they asked for it again. Most touching damn thing I ever saw. I almost started crying right there on stage. We really hit something inside each person there."[92] A few years later, he explained to another white reporter, Edward R. Murrow, that his Russian fans had claimed him as *"our Louie,"* and in 1961, he spoke to *Ebony* about a racially integrated show he had played in Miami in 1948: "I saw thousands of people, colored and white on the main floor. Not segregated. [. . .] Just all together—naturally."[93]

These assessments should trouble all too easy dismissals of Armstrong as a racial clown and political pushover. Yet his performance as King of the Zulus in the Mardi Gras parade in 1949 and his appearance on the cover of *Time* magazine in the same month have been interpreted as fault lines separating the musician's culturally and politically relevant phase from a kind of post-Edenic, fallen state in which he pandered shamelessly to the minstrel mode, grinning on television and playing the Sambo for his white mainstream audience. In the same year, jazz writer Rudi Blesh argued that Armstrong's failure to realize the political potential of his music was of mythic proportions and that it had already occurred much earlier: "Had Armstrong understood his responsibility as clearly as he perceived his own growing artistic power—had his individual genius been deeply integrated with that of the music, and thus ultimately with the destiny, of his race—designated leadership would have been just." Blesh is particularly dissatisfied with Armstrong's status as a popular entertainer: "Around Louis clustered growing public cognizance of hot music and those commercial forces [. . .] which utilize the musical communications system of the phonograph record, the then new radio and talking motion picture, and the printed sheets of the Tin Pan Alley tunesmiths. And behind this new symbolic figure was aligned the overwhelming and immemorial need of his own race to find a Moses to lead it out of Egypt."[94] For Blesh, the artistic powers of Armstrong's music are connected with the mythical powers afforded to him as a symbolic figure. In musical terms, his responsibility would have been to resist the commercial lure of Tin Pan Alley song production and American popular music. In political terms, his responsibility may be said to have been even greater: to be a Moses to his African American people and to have led this people from oppression to freedom. Implicitly connecting Armstrong with the nineteenth-century spiritual "Go

Down, Moses," Blesh subscribes to a teleological reading of American history that conceives of the black struggle first for freedom and then for equal civil rights as a grand narrative from enslavement to liberation. That Armstrong does not figure all too easily into this narrative and that his performances tended to produce ambiguous rather than straightforward political messages points to the difficulties faced by black musicians and entertainers who performed for heterogeneous audiences and sold their material in a marketplace of racialized expectations and commercial demands. Armstrong recorded "Go Down, Moses" (Feb. 7, 1958) and other spirituals for his *Louis and the Good Book* album about a decade after Blesh's writing, but the political impact of these recordings is difficult to gauge. However one judges Blesh's opinions—his romantic vision of musical and personal genius, the jeremiadic overtones against commercial music, his essentialist construction of race and people, as well as his belief in the political powers of popular musicians—one thing is clear: his understanding of jazz is shaped by the discourses and symbols that "clustered" around Louis Armstrong. For many, these discourses and symbols included the Sambo, Uncle Tom, and Ambassador Satch. Peter Dana, for instance, called Armstrong "King Louis" and "the world's great minstrel man" in one and the same article; Phyl Garland wrote in his obituary that "too few of his followers were aware of the creative genius lurking behind the grinning black face, rolling eyes and other attributes of showmanship"; and Richard Meryman thought of "the whole Satchmo act: the acre of white teeth, the 'Yeaaaaas,' the many choruses of *Hello, Dolly!*, the grotesque waggling of his head so that his shaking lips would give the voice vibrato, the brief bars on the trumpet. The more the crowd applauded, the more he mugged and pranced and growled—playing the clown."[95]

Blesh, Dana, Garland, and Meryman were certainly not alone in hearing a convolution of echoes and resonances in Armstrong's life and music. The many cultural complexities and contradictions that shaped the musician's cultural politics are encapsulated in the controversy surrounding the commission and creation of a statue honoring the musician. When sculptor Elizabeth Catlett began working on the statue in the early 1970s, she decided against producing a smiling or grinning Armstrong: "As a black person living at that time, I understand the reasons behind Louie's clowning, but I don't want to perpetuate it and it shouldn't be part of a monument," she justified her decision.[96] Following the wishes of the monument committee, Catlett had initially depicted a waving Armstrong, but she was forced to acknowledge the comparisons many people in Louisiana drew to a "Happy Darky" statue in Baton Rouge. That Catlett then changed the musician's posture is one thing, but the fact that it had been so difficult to produce a statue that looked like Armstrong without conjuring up echoes of blackface minstrelsy teaches us an important lesson about the cultural power and ubiquity of the minstrel poetics. It also teaches us a thing or two about Armstrong's productively ambiguous, and politically controversial, involvement with this poetics.

"What do you know about that?"

Final Thoughts on "Laughin' Louie"

In one of the most impressive studies of black music in the United States published in recent years, Ronald Radano turns to the historical and musical significances of Louis Armstrong's music twice. Two brief passages of *Lying Up a Nation: Race and Black Music* (2003) discuss Armstrong's recordings of "Heebie Jeebies" (Feb. 26, 1926) and "Heah Me Talkin' to Ya?" (Dec. 12, 1928), respectively, and they present more than isolated snippets of intellectual insight. They address many of the issues with which this book has been concerned, and because of their centrality and complexity, they shall be quoted at length here. First, Radano's reading of "Heebie Jeebies":

> When we witness the subversive, disruptive, "scatological" vocalizations in "Heebie Jeebies," in which Louis Armstrong plays the line between speech and song, we engage not merely the pure musicality of the grain [of the voice] but the compression of linguistic signification that is rich with racial meaning as well. We "hear" the Sambo stereotype, the exotic images—the savage, the ghostly apparition—of Armstrong's early filmic appearances, the virtuoso of a famous 1920s studio band, together with the sublime figurations of a black sound that in its public celebrations revealed the sameness that crosses race. And we hear countless other signs and images that no casual analytical gesture [. . .] can properly indicate. These articulations, which at once inform and reflect the discursive, produce the remarkable sense of authenticity and completion we associate with a miraculous sound that seemingly "jes grew."[1]

The richness of Radano's thoughts mandates a close reading of this passage. These thoughts point to Armstrong's prominent scat aesthetics, which invests his musical and physical performances with (racially) productive ambiguities and creates the fluidity and provocative elusiveness that characterize his musicking as well as his verbal communication (spoken or written). Armstrong's scatological vocalizations are disruptive and potentially subversive. They not only disrupt the scripted melody and lyrics of a musical piece but may also be said to subvert them by personalizing the performance as an intermedial presentation of a creative self. Similar effects can be identified in the musician's autobiographical writings, where indexical markers and annotations suggest performative excess. The racial meanings we hear and see in a performance are productively ambiguous as well ("the Sambo stereotype," "the exotic [. . .] savage," "sublime figurations of a black sound"), but they can only be identified once we move into the realm of cultural intermediality ("countless other signs and images"), where, as Radano aptly puts it, "no casual analytical gesture" will suffice. While racial meanings appear in media other than music, for instance, in autobiographical discourse and in film, they depend for their emergence on a cultural poetics of "blackness" that is intermedially coded as a cultural space in which the Sambo figure, savage exoticism, and seemingly authentic sublimity may be produced by the same performance. Thus, what is celebrated as Armstrong's authenticity and genius, on the one hand, and as his pandering to minstrel primitivism, on the other, is revealed as something both articulated and produced by the constant and contested interplay between music and the racial discourses that allow it to emerge as "miraculous sound."

A few pages further into his study, Radano focuses on Armstrong's admonition "Hear me talking to you," with which the musician introduces the song "Heah Me Talkin' to Ya?" and which remains the only verbal utterance on the recording:

> It is an obvious reference to the title, and at first sight it may seem inconsequential to the ensuing performance. But what if we were to take this playful gesture literally? Hear me talking to you? What are we supposed to hear? What's the story? And who's doing the talking? Judging from what jazz musicians have repeatedly claimed, the "story" would seem to be the music itself, in the collective ensemble work and in the solos that arise from it. [. . .] To tell a good story is to play a meaningful, memorable performance. It is to construct an improvisation so powerful, so emotionally and intellectually challenging that it seems to go beyond words, to reveal a deeper, more telling secret. The conceit of storytelling represents one of

the enduring rhetorical gestures among musicians, the principal trope conceptualizing the art of Lester Young, Charlie Parker, and so many others. So too does the conceit lie at the heart of black music's mystification. It serves to justify claims of musical transcendence, of a power projecting meaning beyond language. For many, it is through this beyondness that one discovers much about life generally. Black music emerges as an unspoken tale that nonetheless voices a truth about life and nation.[2]

The absence of speech that characterizes the song after Armstrong's initial utterance points to the fact that the musician's story is not easily told and that it emerges only through his intermedial autobiographics. For one, the story is supplied by the music. In this sense, the performance lets the listener know that music, as a medium distinct from others, communicates in its own ways (here: nonverbally), that it enables communication between the musician and his audience ("Heah *Me* Talkin' to *Ya?*"), and that the transmedial impulse that drives the music can be identified in other media as well (the musicking, versioning, and scat aesthetics/swing typing that motivate and structure Armstrong's autobiographical narratives). At the same time, Nat Shapiro and Nat Hentoff's oral history of jazz, published decades after Armstrong's recording, is titled *Hear Me Talkin' to Ya*, and one could argue that the stories of musicians like Armstrong, who is one of Shapiro and Hentoff's interviewees, supply the speech acts absent from the song. Thus, black music's unspoken tale may paradoxically and simultaneously be present in, and absent from, the music. It is absent because the recording can only suggest a mystified meaning beyond language, and it is present because it forces the listener to ponder the music's meaning. A reversed reading is possible as well: the unspoken tale is absent from the music because it is spoken and written elsewhere, yet it is also present because it is encoded, nonverbally, in the music and signaled by the opening encouragement to listen. It thus makes sense to follow Radano, who argues: "If we take the musicians at their word—to hear them 'talking' to us and acknowledge what they have to say, we can begin to imagine a different story from the one most commonly narrated."[3]

Several conclusions follow from these suggestions. First of all, the story of jazz that journalists, biographers, academic critics, and creative writers have constructed over the decades does not necessarily jibe with the stories told by individual musicians. In Armstrong's case, the musician himself has often been the source of his life story, not in the sense that he controlled and authorized one interpretation of his life and music but in the sense that his continued performances across media provided (and still provide) the source material for various and often contradictory readings—take the growing corpus of biographies that have been published over the last sixty-five years: Robert Goffin's *Horn of Plenty*, Max Jones and John Chilton's *Louis: The Louis Armstrong Story 1900–1971*, Hugues Panassié's *Louis Armstrong*, James Lincoln Collier's *Louis Armstrong: An American Genius*, Gary Giddins's *Satchmo: The Genius of Louis Armstrong*, Laurence Bergreen's *Louis Armstrong: An Extravagant Life*, Scott Allen Nollen's *Louis Armstrong: The Life, Music and Screen Career*, Terry Teachout's *Pops: A Life of Louis Armstrong*, and Ricky Riccardi's *What a Wonderful World*, not to mention lesser-known works such as Mike Pinfold's *Louis Armstrong*, Sam Tanenhaus's *Louis Armstrong: Musician*, and Dempsey J. Travis's *The Louis Armstrong Odyssey: From Jane Alley to America's Jazz Ambassador*.[4]

Second, if these readings and the stories they unveil ultimately exceed the intentions of the artist, then we must leave the analytical realm of author-controlled signification and enter the arenas of intertextual references, intermedial echoes, and cultural resonances. Armstrong's story certainly heeded the demands of jazz improvisation by remaining unfinished because it was endlessly versioned and extended through various media. But it also exceeded the musician's intentions. While it derived some of its performative energy from the conscious mobilization of minstrel sights and sounds, it also unfolded within an evolving intermedial web of significances that was beyond Armstrong's making. Speaking of Armstrong's autobiographics thus ultimately includes more than the total sum of the musician's recordings, visual performances, and writings: it also includes the minstrel poetics that preceded, accompanied, and followed Armstrong's performances across media and charged them with shifting sets of productive ambiguities. Furthermore, it includes the popular debates, critical discourses, and creative responses spawned by these intermedial performances.

Third, if we take Armstrong at his word and make an honest attempt to hear him "talking" to us through his music—or rather, if we take his intermedial autobiographics seriously and listen to its cultural resonances—we really can imagine a story previously untold. This story is especially audible in the two takes of "Laughin' Louie" that Armstrong and his band recorded on April 24, 1933. Armstrong was well-known for his fondness of marijuana. Considering his arrest for possessing and smoking marijuana in

1930 and his repeated musical celebrations of pot smoking in songs such as "Muggles" (Dec. 7, 1928) and "Sweet Sue—Just You" (Apr. 26, 1933), it is safe to say that these two takes were most likely the result of a particularly potent smoking session: "we wouldn't allow anybody on the recording sessions [. . .] unless they were real personal friends, because Louie would like to get high, and he'd like for the band to get high. . . . So he says, 'We going to record "Laughing Louie" today, gentlemen.' And he says, 'I want everybody to smoke a joint,'" tenor saxophonist Budd Johnson remembered.[5] As Armstrong's most baffling performances preserved on sound recording, the two "Laughin' Louie" takes are easily dismissed as "a burlesque of sad jokes and buffoonery" or conveniently celebrated as examples of the musician's exuberant pride in his powers as a charismatic performer.[6] A more promising critical engagement, however, can be offered by way of an Ellisonian approach.[7]

In the much-cited prologue to *Invisible Man*, Ellison's narrator-protagonist smokes marijuana and listens to Armstrong's 1929 recording of "(What Did I Do to Be So) Black and Blue?" Invisible Man confesses: "So under the spell of the reefer I discovered a new analytical way of listening to music. The unheard sounds came through, and each melodic line existed of itself, stood out clearly from all the rest, said its piece, and waited patiently for the other voices to speak. That night I found myself hearing not only in time, but in space as well." What Invisible Man hears beneath the tempo of the song includes "*an old woman singing a spiritual [. . . , a] beautiful girl the color of ivory [. . .] as she stood before a group of slaveowners who bid for her naked body,*" and a black preacher's Melvillean sermon on the "*Blackness of Blackness.*"[8] As Kimberly Benston observes, dislocated by music and the drug, Invisible Man "plunges toward a site where language [. . .] has both the impulse to summon a presence and the power to declare its own absence, to proffer a story of the past while thematizing the performative or fictional character of all such telling."[9] In other words, the preacher's ambiguous evocation of "blackness"—"*black is [. . .] an' black ain't*"; "*Black will make you [. . .] or black will un-make you*"—compels the reader "to consider blackness as a mediated, socially constructed *practice*, a process and not a product of discursive conditions of struggle."[10]

And indeed, what we encounter here is the ambiguity of the blues as an "autobiographical chronicle of personal catastrophe expressed lyrically," that "near-tragic, near-comic lyricism" that Ellison associates with the impulse to "keep the painful details and episodes of a brutal experience alive in one's aching consciousness" and that also constitutes the ontological core of this passage.[11] According to this ontology, the question of what it means to be so black and blue can never be finally answered. As a mediated and socially constructed practice, "blackness" is always subject to the blues: to constant negotiation and struggle. As such, however, it is also the locus of a "generative energy" that has driven black cultural production since the slave era and has picked up speed in the early decades of the twentieth century through the increasing availability and reach of mass media, especially sound recording and radio, but movies and later television as well.[12]

Before we enter into Invisible Man's reefer-induced state and listen to the unheard sounds and spaces of Armstrong's gage-induced "Laughin' Louie," let us consider the actual performance. The official take of "Laughin' Louie" begins with a short musical opening very much in the swing vein of Armstrong's other recordings of the early 1930s. The music is soon interrupted by the band members, who chant, "Yeah, here's some Laughin' Louie." What follows is a short speech by Armstrong in which he greets the audience and announces the title of the tune. All of this is accompanied by frequent laughter, from both Armstrong and his band members. Then the band segues back into the song, with Armstrong singing a comical verse, which is soon accompanied by another spoken segment. Here, Armstrong complains that his band will not let him swing and that others must therefore demonstrate their musical abilities, which they do as saxophone and trombone solos follow. These solos again prompt laughter from all, and Armstrong accepts the challenge implied by his band's musical display. Showcasing himself as a solo artist and thus as the star of the ensemble, he plays an unaccompanied solo of operatic proportions. Before he does so, however, he plays two single notes, pretending that he is suffering from a bad case of stage fright. The band members taunt him: "Mel-low," one of them responds, while another one shouts "look out there, Pops." The performance ends with a harmonious final chord.

What can we hear in "Laughin' Louie"? Who is telling what kind of story, and how is this story told? How can we begin to extract an understanding of Armstrong's jazz autobiographics from this seemingly innocent comic tune? "Laughin' Louie," which was composed by Clarence Gaskill, evokes the space of Armstrong's autobiographics through the title, which not only states the musicians first name ("Louie") but also conjures up one of the musician's most visible and audible gestures: the laugh. Moreover, the name as it is evoked here ("Louie") is not identical with Armstrong's actual first name, Louis. It is different in that it suggests a folksy intimacy that has a racial subtext: "All White Folks call me Louie," Armstrong observed in the 1940s, whereas most of his black friends and colleagues referred to him either as "Pops" or as "Louis," as he himself did as well, for instance on "Hello Dolly" (Dec. 3, 1963).[13] The recording is thus labeled as a black musician's performance for a predominantly white audience.

The recording captures musicking in process by documenting the musicians' bantering in the studio and rating the momentary snapshot of musical and comical interaction higher than the polished piece of music in which this performance could have resulted—after all, it begins like a regular swing tune and contains periods of accomplished and arranged solo-group interaction. As sonic evidence of musicking, the recording indelibly connects the music with those who play it. The musicians reject their status as verbally mute instrumental players and suppliers of dance music by speaking, sometimes in dialogue with Armstrong, sometimes in the form of a chorus. These call-and-response effects, which follow from verbal and musical interaction (soloist and band interact; Armstrong comments on his fellow players' solos), posit music as a performance marked by dialogue and collaboration among like-minded and equally stoned individuals who share a particular sense of humorous rivalry. In fact, verbal and musical interaction put into play the dynamics of the cutting contest; before launching his own solo, Armstrong accuses his colleagues of thinking too much of themselves.

Enticed by Armstrong's announcement to his imaginary audience that they are about to hear "one of them old time good ones," we may also hear echoes of the second line here, evoking the spirit of Mardi Gras (the marijuana-induced atmosphere suggesting a rambling party) and making room for the doings that surrounded such parades. Moreover, we definitely hear the actual space in which the performance takes place. The studio becomes audible and our hearing becomes spatial because the different positions of the speakers are captured by the microphones. We can imagine the actual studio room, and resonance here means the specific reverberation of voices and musical sounds that makes us visualize the space of performance. The lyrics Armstrong sings support this visual dimension: "I wake up every morning and I have to laugh / 'cause I look on the wall and I see my photograph," he intones. We might even imagine a less public space than a Mardi Gras parade. Perhaps we are meant to catch Armstrong and his musicians in a backstage moment and think that we are getting a glimpse of the musicians' hidden transcript, hearing Armstrong's trumpeting as warm-up exercises (he does, after all, exclaim that he will use the performance to "do a little practicin'"). Listeners are invited directly into the performative universe of Armstrong's autobiographics, and this universe is characterized by a sense of performative energy and exuberance.[14]

As an example of Armstrong's versioning impulse, "Laughin' Louie" resists glorification as a singular moment of comic geniality. The piece was recorded twice in the same session. Because they are versioned performances, the versions are neither identical nor completely different. Thus, we hear no totally spontaneous geniality, even if each individual performance may suggest this to some listeners. What is more, the operatic model for Armstrong's solo was Minnie T. Wright's *Love Scene* (1920), which Armstrong may have encountered in the late 1920s during his stint with the Erskine Tate Orchestra in Chicago. And, complicating things even further, Dan Morgenstern points out that "Laughin' Louie" is based on a genre of comic recordings popular in the 1920s, for instance, *The Original Okeh Laughing Record* (1923). The setup is more or less the same: "a hapless cornetist whose every attempted note is greeted first with solitary giggles, then with laughter from a growing number of listeners."[15] Armstrong apparently owned several copies of this record, which indicates that his reference to the tune as "one of them old time good ones" is either simply a joke or perhaps an attempt to claim the material as his own by connecting it with his youth in New Orleans. Knowing this prevents simplistic interpretations of the performance as a piece of musical autobiography. The performance further contains a mock announcement by one of Armstrong's colleagues, who seems to pretend that he is the record producer: "Take off, Gate," he exclaims in a satirized official tone. Jazz, we are told indirectly, is subject to the control and demands of record producers and managers, whose commercial interests sanctioned Armstrong's comic self-display but would most likely have censored politically outspoken or racially controversial material. Finally, Armstrong's reference to "this little Selmer trumpet" reminds the listener of the commercial sponsorship of radio shows common in the 1930s. Mentioning the name of the company that manufactured his trumpets, Armstrong foregrounds his star power (the Selmer company wants him to play their instruments because he will make them famous) but also indicates that his music is played in an economic environment in which musicians occupy a middle ground between the music industry and the listening public.

Armstrong's scat aesthetics is equally prominent. Responding to his band members' introduction of the number ("Yeah, here's some 'Laughin' Louie'"), Armstrong remarks: "Well, what do you know about that?" The fact that he used this phrase in his autobiographical writings—for example, the letter Armstrong wrote to Hugues Panassié in 1934—emphasizes the transmedial impulse behind the performance and the intermedial references resulting from this impulse. The performance also thrives on a series of jive terms ("Gate," "Cats," "Pops"), thus anchoring it in an experience that requires its own vernacular speech patterns and expressions. Armstrong further offers some of his trademark scatting as a musical device that allows him to lead his band members into the tune. There is a moment of ventriloquizing at the beginning of the performance, too, when he states the title of the tune twice: "I want to check this little number about 'Laughin' Louie,' 'Laughin' Louie.'" Furthermore, Armstrong adds self-reflexive commentary. He personifies the Selmer trumpet ("bless his little heart") as a medial extension of his body and mind; he references the photograph on the wall (he knows he is being represented in many media; he knows that many of his listeners have seen photographs of him); and he greets the ladies and gentlemen who make up his imaginary audience and who will eventually be supplanted by the actual buyers of the recording. Armstrong's comedy and artistry, the latter expressed by his operatic solo as well as the technically demanding and emotionally charged high-register playing, are presented as integrally connected. The person, signified by his voice, trumpet playing, and the photograph, cannot be separated from the music.

Moving toward a more cultural reading of the tune, we must concede that the minstrel overtones of "Laughin' Louie" are hard to deny. The whole atmosphere of comedy and mirth conjures up images of animated clowning and exuberant rhythmicality audiences would have known from nineteenth-century representations of the musical slave and early twentieth-century representations of the black jazz musician. Not only were slaves viewed as gifted singers and dancers, as the British John Finch noted in 1833 when he stated that "every negro is a musician from birth"; they were also taken to be a funny people, "mirthful by nature," as Thomas R. R. Cobb wrote in 1858. Writing about an earlier time, J. Hector St. John de Crèvecoeur already pointed to the crossracial fantasies that would come to full fruition with blackface minstrelsy: "You may see them [black slaves] at particular places as happy and merry as if they were freemen and freeholders. The sight of their happiness always increases mine."[16] Frederick Douglass's interpretation of the slaves' "sorrow songs" in his first auto-biography was a notable attempt to counter such minstrel images of eternal happiness and laughter: "Slaves sing most when they are most unhappy. The songs of the slave represent the sorrows of his heart," and "I have often sung to drown my sorrow, but seldom to express my happiness," he wrote in 1845, and his observations were followed by W. E. B. Du Bois in the final chapter of *The Souls of Black Folk*, in which he heard the "rhythmic cry of the slave" as "the most beautiful expression of human experience born this side [of] the seas" and lamented that the expressive power of the "sorrow songs" had been spoiled by minstrel caricature.[17]

The need in American antebellum culture to submit slave music and laughter to an appeasing explanation, to drown out, however imperfectly, the rhythmic cry of the slave's sorrows, is illustrated by Frederick Law Olmsted's recollection of a scene in South Carolina. Spotting a group of slave cabins from a train, Olmsted hears a slave

> raise [. . .] such a sound as I never heard before; a long, loud, musical shout, rising, and falling, and breaking into falsetto, his voice ringing through the woods in the clear, frosty night air, like a bugle-call. As he finished, the melody was caught up by another, and then, another, and then, by several in chorus. When there was silence again, one of them cried out, as if bursting with amusement: "Did yer see de dog?—when I began echoing, he turn 'round an' look at me straight into der face; ha! ha! ha!" and the whole party broke into the loudest peals of laughter, as if it was the very best joke they had ever heard.[18]

The musical Otherness of this laughter includes an association with the bugle, the first brass instrument Armstrong learned to play in the Colored Waif's Home, but also the "long, loud, musical shout" of the falsetto voice. Moreover, the joke the white traveler does not understand calls for an explanation because it stands in contrast to the slave's unfreedom. Uninhibited laughter rising from physical bondage is troubling, indeed. The most plausible and politically viable explanation the Southern planter class issued was that the slaves possessed a racially inherent propensity for all forms of play: a "cheerful and lighthearted manner, penchant for frivolity, rhythmical movements, unusual mannerisms, and even their patter of language."[19]

As Olmsted's experience exemplifies, "Laughin' Louie" stands in a long tradition of minstrel explanations for black laughter. The song's musical genealogy includes "Laughing Chorus" (1848) by the Campbell's Minstrels II, which must have featured blackface actors laughing collectively (perhaps accompanied by music) and must have helped institute "black" laughter as a product of popular blackface representation. Roughly half a century later, one of the first widely successful African American singers and a former slave, George W. Johnson, recorded tunes like "The Laughing Song" (ca. 1894–98) and "The Laughing Coon" (ca. 1898), thereby confirming the connection of "black" laughter with minstrel and "coon" images.[20] Exuberant laughter, visualized through the excessive mouth and lips of the minstrel performer and amplified by Armstrong's moniker "Satchmo" as "mo mouth," as well as by the many references to his big lips, thus had a long history. As Constance Rourke had observed only a few years prior to "Laughin' Louie," for the public, "the Negro was only a comic medium" and expressed "a primitive comic sense" according to which "to be black is to be funny."[21]

These observations indicate that the laughter of modern black performers from George W. Johnson and Bert Williams to Louis Armstrong and other jazz players had historically been heard as the mysteriously uncanny laughter of the slave, as an expression of Sambo's contentedness and childish view of life, and as an affirmation of the black joker's benevolence. On "Laughin' Louie," Armstrong's laughter, announced by the title and supplied extensively on the recording itself, derives some of its cultural energy from this history of minstrel laughter. While the degree to which audiences would have heard this laughter through the filter of the minstrel poetics is difficult to determine, it is worth pointing out that the comic patter of the piece recalls the minstrel shows' verbal sparring of the interlocutor and his endmen. Furthermore, Armstrong taps into Sambo's speech patterns with an affirmative "Yes sir," while the photograph that caused repeated and excessive laughter ("every morning") must have depicted a very funny-looking, perhaps caricaturized or even Samboesque, Armstrong. This assumption is, of course, only that: an assumption. Yet this is where the notion of autobiographics is particularly instructive. Armstrong's "Yes sir" and his almost constant laughter do not only resonate with the minstrel poetics; they also connect the musical performance with Armstrong's autobiographical narratives, which frequently mobilize the sounds of minstrelsy through phrases such as "Yes sir" and representations of laughter such as "ha ha ha" and "tee hee."

The minstrel resonances, however, compete with the trickster's laughter in our interpretive forays into the cultural intermediality of "Laughin' Louie." If the trickster figure wears the smile and realizes this smile soni- cally, through laughter, in order to bewitch audiences and secure his own public agenda, then Armstrong's performance can indeed be heard as sub- versive. In order to make such a hearing plausible, we would have to argue that the self-mockery implied in the performance—when Armstrong's hits a single, anticlimactic note and, upon the mock enticement of his col- leagues, who respond with a sarcastic "mel-low," hits the same single note again—makes other sounds and stories apart from the minstrel poetics possible. Alfred Appel points in this direction when he argues that the per- formance emphasizes "the artifice of Armstrong's phonography," display- ing the "master's self-mockery" and not the slave's self-deprecating ges- tures of filial adoration and self-erasure.[22] Sambo's appeasing smile and happy laughter, one could argue, oscillate between what Ellison has provocatively described as "a black laugher's own uncouth uproar" and the "single hoot-and-cackle" with which this same laugher must downplay its radical implications. In other words, "Laughin' Louie" can be taken as the sonic embodiment of Ellison's "laughing barrel," that imaginary contrap- tion into which Southern Negroes in the Jim Crow era allegedly thrust their heads when they had to laugh in order to prevent whites from being offended by their laughter. This contraption, Ellison puns on Du Bois, caused whites to "suspect [. . .] that when a Negro had his head thrust into a laughing barrel he became endowed with a strange form of extrasensory perception—or second sight." Du Bois's interpretation of the second sight as an effect of the color line serves Ellison as the basis for his riffing on the minstrel poetics of American culture: "whites assumed that in some myste- rious fashion the Negro involved was not only laughing at *himself* laughing, but was also laughing at *them* laughing at his laughing against their own most determined wills."[23] Such confused laughter and its complex motiva- tions lead Ellison to speak of the United States as the "United States of Jokeocracy" and as "a land of masking jokers," a place where everybody tends to laugh about everybody else and where laughter, according to Con- stance Rourke, "produced the illusion of leveling obstacles [. . .] created ease, and even more, a sense of unity among a people who were not yet a nation and who were seldom joined in stable communities."[24]

   As far as "Laughin' Louie" is concerned, the inner sanctum of the bar- rel is the recording studio, and the laughter that is translated onto the grooves of the recording allows the musician to "become [. . .] both the source and master of an outrageous and untenable situation."[25] To give this Ellisonian reading of Armstrong's intermedial autobiographics one final spin: if Armstrong's musical performances, autobiographical narratives, tape recordings, and photo-collages offer creative ways of "reduc[ing] the chaos of living to form," they accomplish this not by producing stable and polished products of art but by serving the musician as media through which he can "make life swing."[26] In different media, Armstrong gives his audiences "a slightly different sense of time," leaving them "never quite on the beat" but "[s]ometimes [. . .] ahead and sometimes behind." For Invisible Man, this different sense of time is produced by Armstrong's recordings of "(What Did I Do to Be So) Black and Blue?" which, aided by the effects of the reefer, propel him toward a new consciousness, a new way of hearing, seeing, and feeling the self in the world. For the listener of "Laughin' Louie," this new consciousness emerges from the experience of jazz's swinging sensations: the ambiguities of the infectious groove that exude from the recording, sometimes ahead and sometimes behind the beat, but rarely squarely on it. This swinging groove alters not only one's sense of time; it changes one's understanding of history, as Ellison's reference to "the groove of history" toward the end of the novel illustrates. Inscribed into this groove are the sounds, images, and voices of America's black citizens, who offer alternative views of history because they can enter this groove by "slip[ping] into the breaks and look[ing] around."[27]

The intermedial nature of Armstrong's autobiographics and its performative realization as musicked, versioned, swing-typed, and minstrel-sounded expression represents such a groove approach to public self-performance. Armstrong's autobiographics thus expresses both the beat of American history (racial discourses, stereotypes, and the minstrel poetics) and an African American countergroove (his scat and swing approach to autobiographical, musical, and visual performance). This, then, constitutes an example of Ellison's revisioning of double consciousness, the difference between, but also the fundamental relatedness of, the metronomic beat of Western culture and the swinging countergrooves of its African American relatives. The color line between black and white is loosened up by the groove, which the technology buff and record collector Ellison might have understood as the swing sensations created by the jazz performance and as the translation of these sensations onto the grooves of the material recording, the black shellac and vinyl onto which the sounds of jazz were pressed. Historical time becomes recorded time, and linear views of history as progressive uplift are questioned. The grooves of jazz—as a sonically induced physical reaction and as material grooves on the actual recording—unfold in circles: the world does not move "like an arrow, but [like] a boomerang."[28]

Ellison's narrator is wary "of those who speak of the *spiral* of history" because he knows that "they are preparing a boomerang."[29] The longevity of the minstrel poetics ensured that the Sambo code would still be alive by the time *Invisible Man* was published. That Armstrong backpedaled from his confrontational remarks about Governor Faubus und President Eisenhower, that he refused to sing "(What Did I Do to Be So) Black and Blue?" as a protest song in the 1960s, and that his performances continued to create the productive ambiguities of minstrel sounding until the very end of his career illustrate the boomerang nature of America's history of race. At midcentury, Jim Crow was still a reality in the South, and popular culture still thrived on Sambo stereotypes. But to assume that things had not changed at all would be an ahistorical blunder. Armstrong's performative possibilities, while following a long tradition of minstrel sights and sounds, were ultimately much more substantial than those of earlier black performers during minstrelsy (Juba), the "coon" era (Sam Lucas, Billy Kersands, Bert Williams), and beyond the 1910s and 1920s (Bill Robinson, Lincoln Perry). These possibilities would become more substantial as the "blackening" of America entered an elevated phase during the Jazz Age and continued to spread in the following decades, a process that was certainly propelled by the cultural work of Armstrong's intermedial autobiographics and that impels us to rethink this work as a central enunciation of American modernity rather than as a minor form of black modernism: as a countergroove that comes to move a whole nation.[30]

The civil rights movement, the criticism uttered against Armstrong's performative politics in the 1960s, and Armstrong's own political interventions speak to the powerful implications of this cultural "blackening." On the level of popular culture, Ellison wrote in "What America Would Be Like without Blacks" (1970), "the melting pot did indeed melt, creating such deceptive metamorphoses and blending of identities, values, and lifestyles that most American whites are culturally part Negro American without even realizing it."[31] On this view, the performances of "Laughin' Louie" appear as sonic expressions of "a world where marginality has *at last* become a productive space," as Stuart Hall has noted in a related context.[32] The larger story here, one that often remains submerged in our post–civil rights climate, is that America's racial politics and its attending power relations created an environment in which "resistance to oppression took on [. . .] largely cultural, rather than more overtly political, forms."[33] In Armstrong's case, these cultural forms were seldom clearly marked as acts of resistance. The ambiguous resonances his transmedial practice of minstrel sounding produced not only conjure up the cultural poetics of blackface minstrelsy. They also complicate hagiographic narratives of the black jazz musician as a dauntless hero who was forced to associate himself (and it is mostly men who feature in this narrative) with the messy history of minstrelsy but ultimately transcended it by revolutionizing American music and staring down the evils of racism. Such narratives tend to leave out some of the more unpleasant realities in American history and culture, and they ultimately pitch an exceptionalist historiography of jazz. As the close readings of Armstrong's intermedial autobiographics in this book have shown, there exists a different und often untold story, one in which the troubled history of blackface acts, minstrel laughter, and primitivist fictions plays an integral role in the development, performance, and reception of jazz. According to this story, beautiful music, stunning visual performances, and fascinating narratives of unusual lives by unlikely protagonists always also addressed the racial fears and fantasies that have shaped the history and historiography of jazz as a music that remains inextricably tied to notions of race and racism. While Dizzy Gillespie was certainly aware of this history and historiography, he also recognized Armstrong's significance as a national figure of identification and as a jazz musician who managed to weave himself "with the very warp and woof of this nation," as W. E. B. Du Bois demanded in *The Souls of Black Folk*.[34] Speaking to *Down Beat*, Gillespie concluded: "Louis is jazz in person, he's the creator of our language on the trumpet. It's impossible to say what he means to us. He is everything or almost everything, just on his own. To speak his name is to conjure up our whole world."[35]

Notes

Introduction

1. Robert G. O'Meally, preface to *The Jazz Cadence of American Culture*, ed. Robert G. O'Meally (New York: Columbia University Press, 1998), xi.

2. "[T]he problem of the Twentieth Century is the problem of the color-line." W. E. B. Du Bois, *The Souls of Black Folk*, 1903, in *The Oxford W. E. B. Du Bois Reader*, ed. Eric J. Sundquist (New York: Oxford University Press, 1996), 100.

3. See Alfred Appel Jr., *Jazz Modernism from Ellington and Armstrong to Matisse and Joyce* (New York: Knopf, 2002), 206.

4. *Louis Armstrong: Good Evening Ev'rybody*, dir. Sidney J. Stiber, prod. George Wein and Greg Lewerke (Ambassador, 2009); Miles Davis with Quincy Troupe, *Miles: The Autobiography* (New York: Simon and Schuster, 1989), 6.

5. *Masters of American Music: Satchmo*, dir. Gary Giddins and Kendrick Simmons (Sony, 1989); *Jazz: A Film by Ken Burns*, dir. Ken Burns (PBS Home Video, 2001). For a recording of "Portrait of Louis Armstrong," see Lincoln Center Jazz Orchestra, *Portraits by Ellington* (Sony/Columbia, 1992).

6. Lester Bowie in Giddins and Simmons, *Masters of American Music: Satchmo*.

7. Armstrong's influence on American jazz singing is explored in Leslie Gourse, *Louis' Children: American Jazz Singers* (1984; updated ed., New York: Cooper Square, 2001).

8. See Billie Holiday with William Dufty, *Lady Sings the Blues* (Garden City: Doubleday, 1956), 16.

9. *The Edsel Show Starring Bing Crosby, with Frank Sinatra, Rosemary Clooney, and Louis Armstrong* (Quantum Leap, 2005); Bing Crosby qtd. in Ken Murray, "Louis, Bix Had Most Influence on Der Bingle," *Down Beat*, July 14, 1950. Reverend Satchelmouth was one of Armstrong's comedic stage roles and nicknames.

10. Louis Armstrong, *Swing That Music* (New York: Longmans, 1936; New York: Da Capo, 1993); Louis Armstrong, *Satchmo: My Life in New Orleans* (New York: Prentice Hall, 1954; New York: Da Capo, 1986).

11. Qtd. in Joshua Berrett, *Louis Armstrong and Paul Whiteman: Two Kings of Jazz* (New Haven: Yale University Press, 2004), 21.

12. Researcher Tad Jones located Armstrong's birth date in a baptismal registry in the 1980s. See Gary Giddins, *Satchmo: The Genius of Louis Armstrong*, 1988 (New York: Da Capo, 2001), 21–25; Ralph Blumenthal, "Digging for Satchmo's Roots in the City That Spawned Him," *New York Times*, Aug. 15, 2000.

13. Du Bois, *Souls of Black Folk*, 238.

14. Ralph Ellison, *Invisible Man*, 1952 (New York: Random House, 1982), 7.

15. Albert Murray, "The Function of the Heroic Image," 1985, in O'Meally, *Jazz Cadence of American Culture*, 575. Ronald Radano deconstructs this argument in "Myth Today: The Color of Ken Burns Jazz," *Black Renaissance/Renaissance Noir* 3.3 (2001): 43–54.

16. The phrases "modern-day Sambo" and "black genius" are Radano's ("Myth Today," 45).

17. Ken Burns, introduction to Ken Burns and Geoffrey C. Ward, *Jazz: A History of America's Music* (New York: Knopf, 2000), x.

18. Dan Morgenstern, review of *Louis Armstrong: An Extravagant Life*, by Laurence Bergreen, 1997, in Dan Morgenstern, *Living with Jazz: A Reader*, ed. Sheldon Meyer (New York: Pantheon, 2004), 89.

19. Thomas Brothers suggests that "Nenest" probably refers to Ernest "Ninesse" Trepagnier. See Thomas Brothers, ed., *Louis Armstrong, in His Own Words: Selected Writings* (New York: Oxford University Press, 1999), 43.

20. Michael Cogswell, *Louis Armstrong: The Offstage Story of Satchmo* (Portland: Collectors, 2003), 39. The Louis Armstrong House Museum, whose catalog can be searched at www.louisarmstronghouse.org, holds a number of these letters; others are held at the William Ransom Hogan Jazz Archive at Tulane University and the Institute of Jazz Studies at Rutgers University.

21. Kaiser Marshall, "When Armstrong Came to Town," in *Selections from the Gutter: Jazz Portraits from "The Jazz Record*,*"* ed. Art Hodes and Chadwick Hansen (Berkeley: University of California Press, 1977), 85; Teddy Wilson qtd. in Terry Teachout, *Pops: A Life of Louis Armstrong* (Boston: Houghton Mifflin, 2009), 192.

22. Louis Armstrong to Joe Glaser, Aug. 2, 1955, in Brothers, *In His Own Words*, 158–63; "Louis Armstrong + the Jewish Family in New Orleans, La., the Year of 1907," Mar. 31, 1969–70, in ibid., 5–36.

23. The letter is reprinted in Hugues Panassié, *Louis Armstrong* (1969; New York: Scribner's Sons, 1971), 19. An earlier article attributed to Armstrong ran in the Aug. 1932 issue of the British magazine *Rhythm* ("Greetings to Britain!"). It contains very few of his stylistic idiosyncrasies and is most likely based only very loosely on an original letter. An excerpt is reprinted in Joshua Berrett, ed., *The Louis Armstrong Companion: Eight Decades of Commentary* (New York: Schirmer, 1999), 47–48.

24. Louis Armstrong to Ken "Stuff" Murry, May 24, 1950, facsimile in Scott Allen Nollen, *Louis Armstrong: The Life, Music and Screen Career* (Jefferson: McFarland, 2004), 101. Armstrong misspells Murray as "Murry."

25. "King Oliver Is Dead," *Jazz Hot*, Apr.–May 1938; "Special Jive," *Harlem*

Tattler, July 2, 1940; "Special Jive," *Harlem Tattler*, July 19, 1940; "Chicago, Chicago, That Toddlin' Town: How King and Ol' Satch Dug It in the Twenties," in *Esquire's 1947 Jazz Book* (London: Davies, 1947); "Storyville—Where the Blues Were Born," *True*, Nov. 1947; "Stomping Piano Man," review of *Mr. Jelly Roll: The Fortunes of Jelly Roll Morton, New Orleans Creole and Inventor of Jazz*, by Alan Lomax and Jelly Roll Morton, *New York Times*, June 18, 1950; "Europe—With Kicks," *Holiday*, June 1950; "Ulceratedly Yours," *Down Beat*, July 14, 1950; "Bunk Didn't Teach Me," *Record Changer*, July–Aug. 1950, in Brothers, *In His Own Words*, 40–41; "Joe Oliver Is Still King," *Record Changer*, July–Aug. 1950, in Brothers, *In His Own Words*, 37–39; "Jazz on a High Note," *Esquire*, Dec. 1951, in Brothers, *In His Own Words*, 128–36; "Why I Like Dark Women," *Ebony*, Aug. 1954, 61–68; "Scanning the History of Jazz," *Jazz Review*, July 1960, in Brothers, *In His Own Words*, 173–75; "Jazz Is a Language," *Music Journal*, 1961, in Lewis Porter, *Jazz: A Century of Change. Readings and New Essays* (New York: Schirmer, 1997), 185–87; Richard Meryman, "An Authentic American Genius: An Interview with Louis Armstrong," *Life*, Apr. 15, 1966, 92–116; Richard Meryman, *Louis Armstrong—A Self-Portrait: The Interview by Richard Meryman* (New York: Eakins, 1971).

26. Dan Morgenstern, review of *Louis Armstrong: An American Genius*, by James Lincoln Collier, 1985, in Morgenstern, *Living with Jazz*, 88; Laurence Bergreen, *Louis Armstrong: An Extravagant Life* (New York: Broadway, 1997), 3.

27. See Charles Mingus, *Beneath the Underdog: His World as Composed by Mingus*, ed. Nel King (New York: Knopf, 1971); Artie Shaw, *The Trouble with Cinderella: An Outline of Identity* (New York: Farrar, 1952); Sidney Bechet with Desmond Flower, *Treat It Gentle* (1960; New York: Da Capo, 1978); George "Pops" Foster, as told to Tom Stoddard, *The Autobiography of Pops Foster: New Orleans Jazzman* (1971; San Francisco: Backbeat, 2005); Alan Lomax and Jelly Roll Morton, *Mister Jelly Roll: The Fortunes of Jelly Roll Morton, New Orleans Creole and "Inventor of Jazz"* (1950; Berkeley: University of California Press, 2001); Edward "Duke" Ellington, *Music Is My Mistress* (1973; New York: Da Capo, 2002); Count Basie, as told to Albert Murray, *The Autobiography of Count Basie* (New York: Random House, 1985).

28. Louis Armstrong, "The 'Goffin Notebooks,'" ca. 1944, in Brothers, *In His Own Words*, 93; Louis Armstrong, "Forward," in *Joke Book*, unpublished manuscript, ca. 1950s (Louis Armstrong House Museum, New York).

29. "A Word from Louis Armstrong," in Hugues Panassié, *Le Jazz Hot* (Paris: Éditions Corrêa, 1934), published in the United States as *Hot Jazz: The Guide to Swing Music*, 1936, trans. Lyle Dowling and Eleanor Dowling (Westport: Negro Universities Press, 1975), xi.

30. James Lincoln Collier, *Louis Armstrong: An American Genius* (New York: Oxford University Press, 1983), 22; Max Jones and John Chilton, *Louis: The Louis Armstrong Story 1900–1971* (1971; New York: Da Capo, 1988), 157; Giddins, *Satchmo*, xvii; Bergreen, *Louis Armstrong*, 386; Teachout, *Pops*, 219.

31. W. H. Barefield Gordon, "What Is Swing Music? Reviewer Gordon Finds Answer in Louis Armstrong's Autobiography," *Chicago Defender* (national ed.), Apr.

3, 1937, 12. Jazz critic Otis Ferguson missed the edited nature of the text when he described the autobiography as "talking as naturally as Louis himself." See Otis Ferguson, "Speaking of Jazz: I," *New Republic*, Aug. 2, 1939, in *The Otis Ferguson Reader*, ed. Dorothy Chamberlain and Robert Wilson (Highland Park: December, 1982), 186.

32. Alain Locke, *The Negro and His Music* (1936; Port Washington: Kennikat, 1968); Winthrop Sargeant, *Jazz: Hot and Hybrid* (New York: Arrow, 1938); Robert Goffin, *Jazz: From the Congo to the Metropolitan* (Garden City: Doubleday, 1944); Marshall W. Stearns, *The Story of Jazz* (1956; New York: Oxford University Press, 1970); J. S. Slotkin, "Jazz and Its Forerunners as an Example of Acculturation," *American Sociological Review* 8.5 (1943): 570–75; Eric Porter, *What Is This Thing Called Jazz? African American Musicians as Artists, Critics, and Activists* (Berkeley: University of California Press, 2002), 43–45; Jorge Daniel Veneciano, "Louis Armstrong, Bricolage, and the Aesthetics of Swing," in *Uptown Conversation: The New Jazz Studies*, ed. Robert G. O'Meally, Brent Hayes Edwards, and Farah Jasmine Griffin (New York: Columbia University Press, 2004), 256–77.

33. Qtd. in Thomas Brothers, "'Swing a Lot of Type Writing': An Introduction to Louis Armstrong's Writings," in Brothers, *In His Own Words*, x.

34. Louis Armstrong, "The Armstrong Story," 1954, in Brothers, *In His Own Words*, 48–76. Another manuscript version, "Life of Louis Armstrong," is held by the Institute of Jazz Studies, Rutgers University.

35. Dan Morgenstern, introduction to Armstrong, *Satchmo*, viii; William H. Kenney III, "Negotiating the Color Line: Louis Armstrong's Autobiographies," in *Jazz in Mind: Essays on the History and Meanings of Jazz*, ed. Reginald T. Buckner and Steven Weiland (Detroit: Wayne State University Press, 1991), 48.

36. Whitney Balliett, "Good King Louis," *Saturday Review* 37 (1954): 54.

37. Although it "contains many minor mistakes in grammar and punctuation, we, as editors, believe it contains some of the finest writing we have ever seen," the editors of *True* magazine acknowledged about the manuscript of Armstrong's 1947 essay "Storyville—Where the Blues Were Born." Qtd. in Albert Murray, "Louis Armstrong in His Own Words," in *From the Briarpatch File: On Context, Procedure, and American Identity* (New York: Pantheon, 2001), 119.

38. On the compositional processes that shaped Mingus's and Holiday's autobiographies, see E. Porter, *What Is This Thing Called Jazz?* 138–47; Robert O'Meally, *Lady Day: The Many Faces of Billie Holiday*, 1991 (New York: Da Capo, 2000), 21.

39. Louis Armstrong, "The Satchmo Story 2nd Edition," 1959, in Brothers, *In His Own Words*, 114.

40. Armstrong, "Goffin Notebooks"; Armstrong, "Satchmo Says," ca. 1970, in Jones and Chilton, *Louis*, 232–46; Robert Goffin, *Horn of Plenty: The Story of Louis Armstrong*, 1947, trans. James F. Bezou (Westport: Greenwood, 1978).

41. I borrow the phrase "limits of autobiography" from Georges Gusdorf, "Conditions and Limits of Autobiography," 1956, trans. James Olney, in *Autobiography: Essays Theoretical and Critical*, ed. James Olney (Princeton: Princeton University Press, 1980), 28–48.

42. Sidonie Smith and Julia Watson, *Reading Autobiography: A Guide for Interpreting Life Narratives* (Minneapolis: University of Minnesota Press, 2001), 13.

43. Sidonie Smith, "Performativity, Autobiographical Practice, Resistance," *a/b: Auto/Biography Studies* 10.1 (1995): 20.

44. See Smith, "Performativity," 19.

45. Leigh Gilmore, *Autobiographics: A Feminist Theory of Women's Self-Representation* (Ithaca: Cornell University Press, 1994), 42.

46. The LP *His Last Recordings: Louis Armstrong and His Friends* (1970) contains "Boy from New Orleans," which covers Armstrong's birth and childhood, as well as later events such as his travels as Ambassador Satch.

47. See Teachout, *Pops*, 320.

48. William Russell, "Louis Armstrong," in *Jazzmen*, ed. Frederic Ramsey Jr. and Charles Edward Smith (1939; New York: Limelight, 1985), 119–42.

49. Louis Armstrong, "Daddy, How the Country Has Changed!" as told to David Dachs, *Ebony*, May 1961, 84.

50. According to Eakin, "narrative is not merely something we tell, listen to, read, or invent; it is an essential part of our sense of who we are." Paul John Eakin, *Living Autobiographically: How We Create Identity in Narrative* (Ithaca: Cornell University Press, 2008), ix.

51. Armstrong speaks of "red beans and rice" in the letter to the *Melody Maker* in 1933 (qtd. in Panassié, *Louis Armstrong*, 19). See also Armstrong to Madeleine Bérard, Nov. 25, 1946, in Berrett, *Louis Armstrong Companion*, 133; Armstrong to Leonard Feather, Aug. 5, 1941, in Leonard Feather, *From Satchmo to Miles* (1972; New York: Stein, 1974), 22; Armstrong to Leonard Feather, Sept. 18, 1941, in Brothers, *In His Own Words*, 149; Armstrong to Betty Jane Holder, Feb. 9, 1952, in Brothers, *In His Own Words*, 156. Brothers's bibliography lists an article by Armstrong in the *Melody Maker* titled "Red Beans and Rice: One of the Only Birthmarks I Can Remember" (July 1952).

52. I take the term *interface* from Sidonie Smith and Julia Watson, who speak of an "interface of textual and visual modes that enables self-imagining, auto-inquiry, and cultural critique." The authors argue that in autobiographical works that combine textual and visual modes of expression, "textuality implicates visuality as [. . .] the visual image engages components of textuality at material, voiced, and/or virtual sites." In Armstrong's autobiographics, the interface is visual, textual, and musical. Sidonie Smith and Julia Watson, ed., *Interfaces: Women, Autobiography, Image, Performance* (Ann Arbor: University of Michigan Press, 2002), 7.

53. See Clifford Geertz, "Thick Description: Toward an Interpretive Theory of Culture," in *The Interpretation of Cultures: Selected Essays by Clifford Geertz* (1973; New York: Basic, 2000), 5.

54. The theory of the autobiographical pact goes back to the French scholar Philippe Lejeune, who observed that "for there to be autobiography [. . .] , the *author,* the *narrator,* and the *protagonist* must be identical." See Philippe Lejeune, "The

Autobiographical Pact," 1975, in *On Autobiography*, trans. Katherine Leary, ed. Paul John Eakin (Minneapolis: University of Minnesota Press, 1989), 5.

55. Timothy Dow Adams, *Light Writing and Life Writing: Photography in Autobiography* (Chapel Hill: University of North Carolina Press, 2000), xvi, xxi.

56. E. J. Nichols and W. L. Werner, "Hot Jazz Jargon," *Vanity Fair*, Nov. 1935, 39.

57. Armstrong, *Swing That Music*, 100.

58. The identity of the ghostwriter remains uncertain; Morgenstern argues that is was most likely Gerlach. See Dan Morgenstern, foreword to Armstrong, *Swing That Music*, xi.

59. Armstrong, *Swing That Music*, 95.

60. *Louis Armstrong: Fleischmann's Yeast Show & Louis' Home-Recorded Tapes* (Jazz Heritage Society, 2008).

61. Roland Barthes, *Image—Music—Text*, selected and trans. Stephen Heath (New York: Hill and Wang, 1977).

62. Armstrong, *Satchmo*, 86. Armstrong recorded the tune with Clarence Williams' Blue Five (Oct. 8, 1925) and with his own band (May 27, 1940).

63. See also Krin Gabbard's chapter on Armstrong's films in *Jammin' at the Margins: Jazz and the American Cinema* (Chicago: University of Chicago Press, 1996), 204–38.

64. See Nollen, *Louis Armstrong*, 66–67; Louis Armstrong to Orson Welles, Oct. 22, 1945, Orson Welles Collection, Lilly Library, Indiana University. I thank John Szwed for clarifying the production history of the film for me.

65. Armstrong to Feather, Sept. 18, 1941, 147; Armstrong to Leonard Feather, Oct. 1, 1941, in Berrett, *Louis Armstrong Companion*, 118; Armstrong to Robert Goffin, May 7, 1944, in Brothers, *In His Own Words*, 78.

66. Armstrong narrates parts of his life story in Wein, Stiber, and Lewerke's documentary about his seventieth-birthday concert. Biopics and fictionalized accounts of Armstrong's life include Dan Pritzker's silent movie *Louis* (2010) and the television film *Louis Armstrong, Chicago Style* (Lee Philips, ABC, 1976), the latter of which covers Armstrong's career in the early 1930s and illustrates the difficulties any biographical film about Armstrong faces: Ben Vereen's attempts to mimic Armstrong's singing, dancing, and trumpet blowing and his efforts to capture the musician's off-stage persona seldom venture beyond involuntary caricature. Almost four decades later, Forest Whitaker is reported to be working on a biopic about Armstrong, and one is left to wonder how he will solve the problem of re-creating the trumpeter's unique personality and stage presence.

67. Louis Armstrong to Marili Mardon, Sept. 27, 1953, qtd. in Marc H. Miller, "Louis Armstrong: A Portrait Record," in *Louis Armstrong: A Cultural Legacy*, ed. Mark H. Miller (New York: Queens Museum of Art/Seattle: University of Washington Press, 1994), 212.

68. Armstrong owned eighty-five scrapbooks, most of which were filled with his photo-collages; he hand-decorated 650 reel-to-reel tape-box covers with similar

works. See Cogswell, *Louis Armstrong*, 103, 38. For reproductions, see Steven Brower, *Satchmo: The Wonderful World and Art of Louis Armstrong* (New York: Abrams, 2009); these images can also be viewed in the online catalog of the Louis Armstrong House Museum.

69. Veneciano, "Louis Armstrong, Bricolage," 258. Others have compared the photo-collages to the genre of the diary. See Miller, "Louis Armstrong: A Portrait Record," 212; Thomas Brothers, *Louis Armstrong's New Orleans* (New York: Norton, 2006), 161.

70. Ben Alexander, "'For Posterity': The Personal Audio Recordings of Louis Armstrong," *American Archivist* 71.1 (2008): 58; Berrett, *Louis Armstrong and Paul Whiteman*, 27. The tapes are stored at the Louis Armstrong House Museum. Ricky Riccardi's new biography analyzes a wide variety of materials Armstrong recorded on these tapes. See *What a Wonderful World: The Magic of Louis Armstrong's Later Years* (New York: Pantheon, 2011). For further analysis, see Alexander, "'For Posterity.'"

71. The first remark can be heard on "Max Jones 1," *Louis Armstrong: Fleischmann's Yeast Show & Louis' Home-Recorded Tapes;* the second remark is quoted in Alexander, "'For Posterity,'" 51. See also: "I tape all of my recordings. [. . .] I know within myself that if I record them on tape and index them (my system) they will be here for ever. Even after I am dead and buried" (Louis Armstrong to Max Jones, ca. 1970, in Jones and Chilton, *Louis,* 15–16).

72. The publication of multiple life narratives is not an uncommon occurrence in African American literature; think of writers such as Frederick Douglass, Booker T. Washington, and Maya Angelou, all of whom produced several versions of their life story.

73. According to Werner Wolf, "'intermediality' applies to any transgression of boundaries between conventionally distinct media of communication: such transgressions cannot only occur in one work or semiotic complex but also as a consequence of relations or comparisons between different works or semiotic complexes." See Werner Wolf, "Intermediality Revisited: Reflections on Word and Music Relations in the Context of a General Typology of Intermediality," in *Word and Music Studies: Essays in Honor of Steven Paul Scher and on Cultural Identity and the Musical Stage*, ed. Suzanne M. Lodato, Suzanne Aspden, and Walter Bernhart (Amsterdam: Rodopi, 2002), 17.

74. The figure of "orchestration" is doubly coded here; it follows Jorge Daniel Veneciano, who speaks of Armstrong's "orchestrating hands" as a performer in many media, and Victor Turner, according to whom "performative genres are often orchestrations of media, not expressions in a single medium." See Veneciano, "Louis Armstrong, Bricolage," 257; Victor Turner, *The Anthropology of Performance* (New York: Performing Arts Journal, 1986), 23.

75. I derive my understanding of material mediality and its significance for intermedia theory from Gabriele Rippl, "Text-Bild-Beziehungen zwischen Semiotik und Medientheorie: Ein Verortungsvorschlag," in *Ikono/Philo/Logie: Wechselspiele von Texten und Bildern*, ed. Renate Brosch (Berlin: Trafo, 2004), 43–60.

76. E. Porter, *What Is This Thing Called Jazz?* xviii, 139.

77. John R. Gennari, "But Is It Jazz?" *Reviews in American History* 23.1 (1995): 91.

78. Gary Giddins, introduction to Hampton Hawes and Don Asher, *Raise Up Off Me: A Portrait of Hampton Hawes* (1979; New York: Thunder's Mouth, 2001), vi; William Howland Kenney III, "Jazz: A Bibliographic Essay," *American Studies International* 25.1 (1987): 3–27.

79. Paul Whiteman and Mary Margaret McBride, *Jazz* (New York: Sears, 1926). I reference much of the secondary literature on jazz autobiography throughout this book and list additional works in the suggested further reading section.

80. John F. Szwed, foreword to Clyde E. B. Bernhardt, as told to Sheldon Harris, *I Remember: Eighty Years of Black Entertainment, Big Bands, and the Blues* (1986; Philadelphia: University of Pennsylvania Press, 1989), ix.

81. Ibid., ix. The first major study of American biography, Rebecca Chalmers Barton's *Witnesses for Freedom: Negro Americans in Autobiography* (New York: Harper, 1948), discusses W. C. Handy's *Father of the Blues* (1941), but this is a rare instance in which a black musician's autobiography is picked up in autobiography studies. Another instance is Elizabeth Schultz's discussion of Mingus's *Beneath the Underdog* in "To Be Black and Blue: The Blues Genre in Black American Autobiography," *Kansas Quarterly* 7.3 (1975): 81–96.

82. Robert G. O'Meally, Brent Hayes Edwards, and Farah Jasmine Griffin, introductory notes to O'Meally, Edwards, and Griffin, *Uptown Conversation*, 5.

83. Alfred Hornung, "Auto/Biography and Mediation: Introduction," in *Auto/Biography and Mediation*, ed. Alfred Hornung (Heidelberg: Winter, 2010), xii.

84. For examples of the popular-entertainer-versus-master-musician dichotomy, see especially Giddins, *Satchmo*. The genius-and-great-art narrative is present in almost all major Armstrong biographies, most recently in Teachout's *Pops* and Riccardi's *What a Wonderful World*. The theoretical basis for my conception of an intermedial cultural poetics of blackface minstrelsy comes from Stephen Greenblatt's, Catherine Gallagher's, and Louis Montrose's New Historicist analyses. See also my essay "From Text-Centered Intermediality to Cultural Intermediality; or, How to Make Intermedia Studies more Cultural," in *American Studies as Media Studies*, ed. Frank Kelleter and Daniel Stein (Heidelberg: Winter, 2008), 181–90.

Chapter 1

1. Henry A. Kmen, review of *Satchmo: My Life in New Orleans*, by Louis Armstrong, *Journal of Southern History* 21.2 (1955): 280–81.

2. The notion that what critics tend to call "the jazz tradition" is a construct with specific ideological implications was influentially discussed by Scott DeVeaux and John Gennari in the early 1990s. See Scott DeVeaux, "Constructing the Jazz Tradition: Jazz Historiography," *Black American Literature Forum* 25.3 (1991):

525–60; John Gennari, "Jazz Criticism: Its Development and Ideologies," *Black American Literature Forum* 25.3 (1991): 449–523.

3. Armstrong to Feather, Sept. 18, 1941, 147; "Max Jones 1."

4. Meryman, *Louis Armstrong—A Self-Portrait*, 55. Christopher Harlos views jazz autobiography "as a genuine opportunity to seize narrative authority." See Christopher Harlos, "Jazz Autobiography: Theory, Practice, Politics," in *Representing Jazz*, ed. Krin Gabbard (Durham: Duke University Press, 1995), 134.

5. Foster, *Autobiography of Pops Foster*, 1; Bechet with Flower, *Treat It Gentle*, 1; Danny Barker, *A Life in Jazz*, ed. Alyn Shipton (1986; New York: Oxford University Press, 1988), vi.

6. Harlos, "Jazz Autobiography," 137. Krin Gabbard characterizes jazz autobiographies as alternate takes in "How Many Miles? Alternate Takes on the Jazz Life," in *Thriving on a Riff: Jazz and Blues Influences in African American Literature*, ed. Graham Lock and David Murray (New York: Oxford University Press, 2009), 184–200.

7. John Gennari, *Blowin' Hot and Cool: Jazz and Its Critics* (Chicago: University of Chicago Press, 2006), 5.

8. Armstrong, "Jazz on a High Note," 130–31.

9. Berrett, *Louis Armstrong and Paul Whiteman*, 72.

10. Mark Osteen lays out this argument in "Introduction: Blue Notes Toward a New Jazz Discourse," in *Blue Notes: Toward a New Jazz Discourse*, ed. Mark Osteen, special issue of *Genre: Forms of Discourse and Culture* 37.1 (2004): 1–46.

11. I understand *vernacular* in Roger Abrahams's terms as a "commonsense system operating beneath the surface of everyday conviviality"; as the shifting synthesis of "work songs, group seculars, field hollers, sacred harmonies, proverbial wisdom, folk philosophy, political commentary, ribald humor, [and] elegiac lament" that Houston Baker associates with the African American blues experience; and in the sense of Sieglinde Lemke's wish to bring written language "closer to lived and spoken language, to words spoken from bodies in specific places." See Roger D. Abrahams, *Everyday Life: A Poetics of Vernacular Practices* (Philadelphia: University of Pennsylvania Press, 2005), 12; Houston A. Baker Jr., *Blues, Ideology, and Afro-American Literature: A Vernacular Theory* (Chicago: University of Chicago Press, 1984), 5; Sieglinde Lemke, *The Vernacular Matters of American Literature* (New York: Palgrave, 2009), 5.

12. Qtd. in Teachout, *Pops*, 167.

13. Christopher Small, *Musicking: The Meanings of Performing and Listening* (Hanover: Wesleyan University Press, 1998), 2. This idea is anticipated in Sidney Finkelstein, *Jazz: A People's Music* (1948; New York: Da Capo, 1975), 27.

14. Small, *Musicking*, 10. Armstrong's life narratives follow a mode of self-representation that Paul John Eakin reads as "relational autobiography." See Paul John Eakin, *How Our Lives Become Stories: Making Selves* (Ithaca: Cornell University Press, 1999), chap. 2.

15. Small, *Musicking*, 9.

16. Brothers, *Louis Armstrong's New Orleans*, 279; Gennari, *Blowin' Hot and Cool*, 6. On the birth of a first-person blues perspective in African American literature and culture, see also my essay "The Things That Jes' Grew? The Blues 'I' and African American Autobiographies," in *Blues and Jazz*, ed. Lisa Graley, special issue of *Interdisciplinary Humanities* 23.2 (2006): 43–54.

17. Armstrong, *Satchmo*, 148; Armstrong, "Jewish Family," 27; Armstrong qtd. in Berrett, *Louis Armstrong Companion*, xv. See also Albert "Papa" French's claim that "music was in my family—I mean it was in my blood, so I had to play." See Jack V. Buerkle and Danny Barker, *Bourbon Street Black: The New Orleans Black Jazzman* (1973; New York: Oxford University Press, 1974), 54.

18. Qtd. in Jones and Chilton, *Louis*, 50.

19. Armstrong, *Swing That Music*, 72.

20. Ibid.

21. Armstrong, *Satchmo*, 181–82.

22. This is a common argument in early jazz histories. Rudi Blesh argues that New Orleans jazzmen used their "lack of formal musical education as a freeing factor in hot and spontaneous creation." See Rudi Blesh, *Shining Trumpets: A History of Jazz* (New York: Knopf, 1949), 11.

23. Armstrong, *Swing That Music*, 32.

24. "They Cross Iron Curtain to Hear American Jazz," *U.S. News & World Report*, Dec. 2, 1955, 60.

25. In *Swing That Music*, Buddy Bolden is referred to as "a one-man genius"; clarinetist Sidney Bechet (misspelled "Sydney Bachet") is called "a young genius" (Armstrong, *Swing That Music*, 12, 14).

26. Armstrong, *Swing That Music*, 74, 125. Scott DeVeaux argues that jazz historiography has assumed "an organic relationship" among diverse styles and has imagined "a seamless continuum" of musical development that ignores essential historical complexities ("Constructing the Jazz Tradition," 530). The presentation of Armstrong's life and music in *Swing That Music* suggests an (auto)biographical relationship: "swing and I were born"; "[j]azz is the granddaddy of today's swing music"; jazz was "the daddy of swing" (Armstrong, *Swing That Music*, 72, 9, 123).

27. Armstrong, *Swing That Music*, 9, 125.

28. Ibid., 73, 74. The value-laden binary distinctions between "jazz" and "culture" in the early reception of the music ultimately led to categories such as "highbrow" and "lowbrow." See also Lawrence W. Levine, "Jazz and American Culture," in O'Meally, *Jazz Cadence of American Culture*, 432–34.

29. Armstrong, "Jewish Family," 21–22.

30. Ibid., 33.

31. Ibid., 16. George "Pops" Foster uses the term "Niggertown" (*Autobiography of Pops Foster*, 15).

32. Armstrong, "Jewish Family," 24.

33. Brothers, *Louis Armstrong's New Orleans*, 164. Creoles were people of mixed European (mostly French and/or Spanish) and African descent; important Creole jazz musicians and autobiographers are Sidney Bechet and Jelly Roll Morton.

34. Qtd. in Brothers, *Louis Armstrong's New Orleans*, 15.

35. Armstrong, "Jewish Family," 32.

36. Barker, *Life in Jazz*, 28.

37. Brothers, *Louis Armstrong's New Orleans*, 180, 181–82, 67, 181.

38. Qtd. in ibid., 194, 195.

39. Armstrong, *Satchmo*, 109–10; Armstrong qtd. in Larry L. King, "Everybody's Louie," *Harper's Magazine*, Nov. 1967, 62–63. See also Meryman, "Authentic American Genius," 100. Danny Barker recalls "people walking along singing popular jazz songs, sad mournful spirituals" (*Life in Jazz*, 7).

40. Goffin, *Horn of Plenty*, 38.

41. Armstrong, "Armstrong Story," 68.

42. Meryman, "Authentic American Genius," 96.

43. Brothers, *Louis Armstrong's New Orleans*, 88–89.

44. Qtd. in Russell and Smith, "New Orleans Music," in Ramsey and Smith, *Jazzmen*, 13.

45. The tape cover is reproduced in Brower, *Satchmo*, 183; Laurence Bergreen argues that Armstrong's pornographic stories were basically retellings and adaptations of material he had read and that he recited these stories to Lucille and friends. See Bergreen, *Louis Armstrong*, 463.

46. Qtd. in Bergreen, *Louis Armstrong*, 105. In Albert Murray's nomenclature, the Funky Butt dances are part of "the old downhome Saturday Night Function." See Albert Murray, *Stomping the Blues* (1976; New York: Da Capo, 2000), 23.

47. See also Jelly Roll Morton: "everybody in the City of New Orleans was always organization minded" (Lomax and Morton, *Mister Jelly Roll*, 16).

48. See Meryman, "Authentic American Genius," 96.

49. Ibid., 96, 98.

50. Armstrong, "Jewish Family," 17.

51. Armstrong, *Satchmo*, 226, 219.

52. Brothers, *Louis Armstrong's New Orleans*, 18–19.

53. *The Edsel Show Starring Bing Crosby, with Frank Sinatra, Rosemary Clooney, and Louis Armstrong; Louis Armstrong: Live in Australia 1964* (Medici Arts, 2008).

54. Armstrong, *Satchmo*, 24. The second line may be a straightened version of the ring shout, "an activity in which music and dance commingled, merged, and fused to become a single distinctive cultural ritual in which the slaves made music and derived their musical styles." See Samuel A. Floyd Jr., "Ring Shout! Literary Studies, Historical Studies, and Black Music Inquiry," *Black Music Research Journal* 11.2 (1991): 266.

55. Armstrong, *Satchmo*, 219. See Bechet: "It's what you want from a parade: you want to *see* it as well as hear it" (Bechet with Flower, *Treat It Gentle*, 66).

56. Armstrong, *Satchmo*, 90–91.

57. On the role of jazz revivalists in the construction of jazz historiography, see Bruce Boyd Raeburn, *New Orleans Style and the Writing of American Jazz History* (Ann Arbor: University of Michigan Press, 2009).

58. Meryman, "Authentic American Genius," 99–100.

59. Armstrong, *Satchmo*, 97.

60. Brothers, *Louis Armstrong's New Orleans*, 202; Lynne Fauley Emery, *Black Dance from 1619 to Today*, 2nd rev. ed. (Princeton: Princeton Book Co., 1988), 91.

61. See Brian Harker, "Louis Armstrong and the Clarinet," *American Music* 21.2 (2003): 139–40; the performance is captured on *Louis Armstrong: Live in '59* (Reelin' in the Years Productions, 2006).

62. Kathy Ogren, "'Jazz Isn't Just Me': Jazz Autobiographies as Performance Personas," in Buckner and Weiland, *Jazz in Mind*, 114, 121. On the performativity of jazz autobiography, see also my essay "The Performance of Jazz Autobiography," in Osteen, *Blue Notes*, 37.2, 173–99.

63. Armstrong, *Satchmo*, 11; Armstrong qtd. in Jones and Chilton, *Louis*, 45–46.

64. Armstrong to L/Cpl. Villec, 1967, in Brothers, *In His Own Words*, 170. On Armstrong's church life, see also Brothers, *Louis Armstrong's New Orleans*, chap. 2.

65. Studs Terkel, interview with Louis Armstrong, 1962, in *And They All Sang: The Great Musicians of the 20th Century Talk about Their Music* (2005; London: Granta, 2006), 146.

66. The musicking of the Sanctified Church may also have had an impact on Armstrong's autobiographical practices, as I shall explain in later chapters. Examples are the "fill[ing] in around the breaks in phrasing of the main statement of the tune" and an aesthetics that privileges "limitless variations" and "makeshift constructions" of precomposed material. Brothers, *Louis Armstrong's New Orleans*, 42; Charles Hersch, *Subversive Sounds: Race and the Birth of Jazz in New Orleans* (Chicago: University of Chicago Press, 2007), 148, 149.

67. "They Cross Iron Curtain," 58.

68. Armstrong, *Satchmo*, 58.

69. The 1954 performance can be seen on *Louis Armstrong: 100th Anniversary* (Passport Video, 2002).

70. Meryman, "Authentic American Genius," 107.

71. Armstrong, "Satchmo Story," 124.

72. See Brothers, *Louis Armstrong's New Orleans*, 138, 150–52. Brothers cites "dirt music" from musician Bud Scott. George "Pops" Foster says about Buddy Bolden: "He played nothing but blues and all that stink music" (*Autobiography of Pops Foster*, 15).

73. Armstrong, *Satchmo*, 34; see also Meryman, "Authentic American Genius," 102.

74. Meryman, *Louis Armstrong—A Self-Portrait*, 46. See also David Yaffe's understanding of jazz autobiography as "hustling the jazz memoir" in *Fascinating*

Rhythm: Reading Jazz in American Writing (Princeton: Princeton University Press, 2006), 150–97.

75. *Louis Armstrong: Live in Stockholm 1962* (Impro-Jazz, 2007).

76. Armstrong, *Satchmo*, 42, 45, 47–48.

77. Ibid., 38, 39, 40.

78. Armstrong, "Jewish Family," 23.

79. See Meryman, "Authentic American Genius," 108.

80. Meryman, *Louis Armstrong—A Self-Portrait*, 26; Armstrong, *Satchmo*, 184. According to Zutty Singleton, musicians referred to their time on these ships as "going to the conservatory." Qtd. in Nat Shapiro and Nat Hentoff, *Hear Me Talkin' to Ya: The Story of Jazz by the Men Who Made It*, 1955 (London: Davis, n.d.), 76.

81. See Armstrong, *Satchmo*, 58, 118. Black musicians routinely performed for white audiences. The Waif's Home orchestra was hired out to play for white picnics and private parties, events that sometimes veered dangerously close to racially motivated violence (see ibid., 48–49).

82. Ibid., 187. William Kenney argues that Armstrong's experiences on the Streckfus ships shaped his minstrel-inflected stage persona. See William Howland Kenney, *Jazz on the River* (Chicago: University of Chicago Press, 2005), 67.

83. Armstrong, "Armstrong Story," 70.

84. Qtd. in King, "Everybody's Louie," 68–69; Meryman, "Authentic American Genius," 116.

85. Warren "Baby" Dodds and Larry Gara, *The Baby Dodds Story*, 1959, rev. ed. (Alma: Rebeats, 2002), 22; Foster qtd. in Kathy J. Ogren, *The Jazz Revolution: Twenties America and the Meaning of Jazz*, 1989 (New York: Oxford University Press, 1992), 49.

86. On these issues, see also Jed Rasula, "The Media of Memory: The Seductive Menace of Records in Jazz History," in *Jazz among the Discourses*, ed. Krin Gabbard (Durham: Duke University Press, 1995), 134–62.

87. Meryman, "Authentic American Genius," 104.

88. "They Cross Iron Curtain," 60. For Armstrong's thoughts on the shifting labels applied to black music, see also Meryman, "Authentic American Genius," 104.

89. Louis Armstrong, with Leonard Feather, "Lombardo Grooves Louis!" *Metronome*, Sept. 1949, in Brothers, *In His Own Words*, 166, 165.

90. Armstrong, *Satchmo*, 168; Dan Morgenstern, "A Sixty-fifth Birthday Interview," 1965, in Morgenstern, *Living with Jazz*, 60.

91. Elsewhere, Armstrong speaks about "real good jazz' telling it—like it was" ("Jewish Family," 25). He expresses a similar sentiment in "They Cross Iron Curtain" (62). On narrative elements in Armstrong's early recordings, see Brian Harker, "'Telling a Story': Louis Armstrong and Coherence in Early Jazz," *Current Musicology* 63 (1999): 46–83; for a theoretical discussion of jazz improvisation as "saying something," see Ingrid Monson, *Saying Something: Jazz Improvisation and Interaction* (Chicago: University of Chicago Press, 1996).

92. "[E]ven when I was very young I was conscientious about everything I did. At church my heart went into every hymn I sang" (Armstrong, *Satchmo*, 11).

93. Ibid., 221.

94. Qtd. in King, "Everybody's Louie," 69.

95. Alexander, "'For Posterity,'" 86.

96. Armstrong, "Rocky Marciano," on *Louis Armstrong: Fleischmann's Yeast Show & Louis' Home-Recorded Tapes;* Armstrong to *Melody Maker Magazine*, Dec. 21, 1946, Louis Armstrong House Museum.

97. Qtd. in Brothers, *Louis Armstrong's New Orleans*, 110; Armstrong, "Joe Oliver Is Still King," 37; Armstrong qtd. in Brothers, *Louis Armstrong's New Orleans*, 129; Armstrong, "Scanning the History of Jazz," 174; Armstrong, *Swing That Music*, 26. See also Meryman, "Authentic American Genius," 112.

98. Armstrong, *Satchmo*, 24.

99. See Meryman, "Authentic American Genius," 104.

100. Jan. 23, 1963: *Ralph Gleason's Jazz Casual: Louis Armstrong and Earl "Fatha" Hines* (Idem Home Video, 2001).

101. Armstrong, "Armstrong Story," 67.

102. Armstrong, *Satchmo*, 24–25; Armstrong, "Joe Oliver Is Still King," 37–38.

103. Gunther Schuller, *Early Jazz: Its Roots and Musical Development* (New York: Oxford University Press, 1968), 89.

104. Gunther Schuller, *The Swing Era: The Development of Jazz 1930–1945* (New York: Oxford University Press, 1989), 169.

105. Schuller, *Early Jazz*, 3.

106. Armstrong, "Armstrong Story," 50. For a similar statement, see Meryman, "Authentic American Genius," 110. On the double breaks, see the interview with Ralph Gleason on the *Jazz Casual* program; Terkel's interview with Louis Armstrong, 147; Armstrong, *Satchmo*, 239.

107. On these social networks, see William Howland Kenney, *Chicago Jazz: A Cultural History, 1904–1930* (1993; New York: Oxford University Press, 1994), 35–60; Burton W. Peretti, *The Creation of Jazz: Music, Race, and Culture in Urban America* (Urbana: University of Illinois Press, 1992), 58–75.

108. For a fuller picture of these developments, see also Ogren, *Jazz Revolution*.

109. Armstrong, "Goffin Notebooks," 95.

110. Milton "Mezz" Mezzrow and Bernard Wolfe, *Really the Blues* (1946; New York: Citadel, 2001), 119–20.

111. Armstrong, "Jazz on a High Note," 131–32.

112. Qtd. in Bergreen, *Louis Armstrong*, 267. These comedians would have been black vaudeville or minstrel performers.

113. See Armstrong, "Jazz on a High Note," 133.

114. Walter Benjamin, "The Work of Art in the Age of Mechanical Reproduction," 1936, trans. Harry Zohn, in *Illuminations: Essays and Reflections*, ed. and with an introduction by Hannah Arendt (1968; New York: Schocken, 1985), 220–21.

115. See Theodor W. Adorno, "Die Form der Schallplatte," 1934, in *Gesam-*

melte Schriften, vol. 19, *Musikalische Schriften* VI, ed. Rolf Tiedemann (Frankfurt/Main: Suhrkamp, 1984), 532. Martin Williams calls this "an ultimate twentieth-century American paradox" in "Jazz, the Phonograph, and Scholarship," in *Jazz Heritage* (New York: Oxford University Press, 1985), 224.

116. Brent Hayes Edwards discusses these and many related issues in "Louis Armstrong and the Syntax of Scat," *Critical Inquiry* 28.3 (2002): 618–20.

117. Charles Hiroshi Garrett, *Struggling to Define a Nation: American Music and the Twentieth Century* (Berkeley: University of California Press, 2008), 93.

Chapter 2

1. Armstrong to Holder, Feb. 9, 1952, 155.

2. Armstrong to Mardon, Sept. 27, 1953, 115; Armstrong to Leonard Feather, Dec. 5, 1946, Louis Armstrong House Museum.

3. The photographs of Armstrong at the Basin Street Club and the Band Box are reproduced in Cogswell, *Louis Armstrong*, 83, 150. I thank Frank Kelleter for alerting me to the connection between these photographs and the title formula of the slave narratives.

4. Armstrong to Slim Evans, Sept. 31, 1967, Louis Armstrong House Museum; Armstrong, "Forward."

5. See Armstrong to Jones, 16. On the three components of auto/bio/graphy, see James Olney, "Autobiography and the Cultural Moment: A Thematic, Historical, and Bibliographical Introduction," in Olney, *Autobiography*, 3–27.

6. See Armstrong, *Satchmo*, 157, 159, 200; Armstrong, "Jewish Family," 10.

7. Armstrong, *Swing That Music*, 57.

8. Ibid., 35, 42, 44, 45, 57, 58.

9. See Armstrong, "Stomping Piano Man"; Meryman, "Authentic American Genius," 114. Armstrong owned the oral history recordings Morton had made for the Library of Congress in 1938. See Armstrong, "Jewish Family," 24.

10. See Berrett, *Louis Armstrong Companion*, 102–3.

11. Howard Taubman, "Satchmo Wears His Crown Gaily," *New York Times Magazine*, Jan. 29, 1950, 12; see Cogswell, *Louis Armstrong*, 89.

12. Armstrong, *Satchmo*, 240.

13. Armstrong, "Armstrong Story," 52.

14. Louis Armstrong, *Satchmo: My Life in New Orleans* (1954; New York: Signet, 1955); Charles L. Sanders, "Louis Armstrong—The Reluctant Millionaire," *Ebony*, Nov. 1964, 138.

15. Armstrong mentions the Prince of Wales, King Edward, the Duke of York, and the crown princess of Italy as royalty he impressed with his music. See Armstrong, *Swing That Music*, 1–2. He also met with Richard Nixon and Lyndon B. Johnson, with the future German chancellor Willy Brandt (when Brandt was still major of Berlin), as well as with popes Pius XII (1949) and Paul VI (1968).

16. Armstrong, *Swing That Music*, 1–2.

17. Kenney, "Negotiating the Color Line," 57; Martin Williams, *Jazz Masters of New Orleans* (1967; New York: Da Capo, 1978), 167; Miller, "Louis Armstrong: A Cultural Legacy," in Miller, *Louis Armstrong*, 18.

18. On the parallels and discrepancies between Armstrong and Franklin, see also Hersch, *Subversive Sounds*, 188–89.

19. Benjamin Franklin, *The Autobiography*, in *Franklin: Autobiography, Poor Richard, and Later Writings*, ed. J. A. Leo Lemay (New York: Library of America, 2008), 644; Armstrong, *Satchmo*, 209.

20. Franklin, *Autobiography*, 645; Armstrong to Glaser, Aug. 2, 1955, 160.

21. Benjamin Franklin, *Poor Richard Improved*, 1758, in Lemay, *Franklin*, 556; Armstrong, "Pluto Again," in *Joke Book*.

22. Qtd. in Gilbert Millstein, "The Most Un-Average Cat," liner notes to *Satchmo: A Musical Autobiography* (Verve, 2001).

23. Armstrong, "Jewish Family," 9.

24. On Washington's potential influence on Armstrong, see also Brian Harker, review of *Louis Armstrong, In His Own Words: Selected Writings*, by Thomas Brothers, and *The Louis Armstrong Companion: Eight Decades of Commentary*, by Joshua Berrett, *Notes* 57.4 (2001): 913, 914.

25. See Armstrong, *Satchmo*, 13, 84; Meryman, "Authentic American Genius," 113. Armstrong claims: "My Mother May Ann and my Uncle *Ike* Miles used to tell us about Slavery Times. They said—Slavery wasn't half as bad as some of the History books, would like for you to believe" ("Jewish Family," 16). Washington wrote: "Ever since I have been old enough to think for myself, I have entertained the idea that, notwithstanding the cruel wrongs inflicted upon us, the black man got nearly as much out of slavery as the white man did." See Booker T. Washington, *Up from Slavery*, 1901, ed. William L. Andrews (New York: Norton, 1996), 14.

26. Feather, *From Satchmo to Miles*, 22; Brothers, "'Swing a Lot of Type Writing,'" ix.

27. Armstrong, *Satchmo*, 199.

28. Armstrong, "Why I Like Dark Women," 61; Armstrong to Glaser, Aug. 2, 1955, 159; Armstrong to Joe Glaser, Jan. 9, 1956, Louis Armstrong House Museum.

29. Armstrong to Glaser, Aug. 2, 1955, 160; Armstrong, *Satchmo*, 86.

30. Qtd. in King, "Everybody's Louie," 63.

31. Armstrong to Goffin, May 7, 1944, 78.

32. See Smith and Watson, *Reading Autobiography*, 50–56.

33. Panassié, *Louis Armstrong*, 23.

34. A good example of autobiographical coaxing is an interview in which Fred Robbins narrates most of Armstrong's life story and then asks the musician to substantiate this version. See Fred Robbins, "Mr. Armstrong and Mr. Robbins," radio interview, Jan. 26, 1944, transcribed by Lorraine Lion, in Hodes and Hansen, *Selections from the Gutter*, 76–82.

35. Meryman, "Authentic American Genius," 113.

36. Kenney suggests this interpretation; see "Negotiating the Color Line," 40.

On the eclectic slave narrative, see Robert B. Stepto, *From Behind the Veil: A Study of Afro-American Narrative* (Urbana: University of Illinois Press, 1979), 6–10.

37. Kenney distinguishes four voices. See Kenney, "Negotiating the Color Line," 41–43.

38. Rudy Vallée and Gil McKean, *My Time Is Your Time: The Story of Rudy Vallée* (1930; New York: Obelensky, 1962).

39. Qtd. in Nollen, *Louis Armstrong*, 54.

40. Rudy Vallée, introduction to Armstrong, *Swing That Music*, xv–xviii. On primitivism in jazz, see Ted Gioia, "Jazz and the Primitivist Myth," in *The Imperfect Art: Reflections on Jazz and Modern Culture* (1988; New York: Oxford University Press, 1990), 19–49; Gerald Early, "Pulp and Circumstance: The Story of Jazz in High Places," in *The Culture of Bruising: Essays on Prizefighting, Literature, and Modern American Culture* (New Jersey, Ecco, 1994), 163–205. See also my essay "Negotiating Primitivist Modernisms: Louis Armstrong, Robert Goffin, and the Transatlantic Jazz Debate," Oslo conference special issue, *European Journal of American Studies* 2 (2011), doc. 8, http://ejas.revues.org/9395."

41. Qtd. in Kenney, "Negotiating the Color Line," 48. My remarks in this paragraph follow Kenney's reading of these editorial interventions.

42. Armstrong, *Satchmo*, 237.

43. Armstrong, "Armstrong Story," 49.

44. Armstrong, *Satchmo*, 177.

45. For a close reading of the poem and Holiday's adaptations, see my essay "Teaching Poetry through Song Adaptation: Abel Meeropol's and Billie Holiday's 'Strange Fruit,'" in *Adaptation and American Studies: Perspectives on Research and Teaching*, ed. Nassim Winnie Balestrini (Heidelberg: Winter, 2011), 171–94.

46. Armstrong, *Satchmo*, 194–95.

47. Armstrong, *Swing That Music*, 47.

48. Armstrong, *Satchmo*, 189.

49. Kenney, "Negotiating the Color Line," 55.

50. Situating *Swing That Music* in a European context goes beyond the scope of my argument, but the chapters on record collectors and European Hot Clubs most likely result from Gerlach's British perspective.

51. Kenney, "Negotiating the Color Line," 39.

52. See Armstrong, *Swing That Music*, 75, 125, 131–32.

53. Ibid., 20, 55, 88, 113.

54. Qtd. in Donald Bogle, "Louis Armstrong: The Films," in Miller, *Louis Armstrong*, 154. Armstrong performed "Lazybones" many times; he recorded it on Feb. 20, 1939, and played it on the radio with Bing Crosby on Feb. 21, 1949.

55. Armstrong, *Swing That Music*, 19. Another intertext is George Gershwin, Ira Gershwin, and DuBose Heyward's folk opera *Porgy and Bess*, which was also based on a novel from 1926 (Heyward's *Porgy*) and was adapted to the Broadway stage in 1935, just a year before the publication of *Swing That Music*. See also Armstrong and Ella Fitzgerald's recording, made for Verve on Aug. 18, 1957, and Aug. 19, 1957.

56. Armstrong, *Swing That Music*, 2.

57. Ibid., 3–4. The discourse will change in *Satchmo*, where Armstrong's mother is no longer a "house servant in a fine old white family" but goes "to work for some rich white folks on Canal Street" (Armstrong, *Satchmo*, 22).

58. David W. Stowe, *Swing Changes: Big-Band Jazz in New Deal America* (Cambridge: Harvard University Press, 1994), 2.

59. Hermann Deutsch, "Louis Armstrong," *Vanity Fair*, Oct. 1935, 70.

60. "Impossible Interview: Fritz Kreisler vs. Louis Armstrong," *Vanity Fair*, Feb. 1936, 33.

61. The caricature is also reproduced in Miller, *Louis Armstrong*, 210.

62. Lawrence F. Lamar, "Orson Welles to Feature Louis Armstrong in Film," *Chicago Defender* (national ed.), Sept. 6, 1941, 20.

63. Armstrong to Welles, Oct. 22, 1945, courtesy of the Lilly Library. I thank the Lilly Library for permission to cite from this letter.

64. Qtd. in Teachout, *Pops*, 300.

65. I reconstruct and assess this negotiation in my essay "Negotiating Primitivist Modernisms." Hugues Panassié also published a shorter Armstrong biography in 1947 (Paris: Éditions de Belvédère), but since it was not translated into English, I will focus my remarks on Goffin's *Horn of Plenty*.

66. Goffin's knowledge of *Swing That Music* is indicated by an explicit reference to the text and by several sentences that are clearly inspired by the autobiography. See Goffin, *Horn of Plenty*, 140, 157, 174.

67. Ibid., 146. It is likely that Goffin knew about Armstrong's early letters from Armstrong himself but arrived at his judgment on the basis of the "Goffin Notebooks" and his own correspondence with the musician.

68. Goffin knew and admired Mezzrow; *Horn of Plenty* is indebted to Mezzrow's primitivist depictions of Armstrong in *Really the Blues*.

69. Goffin, *Horn of Plenty*, 6, 141, 136, 201, 159.

70. Goffin draws heavily on minstrel and "coon" terminology, using expressions such as "pickaninnies," "bucks," "darkies," "wenches," "sluts," and "mammies." This terminology was amplified by the translator, James Bezou, who often picked minstrel-related terms even when Goffin did not.

71. Armstrong, "Goffin Notebooks," 95. He boasted about his stint with the Carroll Dickerson Band at the Sunset Café in the mid-1920s: "I was young and strong, a flying cat, and, God, I blew the people right out of that place" (Meryman, "Authentic American Genius," 112).

72. Goffin, *Horn of Plenty*, 217.

73. Ibid., 167.

74. Jones and Chilton, *Louis*, 105; Teachout, *Pops*, 8.

75. Goffin, *Horn of Plenty*, 251.

76. Ibid., 22.

77. Ibid., 17.

78. Qtd. in Sanders, "Louis Armstrong," 142. This relates to my earlier discus-

sion of Pops Foster's reference to Bolden's style as "stink music" and the African origins of the term *funk* (*Autobiography of Pops Foster*, 15). Jelly Roll Morton recalls the lyrics to a tune about Buddy Bolden: "Thought I heard Buddy Bolden say, / Funky Butt, funky butt, take it away . . . / Thought I heard Buddy Bolden say / Dirty, nasty stinky butt, take it away [. . .] / And let Mister Bolden play" (qtd. in Hersch, *Subversive Sounds*, 46).

79. An earlier appearance at Carnegie Hall had featured one set with a small band and a second set with Armstrong's big band. Due to the success of jazz revivalism, Armstrong had made small-band New Orleans jazz recordings, "Coal Cart Blues," "Perdido Street Blues," "Down in Honky Tonk Town," and "2:19 Blues (Mamie's Blues)," with Sidney Bechet and Zutty Singleton on May 27, 1940.

80. "Satchmo Comes Back," *Time*, Sept. 1, 1947; "Satchmo's Genius Still Lives," *Down Beat*, June 4, 1947. See also Wolfram Knauer, *Louis Armstrong* (Stuttgart: Reclam, 2010), 184–85.

81. Collier, *Louis Armstrong*, 308.

82. The All Stars debuted on television in Nov. 1948, the year in which network television began, as part of the CBS program *Toast of the Town*, hosted by Ed Sullivan. Between Sept. 5, 1946, and Oct. 8, 1946, Armstrong had recorded "Where the Blues Were Born in New Orleans," the song that delivered the title for the essay in *True*, as part of the soundtrack for the movie *New Orleans*. He recorded the song again on Oct. 17, 1946.

83. "Music Is Music," *Time*, May 22, 1950.

84. Louis Armstrong and Bing Crosby, *Fun with Bing and Louis, 1949–1951* (Jasmine, 1997).

85. Morton Roberts's paintings that accompany the article are also a far cry from Miguel Covarrubias's caricature of Armstrong in the *Vanity Fair* piece. See "Jazz: America's Own Music in Its Lusty Youth," *Life*, Dec. 22, 1958, 64–73.

86. For a reconstruction of the debate, see Bernard Gendron, "'Moldy Figs' and Modernists: Jazz at War (1942–1946)," in Gabbard, *Jazz among the Discourses*, 31–56; Raeburn, *New Orleans Style*, chaps. 5 and 6.

87. George T. Simon, "Bebop's the Easy Way Out, Claims Louis," *Metronome*, Mar. 1948, in Berrett, *Louis Armstrong Companion*, 142.

88. Benny Goodman and Irving Kolodin, *Kingdom of Swing* (New York: Stackpole, 1939); Eddie Condon with Thomas Sugrue, *We Called It Music: A Generation of Jazz* (New York: Holt, 1947); Wingy Manone and Paul Vandervoot, *Trumpet on the Wing* (New York: Doubleday, 1948).

89. Armstrong, "Joe Oliver Is Still King," 37; Armstrong, "Bunk Didn't Teach Me," 40–41. See also Park Breck, "This Isn't Bunk; Bunk Taught Louis," *Down Beat*, June 1939, in *Down Beat: 60 Years of Jazz*, ed. Frank Alkyer (Milwaukee: Hal Leonard, 1995), 39–40.

90. Armstrong, "Rocky Marciano."

91. Armstrong, "Joe Oliver Is Still King," 39.

92. See Armstrong, "Jazz on High Note," 128–32.

93. Armstrong, "Max Jones 2," *Louis Armstrong: Fleischmann's Yeast Show & Louis' Home-Recorded Tapes;* Armstrong qtd. in Ernest Borneman, "'Bop Will Kill Business Unless It Kills Itself First'—Louis Armstrong," *Down Beat,* Apr. 7, 1948, in Alkyer, *Down Beat,* 65; Armstrong, "Armstrong Story," 66.

94. The live performance at the Crescendo can be heard on *Louis Armstrong: The California Concerts* (Verve, 1992); the Hollywood Bowl performance of the "Whiffenpoof Song" is included on *Louis Armstrong: 100th Anniversary.*

95. Armstrong to Dizzy and Lorraine Gillespie, July 1, 1959, facsimile in Brower, *Satchmo,* 202; Armstrong, "Jazz Is a Language," 186.

96. Qtd. in Brothers, *In His Own Words,* 201.

97. Louis Armstrong, *Ma Vie: Ma Nouvelle Orléans,* trans. Madeleine Gautier (Paris: Julliard, 1952); the tape cover is reproduced in Brower, *Satchmo,* 136.

98. Goffin, *Horn of Plenty,* 1; Armstrong, *Satchmo,* 7.

99. Armstrong, *Satchmo,* 7.

100. Goffin, *Horn of Plenty,* 63.

101. Armstrong, *Satchmo,* 41.

102. Goffin, *Horn of Plenty,* 64; Armstrong, *Satchmo,* 42. In his interview with Richard Meryman, Armstrong reiterates the claim that Davis had handed him the tambourine. See Meryman, "Authentic American Genius," 102. In his interview with Joachim-Ernst Behrendt, however, he suggests that he himself selected the tambourine, but that Davis told him to "pick something you can blow." See Joachim-Ernst Behrendt, on *Satchmo: Louis Armstrong, Historical Live Performance and Interview* (Jazz Door, 2005). He does so as well in his letter to Orson Welles (Oct. 22, 1945).

103. Goffin, *Horn of Plenty,* 152.

104. Armstrong, *Satchmo,* 230, 231. He told a similar version of these events to Ralph Gleason on the *Jazz Casual* program in 1963.

105. Goffin, *Horn of Plenty,* 156.

106. Armstrong, *Satchmo,* 232.

107. Armstrong, "Goffin Notebooks," 86, 84. The difference between vernacular recollection and minstrel vocabulary is captured by Armstrong's reference to the neighborhood boys as "a half a dozen ragged, snot-nosed kids" and Goffin's depiction of "neighborhood pickaninnies [. . .] rolling their eyeballs." See Armstrong, *Satchmo,* 17; Goffin, *Horn of Plenty,* 12.

108. Armstrong, "Why I Like Dark Women," 61, 62, 68.

109. Ibid., 62, 64, 65, 61, 62, 66.

110. Ibid., 61. On the phallic implications of Armstrong's trumpet, see Gabbard, *Jammin' at the Margins,* chap. 4.

111. Bergreen, *Louis Armstrong,* 4.

112. Armstrong, "Satchmo Story," 112, 113, also 115–16; "Muggles," *Time,* Sept. 7, 1931; "Black Rascal," *Time,* June 13, 1932; "Hot Ambassador," *Time,* June

12, 1933; Armstrong to Max Jones and John Chilton, date unknown, in Jones and Chilton, *Louis*, 132–38; "Max Jones 1."

113. Armstrong, "Satchmo Story," 114, 117, 120.

114. Ibid., 119.

115. Geneva Smitherman, *Talkin and Testifyin: The Language of Black America*, (1977; Detroit: Wayne State University Press, 1986), 147–49. Albert Murray dismisses Armstrong's performative vernacular when he writes about another autobiographical anecdote: "Somehow the idea or the anecdote that he has in mind comes across, but it reads more like a very rough first draft, rougher even than a hurriedly dashed-off letter of gossip or a postcard. [. . .] His grammar and his punctuation are hit-and-miss when they are not just eccentric." Later on, Murray even speaks of "[t]he painfully obvious shortcomings of his writings" ("Louis Armstrong in His Own Words," 113, 123).

116. Kenney, "Negotiating the Color Line," 54. The *Life* interview is presented as a continuous autobiographical narrative without Meryman's questions.

117. Meryman, "Authentic American Genius," 94, 116; Meryman, *Louis Armstrong—A Self-Portrait*, 56–57.

118. Meryman, *Louis Armstrong—A Self-Portrait*, 55.

119. Meryman, "Authentic American Genius," n.p. (emphasis added).

120. Armstrong, "Jewish Family," 9.

121. Ibid., 9, 10.

122. Dick Hebdige, *Cut 'n' Mix: Culture, Identity and Caribbean Music* (London: Methuen, 1987), 12, 13, 12.

123. Lawrence Gushee, "The Improvisation of Louis Armstrong," in *In the Course of Performance: Studies in the World of Musical Improvisation*, ed. Bruno Nettl and Melinda Russell (Chicago: University of Chicago Press, 1998), 292.

124. Collier, *Louis Armstrong*, 130.

125. Jazz inflection includes the way in which a musician "attacks each note, the quality and exact duration of each pitch, the manner in which he releases the note, and the subsequent split-second silence before the next note—in other words the entire acoustical pattern" (Schuller, *Early Jazz*, 116).

126. Panassié, *Louis Armstrong*, 48; Schuller, *Early Jazz*, 66, 91; Harker, "'Telling a Story,'" 51.

127. Qtd. in Humphrey Lyttelton, liner notes, *Satch Plays Fats*, by Louis Armstrong and His All-Stars, 1955 (CBS, 1986), 6. Analyzing the recordings on *Satchmo: A Musical Autobiography*, Panassié speaks of "variations on variations" (*Louis Armstrong*, 137).

128. Meryman, *Louis Armstrong—A Self-Portrait*, 43. Playing too many variations, Armstrong once explained, leads to bebop, a music he never really appreciated. See Richard Hadlock, *Jazz Masters of the Twenties* (1965; New York: Da Capo, 1986), 14–15.

129. See Harker, "'Telling a Story,'" 50.

130. Gushee, "Improvisation of Louis Armstrong," 304; Armstrong, "Armstrong Story," 61; Morgenstern, foreword to Armstrong, *Swing That Music*, vii.

131. Paul Allen Anderson, "Ralph Ellison on Lyricism and Swing," *American Literary History* 17.2 (2005): 286–87. Anderson cites "fixed equations" from Nathaniel Mackey, *Discrepant Engagement: Dissonance, Cross-Culturality, and Experimental Writing* (Cambridge: Cambridge University Press, 1993), 267; he cites "slightly different sense of time" from Ellison, *Invisible Man*, 7.

132. Henry Louis Gates Jr., *The Signifying Monkey: A Theory of African-American Literary Criticism* (New York: Oxford University Press, 1988), xxiv.

133. Veneciano, "Louis Armstrong, Bricolage," 258–59, 257.

134. Gates, *Signifying Monkey*, xxii–xxiii.

135. Walter J. Ong, *Orality and Literacy: The Technologizing of the World* (1982; New York, Routledge, 2002), 41–42.

136. William L. Andrews, "Toward a Poetics of Afro-American Autobiography," in *Afro-American Literary Study in the 1990s*, ed. Houston A. Baker Jr. and Patricia Redmond (Chicago: University of Chicago Press, 1989), 87. See also Winfried Herget, "Black Itinerant Women Preachers: Conversion to Empowerment—The Example of Jarena Lee," in *Religion in African-American Culture*, ed. Winfried Herget and Alfred Hornung (Heidelberg: Winter, 2006), 43–73.

137. Kenney, "Negotiating the Color Line," 48.

Chapter 3

1. Cleveland Amory, "Straight from the Trumpet's Mouth," *New York Times*, Oct. 10, 1954; Tallulah Bankhead qtd. in Miller, "Louis Armstrong: A Portrait Record," 182; Bergreen, *Louis Armstrong*, 2; Berrett, *Louis Armstrong Companion*, 3, 105–6; Cogswell, *Louis Armstrong*, 10; Brothers, "'Swing a Lot of Type Writing,'" xiii; Morgenstern, introduction to Armstrong, *Satchmo*, x; Kenney, "Negotiating the Color Line," 46.

2. Murray, "Louis Armstrong in His Own Words," 113.

3. I use the linguistic meaning of "indexical" as "deictic" (expressions that are relative to the situation of their utterance, including the speaker, the addressee, accompanying gestures, and the discursive context) and understand "annotations" as commentary and corrections added by Armstrong in the process of revising his drafts. These annotations were often done in a different color, probably because he wanted to indicate to himself whether a letter had been checked or not. He once explained: "I never write a letter unless I check it" (Armstrong, "Max Jones 1").

4. Armstrong, *Swing That Music*, 78.

5. Armstrong, "Word from Louis Armstrong," xi.

6. Werner Sollors, *Beyond Ethnicity: Consent and Descent in American Culture* (New York: Oxford University Press, 1986), 252, 249.

7. Armstrong to Bérard, Nov. 25, 1946, 129.

8. Armstrong, "Forward."

9. Edward R. Murrow, "Paris Interview," on *Satchmo the Great*, 1957 (Sony/Columbia/Legacy, 2000).

10. Qtd. in Brothers, "'Swing a Lot of Type Writing,'" x.

11. "The Jive Language," *Metronome* 55, June 1939, 20.

12. Roger D. Abrahams qtd. in Mel Watkins, *On the Real Side: Laughing, Lying, and Signifying—The Underground Tradition of African-American Humor That Transformed American Culture, from Slavery to Richard Pryor* (New York: Simon and Schuster, 1994), 453.

13. "Black Rascal," *Time*, June 13, 1932.

14. The tape covers are reproduced in Brower, *Satchmo*, 121, 145.

15. Brothers, "'Swing a Lot of Type Writing,'" xii.

16. Neil Leonard, "The Jazzman's Verbal Usage," *Black American Literature Forum* 20.1–2 (1986): 152, 153.

17. John "Dizzy" Birks Gillespie with Al Fraser, *to BE, or not . . . to BOP: Memoirs* (1979; New York: Da Capo, 1985), 281.

18. See Leonard: "what you said might matter less than *how* you said it, with semantics depending largely on spontaneous integration of appropriate linguistic, kinesic, proximal, and other codes" ("Jazzman's Verbal Usage," 155).

19. See Armstrong, *Swing That Music*, 135–36. On the jive and slang terms Armstrong used in *Satchmo*, see Berrett, "Cat, Daddy, and All That Jive," in Berrett, *Louis Armstrong Companion*, 20–23.

20. Cab Calloway and Bryant Rollins, *Of Minnie the Moocher and Me* (New York: Crowell, 1976), 251–61; Mezzrow and Wolfe, *Really the Blues*, 371–80. Calloway further popularized his jiving on tunes such as "Jumpin' Jive" (1939) and "Are You Hep to the Jive?" (1940). Armstrong picked up on the second of these titles: "As the days rolled on I commenced getting hep to the jive" (*Satchmo*, 192).

21. See Armstrong, *Satchmo*, 140; Armstrong, *Swing That Music*, 8, 26, 41; Armstrong, "Goffin Notebooks," 104, 107; Armstrong, "Jazz on a High Note," 128; "They Cross Iron Curtain," 58; Armstrong to Frances Church, Mar. 10, 1946, in Berrett, *Louis Armstrong Companion*, 125. Armstrong rarely employed expletives such as "motherfucker" publicly. He uses the term repeatedly in an interview with George Avakian. See Louis Armstrong, "Contention with Collins," Nov. 11, 1953, in Berrett, *Louis Armstrong Companion*, 85. In "Satchmo Says," he uses "motherfucking thing" in reported speech; reading letters to Max Jones into his tape recorder, he curses repeatedly, speaking of "funky shit," "bullshit," and so forth. He also retells the story of the rabbit in the briar patch. See Armstrong, "Satchmo Says," 238; Armstrong, "Max Jones 1" and "Max Jones 2." He addresses a letter to "Bre'r Villec" and calls colleague David Jones "Bre'r Jones." See Armstrong to L/Cpl. Villec, 171; Armstrong qtd. in Bergreen, *Louis Armstrong*, 160; Armstrong, "Satchmo Says," 242.

22. Armstrong, *Satchmo*, 189; Armstrong, "Jewish Family," 9, 17; Armstrong to Church, Mar. 10, 1946, 125; Armstrong, "Goffin Notebooks," 109; Armstrong, "Satchmo Story," 117.

23. Qtd. in Shapiro and Hentoff, *Hear Me Talkin' to Ya*, 185–86.

24. Buck Clayton qtd. in Chris Searle, *Forward Groove: Jazz and the Real World from Louis Armstrong to Gilad Atzmon* (London: Northway, 2008), 50.

25. Armstrong, *Swing That Music*, 64. Maybe Armstrong did not mention Daisy Parker's profession, but since he speaks about it freely in later accounts, the editors may have simply dropped the reference.

26. Armstrong to Mezz Mezzrow, Sept. 18, 1932, Louis Armstrong House Museum. I thank Michael Cogswell for pointing me to this letter and suggesting this interpretation.

27. Art Hodes and Chadwick Hansen, *Hot Man: The Life of Art Hodes* (Urbana: University of Illinois Press, 1992), 22.

28. Gillespie with Fraser, *to BE, or not . . . to BOP*, 303–4.

29. Armstrong to Church, Mar. 10, 1946, 125.

30. Armstrong recalls the event in "Satchmo Says," 238–40; see also Bergreen, *Louis Armstrong*, 346–47; Jones and Chilton, *Louis*, 152–53; Teachout, *Pops*, 171.

31. Qtd. in Brothers, *Louis Armstrong's New Orleans*, 82–83.

32. See Armstrong, *Satchmo*, 73, 156, 212; Armstrong to Feather, Oct. 1, 1941, 109; Armstrong to Church, Mar. 10, 1946, 125; Armstrong, "Satchmo Story," 118; Armstrong, "Open Letter to Fans," June 1, 1970, in Brothers, *In His Own Words*, 187; Armstrong, "Barber Shops," facsimile in Brower, *Satchmo*, 227.

33. See Smitherman, *Talkin and Testifyin*, 94–100.

34. Armstrong, "Satchmo Story," 115 (emphasis added). Armstrong writes about Jelly Roll Morton: "He was a big Bragadossa. Lots of big talk" ("Jewish Family," 24).

35. Dan Burley, *Dan Burley's Original Handbook of Harlem Jive*, 1944, rpt. as "The Technique of Jive," in *Mother Wit from the Laughing Barrel: Readings in the Interpretation of Afro-American Folklore*, ed. Alan Dundes (Englewood Cliffs: Prentice Hall, 1973), 208. Burley might have gotten the term from the "Special Jive" columns Armstrong had written for the *Harlem Tattler* in 1940; I was unable to locate these columns, so the issue cannot be resolved here. The reprint of Armstrong's letter to Bérard excises the reference to "'s'language"; it is included in the facsimile in Edwards, "Louis Armstrong and the Syntax of Scat," 638. Edwards also discusses its significance for Armstrongs' scat aesthetics. Armstrong uses the neologism again in "Barber Shops," 227.

36. Musical examples of the monkey tales are Cab Calloway's "The Jungle King (You Ain't a Doggone Thing)" (1947) and Willie Dixon's "The Signifying Monkey" (1947); for folk recordings of oral renditions, see Bruce Jackson, ed., *Get Your Ass in the Water and Swim Like Me: Narrative Poetry from Black Oral Tradition* (Cambridge: Harvard University Press, 1974) and the CD of the same title (Rounder, 1998).

37. Gates, *Signifying Monkey*, 56, 53.

38. Ibid., 53. Thomas Kochman speaks of an "indeterminate strategic ambiguity." See Thomas Kochman, "Strategic Ambiguity in Black Speech Genres: Cross-Cultural Inference in Participant-Observation Research," *Text* 6.2 (1986): 156.

39. Claudia Mitchell-Kernan, "Signifying and Marking: Two Afro-American Speech Acts," in *Directions in Sociolinguistics: The Ethnography of Communication*, ed. John J. Gumperz and Dell Hymes (1972; Oxford: Basil Blackwell, 1986), 165.

40. Floyd, "Ring Shout!" 273.

41. See Kenney, *Chicago Jazz*, 58–59.

42. Qtd. in Dan Morgenstern, "Satchmo and the Critics," 2001, in Morgenstern, *Living with Jazz*, 73.

43. Armstrong, "Satchmo Story," 114, 112; Armstrong, "Goffin Notebooks," 109; Armstrong, "Satchmo Story," 114; Armstrong, postcard to Lossie Smith, June 8, 1954, facsimile in Cogswell, *Louis Armstrong*, 128. Giddins connects Armstrong's use of ellipses with the writing style of gossip columnist Walter Winchell (*Satchmo*, xx).

44. Brothers, "'Swing a Lot of Type Writing,'" xiii; Edwards, "Louis Armstrong and the Syntax of Scat," 639; Panassié, *Louis Armstrong*, 21.

45. Murrow, "Paris Interview."

46. Qtd. in Panassié, *Louis Armstrong*, 21–22.

47. Smitherman, *Talkin and Testifyin*, 134. Brothers speaks of an "attempt to add Armstrong's *voice* to his words" and "bring [. . .] improvisatory—or *performative*—techniques to his writing hobby" ("'Swing a Lot of Type Writing,'" xv).

48. Armstrong to Murry, May 24, 1950, 101.

49. Veneciano, "Louis Armstrong, Bricolage," 273, 259.

50. Panassié, *Louis Armstrong*, 22.

51. See Kenney, "Negotiating the Color Line," 46–47.

52. Armstrong to Feather, Sept. 18, 1941, 146.

53. Watkins defines "cacography" as "deliberate misspelling for humorous effect" (*On the Real Side*, 60).

54. Qtd. in Kenney, "Negotiating the Color Line," 49.

55. Armstrong, *Satchmo*, 189.

56. Edwards, "Louis Armstrong and the Syntax of Scat," 618, 622.

57. Ibid., 624, 625. Edwards cites from Nathaniel Mackey, *Bedouin Hornbook* (1986; Los Angeles: Sun & Moon, 1997), 62.

58. Armstrong, "Armstrong Story," 64.

59. Edwards, "Louis Armstrong and the Syntax of Scat," 621.

60. Ibid.

61. Mezzrow and Wolfe, *Really the Blues*, 120.

62. M. M. Bakhtin, *The Dialogic Imagination: Four Essays*, ed. Michael Holquist, trans. Caryl Emerson and Michael Holquist (Austin: University of Texas Press, 1981), 364.

63. Armstrong created a similar effect in live performance, something that critics noted as early as 1946: "He always repeated the title twice, the first time announcing it in a normal way, the second time always with a tone and gesture that were in some way unusual; for example, opening his eyes very wide as if he were astonished by what he had just said and was listening to himself repeat it in order to

take account of what he had said; or, the second time, the title might be announced in a foreboding way and the final syllables would be lost in a light laugh, as if to say: 'Ha, do you understand what I mean?'" Hugues Panassié, "Louis Armstrong at the Salle Pleyel," 1946, trans. Joshua Berrett, in Berrett, *Louis Armstrong Companion*, 70.

64. Appel, *Jazz Modernism*, 156.

65. Meryman, "Authentic American Genius," 96.

66. The musical director on this recording, Zilner Randolph, connects the performance with Armstrong's marijuana-induced high. See Giddins and Simmons, *Masters of American Music: Satchmo*. The narrative of animalism and jungle life resonates with primitivist depictions of jazz. On "New Tiger Rag" (Mar. 11, 1932), Armstrong invites his audience to join him on "a little trip to the jungles," where they will chase a tiger that "is runnin' so fast" that it "takes about seven choruses to get that baby."

67. *Swing That Music* defines "mugging lightly" as "[s]oft, staccato swinging" (Armstrong, *Swing That Music*, 136).

68. Appel, *Jazz Modernism*, 138, 137. Armstrong writes about the Hot Five and Hot Seven recordings: "A lot of those comments on the records were just as though we were talking to one another on a club date" ("Satchmo Says," 237).

69. Mark Katz calls the changes in music-making initiated by the medium of recording "phonograph effects." See Mark Katz, *Capturing Sound: How Technology Has Changed Music* (2004; Berkeley: University of California Press, 2010), 2.

70. Stephen J. Casmier and Donald H. Matthews, "Why Scatting Is Like Speaking in Tongues: Post-Modern Reflections on Jazz, Pentecostalism and 'Africomysticism,'" *Literature and Theology: An International Journal of Religion, Theory and Culture* 13.2 (1999): 170, 168. The authors place Armstrong's scatting in the context of glossolalia, the speaking in tongues of the Pentecostal church.

71. Nathaniel Mackey, "Other: From Noun to Verb," in Gabbard, *Jazz among the Discourses*, 85; see also Appel, *Jazz Modernism*, 140, 142.

72. The soundie is included on *Louis Armstrong: St. Louis Blues* (All Stars, 2005). Soundies were music videos that could be played on specially equipped jukeboxes. Armstrong also recorded Sammy Cahn and Saul Chaplin's "Shoe Shine Boy" (Dec. 19, 1935) and played it live repeatedly in the 1930s and 1940s. The tune was written for the *Connie's Hot Chocolates of 1936* show, and its lyrics describe a black shoeshine boy who is content with his low social status.

73. Armstrong to Glaser, Aug. 2, 1955, 160. Armstrong's letters do not always contain the same amount of indexical markers and annotations. Jones and Chilton reprint a handwritten letter that contains some stylistic peculiarities but is mostly straightforward. This suggests that Armstrong frequently used indexical markers *strategically*; writing to Jones and Chilton had not mandated a strategic self-positioning to the same extent that his letter to Glaser had. See Jones and Chilton, *Louis*, 194.

74. John Edgar Wideman, "Charles Chesnutt and the WPA Narratives: The

Oral and Literate Roots of Afro-American Literature," in *The Slave's Narrative*, ed. Charles T. Davis and Henry Louis Gates Jr. (New York: Oxford University Press, 1985), 74.

75. King, "Everybody's Louie," 65; Goffin, *Horn of Plenty*, 146.

76. I take the notion of ethnic self-dramatization in African (American) autobiography from Frank Kelleter, "Ethnic Self-Dramatization and Technologies of Travel in *The Interesting Narrative of the Life of Olaudah Equiano, or Gustavus Vassa, the African, Written by Himself* (1789)," *Early American Literature* 39.1 (2004): 67–84.

77. Edwards, "Louis Armstrong and the Syntax of Scat," 641, 645.

78. Armstrong to Mardon, Sept. 27, 1953, 212.

79. Ellison, *Invisible Man*, 6.

80. Max Kaminsky and V. E. Hughes, *Jazz Band: My Life in Jazz* (1963; New York: Da Capo, 1981), 40.

81. Zora Neale Hurston, "Characteristics of Negro Expression," in *Negro: An Anthology*, ed, Nancy Cunard, 1934, ed. and abridged by Hugh Ford (New York: Ungar, 1984), 24, 25.

82. See also Hersch's analysis of the performance in *Subversive Sounds*, 195–96.

83. Armstrong to Evans, Sept. 31, 1967.

84. Qtd. in Benjamin Givan, "Duets for One: Louis Armstrong's Vocal Recordings," *Musical Quarterly* 87.2 (2004): 188.

85. Qtd. in ibid., 188.

86. *Ralph Gleason's Jazz Casual*, Jan. 23, 1963.

87. Giddins, *Satchmo*, 89.

88. Video footage of the performance is included on Giddins and Simmons, *Masters of American Music: Satchmo*. It originally appeared as part of the film *København, Kalundborg og—?*

89. Edwards, "Louis Armstrong and the Syntax of Scat," 647.

90. This is not to suggest that he did not enjoy opera. See Joshua Berrett, "Louis Armstrong and Opera," *Musical Quarterly* 76.2 (1992): 216–41. Publicity shots taken during the 1933 European tour show Armstrong wearing clothes in the style of the English gentleman; here, he is playing with visual codes of self-representation. These photographs are reproduced in Miller, *Louis Armstrong*, 56; Teachout, *Pops*, 184.

91. Dan Morgenstern, "Louis and the Duke: The Great Summit," 2001, in Morgenstern, *Living with Jazz*, 98.

92. Edwards, "Louis Armstrong and the Syntax of Scat," 648–49.

93. Cf. also Veneciano: "Scat syllables are audible fragments collaged into song" ("Louis Armstrong, Bricolage," 265).

94. Armstrong, "Jazz on a High Note," 130; Charles Keil, "Participatory Discrepancies and the Power of Music," *Cultural Anthropology* 2.3 (1987): 275; Armstrong to Evans, Sept. 31, 1967.

95. Armstrong to Glaser, Aug. 2, 1955, 158.

96. Morgenstern, introduction to Armstrong, *Satchmo*, ix (emphasis added).

97. Edwards suggests that the phrase "'Gappings' on ya," which follows Armstrong's comment on "swing[ing] a lot of Type Writing," signifies a wish "to appropriate a rational technology of the interval ('gappings'—in the sense that the typewriter structures and spatializes an access to language) from a particular, paradigmatically black aesthetic ('swing')." Edwards, "Louis Armstrong and the Syntax of Scat," 640.

98. Finkelstein, *Jazz*, 32.

99. Jean-Jacques Nattiez, *Music and Discourse: Toward a Semiology of Music*, 1987, trans. Carolyn Abbate (Princeton: Princeton University Press, 1990), 44.

100. See Roland Barthes, "The Grain of the Voice," in *Image—Music—Text*, 179–89. This passage is indebted to Heinrich Detering, who has shaped my thinking about the physiognomy of the human voice and its complex cultural connotations. See also Detering, *Bob Dylan* (Stuttgart: Reclam, 2007).

101. Ong, *Orality and Literacy*, 79, 100.

102. Edwards, "Louis Armstrong and the Syntax of Scat," 647.

103. Armstrong printed postcards and sent them to friends and acquaintances. He often gave away free samples of Swiss Kriss. My argument about the scatological significances in Armstrong's autobiographics takes off from Brent Edwards's brilliant analysis in "Louis Armstrong and the Syntax of Scat," 631–36.

104. Armstrong, "Jewish Family," 36; Armstrong to L/Cpl. Villec, 169; Armstrong, "Lose Weight the Satchmo Way," in Berrett, *Louis Armstrong Companion*, 101; Armstrong, "Max Jones 2." Hersch explains Armstrong's choice of John Philip Sousa's "Stars and Stripes Forever" with the sonic similarities between a bowel movement and the "low-pitched emanations of trombones and tubas." See Charles Hersch, "Poisoning Their Coffee: Louis Armstrong and Civil Rights," *Polity* 34.3 (2002): 376.

105. Edwards, "Louis Armstrong and the Syntax of Scat," 633.

106. Armstrong to Joe Glaser, Sept. 8, 1955, facsimile in Edwards, "Louis Armstrong and the Syntax of Scat," 635; Armstrong to William Russell, Oct. 3, 1939, qtd. in Brothers, *In His Own Words*, 198; Armstrong to Mr. Kline, Oct. 22, 1939, qtd. in Kenney, "Negotiating the Color Line," 46; Armstrong to Bérard, Nov. 25, 1946, 133; Armstrong to Joe Glaser, telegram, qtd. in Gilbert Millstein, "Africa Harks to Satch's Horn," *New York Times Magazine*, Nov. 20, 1960, 24.

107. Qtd. in Millstein, "Most Un-Average Cat."

108. The promotional photograph is reproduced in Cogswell, *Louis Armstrong*, 117.

109. Whitney Balliett, *The Sound of Surprise: 46 Pieces on Jazz* (New York: Dutton, 1959).

110. Armstrong, "Satchmo Story," 115.

111. Qtd. in King, "Everybody's Louie," 69 (emphasis added).

112. See Armstrong, "Lombardo Grooves Louis!" 165–66.

113. Anne Faber, *Louis Armstrong* (Dressler: Hamburg, 1977), 32 (my transla-

tion). Faber probably refers to a passage in Meryman, "Authentic American Genius," 114.

114. Ong, *Orality and Literacy*, 82; Armstrong qtd. in Taubman, "Satchmo Wears His Crown Gaily," 12.

115. Marshall McLuhan, *Understanding Media: The Extensions of Man* (New York: McGraw, 1964); Ralph Ellison, "What America Would Be Like without Blacks," *Time*, Apr. 6, 1970, in *The Collected Essays of Ralph Ellison*, ed. James F. Callahan (New York: Modern Library, 1995), 582.

Chapter 4

1. The caricature is reproduced in Cogswell, *Louis Armstrong*, 170; Miller, *Louis Armstrong*, 211.

2. Armstrong to Glaser, Aug. 2, 1955, 160.

3. Meryman, "Authentic American Genius," 110.

4. Armstrong, 17. Similar sentiments appear in King, "Everybody's Louie," 67; Armstrong, "Jewish Family," 20. According to Tony Bennett, he also related the advice to Prince Philip at a gathering at Buckingham Palace. See Giddins and Simmons, *Masters of American Music: Satchmo*.

5. George Fitzhugh, *Cannibals All! or, Slaves without Masters* (Richmond: Morris, 1857), 126.

6. Jones and Chilton, *Louis*, 156.

7. Jones and Chilton give no date for the letter, but on the tape recording on which Armstrong proofreads the letter, he mentions Aug. 15, 1970. See Armstrong, "Max Jones 1."

8. Cogswell, *Louis Armstrong*, 166; Louis Armstrong and Joe Glaser, 1949, photograph by Bill Mark, reproduced in Miller, *Louis Armstrong*, 106; Louis Armstrong and Johnny Collins, early 1930s, photographer unknown, reproduced in Cogswell, *Louis Armstrong*, 161.

9. The tape cover is reproduced in Brower, *Satchmo*, 213.

10. Louis Armstrong, "Louis Armstrong + the Jewish Family in New Orleans, La. The Year of 1907," manuscript, Louis Armstrong House Museum. This reading of the opening page was suggested to me by Michael Cogswell.

11. See Armstrong to Evans, Sept. 31, 1967; Meryman, "Authentic American Genius," 112; Armstrong to Little Brother Montgomery, July 29, 1969, qtd. in Bergreen, *Louis Armstrong*, 490; Armstrong, "Goffin Notebooks," 99.

12. Armstrong to Bérard, Nov. 25, 1946, 132; Armstrong to Church, Mar. 10, 1946, 126; Armstrong qtd. in Jones and Chilton, *Louis*, 202; Armstrong to Feather, Dec. 5, 1946.

13. Armstrong to Joe Glaser, May 17, 1960, Louis Armstrong House Museum.

14. Meryman, "Authentic American Genius," 113.

15. Zora Neale Hurston, "The 'Pet' Negro System," *American Mercury*, Mar. 1943, in *I Love Myself When I Am Laughing . . . and Then Again When I Am Looking*

Mean and Impressive: A Zora Neale Hurston Reader, ed. Alice Walker (New York: Feminist Press, 1979), 156–62.

16. Armstrong to Glaser, Aug. 2, 1955, 160, 163, 161, 162, 163. This usage is not confined to Joe Glaser; Armstrong called his earlier manager "Papa Collins." Armstrong to Mezzrow, Sept. 18, 1932.

17. Armstrong ends a later letter to Glaser in a similar fashion: "Well, I guess I've bothered (you) enough at one' sitting. So seldom that I bother you until I feel that you don't mind. All off my bother is sincerities (HMP)" (Armstrong to Glaser, May 17, 1960). Elsewhere, he wrote: "telling you 'many *many* 'Thanks for the *Loot*/MONEY." Armstrong to Joe Glaser, Feb. 11, 1957, Louis Armstrong House Museum.

18. See Nat Hentoff, "Louis: Black and Blue and Triumphant," *Jazz Times*, Oct. 2000.

19. Meryman, "Authentic American Genius," 114; "Louis the First," *Time*, Feb. 21, 1949. Glaser's letter to Armstrong is dated Nov. 28, 1956, and is held by the Louis Armstrong House Museum.

20. Hurston qtd. in Ann Douglas, *Terrible Honesty: Mongrel Manhattan in the 1920s* (New York: Farrar, 1995), 283; Armstrong qtd. in "Joseph G. Glaser Is Dead at 72; Booking Agent for Many Stars," *New York Times*, June 6, 1969. Armstrong's relationship with manager Johnny Collins was much less playful. See Armstrong, "Contention with Collins," 85–86.

21. Collier, *Louis Armstrong*, 202–3.

22. Ibid., 245–46. In his otherwise astute review of Collier's biography, Gerald Early problematically describes the post-1949 Armstrong as a "darkie minstrel" who "needed to be 'some white man's nigger,'" that is, taken under the protective, paternalistic wing of a white man who would 'look out for him.'" See Gerald Early, "'And I Will Sing of Joy and Pain for You': Louis Armstrong and the Great Jazz Traditions," 1984, in *Tuxedo Junction: Essays on American Culture* (New York: Ecco, 1989), 293, 295.

23. Teachout, *Pops*, 16, 17.

24. William J. Mahar, *Behind the Burnt Cork Mask: Early Blackface Minstrelsy and Antebellum American Popular Culture* (Urbana: University of Illinois Press, 1999), 353. See also Eric Lott, *Love and Theft: Blackface Minstrelsy and the American Working Class* (1993; New York: Oxford University Press, 1995), 71.

25. Armstrong, *Satchmo*, 92, 92–93, 93.

26. See Armstrong, "Max Jones 2."

27. For more historical context, see Eric Lott, "Double V, Double Time: Bebop's Politics of Style," in Gabbard, *Jazz among the Discourses*, 243–55.

28. Collier, *Louis Armstrong*, 72.

29. Other examples are Stephen Foster and George Cooper's "A Soldier in De Colored Brigade" (1863), Ned Straight's "The Darkies Dress Parade" (1894), and Will Accooe's "Ma Dandy Soldier Coon: A Humorous March Song" (1900). Sheet music covers established a visual discourse.

30. Houston A. Baker Jr., *Modernism and the Harlem Renaissance* (Chicago: University of Chicago Press, 1987), xvi.

31. Armstrong, *Satchmo*, 112, 144.

32. Baker, *Modernism and the Harlem Renaissance*, 17.

33. Joseph Boskin, *Sambo: The Rise and Demise of an American Jester* (New York: Oxford University Press, 1986), 42, 10–11.

34. See Dale Cockrell, *Demons of Disorder: Early Blackface Minstrels and Their World* (Cambridge: Cambridge University Press, 1997), 15.

35. On the significance and longevity of minstrel blackface representations in American culture, see W. T. Lhamon Jr., *Raising Cain: Blackface Performance from Jim Crow to Hip Hop* (Cambridge: Harvard University Press, 1998).

36. Before the end of the Civil War, African American actors were rarely seen on stage. An exception is New York's African Grove Theater, the first black theater in the United States in the early 1820s.

37. Boskin, *Sambo*, 37, 52, 79; Bernard qtd. in Boskin, *Sambo*, 61. Bernard's *Retrospections of America, 1797–1811* was published in 1887.

38. See Lawrence W. Levine, *Black Culture and Black Consciousness: Afro-American Folk Thought from Slavery to Freedom* (New York: Oxford University Press, 1977), chap. 5.

39. See John W. Blassingame, *The Slave Community: Plantation Life in the Antebellum South* (New York: Oxford University Press, 1972), chap. 5. Examples of Sambo literature are John Pendleton Kennedy's *Swallow Barn, or a Sojourn in the Old Dominion* (1832) and Martha S. Gielow's postbellum *Mammy's Reminiscences and Other Sketches* (1898). Harriet Beecher Stowe's *Uncle Tom's Cabin* (1851–52) combines minstrel images with melodramatic and sentimental narrative modes.

40. Blassingame, *Slave Community*, 134.

41. Boskin, *Sambo*, 75–76.

42. Robert G. O'Meally, "Checking Our Balances: Louis Armstrong, Ralph Ellison, and Betty Boop," in O'Meally, Edwards, and Griffin, *Uptown Conversation*, 279.

43. Armstrong, "Jewish Family," 20–21.

44. *Satchmo: Louis Armstrong, Historical Live Performance and Interview.*

45. See Sanders, "Louis Armstrong," 136; a letter to Leonard Feather from Sept. 18, 1941, is written on personalized stationery.

46. Ralph Ellison, "On Bird, Bird-Watching and Jazz," *Saturday Review*, July 28, 1962, in Callahan, *Collected Essays of Ralph Ellison*, 257.

47. In the Aug. 1932 edition of *Melody Maker*, Dan S. Ingman acknowledged that "Satchmo" is "a contraction, I am told, of 'Satchel Mouth,'" but others dipped deeply into the minstrel poetics, especially its primitivist variants, to make sense of Armstrong's arrival in England. An advertising poster for his 1932 appearance at the London Palladium depicted him "as a tuxedo-clad monkey blowing a horn"; the journalist Hannen Swaffer wrote in the *Daily Herald* on July 18, 1932, that "Armstrong is the ugliest man I have seen on the music hall stage. He looks, and

behaves, like an untrained gorilla. He might have come straight from some African jungle and thereafter to a slop tailor's for a ready-made dress suit, been put on the stage and been told to sing." Writing substantially later, Wilfred Lowe opined in the British *Jazz Journal* in 1954: "His concerts seldom rise above the plane of a coon carnival." See Dan S. Ingman, "England's Welcome to Louis Armstrong," *Melody Maker*, Aug. 1932, in Berrett, *Louis Armstrong Companion*, 55. Swaffer is quoted in Berrett, *Louis Armstrong Companion*, 50; the poster is described in Nollen, *Louis Armstrong*, 43; Lowe is quoted in Riccardi, *What a Wonderful World*, 106.

48. Qtd. in Cockrell, *Demons of Disorder*, 21.

49. See James H. Dormon, "Shaping the Popular Image of Post-Reconstruction American Blacks: The 'Coon Song' Phenomenon of the Gilded Age," *American Quarterly* 40.4 (1988): 453.

50. The illustrations are reproduced in Kenneth W. Goings, *Mammy and Uncle Mose: Black Collectibles and American Stereotyping* (Bloomington: Indiana University Press, 1994), n.p.

51. Dormon, "Shaping the Popular Image," 455.

52. The advertisement is mentioned in Millstein, "Africa Harks to Satch's Horn," 66; the toilet bowl reference is quoted in Bergreen, *Louis Armstrong*, 113. Not all of these references conjured up images of minstrelsy; in an article in *Down Beat*, Armstrong talks about the physical strain that his virtuoso trumpet playing had exerted on his lips. See "'My Chops Was Beat—But I'm Dying to Swing Again," *Down Beat*, June 1935, in Alkyer, *Down Beat*, 22.

53. Hoagy Carmichael, *The Stardust Road* and *Sometimes I Wonder: The Autobiographies of Hoagy Carmichael*, ed. John Edward Hasse (New York: Da Capo, 1999), 140.

54. Armstrong and Crosby, *Fun with Bing and Louis*, broadcast on Mar. 16, 1949.

55. Dormon, "Shaping the Popular Image," 466.

56. Ibid., 452.

57. For a reproduction of the sheet music cover, see J. Stanley Lemons, "Black Stereotypes as Reflected in Popular Culture, 1880–1920," *American Quarterly* 29.1 (1977): 105.

58. The lyrics are quoted in Dormon, "Shaping the Popular Image," 452, 456.

59. Qtd. in Jones and Chilton, *Louis*, 214.

60. See Henry Louis Gates Jr., "The Trope of a New Negro and the Reconstruction of the Image of the Black," *Representations* 24 (1988): 129, 136–37. Black composers and lyricists such as Will Marion Cook, Paul Laurence Dunbar, Bob Cole, J. Rosamond Johnson, James Weldon Johnson, Alex Rogers, and Jesse Shipp expressly set out "to clean up the caricature of the black race" (J. Rosamond Johnson qtd. in Lemons, "Black Stereotypes," 115). For an intellectual history of the Harlem Renaissance and the function of music as a source of cultural memory, see Paul Allen Anderson, *Deep River: Music and Memory in Harlem Renaissance Thought* (Durham: Duke University Press, 2001).

61. I follow Eric Lott's understanding of a "love-and-theft" dialectic inherent in

blackface minstrelsy; Berndt Ostendorf's notion of the minstrels' work as an example of "[a]ppreciation and caricature"; and David Roediger's view of minstrelsy as an emblem of "considerable ambiguity, including the presence of subtexts and the simultaneous identification with, and repulsion from, the blackfaced character." See Lott, *Love and Theft*, 6; Berndt Ostendorf, "Minstrelsy and Early Jazz," *Massachusetts Review* 20.3 (1979): 579; David R. Roediger, *The Wages of Whiteness: Race and the Making of the American Working Class*, rev. ed. (London: Verso, 1999), 124.

62. Gates, "Trope of a New Negro," 130.

63. Harry Elam speaks of a "productive ambivalence" according to which black entertainers and actors created slippages through excessive performances in order to "renegotiate the meanings of blackness." The notion of "ambivalence," however, seems too closely focused on the perspective of the performer, whereas the conception of ambiguity acknowledges the many-faceted meanings of cultural resonances that are enabled by the performances but ultimately lie beyond performer's control. See Harry J. Elam Jr., "The Black Performer and the Performance of Blackness: *The Escape; or, A Leap to Freedom* by William Wells Brown and *No Place To Be Somebody* by Charles Gordone," in *African American Performance and Theater History: A Critical Reader*, ed. Harry J. Elam Jr. and David Krasner (New York: Oxford University Press, 2001), 288. Elam's views are preceded by Ostendorf's comments on the "ambivalent interpretability" of African American cultural performances. See Berndt Ostendorf, "Black Poetry, Blues, and Folklore: Double Consciousness in Afro-American Oral Culture," *Amerikastudien/American Studies* 20.2 (1975): 209–59.

64. Berndt Ostendorf, "Is American Culture Jazz-Shaped? African American Rules of Performance," in *Satchmo and Amadeus*, ed. Reinhold Wagnleitner (Innsbruck: Studienverlag, 2006), 270.

65. There is also a duet of "Rockin' Chair" with Jack Teagarden on which Armstrong responds to Teagarden's "I'll tan your hide" with the obbligato "my hide's already tanned," and there is his quip that "we give to 'em in black and white" right before he and Johnny Cash launch into "Blue Yodel No. 9" on the *Johnny Cash Show* in 1970. The performance of "Rockin' Chair" is included on Giddins and Simmons, *Masters of American Music: Satchmo*.

66. Armstrong, "Jewish Family," 30. Brothers suggest that Armstrong misspelled "flour" as "flower" (*In His Own Words*, 212).

67. On the transition from folk-rural to folk-urban culture, see Richard A. Long, "Louis Armstrong and African-American Culture," in Miller, *Louis Armstrong*, 67–93.

68. See Miller, "Louis Armstrong: A Cultural Legacy," 23. The earliest known depiction of a jazz band on the cover of the *Mascot* (Nov. 15, 1890) showed "a nigger brass band." See Al Rose, *Storyville, New Orleans: Being an Authentic, Illustrated Account of the Notorious Red-Light District* (University: University of Alabama Press, 1974), 104.

69. See Brothers, *Louis Armstrong's New Orleans*, 228.

70. See W. C. Handy, *Father of the Blues*, ed. Arna Bontemps (1941; New York: Collier, 1970); Garvin Bushell, as told to Mark Tucker, *Jazz from the Beginning* (Ann Arbor: University of Michigan Press, 1988). Armstrong owned a copy of *Father of the Blues*. Handy visited Armstrong and the All Stars in their Columbia studio when they recorded the tribute album *Louis Armstrong Plays W. C. Handy*.

71. Oscar "Chicken" Henry qtd. in Buerkle and Barker, *Bourbon Street Black*, 60; Armstrong, "Satchmo Story," 125.

72. See Brothers, *Louis Armstrong's New Orleans*, 156.

73. Armstrong, *Swing That Music*, 13, 4; Zutty Singleton qtd. in Williams, *Jazz Masters of New Orleans*, 164.

74. See Goffin, *Horn of Plenty*, 44.

75. Ellington, *Music Is My Mistress*, 441. Ellington's position vis-à-vis the minstrel poetics and primitivist modernism is too complex to be discussed here. The most comprehensive picture of Ellington is drawn in Harvey G. Cohen, *Duke Ellington's America* (Chicago: University of Chicago Press, 2010); on Ellington as a writer, see Brent Hayes Edwards, "The Literary Ellington," *Representations* 77 (Winter 2002): 1–29; on Ellington and questions of cultural difference, see Paul Allen Anderson, "Ellington, Rap Music, and Cultural Difference," *Musical Quarterly* 79.1 (1995): 172–206.

76. Ogren, *Jazz Revolution*, 8.

77. Armstrong, "Satchmo Story," 117; Armstrong, "Armstrong Story," 49; Armstrong, "Goffin Notebooks," 91. For a selection of photos that depict Armstrong as a snazzy musical star in the 1920s and 1930s, see Cogswell, *Louis Armstrong*, 11, 116, 117, 139, 167; Miller, *Louis Armstrong*, 16, 36, 37, 49, 52, 53, 57, 62, 66, 186.

78. Armstrong, "Satchmo Story," 119; Armstrong, "Satchmo Says," 237. On one of his tapes, he refers to the members of the Henderson band as "big magaffas" and "prima donnas" with "too much airs and all that shit" (Armstrong, "Max Jones 1").

79. Ogren, *Jazz Revolution*, 57, 78.

80. Lewis A. Erenberg, *Steppin' Out: New York Nightlife and the Transformation of American Culture, 1890–1930* (Westport: Greenwood, 1981), 254.

81. Travis Dempsey, *An Autobiography of Black Jazz* (Chicago: Urban Research Institute, 1983), 41.

82. Madden qtd. in Alan Pomerance, *Repeal of the Blues: How Black Entertainers Influenced Civil Rights* (1988; New York: Citadel, 1991), 4. Armstrong played at the New York Cotton Club in 1939. See Jim Haskins, *The Cotton Club* (1977; New York: Hippocrene, 1994), 151, 153.

83. The black band leader Dave Peyton discusses Armstrong's appearance at the Sunset Café in one of his columns for the *Chicago Defender*. See "Musical Bunch," *Chicago Defender* (national ed.), Apr. 10, 1926, 6. The handbill that announces "Minstrel Days" is reproduced in Kenney, *Chicago Jazz*, 44.

84. The Hirschfeld drawing is reproduced in Miller, *Louis Armstrong*, 113.

85. The minstrel shows featured an interlocutor who engaged in comic dia-

logues with the two endmen seated at the left and right ends of the semicircle, whose names were Tambo (as in tambourine) and Bones (as in bone castanets).

86. The discourse of "hot jazz" that structured early jazz reception and delivered the name for Armstrong's Hot Five and Hot Seven was prefigured by the debates about ragtime. See Ronald Radano, "Hot Fantasies: American Modernism and the Idea of Black Rhythm," in *Music and the Racial Imagination*, ed. Ronald Radano and Philip V. Bohlman (Chicago: University of Chicago Press, 2000), 459–80.

87. The joke about Massey's performance of Abraham Lincoln in Robert E. Sherwood's *Abe Lincoln in Illinois* play (1938) can be heard on *Louis Armstrong: 100th Anniversary*. The comedy routine with Crosby was broadcast on Dec. 27, 1950; see Armstrong and Crosby, *Fun with Bing and Louis*.

88. Okeh Phonograph Corp., race record advertising of "St. James Infirmary," Dec. 1928, reproduced in Collier, *Louis Armstrong*, n.p. Advertisements for Armstrong's shows and records did not always follow the minstrel mode. See the advertisements and newspaper announcements reproduced in Miller, *Louis Armstrong*, 29, 72, 102, 118, 130; Cogswell, *Louis Armstrong*, 28, 70.

89. In the minstrel shows, the Sambo figure had become diversified into two images of comical "blackness," mirroring the growing urbanization of American society and the migration of African Americans to the North: the "plantation darky" and the "urban dandy." Alan W. C. Green describes a "dandy darky or flashy northern city Negro with his big talk, flashy clothes and devastating ways with the women. The plantation or 'Jim Crow' Negro [. . .] spoke the same dialect as his city cousin, but he was as ragged as the dandy was foppish. [. . .] Once an evening a speech was delivered with great pomposity by one of the dandies, in the course of which he demonstrated abysmal ignorance of language and subject matter." See Alan W. C. Green, "'Jim Crow,' 'Zip Coon': The Northern Origins of Negro Minstrelsy," *Massachusetts Review* (Spring 1970): 392. "Long Tail Blue," composed by George Washington Dixon or William Pennington around 1827, was among the first minstrel songs caricaturing the black dandy.

90. Peretti, *Creation of Jazz*, 186.

91. Sam Dennison finds two subgenres of songs with Southern themes in American music: compositions that celebrate the harmonious relationship between master and slave (or ex-master and ex-slave) and promote images of plaintive and easygoing plantation life (or life in the postbellum era), which he calls "magnolia-theme" songs, and compositions that voice the runaway or freed slave's desire to return to the plantation, which he labels "carry-me-back" songs. See Sam Dennison, *Scandalize My Name: Black Imagery in American Popular Music* (New York: Garland, 1982), 64, 65.

92. Jim Crow hilarity appears on songs such as "I'll Be Glad When You're Dead You Rascal You" (Nov. 16, 1941), where Armstrong delivers humorous verbal insults against the adulterer who has seduced the singer's wife.

93. Armstrong, "Satchmo Story," 116.

94. James Weldon Johnson, *Black Manhattan* (1930; New York: Arno, 1968), 93; Beverly Smith, "Harlem—Negro City," *New York Herald Tribune*, Feb. 10, 1930.

95. Armstrong, "Calypso from *High Society,*" *Louis Armstrong: Fleischmann's Yeast Show & Louis' Home-Recorded Tapes*. In the movie, the musicians play themselves, and Armstrong is both a character in the diegesis, where he has little social interaction with the white Newport socialites, and a meta-reflexive figure who, like the Greek chorus in drama, introduces the action, comments on the development of the plot, and concludes the film with a final statement.

96. Qtd. in Nollen, *Louis Armstrong*, 51. My reading of *Pennies from Heaven* is partially indebted to Krin Gabbard's analysis in *Jammin' at the Margins*, 216–17.

97. Armstrong, *Swing That Music*, 8, 26, 41 (emphasis added).

98. Armstrong, "Jazz on a High Note," 128.

99. Armstrong, *Satchmo*, 140; Armstrong qtd. in Shapiro and Hentoff, *Hear Me Talkin' to Ya*, 185; Armstrong, "Goffin Notebooks," 104, 84. For minstrel variants of "yes, sir" and "no, sir," see Armstrong, *Swing That Music*, 26, 41; Armstrong, "Jewish Family," 26, 28; Armstrong, "Armstrong Story," 61, 65, 71; Armstrong, "Goffin Notebooks," 92, 93; Armstrong, "Jazz on a High Note," 136. The phrase "shucks" appears in Armstrong, "Goffin Notebooks," 84, 85, 86; Armstrong, "Satchmo Story," 115. Armstrong also recorded the Dowell/Razaf composition "Yes Suh!" (Apr. 11, 1941).

100. Armstrong, "Goffin Notebooks," 102; Armstrong, *Satchmo*, 45; Armstrong qtd. in Collier, *Louis Armstrong*, 177.

101. Qtd. in Collier, *Louis Armstrong*, 314.

102. Qtd. in Bergreen, *Louis Armstrong*, 154–55.

103. One photograph of Armstrong with the Fate Marable Band on the S.S. *Capitol* was taken by Arthur P. Bedou around 1920; it is reproduced in Miller, *Louis Armstrong*, 27.

104. The photographs are reproduced in Miller, *Louis Armstrong*, 192.

105. "Latin Blowout for Louis," *Life*, Nov. 25, 1957, 170.

106. Photographer unknown, in Armstrong, "Why I Like Dark Women," 65. The Aunt Jemima figure emerged as a postbellum stock character but has its roots in depictions of the slave mammy in the antebellum era. The figure began as a deferential and happy house slave responsible for child rearing and cooking and became the rotund, matronly, and faithful servant of postbellum advertising. Aunt Jemima is an asexual figure, a member of the slave owner's extended family who poses no threat to the slave system. She is not a real aunt, but a black mother surrogate for the slave owner's children.

107. The tape cover is reproduced in Brower, *Satchmo*, 126.

108. Taubman, "Satchmo Wears His Crown Gaily," 12.

109. The photograph is reproduced in Brower, *Satchmo*, 39.

110. King, "Everybody's Louie," 69.

111. Armstrong, "Joe Oliver Is Still King," 38.

112. See Stearns, *Story of Jazz*, 5.

113. Meryman, "Authentic American Genius," 108. When Buck Clayton asked him about a certain trumpet technique, Armstrong replied: "I'll show you how I do it, but if we were down in New Orleans, I wouldn't. In New Orleans whenever I did it, I'd put a handkerchief over my valves so nobody could see how I did it, but you follow me and I'll show you." Buck Clayton, assisted by Nancy Miller Elliott, *Buck Clayton's Jazz World* (1986; New York: Oxford University Press, 1989), 46.

114. Brothers reproduces a photograph of a river baptism from the 1940s in which the clergymen wear white handkerchiefs on their heads. See Brothers, *Louis Armstrong's New Orleans*, 34.

115. Armstrong to Feather, Oct. 1, 1941, 112.

116. Mezz Mezzrow notes how Armstrong's use of handkerchiefs in the late 1920s "started a real fad—before long all the kids on the Avenue were running up to him with white handkerchiefs in their hands too, to show how much they loved him" (qtd. in Jones and Chilton, *Louis*, 165).

117. Robert C. Toll, *Blacking Up: The Minstrel Show in Nineteenth-Century America* (New York: Oxford University Press, 1974), 28.

118. Qtd. in ibid., 28. Rice's recollection was presented in print by Robert P. Nevin in the *Atlantic Monthly* ("Stephen C. Foster and Negro Minstrelsy," Nov. 20, 1867, 606–16), decades after the event had supposedly taken place.

119. Goffin, *Horn of Plenty*, 44.

120. Arthur Knight, *Disintegrating the Musical: Black Performance and American Musical Film* (Durham: Duke University Press, 2002), 55.

121. Johnny St. Cyr qtd. in Mike Pinfold, *Louis Armstrong: His Life and Times* (New York: Universe, 1987), 26.

122. Qtd. in Knight, *Disintegrating the Musical*, 54–55.

123. Qtd. in Shapiro and Hentoff, *Hear Me Talkin' to Ya*, 105; Meryman, *Louis Armstrong—A Self- Portrait*, 36. Armstrong also played at the Lafayette and the Apollo in Harlem, which featured entertainment for African American audiences. Whether this entertainment differed substantially from downtown performances for white audiences is a matter of controversy. For conflicting assessments, see Watkins, *On the Real Side*, 385–88; Nathan Irvin Huggins, *Harlem Renaissance* (New York: Oxford University Press, 1971), 291.

124. On the acrobatic jazz dancing of the 1920s, see Brian Harker, "Louis Armstrong, Eccentric Dance, and the Evolution of Jazz on the Eve of Swing," *Journal of the American Musicological Society* 61.1 (2008): 67–122.

125. Armstrong, "Jewish Family," 11.

126. Qtd. in Shapiro and Hentoff, *Hear Me Talkin' to Ya*, 106.

127. Goffin, *Horn of Plenty*, 45. Goffin's "toute bouche ouverte avec les dents les plus blanches et les plus régulières" was translated by James Bezou as "lips drawn back to show the pearliest set of teeth in Dixie." The minstrel reference is present

in Goffin's version (the white teeth) but is emphasized by Bezou's inclusion of "Dixie" as a code for the minstrel South. Robert Goffin, *Le roi du jazz* (Paris: Éditions Pierre Seghers, 1947), 53; Goffin, *Horn of Plenty*, 45.

128. Qtd. in Bergreen, *Louis Armstrong*, 77.

Chapter 5

1. Armstrong, *Satchmo*, 7–8.

2. Ibid., 75, 76.

3. Ibid., 76, 78.

4. Meryman, *Louis Armstrong—A Self-Portrait*, 20–21.

5. Ralph Ellison, "A Very Stern Discipline," interview, *Harper's Magazine*, Mar. 1967, in Callahan, *Collected Writings of Ralph Ellison*, 734.

6. Armstrong, *Satchmo*, 115, 202.

7. Armstrong, "Jewish Family," 20.

8. Armstrong, *Satchmo*, 26.

9. Meryman, "Authentic American Genius," 110.

10. Armstrong, "Jewish Family," 9.

11. The recording is included on *Bert Williams: The Middle Years, 1910–1918* (Archeophone, 2002–5); the illustration is reproduced in the booklet. Williams also starred in the film *A Natural Born Gambler* (dir. Bert Williams, 1916).

12. Armstrong, *Swing That Music*, 3; Armstrong, *Satchmo*, 25.

13. Armstrong, *Swing That Music*, 3; Armstrong, *Satchmo*, 25–26.

14. Toni Morrison, "City Limits, Village Values: Concepts of the Neighborhood in Black Fiction," in *Literature and the Urban Experience: Essays on the City and Literature*, ed. Michael C. Jaye and Ann Chalmers Watts (New Brunswick: Rutgers University Press, 1981), 39; Toni Morrison, "Rootedness: The Ancestor in Afro-American Fiction," in *Black Women Writers (1950–1980): A Critical Evaluation*, ed. Mari Evans (New York: Anchor, 1984), 343.

15. Farah Jasmine Griffin writes: "The ancestor is present in ritual, religion, music, food, and performance. His or her legacy is evident in discursive formations like the oral tradition." Farah Jasmine Griffin, *"Who Set You Flowin'?" The African-American Migration Narrative* (New York: Oxford University Press, 1995), 5. See also Guthrie Ramsey's notion of "Southernisms," retentions of Southern cultural and musical practices that shaped modern American race music. Guthrie P. Ramsey Jr., *Race Music: Black Cultures from Bebop to Hip-Hop* (Berkeley: University of California Press, 2003), 29.

16. Virginia Richter, "Laughter and Aggression: Desire and Derision in a Postcolonial Context," in *Cheeky Fictions: Laughter and the Postcolonial*, ed. Susanne Reichl and Mark Stein (Amsterdam: Rodopi, 2005), 64.

17. Susanne Reichl and Mark Stein, introduction to Reichl and Stein, *Cheeky Fictions*, 9.

18. Bart Moore-Gilbert's analysis of postcolonial forms of life writing raises many of the issues discussed throughout my analysis of Armstrong's intermedial autobiographics: the tension between centered and decentered selves; the existence of an autobiographical self that is relational, embodied, and located in a specific environment; the tendency of postcolonial productions to cross generic boundaries; the use of non-Western narrative resources; and the political efficacy of postcolonial life writing. See Bart Moore-Gilbert, *Postcolonial Life-Writing: Culture, Politics and Self-Representation* (New York: Routledge, 2009).

19. Michael Rogin, *Blackface, White Noise: Jewish Immigrants in the Hollywood Melting Pot* (Berkeley: University of California Press, 1996), 23.

20. Reichl and Stein, introduction, 14.

21. Alfred Hornung and Ernstpeter Ruhe, preface to *Postcolonialism and Autobiography* (Amsterdam: Rodopi, 1998), 1. I take the phrase "elastic polarity" from Joseph Boskin, *Rebellious Laughter: People's Humor in American Culture* (1997; New York: Syracuse University Press, 2002), 38.

22. Armstrong, *Satchmo*, 163.

23. Armstrong, "Forward"; see also Meryman, *Louis Armstrong—A Self-Portrait*, 41. He also mentions the music-and-dance duo Buck and Bubbles (Ford Lee Washington and John William Sublett), who starred with him in *A Song Is Born*. See Armstrong to Evans, Sept. 31, 1967. That he also enjoyed the comic clumsiness of white actors is illustrated by a remark about "my favorite movie comedian, Stan Laurel" (Armstrong, *Satchmo*, 188). On Armstrong's role in American film, see also Gabbard, *Jammin' at the Margins*; Bogle, "Louis Armstrong: The Films."

24. Armstrong, "Open Letter to Fans," 183.

25. Ibid., 183–84.

26. For James Weldon Johnson, the tone and timbre of the trombone "represent the old-time Negro preacher's voice." Qtd. in Brent Hayes Edwards, "An Essential Element in the Voice of Jazz," *New York Times*, July 22, 2001. See also Johnson's *God's Trombones: Seven Negro Sermons in Verse* (New York: Viking, 1927) and Ellison's characterization of Reverend A. Z. Hickman as "God's Trombone." See Ralph Ellison, *Juneteenth*, ed. John F. Callahan (New York: Random House, 1999), 3.

27. Armstrong, "Goffin Notebooks," 85. He makes the same joke in "Armstrong Story," 61.

28. Bernhardt, *I Remember*, 91.

29. Armstrong, "Jewish Family," 27.

30. Langston Hughes, ed., *The Book of Negro Humor* (New York: Dodd, 1966), 115–17; see Armstrong, *Satchmo*, 91–93.

31. Qtd. in Jones and Chilton, *Louis*, 227.

32. Armstrong, *Joke Book*. The version of the *Joke Book* at the Louis Armstrong House Museum does not include Robinson's funeral anecdote.

33. Armstrong, "Jewish Family," 27–28.

34. Bergreen, *Louis Armstrong*, 247. According to Morgenstern, Fletcher Hen-

derson allowed Armstrong to do an imitation of Bert Williams in 1924. See Dan Morgenstern, "Louis Armstrong and the Development and Diffusion of Jazz," in Miller, *Louis Armstrong*, 103.

35. Russell, "Louis Armstrong," 129–30.

36. Goffin, *Horn of Plenty*, 128.

37. Qtd. in Rex Stewart, *Jazz Masters of the 30s* (1972; New York: Da Capo, 1983), 48.

38. The performances are collected on *Louis and the Good Book*; Williams's originals are available on *Bert Williams: His Final Releases, 1919–22* (Archeophone, 2001–4).

39. The performance is included on *Louis Armstrong: St. Louis Blues*.

40. Ralph Ellison, "Remembering Jimmy," *Saturday Review*, July 12, 1958, in Callahan, *Collected Essays of Ralph Ellison*, 275.

41. Qtd. in Charles Hamm, *Yesterdays: Popular Song in America* (New York: Norton, 1979), 114. The sheet music cover of "Sambo's Address" features a black preacher wearing the dandy's long tail blue and sporting huge teeth and thick lips. See Dennison, *Scandalize My Name*, 42.

42. See Pigmeat Markham, "The Crap-Shootin' Rev" and "Preachin' the Blues," ca. 1960s, on *The Crap-Shootin' Rev* (Fuel 2000 Records, 2005); Richard Pryor, "Eulogy" and "Our Text for Today," on *. . . is it something i said?* (1975; Reprise/Warner, n.d.); Martin Lawrence, "Open with Rev. Ford" on *Funk it!!* (Eastwest, 1995).

43. Additional performances are "You'll Never Need a Doctor No More" (1920), in which Deacon Jones is the victim of a quack doctor, and "Brother Low Down" (1921), which is set in New Orleans and features the money-hungry Parson Brown. For reproductions of sheet music covers reminiscent of the "coon" era, see Richard Martin and Meagan Hennessey, liner notes, *Bert Williams: His Final Releases, 1919–1922*.

44. Bergreen, *Louis Armstrong*, 391; Gabbard, "Reissuing *Louis and the Good Book*," *Louis and the Good Book* (Verve, 2001), n.p.

45. Williams explained his comedic techniques and philosophy in "The Comic Side of Trouble," *American Magazine*, Jan. 1918, reprinted in the booklet included with *Bert Williams: The Middle Years*, 11–19. For analysis of Williams's complicated life and career, see Louis Chude-Sokei, *The Last "Darky": Bert Williams, Black-on-Black Minstrelsy, and the African Diaspora* (Durham: Duke University Press, 2006). Bill Robinson's life also had its tragic moments. In a *Metronome* article, Armstrong recalled seeing him in tears backstage. See Bill Coss and Herb Snitzer, "On the Road with Louis Armstrong," *Metronome*, Dec. 1960, 13.

46. The second sermon, "Elder Eatmore's Sermon on Generosity," mocks the Elder's financial greed (the text is "The Lord Loveth a cheerful giver," but "tonight, my friends, you can omit the cheerful"), as well as his lusting after culinary and sexual favors ("Sister Jones—yeah, tomorrow? Chicken? Chicken? Chicken? I'll be there").

47. Armstrong to L/Cpl. Villec, 170.

48. Ibid., 170.

49. Armstrong's recollection of his mother's conversion during a sermon led by Elder Cozy similarly combines humorous elements with a serious depiction of religious practices. See Armstrong, *Satchmo*, 31–32.

50. See Garrett, *Struggling to Define a Nation*, 83, 87. See also Peretti, *The Creation of Jazz*, chaps. 3 and 4; Kenney, *Chicago Jazz*, chaps. 1 and 2.

51. Qtd. in Griffin, *"Who Set You Flowin'?"* 49.

52. My approach differs somewhat from Charles Hiroshi Garrett's analysis of Armstrong's "Gully Low Blues" (May 4, 1927) in his chapter "Louis Armstrong and the Great Migration," in *Struggling to Define a Nation*, 83–120. Garrett reads the recording as a sonic articulation of the migration experience, while I focus on the minstrel resonances that Armstrong's performances also produce.

53. Alain Locke, ed., *The New Negro* (1925; New York: Touchstone-Schuster, 1997), 6.

54. I take the terms "verbal minstrelsy" and "sonic blackface" from Watkins, *On the Real Side*, 293; Knight, *Disintegrating the Musical*, 92.

55. James Oliver Horton, "Humor and the American Racial Imagination," *American Quarterly* 45.1 (1993): 167. See also Melvin Patrick Ely, *The Adventures of Amos 'n' Andy: A Social History of an American Phenomenon* (1991; Charlottesville: University of Virginia Press, 2001).

56. Watkins, *On the Real Side*, 275.

57. Armstrong, *Satchmo*, 190–91.

58. Armstrong, "Goffin Notebooks," 83–84.

59. Qtd. in King, "Everybody's Louie," 62.

60. Robert C. Toll, *On with the Show! The First Century of Show Business in America* (New York: Oxford University Press, 1976), 86.

61. Meryman, "Authentic American Genius," 110. Armstrong's reference to his underwear is corroborated by drummer Kaiser Marshall. See Marshall, "When Armstrong Came to Town," 85.

62. Goffin, *Horn of Plenty*, 139; Armstrong, "Goffin Notebooks," 84.

63. Griffin, *"Who Set You Flowin'?"* 3.

64. Armstrong, *Satchmo*, 191; Meryman, "Authentic American Genius," 110.

65. Armstrong, *Satchmo*, 229–30.

66. Armstrong, "Armstrong Story," 67; Armstrong, "Satchmo Story," 112.

67. Armstrong, "Armstrong Story," 55, 64; Armstrong, "Goffin Notebooks," 86, 84.

68. Redman qtd. in Collier, *Louis Armstrong*, 125; Marshall, "When Armstrong Came to Town," 83; Henderson qtd. in Jones and Chilton, *Louis*, 99; Hardin-Armstrong qtd. in Jones and Chilton, *Louis*, 79. These statements exemplify what James Gregory describes as the "lasting discursive connection between the North and respectability, the South and backwardness." See James N. Gregory, *The Southern Diaspora: How the Great Migration of Black and White Southerners Transformed America* (Chapel Hill: University of North Carolina Press, 2005), 123.

69. Stewart, *Jazz Masters of the 30s*, 44; Clayton, *Buck Clayton's Jazz World*, 36.

70. Armstrong, "Armstrong Story," 54.

71. Ibid., 50.

72. Ralph Ellison, "Richard Wright's Blues," *Antioch Review* (Summer 1945), in Callahan, *Collected Essays of Ralph Ellison*, 138.

73. "They Cross Iron Curtain," 59. On the significance of the Southern home in African American literature, see also my essay "Walter Mosley's *RL's Dream* and the Creation of a Bluetopian Community," in *Finding a Way Home: A Critical Assessment of Walter Mosley's Fiction*, ed. Owen E. Brady and Derek C. Maus (Jackson: University Press of Mississippi, 2008), 3–17.

74. Barney Bigard, *With Louis and the Duke: The Autobiography of a Jazz Clarinetist*, ed. Barry Martyn (1980; London: Macmillan, 1985), 123–24. See also Riccardi, *What a Wonderful World*, 59–61.

75. Armstrong, "Daddy, How the Country Has Changed!" 81.

76. He did something similar when he introduced his recording of "Mack the Knife" (Sept. 28, 1955) with the words "Dig, man, there goes Mack the Knife" and told Richard Meryman that he had "seen many a cat in New Orleans lying around with a knife to slip in your back and take your money" ("Authentic American Genius," 116).

77. Griffin, *"Who Set You Flowin'?"* 52.

78. Ralph Ellison, "The Golden Age, Time Past," *Esquire*, Jan. 1959, in Callahan, *Collected Essays of Ralph Ellison*, 238.

79. The soundie is included on *Louis Armstrong: St. Louis Blues*.

80. I spell out this argument in "Hearing, Seeing, and Writing Thelonious Monk: Toward a Theory of Changing Iconotexts," *Amerikastudien/American Studies* 50.4 (2005): 603–27.

81. Locke, *New Negro*, 6. Locke discusses *Swing That Music* a decade later in *The Negro and His Music*.

82. See Teachout, *Pops*, 312.

83. Brothers, *Louis Armstrong's New Orleans*, 83; Adams and Taylor are quoted in Riccardi, *What a Wonderful World*, 35, 189.

84. "Louis the First," *Time*, Feb. 21, 1949.

85. Feather, *From Satchmo to Miles*, 28.

86. Brothers, *Louis Armstrong's New Orleans*, 81.

87. Armstrong to Leonard Feather, June 29, 1953, Louis Armstrong House Museum.

88. See Brothers, *Louis Armstrong's New Orleans*, 211–13; Robin D. G. Kelley, *Race Rebels: Culture, Politics, and the Black Working Class*, 1994 (New York: Free Press, 1996), 38–39.

89. See also "History of the Zulu Aid & Pleasure Club," http://www.kreweofzulu.com/history/.

90. Armstrong to Feather, June 29, 1953; "'Satchmo' Rules Mardi Gras Carnival as 'Zulu King,'" *Chicago Defender* (national ed.), Mar. 12, 1949, 1.

91. I take the phrase "double-edged symbolism" from Brothers, *Louis Armstrong's New Orleans*, 81.

92. "Head Hunters on the Loose," *New Orleans Times-Picayune*, qtd. in Bergreen, *Louis Armstrong*, 443–44. The article later explains that "to kill a few" relates to the drinking of alcoholic beverages, but the discourse evoked here is nonetheless that of a minstrel-inflected primitivism.

93. The correspondent for the *Chicago Defender* found that the musician's willingness to appear "grotesquely made up [. . .] struck a queer note" ("'Satchmo' Rules Mardi Gras Carnival," 2).

94. Zulu Aid and Pleasure Club Mardi Gras Poster, Feb. 1949, reproduced in Miller, *Louis Armstrong*, 130.

95. See Bert Williams, *The Early Years, 1901–1909* (Archeophone, 2004). The sheet music cover is reproduced in Allen G. Debus and Richard Martin's liner notes, 10. Songs such as "My Pretty Zulu Lu" and "My Princess Zulu Lu" (both 1902) painted primitive and animalistic pictures of blacks in love.

96. Three years before the Hot Five recording, Armstrong had recorded the instrumental tune "Zulus Ball" with King Oliver's Creole Jazz Band (Oct. 5, 1923). Russell's chapter on Armstrong in *Jazzmen* contextualizes "King of the Zulus" as a tribute to the Zulu parades as early as 1939. See Russell, "Louis Armstrong," 132–33.

97. Bergreen, *Louis Armstrong*, 287.

98. Ellison, "What America Would Be Like without Blacks," 580. On the racial ambiguities in the *Betty Boop* cartoon, see O'Meally, "Checking Our Balances."

99. Teachout, *Pops*, 174.

100. Manone and Vandervoot, *Trumpet on the Wing*, 213.

101. The photo-collage is reproduced in Miller, *Louis Armstrong*, 131.

102. Armstrong to Holder, Feb. 9. 1952, 152, 153.

103. See Armstrong, "Goffin Notebooks," 110; Armstrong, "Max Jones 2."

104. Armstrong, *Satchmo*, 69, 127–28, 125. Armstrong discusses his potential appearance as Zulu King in a letter to Frances Church as early as Mar. 10, 1946. In a letter to Feather, he elaborates: "On Mardigras day, everybody do a little masking of some what . . . Even when I was a kid, I'd black my face, pick up on some old ragidy clothes, and burlesque' somebody. . . ." He further details how his mother and father had worn masks at Mardi Gras when he was a child, thus claiming masking and parading as family traditions. See Armstrong to Feather, June 29, 1953.

105. Mikhail Bakhtin, *Rabelais and His World*, 1965, trans. Helene Iswolsky (Cambridge: MIT, 1968), 5.

106. Brothers, *Louis Armstrong's New Orleans*, 81.

107. Reid Mitchell, *All on a Mardi Gras Day: Episodes in the History of New Orleans Carnival* (Cambridge: Harvard University Press, 1995), 151.

108. "They Cross Iron Curtain," 56.

109. I thank Frank Kelleter for this suggestion.

110. Herman briefly talks about the appearance in Woody Herman and Stuart

Troup, *The Woodchopper's Ball: The Autobiography of Woody Herman* (New York: Dutton, 1990), chap. 20. I thank John Szwed for bringing Herman's role as Zulu King to my attention.

111. Ellison, "Change the Joke and Slip the Yoke," *Partisan Review* (Spring 1958), in Callahan, *Collected Essays of Ralph Ellison*, 101, 103, 109.

112. Ellison, "On Bird, Bird-Watching and Jazz," 260; Ellison, "Change the Joke and Slip the Yoke," 108.

113. Ellison, "Change the Joke and Slip the Yoke," 106.

114. Ellison, "On Bird, Bird-Watching and Jazz," 261; Ellison, "The Charlie Christian Story," *Saturday Review*, May 17, 1958, in Callahan, *Collected Essays of Ralph Ellison*, 271; Ellison, "Change the Joke and Slip the Yoke," 106.

115. Meryman, "Authentic American Genius," 116; Armstrong, "Jewish Family," 25; Armstrong, "Satchmo Says," 245.

116. Qtd. in Humphrey Lyttelton, *Second Chorus* (London: Jazz Book Club, 1949), 154.

117. Randal Johnson, "*Editor's Introduction:* Pierre Bourdieu on Art, Literature and Culture," in Pierre Bourdieu, *The Field of Cultural Production: Essays on Art and Literature*, trans. Richard Nice et al., ed. Randal Johnson (New York: Columbia University Press, 1993), 5. Bourdieu defines "habitus" in *The Logic of Practice*, 1980, trans. Richard Nice (Stanford: Stanford University Press, 2006), 53. He speaks of habitus as "second nature" in "Outline of a Sociological Theory of Art Perception," in Bourdieu, *Field of Cultural Production*, 234.

118. Du Bois, *Souls of Black Folk*, 102; Ralph Ellison, "An Extravagance of Laughter," in *Going to the Territory*, 1985, in Callahan, *Collected Essays of Ralph Ellison*, 643. On the trickster figure during slavery, see Levine, *Black Culture and Black Consciousness*, chap. 2.

119. Reichl and Stein, introduction, 10.

120. Ulrike Erichsen, "Smiling in the Face of Adversity: How to Use Humour to Defuse Cultural Conflict," in Reichl and Stein, *Cheeky Fictions*, 32.

Chapter 6

1. Phil Carter, "It's Only Make Believe," *Crisis* 53 (Feb. 1946): 44; Wilfred Lowe is quoted in Riccardi, *What a Wonderful World*, xix.

2. Gabbard, *Jammin' at the Margins*, 235.

3. Qtd. in King, "Everybody's Louie," 66.

4. Gillespie and Fraser, *to BE, or not . . . to BOP*, 295–96.

5. Qtd. in Will Friedwald, *Jazz Singing: America's Great Voices from Bessie Smith to Bebop and Beyond* (New York: Scribner, 1990), 40.

6. Stewart, *Jazz Masters of the 30s*, 42–43.

7. James Baldwin, "Sonny's Blues," in *Going to Meet the Man* (New York: Dial, 1965), 120.

8. In Martin Ritt's *Paris Blues* from 1961, Armstrong is depicted as *the* father

figure and ultimate man of jazz, as a musical authority adored by his Parisian audience.

9. Davis with Troupe, *Miles*, 83.

10. Meryman, "Authentic American Genius," 116; Armstrong qtd. in Sanders, "Louis Armstrong," 142.

11. Qtd. in Sanders, "Louis Armstrong," 142.

12. Ellison, "Golden Age, Time Past," 239.

13. King, "Everybody's Louie," 66; Armstrong, "Daddy, How the Country Has Changed!" 85. One civil rights activist reportedly called Armstrong "a damn handkerchief-headed Uncle Tom." Qtd. in Sanders, "Louis Armstrong," 140.

14. Qtd. in King, "Everybody's Louie," 66. Armstrong expresses his anger through racially explicit slurs such as "'nigger knocking'" and "*Peckerwoods.*"

15. Qtd. in Sanders, "Louis Armstrong," 143; the benefit concert is discussed in Ingrid Monson, *Freedom Sounds: Civil Rights Call Out to Jazz and Africa* (New York: Oxford University Press, 2007), 196. Enoc Waters once compared Armstrong to a "happy go lucky" shoeshine boy who dances and sings for his customers but secretly contributes a large part of his earnings to the NAACP. See Enoc P. Waters Jr., "Adventures in Race Relations," *Chicago Defender* (national ed.), Sept. 28, 1957, 10. See also trombonist Tyree Glenn: "He did a lot of things like that because he loved his people. He wasn't involved in no politics or anything like that, but he loved them and helped them when he could" (qtd. in Phyl Garland, "Taps for Satchmo," *Ebony*, Sept. 1971, 40).

16. Manning Marable, *Race, Reform, and Rebellion: The Second Reconstruction in Black America and Beyond, 1945–2006* (Jackson: University Press of Mississippi, 2007); Thomas Borstelmann, *The Cold War and the Color Line: American Race Relations in the Global Arena* (Cambridge: Harvard University Press, 2001), 93.

17. An early article in *Time* refers to Ellington, Armstrong, and other black band leaders who toured through Europe as "hot ambassadors." See "Hot Ambassador," *Time*, June 12, 1933. Tallulah Bankhead called Armstrong "one of the greatest ambassadors America ever had, having become a synonym for America in many European countries long before the 'cats' on Main Street ever heard of him." See "Tallulah Says Satch Is Really a Genius," *Chicago Defender* (national ed.), Nov. 11, 1950, 20.

18. Felix Belair Jr., "United States Has Secret Sonic Weapon—Jazz," *New York Times*, Nov. 6, 1955.

19. Qtd. in Penny Von Eschen, *Satchmo Blows Up the World: Jazz Ambassadors Play the Cold War* (Cambridge: Harvard University Press, 2004), 15, 16, 17. My discussion of the jazz ambassadors is indebted to Von Eschen's analysis, as well as to Lisa E. Davenport, *Jazz Diplomacy: Promoting America in the Cold War Era* (Jackson: University Press of Mississippi, 2009).

20. Qtd. in Von Eschen, *Satchmo Blows Up the World*, 12.

21. "This Trumpet Madness," *Newsweek*, Dec. 19, 1955. On the hegemonic appeal of American popular culture, see also Reinhold Wagnleitner, "'No Commod-

ity Is Quite So Strange As This Thing Called Cultural Exchange': The Foreign Politics of American Pop Culture Hegemony," in *Popular Culture*, ed. Ulla Haselstein, Peter Scheck, and Berndt Ostendorf, special issue of *Amerikastudien/American Studies* 46.3 (2001): 443–70.

22. Qtd. in Von Eschen, *Satchmo Blows Up the World*, 61. The photograph is reproduced in the booklet of *Satchmo the Great*, 14–15; the tape cover is reproduced in Brower, *Satchmo*, 81.

23. Qtd. in Millstein, "Africa Harks to Satch's Horn," 24.

24. Robert Alden, "Advertising: Akwaaba to Satchmo in Ghana," *New York Times*, Oct. 14, 1960.

25. The slogan is quoted in Alden, "Advertising," 44; photographs of Armstrong's advertising for Pepsi are reproduced in Miller, *Louis Armstrong*, 90; Cogswell, *Louis Armstrong*, 133.

26. On these and related issues, see Reinhold Wagnleitner, *Coca-colonization and the Cold War: The Cultural Mission of the United States in Austria after the Second World War*, trans. Diana M. Wolf (Chapel Hill: University of North Carolina Press, 1994); Reinhold Wagnleitner and Elaine Tyler May, ed., *Here, There, and Everywhere: The Foreign Politics of American Popular Culture* (Hanover: University Press of New England, 2000).

27. Armstrong at the Tahseen Al Saha health center in Cairo, Jan. 1961, photographer unknown; Armstrong tutoring young Africans, West Africa, Jan. 1961, photographer unknown. The photographs are reproduced in Von Eschen, *Satchmo Blows Up the World*, 74, 75; the film clip is included in Giddins and Simmons, *Masters of American Music: Satchmo*.

28. Paul Hofmann, "Satchmo Plays for Congo's Cats: Trumpeter Arrives on Red Throne and Crew of Bearers," *New York Times*, Oct. 29, 1960.

29. Leonard Ingalls, "Armstrong's Horn Wins Nairobi, Too," *New York Times*, Nov. 7, 1960; Von Eschen, *Satchmo Blows Up the World*, 71.

30. Baker, *Modernism and the Harlem Renaissance*, 30.

31. Qtd. in Millstein, "Africa Harks to Satch's Horn," 64.

32. An exception is a statement reported by Cleveland Allen, in which Armstrong explained why he was thinking about moving to Europe for good: "They don't know how to treat a fellow over there [in the United States] if he happens to be black." See Cleveland Allen, "East Hears Louis Armstrong Seeks Divorce from His Wife," *Chicago Defender* (national ed.), Apr. 28, 1934, 8.

33. Armstrong, "Jewish Family," 33, 9, 17.

34. "Louis Armstrong, Barring Soviet Tour, Denounces Eisenhower and Gov. Faubus," *New York Times*, Sept. 19, 1957. Armstrong eventually apologized after Eisenhower intervened in Little Rock. "Things are looking better than they did before," he told the *Chicago Defender*. "Satchmo Blows Sweeter Tune," *Chicago Defender* (national ed.), Oct. 5, 1957, 3.

35. David Margolick, "The Day Louis Armstrong Made Noise," *Grand Forks*

Herald, Sept. 30, 2007. Armstrong also sang a reworded version of the national anthem, substituting the original lyrics with obscenities. See Teachout, *Pops,* 331; Riccardi, *What a Wonderful World,* 162. Armstrong's comments to the *Grand Forks Herald* were covered extensively by the *Chicago Defender:* "Louis Armstrong, Barring Soviet Tour"; "Satch Blows Up over Ark. Crisis," *Chicago Defender* (daily ed.), Sept. 19; "Satch Blast Echoed by Other Performers," *Daily Defender* (daily ed.), Sept. 24, 1957, 18; "Ole 'Satchmo' Shook The World," *Chicago Defender* (national ed.), Oct. 5, 1957, 10. See also Robeson's autobiography, *Here I Stand* (New York: Othello, 1958).

36. Qtd. in Giddins, *Satchmo,* 128; qtd. in Brothers, *In His Own Words,* 194.

37. Qtd. in Nollen, *Louis Armstrong,* 140.

38. Qtd. in Margolick, "Day Louis Armstrong Made Noise."

39. These events are reported in Giddins, *Satchmo,* 127; Von Eschen, *Satchmo Blows Up the World,* 64; Nollen, *Louis Armstrong,* 139; Teachout, *Pops,* 332.

40. Armstrong to Dwight D. Eisenhower, telegram, Sept. 24, 1957, in Brothers, *In His Own Words,* 194.

41. Qtd. in King, "Everybody's Louie," 67.

42. Qtd. in ibid., 66; Armstrong, "Satchmo Says," 244. See also Meryman, "Authentic American Genius," 110. "Knockin' a Jug" (Mar. 5, 1929) by Louis Armstrong and His Orchestra was one of the first racially integrated recordings in jazz.

43. "With Deliberate Speed," *Time,* Sept. 30, 1957.

44. See Armstrong, "Daddy, How the Country Has Changed!" 88.

45. See Borstelmann, *Cold War and the Color Line,* 88.

46. Qtd. in ibid., 94.

47. "Ole 'Satchmo' Shook the World," 10.

48. Borstelmann, *Cold War and the Color Line,* 104, 85.

49. Other black performers and celebrities, including Marian Anderson, Lena Horne, Eartha Kitt, and Jackie Robinson, were more supportive. See "Satch Blast Echoed by Other Performers," 18. Armstrong's records were boycotted by radio stations in the South. See "Aim Dixie Boycott at Satch, Others," *Daily Defender* (daily ed.), Sept. 23, 1957, 3.

50. "Satch Blows Up over Ark. Crisis," 3.

51. Qtd. in Von Eschen, *Satchmo Blows Up the World,* 64; qtd. in Giddins, *Satchmo,* 128.

52. "Trumpeter, in Venezuela, Sees U.S. Negroes Better Off," *New York Times,* Nov. 30, 1957.

53. Armstrong, "Daddy, How the Country Has Changed!" 88; "They Cross Iron Curtain," 58.

54. Armstrong, "Satchmo Says," 243.

55. Qtd. in Michel Boujut, *Louis Armstrong,* trans. Charles Penwarden (New York: Rizzoli, 1998), 78–79.

56. Qtd. in ibid., 60.

57. Von Eschen, *Satchmo Blows Up the World*, 76.

58. LeRoi Jones/Amiri Baraka, *Blues People: Negro Music in White America* (1963; New York: Quill, 1999), 154.

59. Sanders, "Louis Armstrong," 143.

60. Armstrong, "Daddy, How the Country Has Changed!" 82, 84, 81.

61. Ibid., 81, 88. See also a similar statement in Sanders, "Louis Armstrong," 143.

62. Armstrong to Myra Menville, Dec. 23, 1956, qtd. in Kenney, "Negotiating the Color Line," 53.

63. Armstrong, *Satchmo*, 14–15.

64. Ibid., 15.

65. Kelley, *Race Rebels*, 49.

66. Earl Lewis, *In Their Own Interests: Race, Class, and Power in Twentieth-Century Norfolk, Virginia* (Berkeley: University of California Press, 1991), 92.

67. Kelley, *Race Rebels*, 8, 35; James C. Scott, *Weapons of the Weak: Everyday Forms of Peasant Resistance* (New Haven: Yale University Press, 1985); James C. Scott, *Domination and the Arts of Resistance: Hidden Transcripts* (New Haven: Yale University Press, 1990).

68. Armstrong, *Satchmo*, 8, 201; Lewis, *In Their Own Interests*, 92.

69. Armstrong, "Barber Shops," 227.

70. See Cogswell, *Louis Armstrong*, 37.

71. "My Neighbors," late 1960s, photographer unknown; "My Neighborhood Barber," late 1960s, photographer unknown; Joe's Artistic Barber Shop, 1965, photograph by John Loengard. The photographs are reproduced in Cogswell, *Louis Armstrong*, 58, 59, 37.

72. Armstrong, "The Satchmo Story," 119. The "conk" derives its name from the substance "congalene," which consisted of potatoes, eggs, and lye. See Ayana D. Byrd and Lori L. Tharps, *Hair Story: Untangling the Roots of Black Hair in America* (New York: St. Martin's, 2001), 43.

73. Armstrong, "Satchmo Story," 119.

74. Another one of Malcolm X's comments about the conk adds an interesting facet to my earlier discussion of Armstrong's fondness for wearing a handkerchief on his head. About poor black ghetto dwellers, Malcolm X writes, "you'll see a black kerchief over the man's head, like Aunt Jemima; he's trying to make his conk last longer, between trips to the barbershop." See Malcolm X, as told to Alex Haley, *The Autobiography of Malcolm X* (New York: Grove, 1965), 55, 56.

75. Hersch suggests this date in *Subversive Sounds*, 192.

76. See Byrd and Tharps, *Hair Story*, 44.

77. Several examples of "coon" postcards from the early 1900s are reproduced in Gates, "Trope of a New Negro," 153; see also the sheet music cover of Libbie Erickson's "Topsy" (the rascal slave girl from Harriet Beecher Stowe's *Uncle Tom's Cabin*), reproduced in Thomas L. Morgan and William Barlow, *From Cakewalks to*

Concert Halls: An Illustrated History of African American Popular Music from 1895 to 1930 (Washington, D.C.: Elliott and Clark, 1992), 20; Farina's unruly hair in the *Our Gang* short films of the 1920s to the 1940s.

78. Meryman, *Louis Armstrong—A Self-Portrait*, 43.

79. "Louis Armstrong Scores Beating of Selma Negroes," *New York Times*, Mar. 11, 1965; "Armstrong Speaks Out on Racial Injustice," *Down Beat*, Apr. 22, 1965, 14.

80. Qtd. in Boujut, *Louis Armstrong*, 64; Meryman, *Louis Armstrong—A Self-Portrait*, 42.

81. Armstrong's involvement with civil rights is complicated; he recorded the movement's anthem, "We Shall Overcome," on Mar. 29, 1970.

82. The song was composed as "a mock-pathetic joke" by Andy Razaf and Fats Waller at the request of a New York gangster (Arthur Flegenheimer, aka Dutch Schultz), who demanded "minstrel-show-style Negro pathos and received [. . .] a protest song gently ribboned in humor." It attained additional political connotations when Armstrong changed the lyrics and recorded them on July 22, 1929. See O'Meally, "Checking Our Balances," 286, 287.

83. Meryman, "Authentic American Genius," 116.

84. Patricia Willard, "Interview: Trummy Young," Sept. 18 and 20, 1976, in Berrett, *Louis Armstrong Companion*, 174; Armstrong qtd. in Von Eschen, *Satchmo Blows Up the World*, 70; Armstrong qtd. in Morgenstern, "Sixty-fifth Birthday Interview," 56; Armstrong qtd. in Millstein, "Africa Harks to Satch's Horn," 64, 66.

85. Armstrong, "Daddy, How the Country Has Changed!" 86.

86. "Sayings of Satchmo," *Ebony*, Dec. 1959, 87.

87. Reinhold Wagnleitner, "Jazz—The Classical Music of Globalization," in Wagnleitner, *Satchmo Meets Amadeus*, 290.

88. Mitchell, *All on a Mardi Gras Day*, 9.

89. Berndt Ostendorf, "Anthropology, Modernism, and Jazz," in *Ralph Ellison*, ed. Harold Bloom (New York: Chelsea, 1986), 156. On the social and political power of vernacular New Orleans creativity and the practices of creolization that continue to mark the culture of the city, see Roger D. Abrahams, with Nick Spitzer, John F. Szwed, and Robert Farris Thompson, *Blues for New Orleans: Mardi Gras and America's Creole Soul* (Philadelphia: University of Pennsylvania Press, 2006).

90. See "Bomb Ends Louis' Cleveland Date," *Chicago Defender* (national ed.), Mar. 21, 1953, 5; see also Giddins, *Satchmo*, 126.

91. Lawrence Kramer, *Classical Music and Postmodern Knowledge* (1995; Berkeley: University of California Press, 1996), 22.

92. Qtd. in David Halberstam, "A Day with Satchmo," *Jazz Journal* 10 (Aug. 1957): 1.

93. Armstrong, "Daddy, How the Country Has Changed!" 84. The remark to Murrow is captured on Giddins and Simmons, *Masters of American Music: Satchmo*.

94. Blesh, *Shining Trumpets*, 257–58.

95. Peter Dana, "King Louis," *Chicago Defender* (national ed.), June 7, 1941, 20; Garland, "Taps for Satchmo," 36; Richard Meryman, "Satchmo, the Greatest of All, Is Gone," *Life*, July 16, 1971, 70.

96. Qtd. in Miller, "Louis Armstrong: A Portrait Record," 224; a photograph of the statue is reproduced in Miller, *Louis Armstrong*, 227.

Conclusion

1. Ronald Radano, *Lying Up a Nation: Race and Black Music* (Chicago: University of Chicago Press, 2003), 22. Radano borrows the phrase "grain [of the voice]" from Barthes, "Grain of the Voice." The phrase "jes grew" is taken from James Weldon Johnson, *The Book of American Negro Poetry*, 1922, rev. ed. (New York: Harcourt, 1931), 12–13.

2. Radano, *Lying Up a Nation*, 25.

3. Ibid.

4. Sam Tanenhaus, *Louis Armstrong: Musician* (New York: Chelsea, 1988); Dempsey J. Travis, *The Louis Armstrong Odyssey: From Jane Alley to America's Jazz Ambassador* (Chicago: Urban Research, 1997). This list is far from exhaustive; it does not even include biographies published in other languages. The most illuminating German biography is Knauer, *Louis Armstrong*.

5. Qtd. in Teachout, *Pops*, 193.

6. Stanley Crouch, "Laughin' Louis," *Village Voice*, Aug. 14, 1978, 45

7. David Yaffe puts it well when he writes, "To be a jazz scholar at the beginning of the twenty-first century is to write in the shadow of Ralph Ellison" (*Fascinating Rhythm*, 86).

8. Ellison, *Invisible Man*, 7.

9. Kimberly W. Benston, *Performing Blackness: Enactments of African-American Modernism* (New York: Routledge, 2000), 9.

10. Ellison, *Invisible Man*, 8; Benston, *Performing Blackness*, 9.

11. Ellison, "Richard Wright's Blues," 129. Ellison speaks of the blues as "an art of ambiguity" ("Remembering Jimmy," 277).

12. I cite "generative energy" from Benston, *Performing Blackness*, 9.

13. Armstrong, "Goffin Notebooks," 109.

14. Appel concludes that "we seem to have some kind of miraculous access to Armstrong's space" (*Jazz Modernism*, 137).

15. Dan Morgenstern, liner notes, *Louis Armstrong: The Complete RCA Victor Recordings* (RCA Victor/BMG, 1997), 24.

16. John Finch qtd. in Watkins, *On the Real Side*, 59; Thomas R. R. Cobb, *An Inquiry into the Law of Negro Slavery*, qtd. in Boskin, *Sambo*. 54; Michel Guillaume Jean de Crèvecoeur, *Sketches of Eighteenth Century America*, ed. Henry L. Bourdin, Ralph Gabriel, and Stanley T. Williams (New Haven: Yale University Press, 1925), 148.

17. Frederick Douglass, *Narrative of the Life of Frederick Douglass, An American*

Slave, Written by Himself, 1845, ed. William L. Andrews and William S. McFeely (New York: Norton, 1997), 19; Du Bois, *Souls of Black Folk*, 231.

18. Frederick Law Olmsted, *A Journey in the Seaboard Slave States, with Remarks on Their Economy*, 1856 (New York: Negro Universities Press, 1968), 394.

19. Boskin, *Sambo*, 54.

20. The recordings can be found on *Lost Sounds: Blacks and the Birth of the Recording Industry 1891–1922* (Archeophone, 2005).

21. Constance Rourke, *American Humor: A Study of the National Character* (New York: Harcourt, 1931), 82.

22. Appel, *Jazz Modernism*, 138.

23. Ellison, "Extravagance of Laughter," 653.

24. Ralph Ellison, "It Always Breaks Out," *Partisan Review* (Spring 1963): 16; Ellison, "Change the Joke and Slip the Yoke," 109; Rourke, *American Humor*, 86. See also Armstrong's instrumental recording "Yes! I'm in the Barrel" (Nov. 12, 1925), whose title picks up a New Orleans saying about gamblers who had lost their clothes shooting dice or playing poker, and Langston Hughes's many references to the sad laughter of the blues, for instance, in his novel *Not without Laughter* (1930) and in his short-story collection *Laughing to Keep from Crying* (1952). Armstrong recounts the story about the saying in "Jazz on a High Note," 132.

25. Ellison, "Extravagance of Laughter," 653.

26. Ellison, "Living with Music," *High Fidelity*, Dec. 1955, in Callahan, *Collected Writings of Ralph Ellison*, 229; Ellison, "What America Would Be Like without Blacks," 582.

27. Ellison, *Invisible Man*, 7, 335, 7.

28. Ibid., 5. See also Alexander G. Weheliye's perceptive analysis: "The novel cleft between sound and source initiated by the technology of the phonograph [. . .] supplies the grooves of sonic Afro-modernity." Alexander G. Weheliye, *Phonographies: Grooves in Sonic Afro-Modernity* (Durham: Duke University Press, 2005), 7.

29. Ellison, *Invisible Man*, 5.

30. Berndt Ostendorf interprets minstrelsy as ushering in "the blackening of America" ("Minstrelsy and Early Jazz," 576). Weheliye suggests a repositioning of black culture and its "reciprocal engagement with sound technologies" as central loci of American modernity (*Phonographies*, 4).

31. Ellison, "What America Would Be Like without Blacks," 580.

32. Qtd. in Ray Pratt, *Rhythm and Resistance: Explorations in the Political Uses of Popular Music* (New York: Praeger, 1990), 56.

33. Pratt, *Rhythm and Resistance*, 50.

34. Du Bois, *Souls of Black Folk*, 238.

35. Qtd. in Boujut, *Louis Armstrong*, 87.

Suggested Listening

Louis Armstrong was an extremely busy musician when it came to studio and live recordings. The majority of songs and performances discussed in the preceding pages are collected on the following CDs and box sets, all of which are currently available (sometimes as reissues by different labels) and many of which carry excellent liner notes. The vast archive of Armstrong recordings is meticulously catalogued in Jos Willems, *All of Me: The Complete Discography of Louis Armstrong* (Lanham: Scarecrow, 2006).

King Oliver. *Off the Record: The Complete 1923 Jazz Band Recordings.* 1923. 2 CDs. Off the Record/Archeophone, 2007.

Louis Armstrong. *Portrait of the Artist as a Young Man.* 1923–34. 4 CDs. Sony/Columbia/Legacy, 1994.

Louis Armstrong. *The Complete Hot Five and Hot Seven Recordings.* 1925–29. 4 CDs. Sony/Columbia/Legacy, 2006.

Louis Armstrong. *The Complete RCA Victor Recordings.* 1932–56. 4 CDs. RCA, 2001.

Louis Armstrong and Friends. *Jazz in Paris.* 1934. Universal France, 2007.

Louis Armstrong. *Fleischmann's Yeast Show & Louis' Home-Recorded Tapes.* 1937/various. 2 CDs. Jazz Heritage, 2008.

Louis Armstrong. *The Complete Decca Studio Master Takes.* 1935–39. 4 CDs. Definitive, 2004.

Louis Armstrong. *The Complete Decca Studio Master Takes.* 1940–49. 2 CDs. Definitive, 2004.

Louis Armstrong. *Complete 1950–1951 All Stars Decca Recordings.* 1950–51. 2 CDs. Definitive, 2004.

Louis Armstrong and Bing Crosby. *Fun with Bing and Louis.* 1949–51. Jasmine Records, 1997.

Louis Armstrong and His All Stars. *Louis Armstrong Plays W. C. Handy.* 1954. Sony/Columbia/Legacy, 1997.

Louis Armstrong and His All Stars. *Satch Plays Fats.* 1955. Sony/Columbia/Legacy, 2000.

Louis Armstrong and His All Stars. *European Concert Recordings by Ambassador Jazz.* 1956. Sony/Columbia/Legacy, 2000.

Louis Armstrong and His All Stars. *The Great Chicago Concert.* 1956. Sony/Columbia/Legacy, 1997.

Louis Armstrong and Ella Fitzgerald. *Best of Ella Fitzgerald and Louis Armstrong.* 1956–57. Verve, 1997.

Louis Armstrong. *Satchmo: A Musical Autobiography.* 1957. 3 CDs. Verve, 2001.

Louis Armstrong. *Satchmo the Great.* 1957. Sony/Columbia/Legacy, 2000.

Louis Armstrong. *Louis and the Good Book.* 1958. Verve, 2001.

Louis Armstrong and the All Stars. *Satchmo Plays King Oliver.* 1959. Fuel Records, 2002.

Louis Armstrong and His Band. With Dave Brubeck, Carmen McRae, and Lambert, Hendricks, and Ross. *The Real Ambassadors.* 1962. CBS, 1990.

Suggested Further Reading

The works listed here contextualize and extend the analyses offered throughout this book. They generally include publications I consulted during my research but (with some exceptions) did not explicitly reference in the preceding pages. The lists are certainly not comprehensive, but they will allow readers to conduct further research on Louis Armstrong and dig more deeply into Armstrong's verbal, visual, and aural legacy.

Louis Armstrong

I have referenced the bulk of Armstrong criticism throughout the preceding chapters. Nonetheless, a few additional suggestions may be useful.

Borshuk, Michael. "'So Black, So Blue': Ralph Ellison, Louis Armstrong and the Bebop Aesthetic." *Blue Notes: Toward a New Jazz Discourse*, ed. Mark Osteen, special issue of *Genre: Forms of Discourse and Culture* 37.2 (2004): 261–83.

Brooks, Edward. *Influence and Assimilation in Louis Armstrong's Cornet and Trumpet Work (1923–1928)*. Lewiston: Mellen, 2000.

Brooks, Edward. *The Young Louis Armstrong on Records: A Critical Survey of the Early Recordings, 1923–1928*. Lanham: Scarecrow, 2002.

Gabbard, Krin. "Louis Armstrong's Beam of Lyrical Sound." In *Hotter Than That: The Trumpet, Jazz, and American Culture*. New York: Faber and Faber, 2008. 70–106.

Harker, Brian. *Louis Armstrong's Hot Five and Hot Seven Recordings*. New York: Oxford University Press, 2011.

Meckna, Michael. "Louis Armstrong Blasts Little Rock, Arkansas." In *Perspectives on American Music since 1950*, ed. James R. Heintze. New York: Garland, 1999. 141–51.

Meckna, Michael. "Louis Armstrong in the Movies, 1931–1969." *Popular Music and Society* 29.3 (2006): 359–73.

Meckna, Michael. *Satchmo: The Louis Armstrong Encyclopedia.* Westport: Green-
    wood, 2004.
Potter, John. "Armstrong to Sinatra: Swing and Sub-text." In *Vocal Authority:
    Singing Style and Ideology.* Cambridge: Cambridge University Press, 1998.
    87–112.
Stratemann, Klaus. *Louis Armstrong on the Screen.* Copenhagen: Jazzmedia, 1996.
Taylor, Jeffrey. "Louis Armstrong, Earl Hines, and 'Weather Bird.'" *Musical Quar-
    terly* 82.1 (1998): 1–40.

Jazz Autobiography

Apart from the essays on jazz autobiography cited throughout the book, the following texts should prove useful for readers and scholars interested in the many autobiographies written by American jazz musicians.

Carmichael, Thomas. "Beneath the Underdog: Charles Mingus, Representation,
    and Jazz Autobiography." *Canadian Review of American Studies/Revue canadienne
    d'études américaines* 25.3 (1995): 29–40.
Farrington, Holly E. "Narrating the Jazz Life: Three Approaches to Jazz Autobi-
    ography." *Popular Music and Society* 29.3 (2006): 375–86.
Gebhardt, Nicholas. "Sidney Bechet: The Virtuosity of Construction." In *Going for
    Jazz: Musical Practices and American Ideology.* Chicago: University of Chicago
    Press, 2001. 33–76.
Grandt, Jürgen E. "The Remembering Song: Toward an Aesthetic of Literary Jazz
    in Sidney Bechet's *Treat It Gentle*." In *Kinds of Blue: The Jazz Aesthetic in African
    American Narrative.* Columbus: Ohio State University Press, 2004. 1–21.
Heble, Ajay. "Performing Identity: Jazz Autobiography and the Politics of Literary
    Improvisation." In *Landing on the Wrong Note: Jazz, Dissonance and Critical
    Practice.* New York: Routledge, 2000. 89–116.
McNeilly, Kevin. "Charles Mingus Splits; or, All the Things You Could Be by Now
    if Sigmund Freud's Wife Was Your Mother." *Canadian Review of American Stud-
    ies/Revue canadienne d'études américaines* 27.2 (1997): 45–70.
Wald, Gayle. "Mezz Mezzrow and the Voluntary Negro Blues." In *Crossing the
    Line: Racial Passing in Twentieth-Century U.S. Literature and Culture.* Durham:
    Duke University Press, 2000. 53–81.

Jazz Literature

While my study of Armstrong's intermedial autobiographics diverges substantially
from the focus of jazz fiction studies, I include a list of important works here because it will enable readers to make further sense of the literary connections between jazz autobiography and jazz fiction.

Bolden, Tony. *Afro-Blue: Improvisations in African American Poetry and Culture.* Urbana: University of Illinois Press, 2004.

Cataliotti, Robert H. *The Songs Became the Stories: The Music in African-American Fiction, 1970–2005.* New York: Lang, 2007.

Eckstein, Lars, and Christoph Reinfandt. "On Dancing about Architecture: Words and Music between Cultural Practice and Transcendence." In *The Cultural Validity of Music in Contemporary Fiction,* ed. Lars Eckstein and Christoph Reinfandt, special issue of *ZAA Zeitschrift für Anglistik und Amerikanistik* 54.1 (2006): 1–8.

Ferguson, Jeffrey B. "A Blue Note on Black American Literary Criticism." In *African American Literary Studies: New Texts, New Approaches, New Challenges,* ed. Glenda R. Carpio and Werner Sollors, special issue of *Amerikastudien/American Studies* 55.4 (2010): 699–714.

Gysin, Fritz. "From 'Liberating Voices' to 'Metathetic Ventriloquism': Boundaries in Recent African-American Jazz Fiction." *Callaloo* 25.1 (2002): 274–87.

Hartman, Charles O. *Jazz Text: Voice and Improvisation in Poetry, Jazz, and Song.* Princeton: Princeton University Press, 1991.

Henson, Kristin K. *Beyond the Sound Barrier: The Jazz Controversy in Twentieth-Century American Fiction.* New York: Routledge, 2003.

Jarrett, Michael. *Drifting on a Read: Jazz as a Model for Writing.* Albany: State University of New York Press, 1999.

Munton, Alan. "Misreading Morrison, Mishearing Jazz: A Response to Toni Morrison's Jazz Critics." *Journal of American Studies* 31.2 (1997): 235–51.

Raussert, Wilfried. *Negotiating Temporal Differences: Blues, Jazz and Narrativity in African American Culture.* Heidelberg: Winter, 2000.

Simawe, Saadi A., ed. *Black Orpheus: Music in African American Fiction from the Harlem Renaissance to Toni Morrison.* New York: Garland, 2000.

Yemisi, Jimoh A. *Spiritual, Blues, and Jazz People in African American Fiction: Living in Paradox.* Knoxville: University of Tennessee Press, 2002.

Intermedia Theory

Intermedia studies is a largely European field of academic inquiry on the musico-textual and the musico-visual that is only gradually gaining a foothold in American discourses. The following texts represent only a small sampling of important English-language sources; a substantial amount of additional research has been published in German.

Bernhart, Walter, Steven Paul Scher, and Werner Wolf, eds. *Word and Music: Defining the Field.* Amsterdam: Rodopi, 1999.

Elleström, Lars, ed. *Media Borders: Multimodality and Intermediality.* Basingstoke: Palgrave Macmillan, 2010.

Emden, Christian J., and Gabriele Rippl, eds. *ImageScapes: Studies in Intermediality*. Bern: Lang, 2010.

Grishakova, Marina, and Marie-Laure Ryan, eds. *Intermediality and Storytelling*. Berlin: De Gruyter, 2010.

Wolf, Werner. *The Musicalization of Fiction: A Study in the Theory and History of Intermediality*. Amsterdam: Rodopi, 1999.

Autobiography

The field of autobiography studies has been growing rapidly for the past few decades. Apart from many thematically focused works, several monographs and essay collections (some of which I have cited above) are good starting points for further research into the autobiographies of jazz musicians like Louis Armstrong.

Anderson, Linda. *Autobiography*. New York: Routledge, 2001.

Ashley, Kathleen, Leigh Gilmore, and Gerald Peters, eds. *Autobiography and Postmodernism*. Amherst: University of Massachusetts Press, 1994.

Broughton, Trev Lynn, ed. *Autobiography*. 4 vols. New York: Routledge, 2007.

Eakin, Paul John. *Living Autobiographically: How We Create Identity in Narrative*. Ithaca: Cornell University Press, 2008.

Folkenflik, Robert, ed. *The Culture of Autobiography: Constructions of Self-Representation*. Stanford: Stanford University Press, 1993.

Gilmore, Leigh. *Autobiographics: A Feminist Theory of Women's Self-Representation*. Ithaca: Cornell University Press, 1994.

Hornung, Alfred, ed. *Auto/Biography and Mediation*. Heidelberg: Winter, 2010.

Hornung, Alfred, and Ernstpeter Ruhe, eds. *Postcolonialism and Autobiography*. Amsterdam: Rodopi, 1998.

Huddart, David. *Postcolonial Theory and Autobiography*. New York: Routledge, 2008.

Marcus, Laura. *Auto/biographical Discourses: Theory, Criticism, Practice*. Manchester: Manchester University Press, 1994.

Moore-Gilbert, Bart. *Postcolonial Life-Writing: Culture, Politics and Self-Representation*. New York: Routledge, 2009.

Smith, Sidonie, and Julia Watson. *Reading Autobiography: A Guide for Interpreting Life Narratives*. 2nd ed. Minneapolis: University of Minnesota Press, 2009.

New Orleans Jazz

Quite a lot has been written about New Orleans jazz, its history, and its cultural origins. Texts that add important perspectives and contexts to my analysis of Armstrong's New Orleans recollections include the following.

Ake, David. "'Blue Horizon': Creole Culture and Early New Orleans Jazz." In *Jazz Cultures*. Berkeley: University of California Press, 2002. 10–41.

Charters, Samuel. *A Trumpet around the Corner: The Story of New Orleans Jazz.* Jackson: University Press of Mississippi, 2008.

Gushee, Lawrence. *Pioneers of Jazz: The Story of the Creole Band.* New York: Oxford University Press, 2005.

Ostendorf Berndt, and Michael Smith. "Jazz Funerals and the Second Line: African-American Celebration and Public Space in New Orleans." In *Ceremonies and Spectacles: Performing American Culture,* ed. Teresa Alves, Teresa Cid, and Heinz Ickstadt. Amsterdam: VU University Press, 2000. 238–72.

Regis, Helen A. "Second Lines, Minstrelsy, and the Contested Landscapes of New Orleans Afro-Creole Festivals." *Cultural Anthropology* 14.4 (1999): 472–504.

Touchet, Leo, and Vernel Bagneris. *Rejoice When You Die: The New Orleans Jazz Funerals.* Baton Rouge: Louisiana State University Press, 1998.

Turner, Richard Brent. *Jazz Religion, the Second Line, and Black New Orleans.* Bloomington: Indiana University Press, 2009.

Jazz History, Historiography, Theory

Scholarly works on American jazz history have been around since the 1930s, and it would make little sense to make an attempt at providing a full bibliography here. Much less has been published on jazz historiography and theory, but even in these fields of inquiry the body of secondary literature is growing.

Berliner, Paul F. *Thinking in Jazz: The Infinite Art of Improvisation.* Chicago: University of Chicago Press, 1994.

Cooke, Mervin, and David Horn, eds. *The Cambridge Companion to Jazz.* New York: Cambridge University Press, 2002.

DeVeaux, Scott. *The Birth of Bebop: A Social and Musical History.* Berkeley: University of California Press, 1997.

Erenberg, Lewis A. *Swingin' the Dream: Big Band Jazz and the Rebirth of American Culture.* Chicago: University of Chicago Press, 1998.

Evans, Nicholas M. *Writing Jazz: Race, Nationalism, and Modern Culture in the 1920s.* New York: Garland, 2000.

Gabbard, Krin, ed. *Jazz among the Discourses.* Durham: Duke University Press, 1995.

Gabbard, Krin, ed. *Representing Jazz.* Durham: Duke University Press, 1995.

Giddins, Gary, and Scott DeVeaux. *Jazz.* New York: Norton, 2009.

Gottlieb, Robert, ed. *Reading Jazz: A Gathering of Autobiography, Reportage, and Criticism from 1919 to Now.* New York: Vintage, 1996.

Jerving, Ryan. "Early Jazz Literature (And Why You Didn't Know)." *American Literary History* 16.4 (2004): 648–74.

Kirchner, Bill, ed. *The Oxford Companion to Jazz.* New York: Oxford University Press, 2000.

Lock, Graham, and David Murray, eds. *Thriving on a Riff: Jazz and Blues Influences in African American Literature and Film*. New York: Oxford University Press, 2009.

Lock, Graham, and David Murray, eds. *The Hearing Eye: Jazz and Blues Influences in African American Visual Art*. New York: Oxford University Press, 2009.

O'Meally, Robert G., ed. *The Jazz Cadence of American Culture*. New York: Columbia University Press, 1998.

O'Meally, Robert G., Brent Hayes Edwards, and Farah Jasmine Griffin, eds. *Uptown Conversation: The New Jazz Studies*. New York: Columbia University Press, 2004.

Panish, Jon. *The Color of Jazz: Race and Representation in Postwar American Culture*. Jackson: University Press of Mississippi, 1997.

Peretti, Burton W. "Oral Histories of Jazz Musicians: The NEA Transcripts as Texts in Context." In *Jazz among the Discourses*, ed. Krin Gabbard. Durham: Duke University Press, 1995. 117–33.

Peretti, Burton W. "Speaking in the Groove: Oral History and Jazz." *Journal of American History* 88.2 (2001): 582–95.

Porter, Lewis, ed. *Jazz: A Century of Change. Readings and New Essays*. New York: Schirmer, 1997.

Saul, Scott. *Freedom Is, Freedom Ain't: Jazz and the Making of the Sixties*. Cambridge: Harvard University Press, 2003.

Shipton, Alyn. *A New History of Jazz*. 2001. London: Continuum, 2002.

Sudhalter, Richard M. *Lost Chords: White Musicians and Their Contribution to Jazz, 1915–1945*. New York: Oxford University Press, 1999.

Walser, Robert, ed., *Keeping Time: Readings in Jazz History*. New York: Oxford University Press, 1999.

African American Cultural History

While it would be almost impossible to list all of the significant studies on the diverse facets of African American cultural history, the following texts should offer a good starting point for further investigation.

Abbott, Lynn, and Doug Seroff. *Out of Sight: The Rise of African American Popular Music 1889–1895*. Jackson: University Press of Mississippi, 2002.

Abbott, Lynn, and Doug Seroff. *Ragged but Right: Black Traveling Shows, "Coon Songs," and the Dark Pathway to Blues and Jazz*. Jackson: University Press of Mississippi, 2007.

Anderson, Paul Allen. *Deep River: Music and Memory in Harlem Renaissance Thought*. Durham: Duke University Press, 2001.

Brooks, Tim. *Lost Sounds: Blacks and the Birth of the Recording Industry 1891–1922*. Urbana: University of Illinois Press, 2004.

Davis, Angela Y. *Blues Legacies and Black Feminism: Gertrude "Ma" Rainey, Bessie Smith, and Billie Holiday*. New York: Pantheon, 1998.

Diedrich, Maria, Carl Pedersen, and Justine Tally, eds. *Mapping African America: History, Narrative Formation, and the Production of Knowledge.* Hamburg: Lit, 1999.

Floyd, Samuel A., Jr., ed. *Black Music in the Harlem Renaissance: A Collection of Essays.* 1990. Knoxville: University of Tennessee Press, 1993.

Floyd, Samuel A., Jr., *The Power of Black Music: Interpreting Its History from Africa to the United States.* New York: Oxford University Press, 1995.

Grandt, Jürgen E. *Shaping Words to Fit the Soul: The Southern Ritual Grounds of Afro-Modernism.* Columbus: Ohio State University Press, 2009.

Gray, Herman S. *Cultural Moves: African Americans and the Politics of Representation.* Berkeley: University of California Press, 2005.

Gubar, Susan. *Racechanges: White Skin, Black Face in American Culture.* New York: Oxford University Press, 1997.

Guillory, Monique, and Richard C. Green, eds. *Soul: Black Power, Politics, and Pleasure.* New York: New York University Press, 1998.

Gussow, Adam. *Seems Like Murder Here: Southern Violence and the Blues Tradition.* Chicago: University of Chicago Press, 2002.

Lemke, Sieglinde. *Primitivist Modernism: Black Culture and the Origins of Transatlantic Modernism.* New York: Oxford University Press, 1998.

Malone, Jacqui. *Steppin' on the Blues: The Visible Rhythms of African American Dance.* Urbana: University of Illinois Press, 1996.

Meer, Sarah. *Uncle Tom Mania: Slavery, Minstrelsy, and Transatlantic Culture in the 1850s.* Athens: University of Georgia Press, 2005.

Melnick, Jeffrey. *A Right to Sing the Blues: African Americans, Jews, and American Popular Song.* Cambridge: Harvard University Press, 1999.

Oliver, Paul. *Songsters and Saints: Vocal Traditions on Race Records.* Cambridge: Cambridge University Press, 1984.

Ramsey, Guthrie P., Jr. *Race Music: Black Cultures from Bebop to Hip-Hop.* Berkeley: University of California Press, 2003.

Riis, Thomas L. *Just before Jazz: Black Musical Theater in New York, 1890–1915.* Washington D.C.: Smithsonian Institution Press, 1989.

Spencer, Jon Michael. *The New Negroes and Their Music: The Success of the Harlem Renaissance.* Knoxville: University of Tennessee Press, 1997.

Szwed, John. *Crossovers: Essays on Race, Music, and American Culture.* Philadelphia: University of Pennsylvania Press, 2005.

Williams, Linda. *Playing the Race Card: Melodramas of Black and White from Uncle Tom to O. J. Simpson.* Princeton: Princeton University Press, 2001.

Woll, Allen. *Black Musical Theatre: From Coontown to Dreamgirls.* 1989. New York: Da Capo, 1991.